The Psychology of Love

The Psychology of Love

EDITED BY
Robert J. Sternberg and Michael L. Barnes

Yale University Press

New Haven and London

Designed by James J. Johnson
and set in Sabon Roman type by
Keystone Typesetting Company, Orwigsburg, Pennsylvania
Printed in the United States of America by
Vail-Ballou Press, Binghamton, New York

Library of Congress Cataloging-in-Publication Data

The Psychology of love.

Bibliography: p.
Includes index.
1. Love—Psychological aspects.   I. Sternberg,
Robert J.   II. Barnes, Michael L.
BF575.L8P78   1988   302   87–10656
ISBN 0–300–03950–6 (alk. paper)

*The paper in this book meets the guidelines for permanence
and durability of the Committee on Production Guidelines
for Book Longevity of the Council on Library Resources.*

1   3   5   7   9   10   8   6   4   2

Contents

Preface

BY ZICK RUBIN

Love had always been one thing—maybe the only thing—that seemed safely beyond the research scientist's ever-extending grasp. "So far as love or affection is concerned," Harry Harlow declared in his presidential address to the American Psychological Association in 1958, "psychologists have failed in their mission. The little we know about love does not transcend simple observation, and the little we write about it has been written better by poets and novelists." Since the poets and novelists had always been notoriously contradictory about love, defining it as everything from "a spirit all compact of fire" to "a state of perceptual anesthesia," this was a pretty serious indictment.

By 1968, when I launched my own dissertation research on measuring romantic love, the situation had changed only slightly. Considerable work had been done on love (or "attachment") between parents and infants, along paths blazed by such researchers as Harlow and John Bowlby. And clinical psychologists from Freud to Fromm to Maslow had all along been recording their insights into the nature of love. But with only a handful of exceptions, psychological researchers had stayed clear of romantic love. "Why do you want to measure *that*?" my dissertation committee asked me. "Why not measure something more popular like cognitive dissonance or identity diffusion?" I gulped and then suggested, "Well, this way I can keep the literature review short."

Two decades later, the days of short literature reviews on the psychology of love are over. Once their initial reluctance to study love had been overcome, psychologists flocked to the subject in droves. Dozens of love studies appear annually in the journals; dozens more are presented at regional and national conventions. There is even a four-year-old journal called the *Journal of Social and Personal Relationships* that fills a large proportion of its pages with studies of love. "How do I love thee?"— Elizabeth Barrett Browning might have written in the late 1980s—"Let me count the articles."

Research on love is especially alluring to undergraduate and graduate student researchers, who can't resist the opportunity to get course credit for investigating a topic that obsesses them in their daily lives. Studying love professionally is one creative response to the challenge (discussed by Williams and Barnes in this volume) of integrating the spheres of love and work in one's life. In love research, as elsewhere in our discipline, not all the studies have been notably illuminating. But if there were a need to demonstrate that psychologists have been gaining on love, the proof lies in this volume. Psychologists have finally come to grips with their "mission" of studying love—what it is, where it comes from, and how it develops.

In planning this volume, Robert Sternberg and Michael Barnes have recruited an impressive roster of contributors. Several are eminent social psychologists (including Levinger, Hatfield, Byrne, and Berscheid) who pioneered the study of "interpersonal attraction" in the 1960s. But current research on love, as represented in this volume, reaches beyond social psychology to other areas and disciplines. Researchers are stalking romantic love with the help of concepts and methods imported from the fields of infant-parent attachment (Shaver, Hazan, and Bradshaw), cognitive psychology (Buss), personality (Dion and Dion), and psychometrics (Sternberg). Connections are being made to evolutionary biology (Buss), the sociology of social networks (Levinger), cultural anthropology (Dion and Dion), and behavioral physiology (Hatfield). Rather than yielding to the temptation to talk only to themselves, psychologists studying love have reached out to the conceptions of classical philosophers and religious mystics (Lee, Brehm).

For all these accomplishments, the science of love is still in its infancy. One sign of this immaturity is the fact that the investigators represented in this volume share so little of a common vocabulary. Love researchers are saddled with the problem that "love" means different things to different people. Is "love" an attitude, an emotion, a set of behaviors? Is it an individual orientation or a dyadic bond? Is it serious or playful, passionate or sedate, needing or giving? And if, as some would insist, it is all these things, how can we proceed to organize our study of it? Because of this organizational problem, many of the contributors to this volume have developed their own taxonomies of love. Each categorizing scheme differs from the next, and there are no ready translation rules from one chapter's formulation to another's. Just as partners with different views of love may find themselves talking past each other (see Sternberg's chapter), I suspect that some of the contributors to this volume may find it difficult to relate to others' perspectives.

Love researchers might do well to move toward a more common conceptual vocabulary. One model for such an undertaking is the systematic framework for describing close relationships set forth by Harold Kelley and his colleagues (1983). The present volume, despite its babel of voices, may help to encourage such conceptual integration. By assembling different languages of love within the same covers, the editors have made it more likely that speakers of one language will catch on to the nuances of another. Even apparently irreconcilable conflicts between researchers may eventually lead to a deeper understanding of love. For example, romantic love is viewed by Branden as a positive ideal that brings out the best in us and by Peele as a form of addiction that borders on pathology. Perhaps future researchers can resolve the conflict by specifying more clearly the links between different sorts of love and emotional well-being.

Where should love research go next? There are many avenues that might be pursued, from the brain chemistry of consciousness to the developmental psychology of giving and caring. Let me offer quick plugs for three such directions. First, we need research, as advocated by Berscheid in this volume, that connects the psychophysiology of sexual arousal to the psychology of love. Today, both sex and love are thriving topics of psychological research. (The taboo against sex research, spurred by the work of Masters and Johnson in the mid-1960s, was broken even before love research became respectable.) But whereas most observers would agree that love and sex are closely linked, love research and sex research have for the most part been separate enterprises. Second, love researchers should devote more attention to the environmental and demographic context within which love unfolds. No matter what else may be discovered about the experience of love, it is clear that people establish relationships with others who are *available*. If demographic constraints are such that, for example, there is a severe shortage of men available to college-educated women past the age of thirty, then researchers who seek to understand love must attend to these constraints. Third, researchers should recognize the importance of love as a provision that can help people get through times of stress and crisis. For this reason, research on love needs to be connected with the booming research literature on social support (for example, Sarason & Sarason, 1985).

So far, I've ducked what to many observers is the critical question: *should* we study love? "I believe that 200 million Americans want to leave some things in life a mystery," Sen. William Proxmire protested a decade ago, "and right at the top of the list of the things we don't want to know is why a man falls in love with a woman and vice versa." Love researchers and their boosters in the media were quick to put the senator down as a know-nothing—"you have to assume he was kidding," James Reston wrote in the *New York Times*—yet the question persists: will the new science of love inevitably rob love of some of its magic? More generally, might research on love have undesirable consequences that will outweigh its benefits?

In my view, these questions should not be glibly dismissed. It is easy to justify love research with pious generalities. Here's a pious generality of my own, penned a decade ago as a retort to Senator Proxmire:

> Especially at a time when many people are confused about what love is or should be, the scientific study of love can make a positive contribution to the quality of life. To shun this task is no more justified than the taboo until several centuries ago against scientific study of the human body, on the grounds that such research would somehow defile it. In the words of one of the most humane of modern psychologists, the late Abraham H. Maslow, "We *must* study love; we must be able to teach it, to understand it, to predict it, or else the world is lost to hostility and to suspicion." (Rubin, 1977, p. 59)

Looking back at my statement ten years later, I'd call it a nice pep talk for love researchers, but hardly a convincing defense of love research. Scientists who broke the taboo against dissecting the human body were ultimately able to justify their sacrilege by developing techniques to prevent and cure disease. Will today's dissectors of the anatomy of love be able to achieve comparable results? The question remains open. I still hold to the article of scientific faith that increasing human knowledge, even about so private a matter as love, is to be encouraged. The first fruits of love research, as reported in this volume, help strengthen this faith. But in advocating further research on love, we must go beyond generalities and recognize that research on love—just like research on nuclear physics or on the genetic code—is likely to have real consequences, both for good and for ill.

We may want to consider, for example, the impact of love research on marital stability. The interest in love research that began in the late 1960s and the 1970s seems, in retrospect, to have been part of a broader cultural phenomenon: a heightened emphasis on the quality of intimate relationships. As Beech and Tesser observe in this volume, this new concern with the quality of love undoubtedly contributed to the soaring divorce rate of the past two decades. Rather than sticking with a partner for better or worse, men and women came to believe that a marriage should survive only if love—and with it, individual fulfillment—continued to flower. Will research on love reinforce this trend of questioning—and toppling—existing relationships? And is such questioning of people's closest ties to be welcomed or to be shunned?

Studies of love may have their most direct effects on the individuals and couples who serve as research subjects. Between 1972 and 1974, for example, Anne Peplau, Charles Hill, and I conducted a longitudinal questionnaire study of 231 college student couples who were dating or going together. We found that participating in the research itself had a major impact on many of the couples' relationships (Rubin & Mitchell, 1976). In some cases, the research cemented relationships; in other cases, it hastened their demise. A few of our participants came to feel that our statistical approach to love demeaned their relationships. More often, however, the students felt that taking part in our study helped them come to a better understanding of their relationship and to make a better decision about whether or not to continue it. "I felt that this study brought our relationship close to where it is now," one student told us. "We were forced to look at ourselves honestly and we discussed our differences and problems more openly." In the process of conducting love research, then, we unwittingly became couples counselors.

Playing on a larger stage, love researchers will find themselves cast as couples counselors to society. The approaches and results of love research, as they are heralded in the mass media, will undoubtedly shape people's expectations about love. If the scientists focus on the companionate nature of love, couples will become preoccupied with their own companionship; if the scientists turn their attention to passionate love, couples will become concerned with their own passion. And if researchers define love in unattainably ideal terms, they may create discontent among people who would otherwise have gladly settled for what they had. But to the extent that the results of love research help people choose partners more wisely, cultivate love more resourcefully, and make more realistic demands on their relationships, the research may increase both the quality and the durability of intimate relationships.

"Should we study love?" may in fact have become a moot question. The rich contributions to this volume suggest that, Senator Proxmire notwithstanding, the research will go on. Psychologists are not about to displace poets or novelists as society's preeminent observers of love, but the researchers are beginning to pierce the veil of love in their own ways. As they pursue this research, psychologists have an opportunity not only to satisfy their own scientific curiosity but also to enrich people's lives.

REFERENCES

Kelley, H. H., Berscheid, E., Christensen, A., Harvey, J. H., Huston, T. L., Levinger, G., McClintock, E., Peplau, L. A., & Peterson, D. R. (1983). *Close relationships*. New York: Freeman.

Rubin, Z. (1977, February). The love research. *Human Behavior*.

Rubin, Z., & Mitchell, C. (1976). Couples research as couples counseling: Some unintended effects of studying close relationships. *American Psychologist, 31*, 17–25.

Sarason, I. G., & Sarason, B. R. (1985). *Social support: Theory, research and applications*. Boston: Martinus Nijhoff.

PART I

Introduction

CHAPTER ONE

An Introduction to the Psychology of Love

BY ROBERT J. STERNBERG AND MICHAEL L. BARNES

For many people, love is the most important thing in their lives. Without it, they feel as though their lives are incomplete. But what is "it"? This question has been addressed by poets, novelists, philosophers, theologians, and, of course, psychologists, among others. This book presents the attempts of contemporary psychologists whose field of expertise is the study of love and close relationships to figure out just what love is.

The book is divided into five parts containing sixteen chapters. Part I consists simply of this introduction. Part II contains seven chapters presenting global theories of love, which attempt to deal with the phenomenon of love in its entirety. Part III comprises four chapters describing theories that concentrate primarily upon romantic love. Part IV includes three chapters emphasizing theories of love and relationship maintenance. Part V consists of a single chapter that provides a critical overview of the field of love research.

PART II: GLOBAL THEORIES OF LOVE

In chapter 2, "A Taxonomy of Love," Bernard I. Murstein presents a global analysis of various taxonomies of the nature of love. Murstein begins his chapter with a detailed review of the many diverse conceptions of love that have been advanced by various theorists. He goes on to critique the most popular views, giving as well his own perspective on how love should be defined. Murstein traces how theorists have attempted to understand love by investigating its aspects, modes, origins, and primary intended beneficiaries. Murstein offers what he believes to be a single definition of love that can unite and subsume the great variety of concepts he has presented. Next, he discusses the developmental stages of love and reviews empirical attempts to discover whether love consists of a single general dimension or several dimensions. Murstein concludes by evaluating the utility of taxonomies of love, addressing the research on and practical applications of such taxonomies.

In chapter 3, "Love-Styles," John Alan Lee describes various conceptions of love and how to find and achieve a fulfilling love relationship. Lee views the diversity of human styles of loving as a natural component and even a consequence of our complex modern society. Using an analogy to color, he describes how love is experienced and defined in a personal way by each individual, much as colors are observed in the natural world. Just as love is a distinct entity from person to person, so are styles of loving distinct from one person to another. Lee presents a humorous review of the problems this multiplicity of "love-styles" creates when we attempt to find a match for our own love-styles in the everyday world. People are encouraged to develop an awareness of their preferred love-style and to recognize the changes that occur in styles over time. Lee reviews different love-styles in current and past literature and popular culture, showing how seemingly contradictory the notions of what constitutes an appropriate and fulfilling love-style can be. Certain combinations of love-styles are viewed by Lee as representing more compatible matches then others. He presents a sampling of his experimental methodology for the study of love and concludes by relating his theory to others in this volume.

In chapter 4, "Love as Attachment: The Integration of Three Behavioral Systems," Phillip Shaver, Cindy Hazan, and Donna Bradshaw draw on the resources of attachment theory, human development studies, and evolutionary biology in discussing the nature of love. The authors view love and its consequences as extending back well into early human history and experience. Biological and evolutionarily selective interpretations of love are presented within the context of modern human love as part of a system of human emotion and attachment behavior. The authors begin with a summary of attachment theory, which they subsequently apply to adult romantic love. Next, the authors list some of the observable and theoretical similarities between infant care—giving attachment and adult romantic love. They review three styles of attachment present in mother-infant interaction and report the results of two studies investigating the relationship of these styles of attachment to adult romantic love. They offer an interpretation of grief within the context of the attachment model to show the usefulness of this approach. Finally, the authors review the limitations of their work and suggest further applications of attachment theory in research on adult romantic relationships.

In chapter 5, "Love Acts: The Evolutionary Biology of Love," David M. Buss presents an evolutionary approach to love based on two premises. The first is that love does not reside solely in a person's subjective thoughts, feelings, and drives but rather results in actions with tangible consequences. Buss's second premise is that the key consequences of love center around reproduction. He hypothesizes that love acts derive from evolutionary forces, and his chapter seeks to uncover the potentially evolutionarily significant love acts in which humans engage. Proximate goals for love acts include display of resources, exclusivity (fidelity and guarding), commitment and marriage, sexual intimacy, reproduction, resource sharing, and parental investment. In support of his evolutionary framework, Buss presents data from two studies of love acts that support several of its assumptions. He discusses specific empirical predictions that are based on the principles of natural selection and reproductive behavior underlying modern demonstrations of love. Buss's method for obtaining examples of love acts from participants in his research is reviewed, as is his procedure for determining which love acts are most prototypical. Finally, Buss discusses several intriguing sex differences in love acts and in their conceptualization.

In chapter 6, "Triangulating Love," Robert J. Sternberg presents his triangular theory of love, according to which love can be understood as involving three components: intimacy, passion, and decision/commitment. Intimacy is primarily emotional in its composition and refers to feelings of caring, support, and involvement toward another. Passion, which is primarily motivational in character, refers to psychophysiological arousal brought on by another person. Decision/commitment, which is primarily cognitive in nature, refers in the short term to one's decision that one loves another and in the long term to one's willingness to stay with the relationship over time. Sternberg points out that different combinations of the three components generate different kinds of love. For example, romantic love derives from the combination of the intimacy and passion components, whereas infatuation derives from passion in the absence of intimacy. Consummate love results from the involvement of all three components in a loving relationship. Each component has a different course over time and the course of each of the three components is discussed. Finally, Sternberg shows that it is necessary in order to understand love to take into account not only feelings and beliefs but the actions that result from them.

In chapter 7, "Can We Picture 'Love'?" George Levinger, starting from Sternberg's triangular theory of love, simultaneously expands upon its range and proposes an alternative pictorial representation. Levinger's representation is in terms of circles with various degrees of overlap (Euler diagrams). Each component of the triangular theory is represented in a different way. For example, intimacy is represented in terms of degree of intersection between the circles, and commitment in terms of permeability of boundaries of the circles. Levinger's representation is particularly useful in emphasizing the interactional as opposed to the individual aspects of a given relationship. Whereas in Sternberg's representation, triangles of the two individuals involved in a relationship are represented separately, in Levinger's the circles are always represented in interaction with each other.

In chapter 8, "Fools for Love: The Romantic Ideal, Psychological Theory, and Addictive Love," Stanton Peele explores psychological approaches to love in the light of his belief that romantic love is a heedless involvement whose genuineness is measured by its intensity and perhaps by its destructiveness to the lovers and others. Peele's view of romantic love as obsessive attachment is discussed in terms of why the concept of romantic love is accepted by psychologists at all, and why psychologists seem unable clearly to observe and study the negative consequences of certain love relationships. Peele examines our current views of love and concludes that many researchers' thoughts on love are misleading and degenerate. He argues that it is difficult to describe the fundamental aspects of the addiction model of obsessive love, and that any explanation of what motivates obsessive love must be careful to take the cultural context into account. Peele cites numerous facts and anecdotes that demonstrate the variability of forms of love throughout the world and at different periods, even within our own society. He concludes that our society creates attitudes that encourage addiction rather than love, and that the ability to love can be enhanced by learning to value friendship and community, to develop broad purposes and goals in life, to examine relationships and the impact of one's behavior on others, to accept responsibility for one's actions, to insist upon responsible treatment from others, and to recognize and reject addictive entanglements.

PART III: THEORIES OF ROMANTIC LOVE

In chapter 9, "Passionate and Companionate Love," Elaine Hatfield compares two forms of love. Passionate love, like other forms of excitement, involves a continual interplay between elation and despair, thrill and terror, positives and negatives. Such heightened feelings are shown to enhance passion. Companionate love is defined as the affection we feel for those with whom our lives are deeply entwined. This form of love and the intimate relationships associated with it are seen as characterized more by positive experiences than by negative ones. Hatfield concludes that in order to experience a good loving relationship, people must be capable of both independence and intimacy. Teaching people how to develop intimacy skills involves encouraging them to accept themselves and their intimates as they are, to express themselves, and to learn how to deal with their intimates' reactions.

In chapter 10, "A Vision of Romantic Love," Nathaniel Branden notes that our twentieth-century North American vision of romantic love is extraordinary in the context of most of human history. We Americans believe it is our right to find complete happiness, including romantic love, here on earth. Branden defines such love as a passionate spiritual-emotional-sexual attachment between two people that reflects each partner's high regard for the value of the other. Critics of romantic love view it as an immature form of love that is not romantic at all, in that it is not rooted in two partners' genuinely appreciating each other. But Branden regards genuine romantic love as an attainable, desirable goal and criticizes the view that it is an impossible dream. He notes that some people do, in fact, succeed in establishing a successful, long-term romantic love relationship. Problems in understanding and achieving romantic love are seen as consequences of the sometimes irrational and irresponsible demands made of it. Branden believes that characteristics of people in successful romantic love relationships include the following: they tend to express love verbally, sexually, and materially, to be physically affectionate, to voice appreciation and admiration, to participate in mutual self-disclosure, to offer each other an emotional support system, to accept demands or put up with shortcomings, and to create time to be alone together. Crucial to all these characteristics is the maintenance of a positive sense of self. For Branden, romantic love is that kind of love that brings out the very best in us.

In chapter 11, "Passionate Love," Sharon Brehm compares Stendhal's view of passionate love with the writings of the Christian mystics, whose passionate love for God she likens to passionate love in modern relationships. Several major literary works are mined for their potential ability to enrich our understanding of modern passionate love. Brehm's view of its function is that it motivates people to construct a vision of a better world and to try to make that vision a reality.

In chapter 12, "Romantic Love: Individual and Cultural Perspectives," Kenneth L. Dion and Karen K. Dion describe the results of their research on the role of personality in romantic love. They open the chapter with a review of personality correlates of romantic love, citing studies that show, for example, that people who tend to make external (environmental) attributions for events in their lives are more likely to experience romantic feelings than are people who tend to make internal (personal) attributions for life events. The Dions then discuss the roles of self-esteem and defensiveness in love, finding, for example, that individuals high in the first quality and low in the second report romantic love most frequently. But people low in self-esteem report more intense experiences of romantic love and find themselves to be less rational in love relationships than are people with higher self-esteem. The Dions also discuss research on the relationship between self-actualization and love. They find that highly self-actualized individuals report richer, more satisfying love experiences than do people who are less self-actualized. But highly self-actualized people are also less idealistic and more pragmatic in their attitudes toward love than are their less self-actualized counterparts. In the second part of the chapter, the Dions review cross-cultural perspectives on love, showing how cultural norms interact with a culture's conception of love.

PART IV: THEORIES OF LOVE AND RELATIONSHIP MAINTENANCE

In chapter 13, "Maintaining Loving Relationships," Donn Byrne and Sarah Murnen present an analysis of the maintenance period of loving relationships, a period they believe has often been overlooked in past research. The authors criticize the assumption, implicit in much research, that the maintenance period of relationships can be understood by extrapolating from the initiation and dissolution periods. Byrne and Murnen believe that the constructs identified as crucial to attraction are also crucial to maintaining or failing to maintain a relationship. Along these lines, they describe a conceptual framework and apply it to three proposed classes of maintenance variables. A model of attraction is presented in which it is assumed that if two people continue to like each other, the relationship should endure. The authors hypothesize that three realms of interpersonal interactions are vital to the maintenance of loving relationships: similarity, habituation, and evaluation. Knowing a partner better before marriage is seen as making a successful marriage more likely, although problems arise in the process of change that characterizes most people's lives. Habituation may lead to oversaturation or boredom with a partner, resulting in diminished arousal and dissatisfaction. In fact, boredom is cited as a major reason for the breakup of relationships. Methods for overcoming boredom should be studied so that couples can be instructed on how to spice up and add novelty to their relationships. Positive evaluation, expressed through positive communication, is cited as a critical feature of happy loving relationships. Emphasis is placed upon teaching individuals to interact in non-destructive ways, so that they express more of the positive than of the negative aspects of their relationship.

In chapter 14, "Love within Life," Wendy M. Williams and Michael L. Barnes propose a model of love relationships according to which three kinds of boundaries determine, in large measure, the success of such relationships. The first kind of boundary is that between the partners within the internal world of the relationship. The second kind is that between the two partners' external lives. And the third boundary separates each person's own external world from his or her part of the internal world of the relationship. Partners need to reach some consensus and balance in terms of how much of their lives will be shared and how much independent, both within the world of the relationship and outside it. Happy relationships are often ones in which a working agreement is reached in terms of a balance between love and work, and between the couple's own relationship and other personal relationships that affect their lives.

In chapter 15, "Love in Marriage: A Cognitive Account," Steven R. H. Beach and Abraham Tesser open their discussion by noting how dissimilar people's conceptions of love and loving relationships are across both time and culture. This variability, they suggest, undermines any attempt to define the concept of love by forcing it into static categories. The authors discuss the components of pair relationships that most people associate with love. They then define and differentiate between these components, using a cognitive theoretical perspective. The authors also discuss the interaction of these components both within the individual and within the couple. They hope that their model will be of value by guiding further efforts to understand love in the context of stable marital relationships. Beach and Tesser, who derive their set of components from a broad range of research by themselves and others, identify them as commitment, intimacy, cohesion, and sexual interaction. The authors consider each component from a cognitive perspective and outline the interactions among cognitions, affects, and behaviors within each. Next, they examine each component's systemic value by analyzing how the components interconnect for a given individual. Finally, Beach and Tesser discuss the interpersonal links between the components of love as they apply to both members of a given relationship.

V. OVERVIEW

In chapter 16, "Some Comments on Love's Anatomy: Or, Whatever Happened to Old-fashioned Lust?" Ellen Berscheid notes that it is difficult to get a sense even of what love is. She suggests that it is not a single, distinct behavioral phenomenon but rather a motley collection of many different behavioral events that may have in common only that they take place in a relationship with another person. Berscheid discusses past dissections of the anatomy of love and concludes that they generally fall short of giving us a comprehensive picture of what love is about. She notes that whereas classification schemes should be a beginning, they all too often are an end. We need to take off from them rather than feel that they provide a final understanding. Berscheid reaches three general conclusions about romantic love. First, in order to understand it, we need to understand the emotional experiences that underlie it. Second, we need to understand how these emotional experiences are interpreted by the lovers. And finally, we need to recognize the role of sexual desire in love, a factor that, according to Berscheid, is too often ignored in contemporary accounts of love.

PART II

Global Theories of Love

CHAPTER TWO

A Taxonomy of Love

BY BERNARD I. MURSTEIN

Without question the major preoccupation of Americans is love. No one can be certain when this love affair with love started, but ever since the advent of hit songs—that mass reflection of the popular mind—their central theme has been love. In the mid-nineteenth century the populace chanted Stephen Foster's "I Dream of Jeanie with the Light Brown Hair." In the early twentieth century it was "Come Josephine in my Flying Machine," in the 1960s Celia was breaking her lover's heart, and in the next century perhaps a rejected suitor will wail that "Zelda took a rocket trip with a concupiscent drip."

Surveys have shown that our songs' preoccupation with love (Horton, 1957; Wilkinson, 1976) only reflects what the American public believes: that "love and marriage go together like a horse and carriage." In an Elmo Roper survey of 1966, 76 percent of a national sample of married couples named love as one of the two major reasons for marrying; the second reason, "desire for children," was named by only 24 percent. Sex was a distant third, with 16 percent of the men and 8 percent of the women picking it as a major reason for marriage (Brown, 1966).

Important as love may be, however, this four-letter word, unlike its four-letter scatological companions, is ambiguous. The word *love* is bandied about more promiscuously than almost any other word in the English language. We "love" Yorkshire pudding, a football team, our lovers, Uncle Otto, babies, and oranges. Table 2.1 shows how various celebrated personalities have viewed love, and they are varied indeed.

In this chapter, I shall briefly trace how some writers have attempted to understand love by investigating or analyzing various aspects of it—its

TABLE 2.1   A Sample of Definitions of Love

Love is the delightful interval between meeting a beautiful girl and discovering that she looks like a haddock.   —JOHN BARRYMORE

What is love? The need to escape from itself.

—CHARLES-PIERRE BAUDELAIRE

As soon as you cannot keep anything from a woman, you love her.

—PAUL GERALDY

There are people who would never have fallen in love if they never heard of love.

—FRANÇOIS DE LA ROCHEFOUCAULD

Love is the triumph of imagination over intelligence.   —H. L. MENCKEN

Love is a game exaggerating the difference between one person and everybody else.

—GEORGE BERNARD SHAW

It is not customary to love what one has.   —ANATOLE FRANCE

Aim-inhibited sex.   —SIGMUND FREUD

Love is a substitute for another desire, for the struggle toward self-fulfillment, for the vain urge to reach one's ego-ideal.   —THEODORE REIK

---

origins, its modes, and whom its primary intended beneficiary is. I then ask the question: is there a single definition of love that can unite and subsume the endless variety of concepts? I offer such a definition and discuss its implications.

Next to be considered are the developmental stages of love and whether love is accurate. Following is a brief review of empirical attempts to study whether love is a single general dimension or several dimensions. Finally, the utility of a taxonomy of love is considered as well as some research and practical applications.

ORIGINS

Most theorists focus on the mother-infant relationship as the prototype of all love relationships. Much has been written by Freud (1952), Sullivan (1953), Harlow (1971), and countless others on how various interaction patterns lead to differing kinds of pathological development or strengths of personality development including the capacity to love. In this chapter, however, I will focus on the immediate origins of love among adults. A review of the literature on love suggests four categories of origins: personality inadequacy, personality adequacy or even superadequacy, the influence of societal norms, and physiological arousal.

Personality Inadequacy

Some individuals (Casler, 1974; Freud, 1952; Martinson, 1955, 1959; Reik, 1957) have attempted to portray the need for love as a sign of inadequacy. Casler states he does not believe that it is pathological to love, but that the *need* to love is. "Love is the fear of losing an important source of need gratification" (1974, p. 10). In sum, "a person who does not have the inner resources to stand alone can usually impose himself upon someone who is equally incapacitated" (p. 7).

Martinson concerns himself with the need to marry, but in the context in which he speaks this need can be seen as a need for a permanent love relationship. Martinson hypothesizes that "persons who marry demonstrate greater feelings of ego deficiency than do persons who remain single" (1955, p. 162).[1]

Freud (1952) and Reik (1974) both saw love as reflecting the perception of one's own unattained ideals in the partner. They differed somewhat in emphasis in that Freud focused on a deflected (aim-inhibited) sex drive as supplying the energy for the projection, whereas Reik believed that ego needs can function independently of the libido.

The conception of love as an addiction is considered by one theorist as an example of personality inadequacy but by another as a basic human reaction. Addiction, as defined by Peele (1975), exists "when a person's attachment to a sensation, an object, or another person is such as to lessen his appreciation of and ability to deal with other things in his environment, or in himself, so that he has become increasingly dependent on that experience as his only source of gratification" (p. 61). Peele draws parallels between the use of drugs and the use of another individual as an escape from one's self. A fear of interpersonal incompetence may drive one to use a drug or a person as a buffer against anxiety.

The concept of love as an addiction is also developed by Solomon and Corbit (1974) as a part of their opponent-process theory of motivation, but it is explained as a natural human reaction. They state that most sensations are followed by opposite sensations. The fear engendered by the first parachute jump is turned to relief when (and if) the jump is successfully accomplished. With repeated practice the aftereffect becomes increasingly more potent and the effect itself less strong. A practiced jumper, therefore, feels

---

1. Martinson found support for this hypothesis with female subjects (1955), but his results were due to using only young persons who had married shortly after high school. When he used male subjects who had married at not so young an age (1959), no significant findings resulted.

momentary and limited fear, almost better explained as nervous anticipation, followed by exhilaration after the jump.

Conversely, something that at the start is intensely pleasurable, such as using heroin, slowly loses its high, but the aversive feeling of doing without it becomes so painful that addicts find they need it ever more while enjoying it ever less.

In sum, the term *inadequacy* is used differently from writer to writer. To Casler, the need to love reflects a basic state of inadequacy, whereas, to theorists like Freud and Reik, inadequacy in the typical lover is not pathological but intrinsic to the human condition in that we cannot fulfill all our ideals.

Personality Adequacy

By far the vast majority of the populace and most writers assume that it is normal to love and that only the *inadequate* personality is unable to do so. Presumably, as noted earlier by Sullivan and Harlow among a host of others, this inadequacy stems from an absence of warmth, trust, security, and tactile contact in the infant's relationship with the mother. Some theorists believe that the capacity and inclination to love can stem from a superabundance of adequacy. Winch (1958) speaks about *deficit* needs leading to attraction to someone who can fulfill these needs, but he also speaks of *surplus* needs such as nurturance. Individuals can be suffused with love which they need to express toward others in general (as do saints, for example) or toward a specific person.

Maslow (1954) and Lewis (1960) speak of the distinction between "deficit" love and "being" (Maslow) or "gift" (Lewis) love. From the foregoing it can be concluded that the need to love is not restricted to the inadequate personality but can emanate from the healthy personality as an inevitable concomitant of the energy available when one is freed from neurotic preoccupation with oneself.

Societal Norms

Up to this point love has been treated as a personal experience, but to restrict ourselves to the area of personality is to overlook the vested interest that society has in love and its frequent result, marriage.

Greenfield (1965) has argued that romantic love is a behavioral complex whose function is

> to motivate individuals—where there is not other means of motivating
> them—to occupy the positions husband-father and wife-mother and

form nuclear families that are essential not only for reproduction and socialization but also to maintain the existing arrangements for distributing and consuming goods and services and, in general, to keep the social system in proper working order and thus maintaining it as a going concern. (p. 377)

Greenfield believes it is necessary to motivate people because the roles of husband-father and wife-mother often involve more burden than gain to the individuals. The interests of society may be opposed to their own. Thus, they learn that there must be more to life than merely material considerations and that "love" is what makes life meaningful. Accordingly, if they marry for "love," which almost everybody must do as a self-fulfilling prophecy, they will add this enriched dimension to their existence.

Physiological Arousal

A novel theory of passionate love has been presented by Walster (1971). Individuals are said to experience passionate love when (1) they are intensely aroused physiologically, and (2) given the context in which the arousal takes place, "love" seems an appropriate label for these feelings.

The theory is derived from the work of Schachter (1964) and leans heavily on an experiment in which subjects were injected with epinephrine, a drug that increases systolic blood pressure, muscle and cerebral blood flow, and heart rate, among other changes. To the individual, the experience is one of tremor of the hands, palpitation, more rapid breathing, and sometimes flushing. This type of reaction is usually experienced in a number of emotional states including fear, anxiety, anger, and the cardiorespiratory state of love or infatuation.

All the subjects were misled and told they had received a new vitamin compound called Suproxin. Half of the subjects received epinephrine, however, and half a placebo. Some of those receiving epinephrine were told of the actual effects that would ensue as a result of the injection; others were misled as to the symptoms (they were told that their feet would feel numb, and they would itch and have a slight headache); and yet another group received no information about their "vitamin" shot.

Some of the participants were then subjected to a "euphoria" condition in which a confederate of the experimenter carried on in a madcap fashion, shooting paper wads and dancing with a hula hoop. Other subjects in the "anger" condition filled out an insulting questionnaire asking who in their family bathed regularly, who was under psychiatric care, and how many lovers their mother had had, of which the least response was "4 and under." The respondents watched a confederate become increasingly indignant and finally stomp out of the room after voicing his irritation. In accordance with the prediction, those subjects who received the epinephrine but no information as to its effect showed greater emotional arousal than those who received placebos or who received the epinephrine but knew what to expect. Generalizing from these data, Walster reasons that when the cognitive appraisal of the situation justifies an interpretation of love (as in the presence of an attractive member of the opposite sex), arousal, *even from an independent source*, can lead to the conclusion that one is in the throes of passionate love.

EVALUATION OF THEORIES ON THE ORIGIN OF LOVE

Personality Inadequacy

If we regard love as not necessarily promoting the growth of the beloved but as merely reflecting a strong emotional attachment usually accompanied by a sexual relationship, then the theory that personality inadequacy is one of the origins of love can scarcely be questioned. Countless therapists have described the overwhelming dependence of their clients who fixate on, lean on, and smother their mates, pressing them into service as buffers against the anxiety of experienced inadequacy.

Sperling (1985a, 1985b) has demonstrated empirically that personality inadequacy can lead to a pathological form of "desperate love," which involves themes such as a feeling of fusion with the lover, an overwhelming desire for and anxiety concerning reciprocation, idealization of the lover, feelings of insecurity outside the relationship, difficulty with interpersonal reality testing, anxiety at separations, and extremes of happiness and sadness (1985b, p. 10).

Whether adequately functioning personalities need to love someone is difficult to answer unless the meaning of *need* is clarified. If *need* is interpreted to mean "cannot function without," then adequately functioning persons can usually live without specific loved ones. They can engage in a multitude of satisfying but emotionally diffused relationships without having one intense, all-embracing relationship.

If we consider what is *preferred* rather than what is *necessary*, it would appear that most adequately functioning men seek love relationships, preferably those that might result in marriage, rather than nonlove ones. The work of Knupfer, Clark, and Room (1966) conclusively shows that single men (specified as past the age of thirty), who might be expected to be less likely to be involved in a love relationship than married men, were far more unhappy and unable to function adequately than married men. The evidence is somewhat mixed for single women as opposed to married women (Murstein, 1986). Yet most single women prefer love relationships. They are, however, able to function better in the absence of such relationships than are men. But humans seem to function best when their emotional and sexual needs are fulfilled in a love relationship. Thus, it seems logical to conclude that both the inadequate and adequate personalities seek and need love relationships, but the inadequate are much more dependent on such relationships to survive psychologically. Unfortunately, their lower number of assets and greater interpersonal liabilities make it less likely that they can attract a desirable individual into a love relationship.

Addiction

Concerning the two theories of love as an addiction, I have some difficulty in accepting either theory. Peele's description rings psychologically true for certain kinds of individuals, but we would do violence to the concept of love to equate it with need for another individual as a palliative against anxiety. At least, however, Peele does differentiate between addictive and nonaddictive love. Solomon and Corbit's attempt to describe love in terms of an opponent-process theory is reductionism carried to the point of absurdity. As Peele has pointed out, it ignores cultural and personality factors and cannot account for those individuals who derive pleasure and enjoyment from interaction with loved ones but do not find this pleasure diminishing with time and are not lost in the absence of their loved ones. Thus, addiction theory serves a useful purpose in pointing out how dependency may mimic love in the need for the beloved, but it is hardly to be taken seriously as a definition of love.

Passionate Love

There have been a number of studies of the theory of passionate love. One of the most widely cited is that of Dutton and Aron (1974). In this experiment, men had to cross a narrow swaying bridge with low guard rails 230 feet above rocks and shallow rapids. They showed more sexual imagery on a personality test and were more attracted to a female confederate of the experiment whom they met on the other side than were control-group men interviewed on a sturdy bridge involving a mere ten-foot drop. When a male confederate was used, there were no differences between the experimental and control groups.

The interpretation of this experiment as supporting arousal theory has been challenged by two learning theorists (Kenrick & Cialdini, 1977), who state that any behavior that is associated with a reduction of a noxious or unpleasant stimulus will be experienced as pleasant. Thus, according to these authors, the results of the bridge experiment were due not to passionate love theory but to the principles of learning. The female confederate was liked because she was seen at the end of a harrowing trip across the bridge and was associated with relief. The frightened male subjects could not have misattributed the source of their arousal to the female confederate because they could clearly label the bridge as the source of their anxiety. Besides, attraction to the female confederate as expressed in their telephoning her to find out more about the experiment (she had invited this call and had offered her phone number to participants) was not the same as passionate involvement.

Subsequent research has attempted to manipulate the source of arousal, changing it to exercise, comedy routines, mutilated missionaries, and so on. These studies have always included only men as subjects and attractive females as confederates. Murstein described several of them in detail (1986) and concluded that men aroused by a neutral stimulus can be influenced to misattribute the source of arousal if the salience of the neutral arousal is minimized and the salience of cues regarding the attractiveness of the target person is maximized. By way of example, if the neutral arousal stimulus—a jump rope the men had used to raise their heartbeat—had a light shining on it later, men were less attracted to a female confederate than if no light shone upon it. Apparently the lighted rope made them more conscious that their arousal was due to exercise (White & Kight, 1984). In the same experiment they were also more attracted to the confederate if they were told they would meet her later than if told they would not see her. (There is nothing to weaken salience like not seeing someone again.)

These and other experiments suggest that arousal from a nonsexual stimulus can heighten men's attraction to women even when the men do not attribute much importance to the neutral arousal situation. It is questionable, nevertheless, whether such research supports the theory of passionate love. The experiments demonstrate that attraction of some degree has occurred, as determined usually by questionnaires. It remains to be demonstrated that *passion* can be aroused by experimental manipulation.

Social-Norm Theory

The social-norm theory seems to have plausibility. Much of our economy is geared to marriage, children, and the manufacture of goods needed to maintain the family. But Greenfield has his cause and effect mixed up. It is doubtful that people would invest themselves so extensively in love and marriage were it not satisfying very basic needs.

People do not adhere to norms merely because they have been inculcated with these norms. Adherence must yield benefits to the adherent, and when it no longer does, conformity drops rapidly. The norm of premarital chastity carried weight as long as religious orthodoxy influenced everyday life, parents could effectively supervise and restrict their children's behavior, no effective peer culture existed to counteract parental influence, and little leisure time or opportunity existed for young people to get together. When the importance of these influences waned, the rewards of nonconformity quickly made premarital sex the norm. The continued strength of love and marriage in our society indicates that the rewards for norm adherence still exist for a majority of persons, and that is why love and marriage continue to be accepted as traditional values.

In sum, the origins of love probably stem from human emotional interdependence. We are programmed that way from birth, and the neurotic need love as much as the normal do—probably more so.

THE PRIMARY INTENDED BENEFICIARY OF LOVE

This heading may appear needless. Is not the beloved the primary intended beneficiary? Actually, it might be safer to say only that the beloved is the main target of the lover. If the major purpose of wooing is to remedy some deficit of the lovers, we can consider their love acquisitive—they get something from it. If it is to benefit the beloved in some way, we can speak of benevolent love. And if lovers intend benefits to both themselves and the beloved, we deal with mixed, or acquisitive-benevolent love (Hazo, 1967). It might seem that every definition of love would be located along the mixed axis, but a consideration of a number of definitions indicates that this is not the case. Consider first the acquisitive theorists.

Acquisitive Love

PLATO. In Plato's *Symposium*, Socrates, speaking to Agathon, says that "love is something which a man wants and has not" (Plato, 1952, p.

162). A careful reading of Plato makes it clear that love implies a deficiency and always has an object, and that the object invariably partakes of the good and the beautiful. Although we may love a person, according to Plato, it is the essence of beauty that draws us to the person.[2] In time, if we are fortunate, we move toward an increasingly higher level of functioning, leading us to an appreciation of the abstract concept of the physically beautiful. But that itself is but a stepping-stone to an appreciation of the morally beautiful, which in turn leads to an appreciation of the intellectually beautiful and at last to an appreciation of the idea of beauty itself. Love is, thus, the soul's dynamic attempt to achieve oneness with the source of its being.

The primary object of love is the abstract notion of beauty. Although human beings may contain traces of beauty, the focus is on the *idea* of beauty rather than on one of the many exemplars of beauty such as persons. Plato thus avoids the language of feeling—bestowal of value, tenderness, warmth, and caring. Sex is but a means of propagating the race and little more.

There is some hint in Plato that love may contain elements of benevolence. For example, love is said to be intermediate between the divine and the mortal. Although the Platonic God has no personal interest in mankind, the mortal aspect of love might refer to nurturing others, and philosophers, who in the Platonic way of thinking are superior to the rest of mankind because they are more sensitive to and more involved in the search for wisdom and beauty than the rest of us, enjoy teaching the less advanced the joys of knowledge of beauty. Thus, there is the possibility of conferring good on others in Plato's philosophy, although, in the totality of his writings, it is muted.

The concept of love as acquisitive is contained in the writings of a multitude of other theorists and theories, but I can mention only a sample: Ovid, Freud, Winch, learning theory, courtly love, love as pathology, and love as addiction. To Ovid (1931), love is essentially a sexual (behavior) sport in which duplicity is used in order that a man might win his way into a woman's heart and subsequently into her boudoir. Andrew Capellanus, whose *The Art of Courtly Love* (1959) is our chief treatise on this twelfth-century art form, defined love as "a certain inborn suffering derived from the sight of an excessive meditation upon the beauty of the opposite sex" (p. 28). The cure is "the embraces of the other." Thus love for him is acquisitive.

2. Beauty and good are synonymous in Platonic thinking.

FREUD. Freud's description of love is likewise acquisitive but much more detailed. Love is at its core the desire for sexual union (Freud, 1952). When the desire is blocked, and when the object desired also possesses many qualities the ego has aspired to but not attained, we find not only a sexual overestimation of the object but also the object serving as a substitute for the unattained ego-ideal. The subject falls in love and idealizes the object. But once the sexual aim is achieved through coitus, love ought to extinguish. Freud, however, knew that this was not always the case. How did love survive? According to Freud, the individual "could calculate with certainty upon the revival of the need . . . and this is the first motive for directing a lasting cathexis upon the sexual object and for *loving* it in the passionless intervals as well" (1952, p. 681).

Such feelings as tenderness, affection, and the like thus tie individuals together during passionless moments. Tender feelings also may result from completely blocked sexual aims. The love between brothers and sisters and parents and children is also aim-inhibited sensual love, maintaining its sensual connection only in the unconscious mind. In sum, Freud acknowledged the presence of benevolent wishes in individuals (tenderness, for example), but since these are derivatives of sensual desire, which is essentially acquisitive in nature, it seems justifiable to classify Freud among those seeing love as an acquisitive drive.

LEARNING THEORY. In their book *Loving*, Miller and Siegel (1972) explain love as a learned response. Specifically, "love is a response to a generalized hope signal, a broad pleasurable expectancy. The love object, be it a 'thing' or a person, is a generalized, secondary, positive reinforcer" (pp. 14–15). This translates into nontechnical language as follows. In association with the beloved, the lover experiences warm, pleasant, "good" feelings and often relief from doubts, fears, and the like. What is primarily satisfying is the pleasant feeling (primary reinforcement). These pleasant feelings, however, do not just happen. They occur only when the beloved is present. Hence, the beloved becomes a secondary positive reinforcer, which is to say that the beloved's presence is associated with these good feelings and the beloved's appearance becomes a hope signal that pleasant feelings are forthcoming.

This definition clearly falls into our acquisitive-behavior framework because the benefits accrue to the lover and a response is the operational manifestation of love. If lovers ceased to enjoy the presence of the beloved, they could terminate the relationship. By definition, the hope signal remains a hope signal because of the benefits to the lover. There is, however, no reason the beloved cannot also be acquiring benefits through his or her own responses.

Benevolent Love

If the purpose of love is defined as aiding, protecting, or improving other persons, if the inclination is to give rather than to get, to seek good for another person rather than for oneself, we are dealing with benevolent love (Hazo, 1967). In its purest form, such love was referred to by the church as agape, and it was said to flow from God to man, infusing man's life with a radiance that led to salvation (Nygren, 1953). Its chief characteristics were (1) it was spontaneous and unmotivated by personal considerations and needs, (2) it was indifferent to value—a beggar could be loved as readily as a king, a monster as much as a saint, (3) it was creative, and (4) it was an initiator of fellowship with God.

The leading exponent of agape as a mode of life was Martin Luther. He saw man as but a tube through which the sacred fluid of God's love flows (Singer, 1966). But to achieve this love, man must renounce self-interest totally. "Good works" as a ladder to heaven is totally rejected. It is presumptuous to pretend that one can achieve a fellowship with God on quasi-equal terms. One must confess total worthlessness and become the instrument of God's will.

It is questionable how many persons would qualify for the role of agapean lover. I can think only of Jesus, and according to most Christian beliefs, Jesus was not a person; he was a manifestation of the Godhead. On a human level, therefore, I shall content myself with considerations of love that are primarily other-oriented but are not necessarily devoid of secondary gains for lovers. Within the confines of this definition of benevolence, for example, lovers could be permitted such recompense for their love as feelings of satisfaction, moral improvement, and recognition by others of their love. Within this "relaxed" model of love, there is no dearth of suitable definitions that might fit it:

> Fromm: "The active concern for the life and growth of that which we love" (1956, p. 22)
>
> Leibniz: "To love is to be inclined to take pleasure in the complete perfection of happiness of the object loved" (Hazo, 1967, p. 378)
>
> Ortega y Gasset: "The affirmation of its object" (1957, p. 17)

Acquisitive-Benevolent Love

If love is assumed and intended to benefit each partner to a more or less equal degree, we deal with a mixture of acquisitiveness and benevolence. The following writers' definitions can be thus classified:

May: "A delight in the presence of the other person and an affirming of his value and development as much as one's own" (1953, p. 241)

Montagu: "The relationship between persons in which they confer mutual benefits on each other" (1975, p. 7)

Foote: "The relationship between one person and another which is most conducive to the optimal growth of both" (1953, p. 246)

It should be noted that the definitions cited accord with the subjective aim of the individual, although the objective outcome may be different than was intended. Thus, a mother may intend benefit to her child by excessively pampering him in order not to dampen his "individualism," but the result to the outside observer may be a spoiled brat. Conversely, it is conceivable that less than altruistic motivations may nevertheless result in beneficial personal growth.

IS THE FOCUS ON THE INTENDED PRIMARY BENEFICIARY USEFUL?

Although differentiating definitions of love as acquisitiveness, benevolence, or a mix of the two aids in distinguishing among the definitions of various theorists, this classification scheme becomes more complex when we try to assign value to these intentions. It was noted earlier that an acquisitive need to possess another might involve the need to nurture the other. Thus acquisition can involve benevolence. It was also noted earlier that benevolent intentions might turn out badly and in fact might involve rationalization to cloak possessive (acquisitive) behavior. A further problem lies in ascertaining what is primary and what is secondary. When Albert Schweitzer consecrated his life to establishing a hospital for Africans, he undoubtedly took pride or at least pleasure in the thought of what he had done and in the accolades tendered him by the admiring world.

If his primary purpose was fame and the hospital was a means to it, then his love for the sick was acquisitive. If, however, he primarily cared for the sick, then his primary love was benevolent, although we could not begrudge him the secondary gain of satisfaction. But who could tell what lay in his heart? Moreover, how could one measure units of praise received against units of affection given to others?

Last, the categorization by intended beneficiary does not allow for contingency behaviors. Individuals may start out by intending wholly acquisitive behavior but may respond to the modeling effect of their partners' benevolent love by modifying their own "love" more toward the benevolent continuum. Thus, categorization by intended beneficiary, although a theoretically useful concept, is difficult to utilize meaningfully in practice.

THE NATURE OF LOVE

Love has been said to involve a host of characteristics such as altruism, intimacy, admiration, respect, sharing, confiding, acceptance, pride in the other, unity, exclusive preoccupation, and so on (Scoresby, 1977; Symonds, 1946; Turner, 1970). Each characteristic, however, can be classified by mode of expression as a *behavior, judgment,* or *feeling.*

For those who consider love as behavior, the key word is response. Love may be caring for another, responding to his or her needs, expressing affection in a physical sense, or gazing at the beloved a long time.

Writers who think of love as a judgment focus on esteem (someone is good in himself or herself) or valuation (someone is good for me) (Hazo, 1967). Love measured as an attitude would fall under the rubric of judgment, although the attitude might be derived from evaluation of behavior or feeling.

Love as a feeling presupposes some physiological correlate, although this may not be readily measurable. Cardiorespiratory love with sweating, tremor, and heart palpitations in the presence of the beloved would be a classic example of love as feeling. The dean of American behaviorists, John B. Watson, thought of love as "an innate emotion elicited by cutaneous stimulation of the erogenous zones" (Harlow, 1958, p. 17). The sensation, however, might be more subtle, such as engaging in hypnotic or dreamlike reveries of the beloved. A definition of love need not be limited to only one of these three possibilities, but might include any two or three in varying interactions.

EVALUATION OF MODES OF EXPRESSION OF LOVE

Love as a Feeling

When one *feels* in love, one is usually sure it *is* love! The feeling of being in love was described by the majority of a sample of college women "as the most important thing in the world" (Ellis, 1950). Many a courtship declaration has begun with such phrases as "The love that I feel for you . . ." But feelings are tremendously variable. Today's passionate love may be regarded tomorrow as yesterday's infatuation. Indeed, the difference between love and infatuation may well be that a successful love affair, perhaps one leading to marriage, is retrospectively declared to be true love, whereas if one is rebuffed, retrospection, in defense of ego, declares the relationship to have been only an infatuation.

In everyday marriage, there are times when the spouses are highly irritated or angry with each other. Should we declare them to be out of love and reinstate them in love's kingdom only if and when they have kissed and made up? If so, we would have to acknowledge that, at any given moment, considerable numbers of individuals are shifting positions of being in or out of love. I believe, therefore, that feelings are too unstable a criterion to use as an index of love.

Is Love an Attitude?

Many writers have considered love as an attitude. Fromm, for example, states that love is "an *attitude*, or *orientation of character* which determines the relatedness of a person to the world as a whole, not toward one 'object' of love" (1956, p. 38). Rubin, who constructed an attitude scale on which the higher one scores, the more one's attitude is said to be that of romantic love, defines it as "love between unmarried opposite-sex peers, of the sort which could possibly lead to marriage" (1970, p. 266). This definition suffers from such problems as imprecision ("love . . . which could *possibly* lead to marriage"; italics mine). I am reminded of a talk given by Edward Shneidman in which he paused in the middle of his assessment of a case and said, "I suppose some of you may be saying isn't Mr. A [the case in question] a latent homosexual? I would remind you that *all* of us here are *latent* homosexuals, except, of course, those of us here who are *practicing* homosexuals." In short, love that possibly could lead to marriage also possibly could not, which does not clarify matters very much. That romantic love is defined as something that could lead to marriage is tautologous because romantic love has no separate meaning of its own. Its existence is defined by its consequence.

A further difficulty with this conception of love is that even some individuals with very high scores would persist in saying that they are not in love. Conversely, some individuals with low scores may, nevertheless, persist in saying that they love the individual in question. In employing attitude as measured on a scale as the criterion of love, therefore, we risk to some degree misclassifying some individuals if we take their statement that they love or do not love someone as the ultimate criterion.

Another problem is that attitude as measured by love scales yields continuous scores, but the behavioral correlates of these quantified attitudes may not be proportionate to the difference in scores. For example, a woman may decide that she likes but does not love Samuel Swain. She decides that she *loves* Wolfgang Wooer. Suppose that she had a romantic love score of 85 with respect to Wolfgang and one of 80 with respect to Samuel. The difference in score is small, but the behavioral consequences of living with Wolfgang and not Samuel are considerably greater. She moves in with Wolfgang, sleeps with him, and does his shirts because being a "one-man woman," she loves Wolfgang, not Samuel.

Love as Behavior?

Exactly the same problem we encountered with the use of attitude as a criterion of love is apparent in the use of behavior as a criterion. Someone might engage in what seems very unloving behavior toward another, such as cuffing the person about the head a bit, but then avow that he truly loves that person. Another might behave very lovingly toward someone but disclaim the label of loving: "we're just good friends." If we therefore superimpose our definition of what love is upon that of the lovers', we may leave them far from satisfied with our definition.

Love as Judgment

Since love cannot be reduced to feeling or behavior, it falls under the rubric of personal judgment. This judgment by the individuals concerned may draw upon feelings and behaviors by themselves and/or the potential loved ones, but its essence is a *cognitive decision by the individuals that they love another*. This decision may be based on conscious criteria against which the partner is compared, or the comparison may be implicit. The implications are far-reaching to individuals, for to acknowledge such a state of affairs is, in effect, as I have noted earlier, to program themselves to behave in a certain way toward their beloved ones. Henceforth, certain attitudes as well as expectations may be held with respect to the beloved, and the lovers may even expect that certain feelings on the part of the self and the partner should now be in evidence.

It is true that these feelings, attitudes, and behavior may have been present and led to the conclusion that the individual was in love, but it is also true that the decision to consider oneself in love may in turn produce new feelings, attitudes, and behavior, as I noted earlier.

Let us sum up the advantages and disadvantages of each mode for defining love. If *feeling* is employed as the criterion, the experience of love may seem very clear to the individual experiencing it, but when the feeling is absent, the love must be declared officially dead, although the feeling may return later on, in which case the individual is said to love again. If *attitude* is employed, there is the question as to who sets the criterion of love. If it is an outsider, as in a scale, the test taker's evaluation may differ from that of the outsider. If individuals themselves set the criterion, they must decide when sufficient positive attitudes have accrued to call their condition "love." Once they decide that, however, they have in essence made a *cognitive decision*.

If *behavior* is the criterion, one must disregard feelings and even cognitive decisions and work backward, judging whether one loved or not by the behavior that followed. Much loving behavior, however, will result from labeling oneself as "in love" or declaring one's love to another. Thus, it may be difficult to tell whether one loved prior to the behavior or as a result of it. Finally, in arguing that love results from a decision to bestow one's love on another, we avoid some of the difficulties inherent in defining love as a feeling or attitude. There is nothing immutable in a decision that one loves, as the history of human relationships must surely indicate. Individuals may decide, in view of feedback from others and themselves, that they were mistaken when they thought they loved, or they may acknowledge that they once loved the other but no longer do. They may arrive at such a conclusion by referring to feelings, attitudes, or behavior, but the evaluation of their present state is still a conscious decision.

THE DEVELOPMENTAL STAGES OF LOVE

A review of the research on love suggests three stages of love: passionate, romantic, and conjugal (companionate). Passionate love involves intense arousal and a strong sexual base, although consummation may not take place because of external barriers or internally imposed ones. An almost invariant major correlate of this intensity is that the members of the couple have not known each other very long or, if the relationship is long-standing, circumstances may have prevented frequent or intimate interaction.

Romantic love is difficult to separate from passionate love. Both are intense. Romantic love, however, is often more focused on idealization of the other than on mainly the sexuality of the other. Both types of love occur fairly early in a relationship. In the absence of much real knowledge of the other, each member of the couple may project fantasized ideal qualities onto the other. The qualities of the other are apt to be exaggerated, and much attention is paid to the beloved and to the experience of love, to the exclusion of almost everything else. There is much sentiment, often bathetic, and there is an omnipresent, insatiable need to be with the be-loved, although circumstances often prevent it.

Conjugal love, the least intense form of love, is what happens to a couple after marriage, or more correctly after they have come to know each other well, which can occur before marriage if the courtship is an extended one. With unimpeded access to each other and as a result of habituation, bit by bit generalized, overriding passion and longing evaporate and are re-placed by liking or trust, although in good marriages, passion may return on specific occasions. Almost with a sigh of relief, the couple turn back to the business of life. Conjugal love, however, does not imply indifference to each other. Rather, the couple are presumably building more stable and permanent bonds of affection and trust based on increasing, real knowledge of the other which replaces fantasy. Out of the evolving network of shared experiences as a couple—children, family, married life—comes something less ephemeral and more permanent than romantic love. Consideration, courtesy, and gallantry may persist, but the terrible need for the other at every possible moment and the emotional intoxication in the presence or at the thought of the other become a thing of the past.

The sequence of these stages has not been studied. One possible scheme is that passionate love or physical attraction is quickly followed by idealization (romantic love) and then moves to conjugal love in long-standing relationships. Some individuals, however, start with friendship and then evolve into romantic or passionate love. The study of these sequences is a subject for future research. We do, however, have some beginnings in this regard.

Love and trust were found to be more highly correlated for married couples than for unmarried ones (Dion & Dion, 1976; Driscoll, Davis, & Lipetz, 1972). Knox (1970) reported that couples married more than twenty years scored higher on romantic love than those married five years. The sample of those married twenty years, however, probably reflects a selective influence in which the survivors (nondivorced) are more apt to be happier and to have better relationships than the typical couple married only five years who have yet to face many of the trials that the longer married couples have passed through. Moreover, inspection of Knox's items reveals that what he means by romanticism is mainly idealization of the partner in addition to a belief in the eternity of love. The concept of romantic love that I hold, however, includes also an emphasis on passion and the physical. Thus, the Knox data are not really in conflict with at least a two-stage concept of love (a difference between sensual-romantic and companionate love), and it appears validated by the research to date.

ACCURACY: A DIMENSION NOT CONSIDERED

We have up to this point bypassed consideration of the question that many people have pondered in their own personal lives. How do you determine whether the love one experiences is based on reality or on distortion? Some extremely distinguished writers think of love as essentially artifact. Stendhal (pseudonym of Henri Beyle), in his book *On Love* (1947), noted that passion is a subjective experience that leads to distortion. He once observed that a bare tree bough that had fallen into a salt pit and lay there for some time acquired a covering of brilliant crystals when it was extracted. The shabby branch appeared at first glance to be a priceless objet d'art, but in reality it was worthless. He drew an analogy to the experience of love, which he called crystallization. Love is a fantasy, a projection of the individual's ego-ideal onto the often undeserving object. When reality intrudes, crystallization ends and so does love.

Freud (1952) saw love as aim-inhibited sex and thus, in essence, distortion, and Schopenhauer (1964) saw it as a device of nature for propagation. On the other hand, the vast majority of writers, as we have seen, do not think of love as basically self- or partner-deception.

The reason it seems fruitless to pursue this avenue further is that it is impossible to tell at the time that love is experienced whether it is based on reality, deception, or some combination of the two. It should be noted also that self-deception in any event is not necessarily a precursor of unhappiness. A tendency to exaggerate the spouse's attributes is characteristic of happy marriages (Kelly, 1941; Murstein & Beck, 1972) and may continue for the entire course of the marriage.

EMPIRICAL RESEARCH ON TAXONOMIES OF LOVE

Many researchers have undertaken factor analyses of love in an effort to determine how many dimensions of love there are. Is there a single general factor we call love, or are there at least nine types of love as Lee (1976) has claimed? An examination of a far from complete list of the efforts to factor analyze love (Dion & Dion, 1973; Knox & Sporakowski, 1968; Mathes, 1980; Rubin, 1970; Sternberg & Grajek, 1984; Swensen, 1961, 1972; Swensen & Gilner, 1964) shows that they have resulted in the conclusion that there is only one major factor of love that includes a wide variety of behaviors, feelings, and attitudes.[3] This factor encompasses all the good

3. A possible exception to the ubiquitous finding of a general factor with every factor analysis is the work of Hendrick and Hendrick (1986), whose first factor extracted was only

things one can think about another, which led Murstein (1976), who factor analyzed marital expectations, to call it the Madonna factor for women and the Jack Armstrong factor for men.[4]

Despite this primary factor, many writers have focused on the substrata or clusters within scales of love. Sternberg (1986) has proposed a triangular theory of love, in which it is said to comprise three components:

1. An *intimacy* component, which encompasses the feelings of closeness, *connectedness*, and bondedness one experiences in loving relationships;
2. A *passion* component, which encompasses the drives that lead to romance, physical attraction, and sexual consummation; and
3. A *decision/commitment* component, which encompasses, in the short term, the decision that one loves another, and in the long term, the commitment to maintain that love (Sternberg, 1986).

He then listed and differentiated among a variety of love relationships such as "love at first sight," "liking," "romantic love," "companionate love," and so on, according to how much of the three components each love contained. "Love at first sight," for example, results from high passionate arousal in the relative absence of emotional intimacy and/or cognitive commitment.

Sternberg's classification system is a major contribution to unifying the various kinds of love he describes. A simple three-component concept, however, cannot hope to account for all the nuances and complexities of love. Thus, little is said about the *source* of love or of the *goal* of love or of the *modes* of love. But using his paradigm as a base, one could expand it to account for these omissions.

Passionate love should be high on feeling, with intimate love second and committed love third. Committed love should be represented as a judgment more than the others. Behavior is difficult to assign to his paradigm. Nor is it possible to know whether love for a given individual means loving another or being self-focused as portrayed in Thomas Mann's novel

---

moderately greater in variance accounted for than the second extracted factor. These authors, however, specifically attempted to create six predetermined factors by carefully constructing six clusters of items to represent the six factors. After several trials they were able to achieve six factors, but it is doubtful that their selected forty-two-item pool (seven for each factor) could be said to represent the universe of feelings, behaviors, judgments, and attitudes that might signify love.

4. For those readers of less than mature years, Jack Armstrong, "the All-American Boy," was a legendary hero of the radio who was a student at Hudson High School and crushed a succession of evil villains when he wasn't indulging himself in a bowl of Wheaties, the Breakfast of Champions and sponsor of the program.

The Magic Mountain. A character in the novel says about a woman, "You ask her if she loves him, and she answers, *he* loves me very much." It is probable, therefore, that Sternberg's triangle may eventually become at least a pentagon or even a hexagon if it is to encompass all the phenomena of love. Nevertheless, it is an impressive start.

CONCLUSION AND IMPLICATIONS

Review

Love is an Austro-Hungarian Empire uniting all sorts of feelings, behaviors, and attitudes, sometimes having little in common, under the rubric of "love." Love can come from a surplus of energetic positive feelings or from feelings of inadequacy and gratitude to the one who lessens these feelings. Attraction, if not love, can be influenced by arousal from a neutral source.

Love can be felt for another who services the individual, it can be agape, or benevolent love for another without personal advantage, or it can be a mixture of the two. Love can manifest itself as a feeling, as behavior, as a judgment (decision). A definition of love that attempts to unify these diverse phenomena results in a simplistic tautological definition that love is what one decides it is.

All factor analyses of love have yielded a major factor that dwarfs the others and includes a glorification of the beloved in numerous ways. Despite this unitary factor, there are undoubtedly many kinds of love. The triangular theory of love judges these on the basis of three components, but I have suggested that the structure of love is more complex than that. What are the implications for research and clinical practice?

Research and Clinical Implications

The various developmental stages of different kinds of love have not been studied. Passionate love evolving to companionate love is well known, but how many follow this route? Can one evolve from companionate love to passionate love? There are no data to answer this question, only anecdotal recollections that suggest a yes answer. Longitudinal research (following couples for a period of years) and cross-sectional research (studying couples varying in numbers of years married and assuming that the samples are generalizable so that a couple married fifteen years is similar to one married five years except for the passage of time) should map out how love changes with time.

But individuals also vary in their concept of love at a given time. How similar are the definitions of love of members of a couple? Do individuals tend to converge into a communal definition of love when they marry? Is the similarity in definitions of love between members of a couple greater than chance? And what are the correlates of agreement in a definition of love? Do couples with similar definitions have a better marriage adjustment? Timothy Hayes and I are currently researching the answers to some of these questions.

My taxonomy of love did not lead to the conclusion that there is a useful single definition. But many couples believe that they share a common definition when in fact they do not. Both may argue that they love the other, but the other does not love them, and if they have different definitions of love, they are probably correct. Couples probably need to be educated to respect their partner's differences, particularly in their concept of love. Perhaps individuals should be judged according to how well they live up to their own definitions of love rather than those of their partners. At the very least couples need to be aware of these differences.

Unfortunately, some individuals believe, like Archie Bunker, that ignorance is bliss. Senator Proxmire in 1975 opposed the use of National Science Foundation funding to study love, stating:

> I believe that 200 million other Americans want to leave some things in life a mystery, and right at the top of things we don't want to know is why a man falls in love with a woman and vice versa. . . . So National Science Foundation—get out of the love racket. Leave that to Elizabeth Barrett Browning and Irving Berlin. Here, if anywhere, Alexander Pope was right when he observed, "If ignorance is bliss, 'tis folly to be wise." (Berscheid & Walster, 1978, p. 150)

Senator Proxmire is not alone. Harry Harlow (1958) remarked a generation ago that most psychologists as far as their work was concerned could live without love—and they deserved it! But times have changed, and we now recognize that love is not only personally meaningful but a very important concept in understanding personality—one that needs to be researched and is at last getting the attention it deserves. Indeed, the expression "Don't leave home without it!" might be more important with reference to love than to one's American Express card.

REFERENCES

Berscheid, E., & Walster, E. (1978). *Interpersonal attraction* (2nd ed.). Reading, MA: Addison-Wesley.

Beyle, M. H. (Stendhal). (1947). *On love*. New York: Liveright.

Brown, S. (1966, December 31). May I ask you a few questions about love? *Saturday Evening Post*, pp. 24–27.

Capellanus, A. (1959). *The art of courtly love* (J. J. Parry, Trans.). New York: Frederick Ungar.

Casler, L. (1974). *Is marriage necessary?* New York: Human Sciences Press.

Dion, K. L., & Dion, K. K. (1973). Correlates of romantic love. *Journal of Consulting and Clinical Psychology, 4,* 51–56.

———. (1976). Love, liking, and trust in heterosexual relationships. *Personality and Social Psychology Bulletin, 2,* 191–206.

Driscoll, R., Davis, K. E., & Lipetz, M. E. (1972). Parental interference and romantic love. *Journal of Personality and Social Psychology, 24,* 1–10.

Dutton, D. G., & Aron, A. P. (1974). Some evidence for heightened sexual attraction under conditions of high anxiety. *Journal of Personality and Social Psychology, 30,* 510–517.

Ellis, A. (1950). Love and family relationships of American college girls. *American Journal of Sociology, 55,* 55–56.

Foote, N. N. (1953). Love. *Psychiatry, 16,* 245–251.

Freud, S. (1952). Group psychology and the analysis of the ego. In *The major works of Sigmund Freud* (pp. 664–696). Chicago: Encyclopaedia Britannica.

Fromm, E. (1956). *The art of loving.* New York: Harper & Row.

Greenfield, S. M. (1965). Love and marriage in modern America: A functional analysis. *Sociological Quarterly, 6,* 361–377.

Harlow, H. F. (1958). The nature of love. *American Psychologist, 13,* 673–685.

———. (1971). *Learning to love.* San Francisco: Albion.

Hazo, R. G. (1967). *The idea of love.* New York: Praeger.

Hendrick, C., & Hendrick, S. (1986). A theory and method of love. *Journal of Personality and Social Psychology, 50,* 392–402.

Horton, D. (1957). The dialogue of courtship in popular songs. *American Journal of Sociology, 62,* 569–578.

Kelly, E. L. (1941). Marital compatibility as related to personality traits of husbands and wives as rated by self and spouse. *Journal of Social Psychology, 13,* 193–198.

Kenrick, D. T., & Cialdini, R. B. (1977). Romantic attraction: Misattribution versus reinforcement explanations. *Journal of Personality and Social Psychology, 35,* 381–391.

Knox, D. H. (1970). Conceptions of love at three developmental levels. *Family Coordinator, 19,* 151–157.

Knox, D., & Sporakowski, M. (1968). Attitudes of college students toward love. *Journal of Marriage and the Family, 30,* 638–642.

Knupfer, G., Clark, W., & Room, R. (1966). The mental health of the unmarried. *American Journal of Psychiatry, 122,* 841–851.

Lasswell, T. E., & Lasswell, M. E. (1976). I love you but I'm not in love with you. *Journal of Marriage and Family Counseling, 2,* 211–224.

Lee, J. A. (1976). *The colors of love.* Englewood Cliffs, NJ: Prentice-Hall.

Lewis, C. S. (1960). *The four loves.* New York: Harcourt, Brace, & World.

Martinson, F. M. (1955). Ego deficiency as a factor in marriage. *American Sociological Review, 20,* 161–164.

———. (1959). Ego deficiency as a factor in marriage—a male sample. *Marriage and Family Living*, 21, 52–58.

Maslow, A. H. (1954). *Motivation and personality*. New York: Harper & Brothers.

Mathes, E. W. (1980). Nine colours or types of romantic love. *Psychological Reports*, 47, 371–376.

May, R. (1953). *Man's search for himself*. New York: Norton.

Miller, H. L., & Siegel, P. S. (1972). *Loving: A psychological approach*. New York: Wiley.

Montagu, A. (1975). A scientist looks at love. In A. Montagu (Ed.), *The practice of love* (pp. 5–16). Englewood Cliffs, NJ: Prentice-Hall.

Murstein, B. I. (1976). *Who will marry whom? Theories and research in marital choice*. New York: Springer.

———. (1986). *Paths to marriage*. Beverly Hills, CA: Sage.

Murstein, B. I., & Beck, G. D. (1972). Person perception, marriage adjustment, and social desirability. *Journal of Consulting and Clinical Psychology*, 39, 396–403.

Nygren, A. (1953). *Agape and Eros*. Philadelphia: Westminster Press.

Ortega y Gasset, J. (1957). *On love*. New York: Meridian Books.

Ovid. (1931). *The art of love* (C. D. Young, Trans.). New York: Horace Liveright.

Peele, S. (1975). *Love and addiction*. New York: Taplinger.

Plato. (1952). *Plato*. Chicago: Encyclopaedia Britannica.

Reik, T. (1957). *Of love and lust*. New York: Farrar, Strauss & Cudahy.

Rubin, Z. (1970). Measurement of romantic love. *Journal of Personality and Social Psychology*, 16, 265–273.

Schachter, S. (1964). The interaction of cognitive and physiological determinants of emotional state. In L. Berkowitz (Ed.), *Advances in experimental social psychology* (Vol. 1, pp. 49–80). New York: Academic Press.

Schopenhauer, A. (1964). Of women. In I. Schneider (Ed.), *The world of love* (Vol. 2, pp. 224–235). New York: George Braziller.

Scoresby, A. L. (1977). *The marriage dialogue*. Reading, MA: Addison-Wesley.

Singer, I. (1966). *The nature of love*. New York: Random House.

Solomon, R. L., & Corbit, J. D. (1974). An opponent-process theory of motivation. I: Temporal dynamics of affect. *Psychological Review*, 81, 119–145.

Sperling, M. B. (1985a). Discriminant measures for desperate love. *Journal of Personality Assessment*, 49, 324–328.

———. (1985b). *Fusional love relations: The developmental origins of desperate love*. Manuscript submitted for publication.

Sternberg, R. J. (1986). A triangular theory of love. *Psychological Review*, 93, 119–135.

Sternberg, R. J. & Grajek, S. (1984). The nature of love. *Journal of Personality and Social Psychology*, 47, 312–329.

Sullivan, H. S. (1953). *The interpersonal theory of psychiatry* (H. S. Perry & M. L. Garvel, Eds.). New York: Norton.

Swensen, C. H. (1961). Love: A self-report analysis with college students. *Journal of Individual Psychology*, 17, 167–171.

———. (1972). The behavior of love. In H. Otto (Ed.), *Love today: A new exploration* (pp. 86–101). New York: Association Press.

Swensen, C. H., & Gilner, F. (1964). Factor analysis of self-report statements of love relationships. *Journal of Individual Psychology, 20,* 186–188.

Symonds, P. M. (1946). *The dynamics of human adjustment.* New York: Appleton-Century.

Turner, R. H. (1970). *Family interaction.* New York: Wiley.

Walster, E. (1971). Passionate love. In B. I. Murstein (Ed.), *Theories of attraction and love* (pp. 85–99). New York: Springer.

White, G. L., & Kight, T. D. (1984). Misattribution of arousal and attraction: Effects of salience of explanations for arousal. *Journal of Experimental Social Psychology, 20,* 55–64.

Wilkinson, M. (1976). Romantic love: The great equalizer? Sexism in popular music. *Family Coordinator, 25,* 161–166.

Winch, R. F. (1958). *Mate selection.* New York: Harper & Brothers.

CHAPTER THREE

Love-Styles

BY JOHN ALAN LEE

WHY I STUDIED LOVE

I have studied love because it is my life's most difficult problem. Although I have made much progress, the "impossible dream" of a truly fulfilling mutual love remains a goal I have yet to achieve. Possibly you are not satisfied with your achievements in the pursuit of love. Erich Fromm warned that "there is hardly any activity, any enterprise, which is started with such tremendous hopes and expectations and yet which fails so regularly as love" (1956).

The problem of finding a fulfilling *mutual* love was never more difficult. In bygone days, people held lower expectations of life. Also, they were much more alike: most had about the same kind of education; few traveled far; there was no great variety of entertainment; and there were relatively few kinds of jobs. Today we live in a fast-changing, pluralistic society. Finding a partner who shares our particular combination of tastes, interests, and opinions—our particular *life-style*—is far more difficult than it once was.

Our experience of different people often leads us to want this one's looks, that one's intelligence, another one's character. If only I could find one person with all the desirable qualities I seek! It doesn't require a course in statistics to demonstrate that the odds are against me—all I have to do is spend a few nights in the city's hot spots looking for the perfect partner. Finally I find someone who "comes close." Alas, I am not what the near-perfect partner is looking for. What frustration! Or my choice is "already taken" by someone else. I know people who have waited for years, hoping the only partner they ever met who seemed really suitable would get divorced and "come back on the market."

My research has found that many married people are troubled, deep down, by a nagging awareness that they "settled" for less than they hoped for in a partner. The trouble is, most people don't get to choose between even a half-dozen possible partners. Quite often, we let one choice go by, in the hopes of a better, only to realize later that the rejected choice was the best. It's usually too late then to go back. How many partners should we review before beginning to worry that we're getting too old and it's time to "settle down"? We're not all as persevering as, say, Lord Bertrand Russell, who went through five marriages and met his ideal woman when he was in his seventies (Russell, 1969).

When your efforts to find a satisfying *job* are frustrated, you don't leave the solution to luck—you study the problem and review all possible options. Why not do the same for *love*? If you're not prepared to "settle" and you can't count on luck to lead you to someone close to your ideal, then you need to study love. To be more precise, you need to study "love-styles."

MORE THAN ONE STYLE OF LOVING

Our language has thousands of words for the different parts of a car, but only one word for the satisfying and fulfilling interpersonal relationship we call love. Certain related words—*infatuation, friendship, affection, liking, attraction*—are not synonymous with *love*. With only one word to use, we tend to think there is only one thing corresponding to the word—one kind of relationship that is truly love.

We do recognize that this thing called love has different objects: love of God, love of mother, love of poetry. In this chapter, I am concerned only with *partnering love*—in which one person looks for another to love as a partner for at least a short period of time and possibly for life. As we shall see, partnering love is related to other kinds of love—love of a friend, charitable love of those in need, and so on. But our focus is on *the search for a partner*.

Because we think of love as one thing, we tend to measure differences in experiences of love as differences in *quantity*: "I love you *more than* anyone else. *How much* do you love me? Do you love me *less* since you discovered I was unfaithful to you? Do you love me *as much as* you loved your former girl/boyfriend? Would you love me *more* if I lost thirty pounds?" Thus, we tend to define *mutual love* as a situation where you love me *as much as* I love you. It's as if we lived in a world of black and white love, with varying amounts of love making the picture more or less gray. But we threw out black and white television sets years ago, in preference for color. Now it's time to look at a *color picture of love*.

A COLOR ANALOGY FOR LOVE

Define color. Go ahead—try explaining what color is to a person blind from birth. You'll probably have to use an analogy: "If you had sight, your eyes would see different qualities in objects, similar to the different surfaces your sense of touch can feel. Just as some objects are rough and some smooth, we call the sight of some objects *red*, others *green*, and so on. But you need sight to see these colors." In short, it is more meaningful to explain different colors than to define color itself.

My study of love takes the same approach. I am not concerned with defining love itself, but with helping lovers distinguish between its "different colors." In my study, color becomes the analogy for explaining love. Thus mutual love becomes a new kind of problem. It is not two people who love each other "as much," but two people whose "colors of love" make a good *match*. Just as we learn how to make pleasing matches in colors, we can learn to match love-styles.

There's good reason for looking at love through the analogy of color. I think I look best when I wear browns, so in clothing, brown is my favorite color. But you'd think me daft if I told you "Brown is the only true color. Everyone should wear brown." You'd remind me that you prefer to wear dark blues, and blue is just as attractive a color as brown. There is no such thing as one true color. Nowadays, we don't believe boys must wear blue and girls pink. People wear whatever color they prefer. In the same way, when we recognize different kinds of love—different love-styles—we are less tempted to claim that another person's love is *not really love*: "You don't really love me. If you did . . ." (you've heard the line and can fill in the rest!). It would be kinder and, I will demonstrate, closer to reality to say "Your kind of loving is not the kind I prefer" just as we would speak about a difference in color preferences.

Here's another good reason for looking at love as we do at color: often, we disown our past experiences of love, simply because they did not work out as we hoped. "Well, I guess I didn't really love Billy; it was just an infatuation." We can learn more from our experience if we say "What I felt for Billy was a kind of loving, but not the kind I prefer. Now what kind do I really want?" The notion of different kinds of love is hardly new—it dates at least from the eleventh-century Arab poet, Ibn Hazim, who wrote "Love is of various kinds." But almost every student of love has shown an untempered bias for one particular kind as more *truly love* than the others. (Notable exceptions are Hazo, 1967; Kolb, 1965.)

Some authors have excluded the loving experience of millions of homosexuals by defining love as a heterosexual relationship (for example, Blood, 1962; Goode, 1959). Some have argued that love must be unselfish and concerned only for the beloved (Kierkegaard, 1963; Nygren, 1952; Sorokin, 1967), whereas others have said love should be self-fulfilling and realistic (Gross, 1944; Reiss, 1967). Some even apply a Puritan work ethic, arguing that true love must be productive (Fromm, 1956) or contribute to growth and development (Foote, 1953; Martinson, 1980). Ironically, the most astute application of my theory of love to marriage counseling problems—*Styles of Loving* (Lasswell & Lobsenz, 1980)—nevertheless concludes with an argument that loving should be more "effective"—obviously a notion from the industrial work ethic. Would it not be equally valid to argue that love should be more fun?

Once you have accepted the notion of different styles of loving, each valid according to each person's taste, the problem of love becomes a matter of studying different kinds in order to choose the love-style you prefer most. Then you can consider how your preferred love-style "matches" with others and learn where you are most likely to find partners who are looking for this particular match.

CHANGING LOVE-STYLES THROUGH A LIFETIME

I have chosen the analogy of color deliberately. My favorite color in clothing is not necessarily my favorite color for decorating my home, and, over the course of my life, my favorite color for either purpose may change. The same is true of love. Love-styles are not like signs of the zodiac. You are not born with a particular preference, and you can have more than one preference in a lifetime. In fact, you can have two different preferences in love-style at the same time, each fulfilled by a different partner.

Loving is not a behavior that "comes naturally," not even for mothers of newborn babes. If it were, every mother would love her baby and there would be no cases of horrifying abuse—even to the point of death—of children by their own mothers. This is even more true for the kind of loving involved in seeking a partner. It does not come naturally, but must be learned. Elsewhere (Lee, 1975) I have shown how our modern ideas about love developed in European society hundreds of year ago. These ideas have changed over time; in fact, ideas about styles of loving have changed considerably in my own lifetime (fifty years).

Sets of ideas that develop over time in a particular society to meet the needs of individuals for explaining the world around them are called ideologies. Christianity, capitalism, science—all involve ideology. But Christianity, for example, no longer involves a single ideology. It has split into several competitive and sometimes antagonistic ideologies—or denominations. A fundamentalist Christian does not think about the world in the same way as a Catholic, for example. The same is true of love: there are several ideologies of loving, and I call each a love-style.

Most people learned a particular religious ideology as they grew up, and most people have grown up learning a particular love-style. In adult life, people often find their childhood religion no longer satisfying, and they change. Perhaps the love-style you learned in childhood is also dissatisfying; if so, why not change? For instance, some adults repeat a cycle of falling in love with incompatible partners, behaving foolishly, suffering a heartrending breakup, taking months to get over it, and then—doing the same thing all over again! This style of love can be quite interesting and even nostalgically enjoyable for some people. But if you want to get out of this love-style into something more relaxed, you must study the conditions that led you to learn this style in the first place, and then change those conditions.

Just as different religions are constantly competing for supporters, so different love-styles are constantly seeking your agreement. You have only to turn on your radio for fifteen minutes to hear several love songs in a row. The first tells you love is not merely the most important thing in life—"love is *all* there is." The next tells you not to be so stupid—love is just heartaches and a way to catch pneumonia. The next tells you to enjoy love, but don't take it seriously and don't become dependent on it. The next tells you love is simply a lifelong friendship, whose closing chapter is two old folks playing checkers in the sun.

Or open half a dozen novels, and see the competing ideologies of love! If one examines the fictional and nonfictional writing about love over the past twenty centuries, it becomes obvious that our civilization has been a battleground for ideologies of love. Advocates of some love-styles have attempted not merely to libel other loves but to drive them out of society. St. Augustine sought the triumph of agape over eros (Nygren, 1952), and Denis de Rougemont (1956) attempted to banish mania by equating it with a "love of death." As you can see, I have already given some names to the styles of love. Let's examine each in closer detail.

EROS. In ancient Greek mythology, the arrows of Eros are shot through the eyes of the lover. "To see her is to love her," Kierkegaard sighed. Dante exclaimed on first beholding Beatrice: *Incipit vita nuova* (my life begins anew). Stendhal called this love based on sight "a sudden sensation of recognition and hope."

An erotic lover is perfect evidence that (for this love-style!) love is *not* blind. Erotic lovers know exactly what physical type turns them on, although some have more than one version of the ideal type. For example, a lover may be attracted to slim mates only, but be willing to balance off certain other attributes against each other—giving equal weight, say, to blonde hair combined with a not-quite-so-pretty face, and brunette hair with a more attractive face. In any event, the erotic lover knows exactly what she or he wants in each major attribute—noting, for instance, that the nose is a little too long and silently debating whether to ignore this flaw. The erotic style of loving always begins with a powerful physical attraction because this lover is aware that his or her ideal partner is rare. Like any other searcher for rare treasure, the erotic lover becomes intensely excited at any encounter with a person who comes close to fulfilling the ideal sought for. On the other hand, many people have no favorite type and may consider it irrelevant whether the partner has brown hair or blonde, a heavy or slim build, hairy or smooth skin. Such people are unlikely to experience eros as their preferred love-style.

Much fun has been made of love at first sight. "Lovers manage in their passion's cause to love their ladies even for their flaws," joked Molière. It has been argued that intense physical attraction soon wears off, and indeed it may. But I have interviewed men and women who loved at first sight and, decades later, still rejoiced in the physical pleasure of the beloved's company. More often, an eros love-style will convert over time into a more relaxed companionship, in a mixture of eros and *storge*.

STORGE. The ancient Greek word for the loving affection that develops slowly over time between siblings or playmates is storge (pronounced stor-gay). "Love without fever or folly" (Proudhon) is a traditional conception of true love in agrarian societies where people can grow up slowly with others like themselves. They become affectionate and committed to each other, and finally settle down together. In the fast lane of modern city life where the average person changes home and job every five years, this "friendly love" is difficult to cultivate.

Those who prefer a more passionate love like eros or mania consider storge a bit dull—"just friendship or affection, not *love*." Storgic lovers don't spend much time looking into each other's eyes. The storgic lover is often so easygoing about the relationship that it would be embarrassing to say "I love you." If the partner asks "Do you love me?" the reply is likely to be "Of course, I love you. Whatever made you ask that question?" The storgic lover has no ideal physical type in mind and never consciously selects a love partner. This lover is not "looking for love." Instead, he or she selects enjoyable activities and, through them, happens to meet others who do the same things—so why not do them together? In short, the truly storgic lover has already found this chapter silly and will probably read no further!

LUDUS. "I have been a rover" begins one love song: I have had interesting relationships with many partners but never settled down with any of them. Another song recounts delightful loves in each decade of the singer's life, beginning when he was seventeen. A character in *Finian's Rainbow* explains how, when he can't be with the one he fancies, he fancies the face he faces. All are examples of the love-style called ludus (pronounced loo-dus), the Latin word for "play" or "game." The ludic lover has no ideal type of beloved in mind and refuses to devote the whole of life to the development of one partnership in love. He is a rover, and she is a collector of love experiences to be looked back on with pleasure, as one might recall annual vacations to many distant lands.

A guide to love published in 1653 was called *Divided love, in which it is proved that one can love several persons equally and perfectly at the same time*. Two centuries later, the poet Shelley understood the ideological competition between different love-styles when he wrote in his poem "Epipsychidion":

> I never was attached to that great sect
> Whose doctrine is, that each one should select
> One of the crowd a mistress or a friend,
> And all the rest, though fair and wise, command
> To cold oblivion.

Some readers will object: "This isn't love at all! This is dalliance, flirtation, a series of affairs." (So maybe you don't like orange; it happens to be my favorite decorating color!) I have interviewed many men and women who look back on a life of ludic relationships with great satisfaction. As a love-style, ludus has a long pedigree. The term was first used for a style of playful, noncommittal loving in the year 1 A.D. by the Roman poet Ovid.

Ludic lovers are pluralistic (detractors would say promiscuous) in love. They know there are plenty of fish in the sea, so jealousy is pointless and always deplored in the beloved. "Why ask where I was Friday night; this is Saturday and I'm loving you now. Isn't that enough?" Ludus can be played as an open game, with the lover honestly warning the partner that there are other irons in the fire. Or it can be played with deception: the lover promises commitment after the manner of Don Juan. He went unrepentant to his death, but most ludic lovers I have interviewed found that lying gets complicated. Fair play is less likely to produce feelings of guilt later on. In the gossipy world of the singles bars where modern ludic lovers often find partners, a reputation for fair dealing is more likely to win new partners: "Well, if you fall in love with *him*, don't expect wedding bells, but at least he won't promise you anything just to get you into bed."

THE PRIMARY COLORS OF LOVE

All colors of the rainbow arise from blends of three primary colors—red, yellow, and blue. In my typology of love, the three primary love-styles are eros, ludus, and storge, and numerous other colors of love result from various combinations of the three primaries. No one can say how many colors there are; experts claim the human eye can distinguish more than eight million (*Psychology Today*, December 1985, p. 8). It seems equally pointless to me to attempt to say how many love-styles there are. It makes more sense to analyze various love-styles into their primary components, just as you do with an unusual shade of color you want to duplicate at the paint store.

It is important to remember that when things are combined, some of the qualities of each ingredient are lost and some new qualities, not found in any one of the ingredients, may emerge. Until you have certain colors made up at the paint store, you'd never guess that they have, say, black pigment in them. Who would know, by tasting salt, that it is a combination of two noxious poisons, sodium and chlorine? In my typology, the same process occurs in love-styles. The results can be quite astonishing, as in *mania*, *pragma*, and *agape*, three of the most familiar secondary love-styles in our society.

SECONDARY COLORS OF LOVE

MANIA. This was the ancient Greek word for a kind of loving that strikes the lover like a bolt from the blue—or from the gods, for the full expression was *theia mania* (the madness from the gods). The manic lover is obsessively preoccupied with the beloved, intensely jealous and possessive, and in need of repeated assurances of being loved. At the same time, the manic lover often holds back, fearful of loving too much before there is a guarantee of being equally loved in return. In many cases, the lover doesn't even *like* the beloved and would not choose him or her as a lasting friend. In

Love and Addiction, Peele and Brodsky (1976) suggest a proof of addictive love: if you ceased being *in love* with the partner, you would not continue to be friends. Of course, Peele is no admirer of mania and compares such love to dependence on heroin.

The contradictory behavior of mania was first noted in literature by Catullus two millennia ago, when he wrote "I love and I hate. And if you ask me how, I do not know. I only feel it, and I'm torn in two." Aldous Huxley describes the same experience: "And he wanted her . . . madly, against his wishes, even against his own feelings, for he didn't like Lucy, he really hated her" (1963, p. 11). In his "autobiographical" novel *Of Human Bondage*, Somerset Maugham tells of Philip falling obsessively in love with Mildred, a woman he doesn't like. The inherent contradiction of mania arises from its peculiar mixing of two primary loves, eros and ludus. The manic lover has the desire for the intense, physically stimulating relationship typical of eros, but lacks the erotic lover's ability to confidently, almost egotistically, sort people out and spot an example of the favorite type. Thus the manic lover is likely to choose quite inappropriate partners and madly *project onto the partner* those qualities that are desired in the beloved, but that any bystander can clearly see are not possessed by the beloved.

The ability to fall in love with almost anyone works nicely in a confident ludic lover, and the manic lover's desire to manipulate the relationship so as not to be in the weaker position (more loving than loved) is certainly ludic. But the manic lover is too much in need of love to play it cool. He may tell himself that it's her turn to call and if she doesn't, he'll wait. But if she is a few minutes late, he is likely to be on the phone, calling her. The manic lover would like to have ludic detachment, but lacks the self-confidence.

Mania, I learned from many examples, tends to be the first love-style of young people who eagerly desire to experience the excitement and adventure of love. Most get over it, label it infatuation, and go on to some other style of loving. The labeling is a mistake—it denies some of the valuable aspects of manic experience. For example, it can be beneficial to realize how deeply, how intensely you are capable of loving another person. Later, in some other choice of love-style, this realization can add considerably to your self-esteem and to your ability to love a worthy partner.

Some lovers, especially from settled domestic backgrounds, may not experience mania until middle age—for example, in an intense affair after a quietly comfortable storgic marriage has lost its interest. These adult experiences of mania are often more unsettling than the teenage variety.

But the potential for self-revelation is still there. If one wants to get off the cycle, or recover from a manic experience and return to the safe harbor of one's marriage, the social origins of the experience must be identified and changed.

A cycle of manic loves is often caused by the lover's desperate need to be in love. The lover is actually "in love with love itself" rather than with any particular beloved. To remedy this situation, the unwilling manic lover must locate the causes of the desperate need. These can include a lack of close friends, deep discontent with one's job, living alone, and similar sources of loneliness and low self-esteem. The solution may be as simple as the acquisition of a roommate, but in some cases I have studied, only drastic measures have worked. One of my respondents finally found himself able to enjoy a different love-style only after leaving his parents' small-town home, moving to a large city, starting a new career, and adopting a new identity for himself.

PRAGMA. A love very different from mania is pragma (the Greek root of "pragmatic"). The pragmatic lover has a more or less conscious "shopping list" of practical, everyday qualities that he or she desires in a beloved. These may include physical characteristics, but there is no special emphasis on the body of the beloved, as there is in eros. Instead, the pragmatic lover is looking for a *compatible* partner, in the sense that sociologists and computer dating agencies use the word. It is known, for example, that people of the same religious, political, and social class backgrounds are more likely to feel compatible with each other. The pragmatic lover's shopping list may include some of these sociological measures, but is also likely to include personal interests, such as a hobby or favorite sport. Pragma is the style of loving most easily described in a classified advertisement for the personals column.

The pragmatic love-style is a combination of ludus and storge. Not having grown up with a beloved of suitable background and interests, the lover sets out consciously, with the manipulative confidence of ludus, to discover suitable candidates for affection. The search is for a sensible, storgic partnership, not an ecstatic romance or exciting affair. The search is a conscious sorting—first, of the qualities to put on the shopping list, and then, of the candidates who appear to possess these qualities. Each candidate must be weighed carefully. A suitable candidate will be invited to share some of the activities of the lover until he or she is satisfied that the candidate would make a compatible partner. The pragmatic lover may often discuss his or her potential choices with a friend or parent: "Who do you think would suit me better, Jean or Chris?" This is a question no erotic, storgic, manic, or ludic lover would dream of discussing with anyone else.

In bygone days, pragmatic ideology was managed largely by the parents and was called *arranged marriage*. Today many urban lovers look after their own arrangements. A computer dating agency is not necessary—one can join a club, a church, a night class, a charity group, or a political party in the hope of finding at least one compatible person there who might be a candidate for a loving relationship.

AGAPE. A familiar ideology, agape is the love-style urged on us by the Christian religion. It also happens to be—at least in my research— the least common love-style actually practiced in adult partnering relationships. Few of us are on the side of the angels when looking for a partner. Agape is selfless, giving, altruistic love. The lover considers it a *duty* to love, even when no loving feelings are present. Thus agape is guided more by the head than the heart; it is more expressive of will than emotion.

This might explain why the ideal of Christian self-sacrifice is not frequently found in relationships where we expect the heart to rule, were it not for the fact that ludus is equally a matter of rational self-control. A more likely explanation of the rarity of agape is the enlightened self-interest that pervades the ideology of our commercial, political, and even educational institutions. A gentle, patient, caring love without motives of self-interest is difficult to find even in those helping professions supposedly organized to supply it in the form of healing and therapy. Ironically, the most agapic expressions of love in our society may come from persons who practice celibacy and have neither lover nor mate.

Agape is a combination of eros and storge. This was first recognized by St. Augustine, who wrote of the need to harness the intense drive of Eros (union with the ideal other) to the Christian belief that the only other worthy of such union was God. Thus, agape redirects erotic yearning for union with the perfect beloved by submission to the perfect will of God. The behavior required by dutiful, giving love is that of the good neighbor, the faithful servant, the devoted friend. This invokes the storgic love-style, but in a generalized way rather than toward a specific person.

The agapic lover feels an intense duty to care affectionately for the beloved, and the beloved is defined as anyone in need of such care. Thus, the agapic lover in a relationship is likely to see the partner as only one of the many people in need. The partner may have to be content with a small portion of the lover's time and energy, for so many others are in need. If the agapic lover comes to the conviction that the partner would be "better off, happier with someone else," he or she is capable of giving up the relationship, even to a "rival."

How many colors of love are there? As many as there are possible mixtures and combinations, as in color itself. There are other kinds of loving still to consider—ludic eros and storgic ludus, for example. Each combines certain features of the primaries, but also permits the emergence of new qualities not found in either primary. (For a detailed explanation of these many colors of love, see Lee, 1973, 1976a.)

DETERMINING YOUR PREFERRED STYLE OF LOVING

Some readers will already have recognized themselves in the brief descriptions above. "That's me! I've been a (manic, erotic, ludic . . .) lover for years!" It's important to recall at this point that love-styles are not fixed. A lover may move from a first experience that is, say, ludic to one that is manic and then to one that is, say, storgic. It is the relationship that is styled, not the lover. It is also possible to be involved in two or more relationships of different love-styles at the same time.

If you should find something of yourself in several love-styles, how can you know which one you prefer? Several methods have been developed to sort out love-style preferences. The first was the detailed description of "symptoms" of eight styles (Lee, 1973) given below. Another method was developed by the Lasswells (1980), who read a general description of my typology of love in *Psychology Today* (Lee, 1974) and from it constructed the SAMPLE profile (Storge, Agape, Mania, Pragma, Ludus, Eros). This is a set of fifty statements with agree-disagree responses. Each statement is intended to contain the ideological content of one of six love-styles. This test can be found in Lasswell and Lobsenz (1980). A third procedure for determining a preferred love-style involves a modification of the original methods I used to study love and is found in chapter 11 of Lee (1976a). Still other methods have been developed by social scientists such as Mathes (1980) and Sandor (1982). At present, none of these methods is really satisfactory because all are shortcuts. They are like a ten-minute talk with your physician when you really need a complete checkup using various tests and instruments.

Besides, as I explain below, various scientific studies of love disagree about the validity of my typology. The last word on love has certainly not been spoken! In the meantime, the best assessment of your preference of love-style is a review of your experience, not a paper-and-pencil test. A careful study of the descriptions of each of eight major love-styles will help you assess which style—or styles, for you can prefer more than one color of love!—you favor most. Each example is of a "typical" lover—that is, one showing characteristics found in at least 75 percent of the cases of that love-style that occurred in my research.

Profiles of Typical Examples of Eight Love-styles

EROS. Typical erotic lovers believe their childhood was happy (it is the *attitude* that counts, not the objective facts), enjoy their work, and are ready for the risks of love, although not anxiously searching. They can clearly describe what body type is most attractive to them, and they feel great excitement on first beholding anyone (even in a photo) who appears close to that type. They are eager to get to know the beloved quickly, intensely—and undressed. They are open-eyed to flaws and potential shortcomings in the beloved, and seek to express their delight in the beloved frequently in verbal and tactile ways. They usually want an exclusive relationship but are not possessive or fearful of rivals. Erotic lovers consider that finding and living with their ideal beloved is the most important activity in their lives.

LUDUS. Typical ludic lovers believe their childhood was average but are often frustrated in adult life. They are unwilling to commit themselves to love ("not ready to settle down"). They find a variety of body types equally attractive and can switch readily from one to another. Ludic lovers go about life as usual after meeting a new partner; they feel no special excitement and certainly do not *fall* in love. There is a reluctance to plan activities for the future, as that raises the question of whether the beloved will be included. Ludic lovers avoid seeing their partners too often, as a means of preventing partners from getting "too involved." They avoid jealous partners, who spoil the fun of love. They see no contradiction in loving several partners equally or at the same time. Sex is for fun, not for expressing commitment, and love is not the most important activity in life.

STORGE. Typical storgic lovers often grew up in large, supportive families, or in stable, friendly communities. They enjoy their friends and are satisfied with life. They expect love will be a special friendship in which more than the usual time and activities are shared. No particular body type is strongly preferred. Storgic lovers are not anxious or preoccupied with an absent beloved. "Time will tell" whether they are meant to be together.

They recoil from an excessive show of emotion in the partner, and prefer to talk about interests they share rather than about their feelings for each other. As the partnership matures, they become possessive in a quiet way unless a real threat to the relationship occurs, forcing them to declare stronger feelings. It's important to get to know the partner first as a friend before getting into sexual relations. Once deep friendship is secured, sexual problems can be "worked out." Mutual love is not a goal of life for itself, but as an aspect of the greater goals of friendship and family.

MANIA. Typical manic lovers feel their childhood was unhappy, and they are usually lonely in adult life and often dissatisfied with their work. They feel a strong need to "be in love," but are also afraid that love will be difficult and painful. They are uncertain what type attracts them, and often look for a combination of contradictory qualities. They are often surprised to find themselves in love with someone they don't even like and would not keep as a friend if love failed. Yet they attempt to see the partner every day, begin to imagine their future together, and are easily upset by delays and postponements. Manic lovers often appear to have lost their senses, going to absurd extremes to prove their love. Demonstrations of love alternate with times of drawing back to "get control" of themselves, usually without success. Thus manic lovers are led to extreme displays of jealousy, and to demands that the partner show more affection and commitment. They rarely find sex with the beloved satisfying or reassuring. Yet they are unable to break off and it is always the partner who finally ends the relationship. The manic lover will take a long time to get over it.

PRAGMA. Typical pragmatic lovers show no distinctive attitude to childhood and current life-style, but they are often adults who feel they can master life and achieve goals through personal effort. Finding a compatible mate is a practical problem to be solved by sensible effort, and is often begun by looking among those at hand in office, club, or community. These lovers prefer to see the partner in a social setting to find out what the person is "really like." They carefully note warning signs, and restrain discussion of commitment and the future until they are more confident they know the partner well. They generally disdain excessive emotional displays and especially jealous scenes, but they appreciate reciprocal signs of thoughtfulness and increasing commitment. Sexual compatibility is important, but it is more a question of technical skills, which can be improved if necessary, than of some elusive chemistry. Finding a compatible mate is desirable for a happy life, but not essential, and no particular partner is worth sacrificing one's common sense for.

STORGIC EROS. This loose combination of the primaries storge and eros is more common than agape. These lovers feel that childhood was meaningful; whether happy or not, they "learned from it." They have "come to terms with themselves," and consider that the act of loving is essential to a mature and fulfilled life, whether or not their love is reciprocated. There is no preferred type—everyone is ideally worthy of love, but these lovers may (somewhat guiltily) avoid what is repulsively ugly. They see love as a duty to respond to the need of others. Although pleased by reciprocation, they are not jealous or possessive. In fact, they are willing to step aside when it appears that some other person would better meet the partner's needs. Storgic erotic lovers never try to compel their partners to show love or commitment. There is little emphasis on sexual intimacy; gentle, warm feelings are more highly valued. Loving another person is the central purpose and meaning of human life, and the particular partner for whom the love is expressed is much less important than the act of loving.

LUDIC EROS. This combination brings together the same primary loves as mania, but in a very different form. (Compare the results of combining flour and water in a white sauce when the water is cold and when it is hot.) Typical ludic erotic lovers are content with life and feel confident to cope with its problems. They meet people easily and want "experience," including a variety of experiences of love. They enjoy partners of various body types. Love relationships are readily fitted into life's everyday pattern without special emotion. There is a desire to enjoy love almost as an art form or theater; the lover tries to help each partner to similarly enjoy the experience without becoming too involved. Feelings are expressed in ways that indicate they are not exclusively felt for that specific partner. Jealousy and possessiveness are avoided, and when a relationship ceases to be enjoyable it is terminated. Love should be a creative experience, and fun for everyone concerned.

STORGIC LUDUS. This combination brings together primaries also found in pragma, but with a different result. Here, the emphasis is on having affairs rather than on the more permanent mating relationship of pragma. Storgic ludic lovers feel no special need to be in love with the partner. (In many cases this is because they already have a love partner in one of the other love-styles; storgic ludic lovers are often already married.) When the opportunity for pleasant dalliance comes along, it is enjoyed, but these lovers expect discretion and self-restraint. Ordinary life is continued as usual, and time is spent with the partner when mutually convenient. These lovers feel no jealousy or possessiveness, and if these qualities are shown by the partner, the storgic ludic lover will break off the relation-ship—especially if it threatens a more valued love. Feelings are not ex-pressed intensely, nor on a wide range of emotions, and there is never any commitment to a long-range future. Storgic ludus is often a second choice of love-styles by lovers who hold some other preference for more enduring love. It is, however, the preferred style of those who would like their lives to be one long series of interesting love affairs.

A word of caution: Keep in mind that lovers are not limited to one particular love-style and that lovers of a particular style are by no means all the same in personality or life history. The above portraits are of *typical* expressions of each style. (There is a *typical* form of dog called a cocker spaniel, but this hardly means that all cocker spaniels are the same.)

FINDING PARTNERS TO MATCH YOUR PREFERRED LOVE-STYLE

Once you have identified your preferred love-style for the present time in your life (remembering that preferences for love, as for color, may change with time and experience), you will naturally want to know what love-styles "match" your choice. Mutual love is not a question of *how much* love the partner returns, but *which kind*. If you are a ludic lover, for example, and your partner is manic, then the more love your partner shows you, the *less* happy you are likely to be! For your partner's love will be insistent, demanding, jealous, possessive—not your idea of loving at all.

The matching of love-styles can be most easily explained in the same format as the variations among color are explained in art: by a color wheel (Lee, 1973) or by geometric forms (Lee, 1976a). The circle and triangle in figure 3.1 represent the structure of love-styles. The three primaries are at the apexes of the triangle. Each pair of primaries may be combined in two ways—along the triangle or around the circle. For instance, eros and ludus may be combined to form either mania or ludic eros. In general, the closer two love-styles are on this chart, the more likely it is that two lovers, one of each style, will match. I call this the rule of proximity. One obvious match is with a partner of exactly the same love-style—but the lovers may find their definitions of love so similar that the relationship eventually loses interest. Many love relationships require a certain amount of conflict to prevent boredom. Another suitable match is with a partner of a nearby love-style. For example, the definitions of "love" held by a storgic lover and a prag-matic lover will have enough in common to make their relationship satisfy-ing for each of them. By contrast, a manic lover and a storgic lover will fill

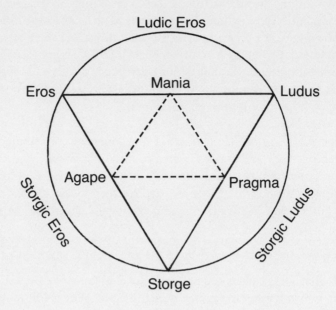

Fig. 3.1.

their days with mutual misunderstandings and accusations that each other's behavior is "not love at all!" The storgic lover will argue, "If you loved me, you'd trust me like a friend, and not be so possessive, always asking where I've been," and the manic partner will reply, "If you loved me, you'd show more jealousy, and worry about me when I'm not around."

There is one exception to the rule of proximity: mania and ludus. They are close enough on the chart, but hold very different definitions of love. If you are looking for a happy, mutual love, these two do not match. The chart, however, is not entirely misleading about these love-styles. It is surprisingly common to find relationships in which one partner is manic, the other ludic. These two loves do have a fatal attraction for each other, and a manic-ludic match is bound to be interesting, if not happy. Manic love thrives on difficulties, and no one is more likely to create them than a ludic partner. In turn, the vanity of the ludic lover will get a certain satisfaction out of all the attention paid by a manic partner. This matching is the stuff of many novels and plays!

Remember that *mutual*, *satisfying* love is not necessarily *lasting* love. A ludic lover and a storgic ludic partner may have a splendid love affair, but neither will expect the relationship to last longer than is mutually enjoyable and convenient. Neither is going to change jobs or cities to go on seeing the other. The color theory of love reminds us that different love-styles are as valid as different color preferences—it all depends on your tastes. But a common assumption in our society is that a happy love is a long-lasting love. We often ask the question of partners, "How long have you been together (married)?" For some styles of loving, the correct answer would be "Who cares? We enjoy each other."

HOW I STUDIED LOVE

Many readers will be content with what has already been said and will go off now to put some of my ideas into practice—hoping to have the kind of love they want, whether it is more fulfilling, more productive, more adventuresome, more fun. But some will ask, how do you know love is like this? How did you find out? What do other social scientists think of your findings—and your methods? My study of love did not begin with a search for its various kinds. Rather, I sought an answer for the question: in an age of medical, psychological, and sociological sciences, why do people ignore scientific explanations of human relationships, and still fall romantically in love?

Measures of love have been developed to distinguish realistic love and liking from romantic attraction (for example, Rubin, 1970). Numerous studies have shown that romance is actually guided by compatibility and "complementary needs" (for example, Winch, 1955), and partnering decisions are generally made on the basis of sociologically predictable patterns. Nevertheless, our culture remains profoundly infused with romantic ideology in novels, theater, films, and television; and most people are still suspicious of "scientific" matchmaking, for example, by the use of computers.

My study began with the most successful teachers of romantic ideology for half a millennium—the great novelists. Then I turned to nonfictional observers of love, from Plato and Ovid to Andreas Cappellanus and Castiglione to the most recent psychologists. Each time I encountered a new statement about the nature of love, I recorded it, so that eventually I accumulated more than four thousand descriptions of some aspect of loving. Then I classified the statements—for example, bringing together all those referring to the role of jealousy in love.

It soon became obvious that no single set of statements would describe love—either fictional or nonfictional, romantic or realistic. Some authors, for example, were adamant that jealousy is a proof of true love (Capellanus), whereas others considered jealousy an immature behavior (Margaret Mead) or not loving at all (St. Paul). My goal shifted to the search for a "constructive typology" (Cattell, 1965; McKinney, 1966) of loving. Such typology looks for the clustering of characteristics in a great variety of facts.

For example, think of five varieties of dogs—such as bulldogs, cocker spaniels, greyhounds, German shepherds, and whippets. You won't do well at distinguishing one breed from another if you concentrate on differences in the number of ears or legs. All dogs come with four legs. But if you concentrate on the proportions of legs to body, you'll begin to develop a recognition of each breed. All dogs have two ears, but attention to the kind of ears will help distinguish breeds. It is the *clustering together of a set of typical characteristics* of leg, ear, head shape, hair type, and so forth, that says "cocker spaniel" or "German shepherd" when you see one. All systematic explanation of experience proceeds by such *typical clusters* or, simply put, *typologies*. Medical diagnosis, for example, looks for the typical cluster of symptoms that says "pneumonia" rather than "heart attack."

What are the equivalent "symptoms" for distinguishing different kinds of love? I sorted my collection of thousands of statements, looking for characteristics frequently used by authors to distinguish what they considered true love from all the impostors. The results included reciprocity, jealousy, fidelity, unselfishness, the power of love to overcome all odds, and fifteen other symptoms. Then I analyzed my thousands of statements for clustering of such symptoms. Each cluster was given a name. Because English has only the word *love*, I borrowed from ancient Latin and Greek. Thus, *mania* was identified as a cluster of physical distress (like loss of sleep), intense preoccupation, jealousy, possessiveness, ambivalence (love-hate), and belief in the power of love to overcome all odds. In turn, each other type of love was sorted as a cluster of ideas.

A typology of love is not a new idea. Robert Burton (1621/1962), Stendhal (1830/1957), and C. S. Lewis (1963) each described four different types of love, but unfortunately not the same four. I eventually decided that a typology of six kinds of love (six ideologies) would embrace all the varieties of love in our literature. Later, I would conclude that six kinds are too few.

It is important to recall that every typology of love—including mine, to this point—was simply an extraction of ideas from literature. Surely it was time for someone to discover whether these alleged types of love actually existed in the population. My first resolution was that the world is not limited to the college classroom. Far too much research is based on a captive audience of undergraduates. I went into the streets of four cities—two in England, two in Canada—to ask people to tell me their experiences of love. It is amazing how much total strangers will tell you about their intimate lives if you offer them an opportunity to talk to you at leisure, in your office, without asking their names or addresses. In fact, quite a few people welcomed this opportunity to share the joys and sorrows of their love lives with me, knowing that I would never see them again or be able to cause them any trouble.

To enable these lovers to tell me their stories in a way I could record systematically, I developed a "Love Story Card Sort." This device is based on the observation that at numerous points in any love relationship, there are only a few choices of what to do next. (Ask any novelist attempting to write a really new love story.) There are, for example, only three possibilities for the "I love you" statement in any story, real or fictional. Your partner says it first; you say it first; or neither of you say it. (Some may claim a photo finish when each partner says it at almost exactly the same time!) Suppose your partner is the first to say "I love you." Again, choices are limited: you say nothing in return; you suggest that the declaration is premature but might be welcomed later; you say it is premature and/or probably in vain; you respond halfway (for example, I like you a lot); or you reciprocate (I love you, too). In my card sort, each of these statements was typed on a three-by-five card, and coded on the back. In telling their love stories, my interviewees simply selected the appropriate card for this point in the story, and I recorded the code.

There are fifteen hundred cards in the Love Story Card Sort, so the whole sort forms an omnibus love story, from which any lover can select the appropriate cards to tell the key points of his or her own story. There are several advantages to this method. It enabled me to keep track of a great variety of love stories by relatively simple coding methods. It stimulated the memory of the lover and ensured that important details were not left out. It turned the attention of the storyteller away from me (I did not lean over them, watching every card—the coding was done later), so that a more honest story was evoked than if everything had to be said directly to me. It was common for my interviewees to get very involved—laughing, crying, feeling nostalgia as the cards prompted their memories of love. After I collected about 100,000 items of data from 120 respondents, the analysis of real love experience could begin. It went through many stages and eventually produced the color analogy outlined above. (Further details will be found in Lee, 1973.)

My first 120 interviewees were all heterosexual lovers. Later, I collected still more experiences, including homosexual loves. There was no difficulty in fitting the gay experiences into my general typology. Gay and lesbian lovers share the general cultural definitions of love in novels, films, and other media. The distribution of kinds of loving in gay and lesbian experience, however, is likely to differ from that of heterosexual lovers (see Lee, 1976b).

TESTING AND CRITICISM OF MY TYPOLOGY

A fundamental problem of researching experience of love is ethnocentrism. A scientific study of love must enable respondents to report relationships that are not defined by prevailing ideologies as "true love." Many people are reluctant to admit that they are out of step with fashions, especially in love. For example, it is less likely now than in past stages of Western society that many people will have St. Paul's prescription of love in mind when they think of one adult loving another. It is also less likely now than in the seventeenth century that they will have La Rochefoucauld's maxims in mind (La Rochefoucauld, 1665/1959). At one time, playful love was not merely au courant, but almost de rigueur—it was a boring spouse who was faithful and had no affairs. But today, many respondents would not think of such relationships as love. It is also less likely that modern lovers will picture true love as the quiet but dull pastoral fidelity of Wordsworth's "Michael" and his wife Isabel (Wordsworth, 1800/1952). A valid method of studying love must encourage respondents to ignore ethnocentric fashions and describe whatever they believe was an experience of love.

Another problem of much modern research on love is ahistoricism. Some modern love research is so devoid of historical awareness that the reader might conclude that romantic love was an American invention. Note that the original version of a particular ideology need not be current today for people to believe in it. Jesus himself might not recognize many versions of modern Christianity, and if Karl Marx returned, he might well look at so-called Marxist regimes and exclaim, "I am not a Marxist!" Much the same is true of love, and those who analyze modern attitude scales of loving without paying attention to historical antecedents do so at their peril.

Each ideology of love is a systematic clustering of ideas used to justify specific social arrangements and institutions. For instance, agape became the official love-style of the Christian church from at least the fourth century (Nygren, 1952). It provided a rationale for Christian conceptions of marriage, conflict (the "just war" theory), and even economic behavior (a ban on usury). Later, a contrary ideology of love arose in Christendom, first called courtly love (*amour courtois*) for its origins in castle society. It was branded as heretical and is still seen as such by some leading Christian thinkers (for example, de Rougemont, 1956), because it legitimated social behavior (such as adultery, divorce) contrary to that required by agape. Yet another distinctive formula of social behavior is legitimated by ludus, and it is a formula sufficiently threatening to other ideologies that its first published author, Ovid, was banished to the edges of empire for his heresy.

When ethnocentrism and ahistoricism are combined, the result is often a tendency to define a given expression of an ideology as outside the boundaries of the true faith. Thus, many Christian sects claim their own beliefs are the true gospel and exorcise most other related beliefs, despite their Christian origin, as heresies. Socialist and communist sects are also good at this kind of exclusionism. Much the same thing has happened in research on love. The search for attitudinal correlates of a culturally limited and historically blinkered conception of love leads, not surprisingly, to a confirmation of the definition of true love held by the authors—and a dismissal of those relationships the authors do not regard as love.

The need to avoid ethnocentrism and ahistoricism in studying love is best resolved by approaching love as a problem of competing ideologies about the optimum arrangement of intimate adult partnering. It is not met, I argue, by limiting one's research to a checklist of attitudinal statements. I have described elsewhere (Lee, 1973, p. 232) my own early experiences in attempting to use Likert scales to measure respondents' experiences in love. Yet much contemporary love research is done this way—including, ironically, some of the validation tests on my typology. Only a very few contemporary students of love (for example, Snead, 1980; Sandor, 1982) have noticed the contradiction in testing an ideological typology of love by an attitude scale. These latter authors (discussed below) have followed my lead in seeking more holistic ideological conceptions of love.

There is obviously no space here to consider the relationship of my typology to all the competing theories of the anatomy of love. I have already discussed in detail elsewhere (Lee, 1973, 1977) the comparison of my theory with many others. What follows is a brief review of some of the possible comparisons to underline my argument on the need for an ideological approach to love.

Swensen and Gilner (1964) conclude that only two factors are common to all kinds of loving, whether parental love, sibling love, love of friends of the same or the opposite sex, or love of spouse. These factors are emotional support of the loved one and toleration of the demands and negative aspects of the loved one. For what we think of as partnering love, the authors find seven basic dimensions, but they draw attention to the fact that shared values, goals, and activities are characteristics of liking, not love. For these authors, storgic lovers—with their emphasis on common activity rather than on expression of affection—are little more than married friends, and agapic lovers would not meet the requirement of physical expression of affection. Manic and ludic lovers would not even be friends! The manic lover does not show the feeling of security in the presence of the beloved that Swensen and Gilner consider a basic dimension of partnering love—thus, like many others, they would dismiss mania as neurosis. The ludic lover is obviously too manipulative to fit the "verbal revelation of intimate facts about the self" required of love by these authors.

At least, Swensen and Gilner's conceptions embrace a wider range of experience than that of, say, Albert Ellis (1949). His study of five hundred college women is loaded from the outset by distinctions between "infatuation" and "love." It is hardly surprising that Ellis found that his respondents considered longer relationships to be love, and shorter ones to be infatuations. It is even more predictable that they should be most likely to consider their recent and current involvements to be love.

Munro and Adams (1977) begin their study with the admission, in the title, that what they are analyzing is love, *American style* (and presumably, late twentieth century). Their title may be an effort to excuse their obvious ahistoricism; their earliest reference to any publication on theories of love is 1953. They are also an example of Snead's (1980, p. 2) caustic observation (after a comprehensive examination of the scientific literature on love) that researchers in this field show a tendency to reinvent the wheel by not reading each other's work. (For example, there is no reference to my 1970–76 publications in Munro and Adams.) Thus, Munro and Adams repeat, unknowingly, the methods and concepts of Gross (1944) by boiling a selection of romantic quotations down to two kinds of loving—romantic and conjugal rational (equivalent to Gross's realistic). Scales of romantic ideals (for example, "love is the highest goal of life") and romantic power ("love surmounts all obstacles") and a conjugal-rational love scale were tested on large samples of high school and college students. The authors conclude that true love goes through a development process from romantic to conjugal over time, but romantic beliefs may emerge again in older years. There is no attempt to raise, much less answer, the question of ideology or cultural-media sources of the varying conceptions of love involved in the items of their scales.

Dion and Dion (1973, 1975) are slightly more historical about love— they list one reference for 1939, but most are only a decade old. Their cultural blinkers are tighter than most. There is no reference to my work, even though I was teaching in another department of the same university. The Dions used responses by introductory psychology students to develop correlates of susceptibility to romantic experiences. Again, *romantic* is narrowly, culturally defined (restlessness, daydreaming, difficulty in sleeping).

The Dions conclude that our culture defines romantic love as an external event, destined to happen to us. (A careful viewing of any number of films, such as *A Man and a Woman, Dr. Zhivago, West Side Story, Love Story*, would have produced the same conclusion—as would a reading of any number of love stories back beyond *Tristram and Iseult* to the ancient Greeks.) They state that romantic love serves a functional role by inducing males into marriage—without acknowledging the existence of this concept of love, in considerable detail, in the earlier work of functionalist sociologists (for example, Greenfield, 1956). The Dion results (1975) show a correlation of low self-esteem and high defensive personality scores with more intense experience of romantic love and more frequent experience of unrequited love. It is obvious from their cited examples of preoccupation, sleeplessness, and the like, that what they have in mind is a manic kind of loving. Thus, the authors inadvertently confirm the typical characteristics that led me to distinguish eros and mania from ludus and storge—but they conclude with only a monolithic conception of romantic love.

The following are examples of research that has taken my typology into account, even if only to reject it.

Mathes et al. (1980) sought evidence of my types of loving among sixty-seven dating couples in introductory psychology classes. Their title gives the result: "How many ways do I love thee? Three." The subjects were asked to complete liking, romantic love, jealousy, and sex attraction scales for three targets: same-sex friends, opposite-sex friends, and dating partners. The authors conclude that liking and romantic love scales measure the same emotion (a conclusion I would agree with, in contrast to Swensen above). A second factor isolated from the results is jealousy, and the third—distinguishing the *dating* partner—was sexual attraction.

Mathes (1980) alone conducted a study in which he asked fifty-six college dating couples for agreement or disagreement (on a five-point scale) with 168 statements. He constructed each statement to represent one of my types of loving. For example, "I know what physical type attracts me and my beloved is that type" (eros). He found three scales reliable for men: ludus, mania, and storgic ludus, and an additional two for women: eros and ludic eros. He concluded, however, that there are really only four kinds of loving relationship in his factor analysis. There is no attempt to square these results with the 1980 study that Mathes co-authored with five other researchers.

Mathes, writing alone, argues that the first kind of love is romantic and expresses eros ideas, while firmly rejecting ludus. He concludes that this is the only *true* love, like Erich Fromm's true loving with its long-term commitment to intimacy (Fromm, 1956). Mathes's second kind is "flirtation without serious commitment"—apparently my ludus, but note that it is demoted to flirtation and is not a kind of loving equally valid with romantic. Mathes does admit that this type showed internal convergence in his analysis. Its characteristics form a cluster, and he considers it worthy of further research as a species of heterosexual relationship—but it is not love, and his references to heterosexuals again emphasize the blindness of many love researchers to gay and lesbian partnerships. Mathes identifies a third kind of relationship as mania, but he dismisses this as neurosis—not really loving at all. He finds a fourth kind, which he says is "uninterpretable" and mixes sex, storgic eros, and durability. This kind seems quite interpretable to me: when dutiful, durable agape was sexually expressed in a partnership by my respondents, I called it storgic eros.

T. E. and M. E. Lasswell (1976) developed a scale of 144 true-false statements derived from my article in *Psychology Today*, without any communication with me directly. They reduced the items to 95, 57, and finally 50, after repeated tests on various samples. As we saw earlier, the final 50-item SAMPLE scale distinguishes among six of my types of loving and is named by an acronym formed from these types (*S*torge, *A*gape, *M*ania, *P*ragma, *L*udus, *E*ros). It is worth noting that their samples included a wide variety of nationalities and religions. The most valuable contribution of the Lasswell research to my own work is the fact that they are the only researchers of love-styles, to date, to submit a large sample of data to the sophisticated test of a Guttman-Lingoes Smallest Space analysis. Their results showed that each of the six conceptualized love-styles is systematically distinguishable from the others. The Lasswells were sufficiently persuaded of the correlation of their scale items to actual experiences of the different kinds of loving to apply the instrument in marital counseling (Lasswell & Lobsenz, 1980).

The fact that the SAMPLE instrument was independently developed and tested, and was found useful on samples of several cultures, is considered by some (such as Sandor, 1982) as an argument in support of the existence of distinguishable ideologies of at least six kinds of loving. I am less sanguine, however, about the diagnostic utility of their fifty-statement SAMPLE instrument in helping lovers determine their own preferred love-style. It would not be difficult for anyone familiar with a description of their six types of love to guess which type each statement is intended to measure. Any valid instrument for assessing ideological conceptions of love (or, for that matter, any other ideology) must avoid being short-circuited by the respondent's awareness of the expected results. In our psychologically sophisticated society, there are many respondents capable of sensing what the researcher is looking for. Even a short version of the storytelling instrument (for example, Lee, 1976a, chap. 11) contains fewer clues than an attitude scale as to how each statement will be scored. But that instrument was offered largely as entertainment, with ample warning (Lee, 1976a, p. 188). There are no satisfactory shortcuts to an adequate analysis of so complex an experience as love. Only elaborate instruments such as the Love Story Card Sort can distinguish between ideologies that are rich in historical variation and overlapping in cultural expression.

Various studies have employed the SAMPLE instrument. For example, Rosenham (1978) tried the SAMPLE profile on 113 college students and found that women were more clear in their definitions of love than men. But only three types (agape, mania, and storge) were convincingly validated in this obviously limited sample. Snead (1980) attempted a "multidimensional analysis of styles of loving" on 30 unmarried heterosexuals. He found "generally strong support for Lee's notion that people prefer different styles of loving" but did not find evidence for all the styles outlined in my original work (Lee, 1970). In a small sample, narrowly selected, this is not surprising. However, his sophisticated mathematical analysis of the sample he collected convinced him that lovers should be less concerned with *how much* the partner loves and focus instead on the *kind* of love.

K. E. Davis and M. Todd (in press) tested a variety of scales (not including the SAMPLE scale) to focus on measurements of friendship, recognizing that some forms of friendship merge into love. They take my typology into consideration, but the ideology of this paper, and especially the language, is an exemplar of all the arguments I make here about the restriction of vision in a black-and-white conceptualization of love.

Davis and Todd eventually argue for a two-type system—friendship and romantic love. They reduce my typology to one of man-woman relationships (again the exclusion of gay and lesbian love). The point of distinguishing types of love is lost; storge becomes heterosexual friendship. Eros is equated with romantic love or passion, so it is not surprising that the authors argue that nothing requires lovers to have an ideal physical image in mind. I quite agree; this is characteristic only of the eros love-style, which is distinguishable from other romantic love, such as mania. They dismiss ludus as "obviously not a mutual or reciprocal relationship." Why not? I have certainly interviewed couples, each of whom enjoyed a nonpossessive, sexually open, playful relationship with the other. These authors label mania a "very destructive" relationship with no saving benefits. Agape is, they say, "not a personal relationship at all, for in it, one is merely granting to one's 'lover' the kind of acceptance or Christian charity that one would grant to anyone." The reader is left to puzzle why an accepting or charitable interaction with another individual is not a "personal relationship," much less love.

To date, the most elaborate application of my styles of loving is that of Sandor (1982). His work in Melbourne, Australia, involved tests and re-tests on samples of 375 high school students and 127 undergraduates (with retest four weeks later on a sample of 66). Sandor noted serious flaws in several of the SAMPLE items. For example, one item asks for a true or false response to a triple-barreled statement. Sandor substituted simpler items in several cases and converted the scale from true-false to a five-point agree/disagree scale. The items were also reworded so as to measure the respondent's definition of love rather than of a specific love relationship with a single partner. That is, Sandor strove to distinguish ideologies of love, but by an adaptation of the SAMPLE instrument.

His results, using factor analysis, showed a strong confirmation of four types: pragma, mania, agape, and ludus (in descending order of strength). A fifth factor mixed pragma and storge. He noted my early warning (Lee, 1973) that empirical distinctions between these types in modern society is difficult. Sandor agreed with the need to analyze the ideological structure of love, and noted that orthogonal rotation by factor analysis is itself inconsistent with my love types, because it assumes independent origin of the types, whereas I have emphasized their joint historical development.

Finally, Sternberg (1986) proposes a triangular theory of love. His focus is the psychosocial rather than socio-ideological dimensions of love, but he is also concerned to integrate his theory with existing research on love, and concludes that my typology is probably "closest in spirit" to his own. I would agree—with reservations.

Sternberg measures love experience along three dimensions—intimacy, passion, and decision-commitment. Although he treats these as "components" rather than "dimensions," his analysis is consistent with that of my Love Story Card Sort, which includes items to measure each dimension along the (obviously implied by Sternberg) fourth dimension of time span. Sternberg develops a typology of eight kinds of relationships ranging from nonlove, in which threshold measures of the three dimensions are not met, to consummate love, in which, presumably, measures of all three components are at a maximum. "Liking" is separated from "stronger loves" by the famous test of absence and is said to have only a significant intimacy component. I would consider this a mistake in analysis; intimate feelings must be teased apart so that interdependent feelings of bonding are not conflated with the essentially *dependent* feelings of need for union that are part of mania. This desire to merge with, almost to be consumed by, the beloved was first recognized by the ancient Greeks as an emotional component of theia mania.

Intermediate ranks are assigned to such types as "infatuation," which is strong on passion only; "empty love," strong on commitment but without significant feelings or sexuality; "companionate love," high on intimacy and commitment but low on passion; and "fatuous love," strong on passion and commitment but low on intimate involvement. These types seem to approximate (in order) mania, agape, storge, and ludus. But, as numerous analyses (such as Reik, 1949) have shown, the drive of mania must not be reduced to mere passion—sexual lust for the other's body. Indeed, mania is best understood as divided, ambivalent motivations. A more serious flaw, in my opinion, is Sternberg's acceptance of the bias toward some kinds of relationships as more truly love than others—the bias for one color over another, with which his article began. The very names adopted—fatuous, empty, consummate—signal the biases. For Sternberg, mania is "infatuated love gone berserk."

Sternberg argues that ludus is not a kind of love, but a style possible in various kinds. "For example, infatuated lovers, romantic, companionate, as well as lovers of other kinds, are all capable of playing games with one another." Quite so, from the observer's point of view—or even from the participant's, at a later time of retrospective interpretation. But at the time, the manic lover does not perceive him- or herself as playing games in the sense implied here. This lover is playing for keeps and is deadly serious (sometimes literally so!). In ludus, by contrast, the pleasure comes in the mere playing of the game, knowingly played as a game—a pastime that is not at all for keeps. In ludus, playing games is not a part of love; love *is* the game.

Sternberg's practical applications of his typology reflect back (perhaps unconsciously, as there is no citation) to the observations of Katz (1977) on the double-binds of loving. The feelings of love are best maintained by change. The drives of love are best perpetuated by a program of intermittent reinforcement. But this approach calls for conscious manipulation of love behavior that some, at least, would consider not really loving.

And there's the rub. So many students of love finally conclude that one kind of love is superior to all others. The argument may be explicit, as in Erich Fromm's (1956) elevation of productive love to supremacy, or implicit, as in C. S. Lewis's *Four Loves* (1963), which shows a clear preference for agape. But almost always the conclusion is there—the kind of love the researcher likes best is the only "true" love.

In many forms of human activity, we seek, develop, and celebrate the richest possible variety of kinds. In art, films, ideas, fashions, books, and flowers, who would accept any researcher's notion that there was only one true kind? How ironic, that in the glorious activity of loving, so many still refuse to celebrate the wondrous human capacity for variety.

REFERENCES

Blood, R. (1962). *Marriage*. New York: Free Press.
Burton, R. (1621/1962). *The anatomy of melancholy*. New York: New English Library.
Cattell, R. (1965). *The scientific analysis of personality*. London: Penguin.
Davis, K. E., & Todd, M. (in press). Friendship and love relationships. In *Advances in descriptive psychology* (Vol. 2).
de Rougemont, Denis (1956). *Love in the Western world*. New York: Pantheon.
Dion, K. L., & Dion, K. K. (1973). Correlates of romantic love. *Journal of Consulting and Clinical Psychology, 41*.
————. (1975). Self-esteem and romantic love. *Journal of Personality, 43*.
Ellis, A. (1949). A study of human love relationships. *Journal of Genetic Psychology, 75*.
Foote, N. (1953). Love. *Psychiatry, 16*.
Fromm, E. (1956). *The art of loving*. New York: Harper.
Goode, W. J. (1959). The theoretical importance of love. *American Sociological Review, 24*.
Greenfield, S. (1956). Love and marriage in modern America; a functional analysis. *Sociological Quarterly, 6*.
Gross, L. (1944). A belief pattern scale for measuring attitudes toward romanticism. *American Sociological Review, 9*.
Hazo, R. (1967). *The idea of love*. New York: Penguin.
Huxley, A. (1963). *Point Counterpoint*. London: Penguin.
Katz, J. (1977). How do you love me? Let me count the ways. *Sociological Quarterly, 46*.
Kierkegaard, S. (1963). *Works of love*. New York: Harper.
Kolb, W. (1965). Family sociology, marriage education and the romantic complex; a critique. *Social Forces, 29*.
La Rochefoucauld, F. (1665/1959). *Maxims*. London: Penguin.
Lasswell, T. E., & Lasswell, M. E. (1976). I love you but I'm not in love with you. *Journal of Marriage and Family Counsellor, 2*.
Lasswell, M. E. & Lobsenz, N. M. (1980). *Styles of loving*. New York: Ballantine.
Lee, J. A. (1970). *A typology of love*. Unpublished thesis, University of Sussex.
————. (1973). *Colors of love*. Toronto: New Press.

————. (1974, October). The styles of loving. *Psychology Today*.

————. (1975). The romantic heresy. *Canadian Review of Sociology and Anthropology, 12*(4).

————. (1976a). *Colours of love*. Toronto: General.

————. (1976b). Forbidden colors of love. *Journal of Homosexuality, 1*.

————. (1977). A typology of styles of loving. *Personality and Social Psychology Bulletin, 3*.

Lewis, C. S. (1963). *The four loves*. London: Fontana.

Martinson, E. W. (1980). Nine "colors" or types of romantic love? *Psychological Reports, 47*.

Mathes, E. W. (1980). *Kinds of loving*. Unpublished manuscript supplied to the author.

Mathes, E. W., Phillips, J. T., Skowron, J., Dick, W., & Beaumont, D. (1980). *How many ways do I love thee? Three*. Unpublished manuscript.

McKinney, J. (1966). Constructive typology. In J. Doby (Ed.), *An introduction to social research*. New York: Appleton.

Munro, B., & Adams, G. (1977). Love American style. *Human Relations, 31*.

Nygren, A. (1952). *Agape and eros*. London: Westminster Press.

Peele, S., & Brodsky, A. (1976). *Love and addiction*. New York: American Library.

Reik, T. (1949). *Of love and lust*. London: Farrar Straus.

Reiss, I. (1967). *Social context of premarital sexual permissiveness*. New York: Holt Rinehart.

Rosenham, M. (1978). Liking, loving, and styles of loving. *Psychological Reports, 42*.

Rubin, Z. (1970). Measurement of romantic love. *Journal of Personality and Social Psychology, 16*.

Russell, B. (1969). *Autobiography*. New York: Bantam.

Sandor, D. (1982). *Love, an investigation*. Unpublished thesis, Department of Psychology, University of Melbourne.

Snead, H. (1980). *Multidimensional analysis of styles of loving*. Unpublished thesis, Department of Psychology, Catholic University of America.

Sorokin, P. (1967). *The ways and power of love*. Chicago: Regnery.

Stendhal, H. (1830/1957). *De l'amour*. Paris: Le Divan.

Sternberg, R. J. (1986). A triangular theory of love. *Psychological Review, 93*, 119–135.

Swensen, C., & Gilner, F. (1964). Factor analysis of self-report statements on love relationships. *Journal of Individual Psychology, 20*.

Winch, R. F. (1955). The theory of complementary needs in mate selection. *American Sociological Review, 20*.

Wordsworth, W. (1800/1952). Michael. In *Upper School Poems*. Toronto: Copp Clark.

CHAPTER FOUR

Love as Attachment

The Integration of Three Behavioral Systems

BY PHILLIP SHAVER, CINDY HAZAN, AND DONNA BRADSHAW

Research on romantic love has been primarily descriptive and atheoretical. Rubin (1973), for example, developed questionnaires to assess degrees of liking and loving but said relatively little about why these states exist. Walster and Walster (1978), following a popular tradition, distinguished passionate from companionate love but said little about the origins or functions of either. Berscheid and Walster (1974), noting that previous investigators had proceeded without much theorizing, attempted to apply Schachter's (1964) two-factor theory of emotion to passionate love. Unfortunately, since Schachter's theory dealt mainly with mislabeled states of arousal, love perforce became a mislabeled arousal state, robbed of independent existence and purpose. Sternberg and Grajek (1984) tested various psychometric theories of love, taking their lead from psychometric models of intelligence. Since this approach relies on existing measures of love (and of liking, in Sternberg and Grajek's case), the resulting conception of love is like the operational definition of intelligence: love is whatever measures of love measure.

Our own approach (Hazan & Shaver, 1987; Shaver, Hazan, & Bradshaw, 1984) has been to situate love within an evolutionary framework, to ask about its dynamics and possible functions, to consider how it relates to loss and grieving, and to explore how its infantile and childhood

In preparing this chapter we have benefited tremendously from conversations with Mary Ainsworth, Rick Canfield, and Roger Kobak, and from correspondence with John Bowlby and Robert Sternberg. We thank Marty Meitus and the editors of the *Rocky Mountain News* for help with one of the studies summarized here. Address correspondence to the authors at Department of Psychology, University of Denver, Denver, CO 80208–0204.

forms might be related to its adolescent and adult forms, on the assumption that, as Konner (1982) put it, "the evolution of the brain would have to be considered unparsimonious if it were not able to draw upon the same basic capacities of emotion and action in the various settings where strong attachment is called for" (p. 298). Fortunately, a rich theoretical framework, *attachment theory* (Ainsworth, Blehar, Waters, & Wall, 1978; Bowlby, 1969, 1973, 1979, 1980; Bretherton, 1985; Sroufe & Waters, 1977), has already been developed to explain various facets of infant care-giver attachment. To the extent that adolescent and adult romantic love are also attachment processes, many of the concepts and principles of attachment theory should apply to them.

Unfortunately, a major preconception held by some social scientists makes it difficult to consider romantic love an attachment process having emotional dynamics and biological functions akin to those of infant care-giver attachment. According to this preconception, romantic love is a fairly recent invention of Western civilization (for example, Averill, 1985; de Rougement, 1940), in particular, a creation of the courtly love tradition that emerged in thirteenth-century Europe. When one consults sources from over a thousand years earlier, however, love is easy to find. In two fragments attributed to Sappho, a well-known sixth-century B.C. poet, for example, we encounter both the pain of unrequited love, thought by some current writers to be a thirteenth-century invention, and the recognition that a lover's reaction to unresponsiveness is like that of a small child:

> It's no use
> Mother dear, I
> can't finish my
> weaving
> You may
> blame Aphrodite
> soft as she is
> she has almost
> killed me with   (Sappho, Fragment 12,
> love for that boy   1958 translation)

> Afraid of losing you
> I ran fluttering
> like a little girl   (Sappho, Fragment 54,
> after her mother   1958 translation)

The same kinds of examples can be found in the great literatures of early historic times, from China and the Middle East to Greece and Rome

(Mellen, 1981). The relative contributions of biology and culture to romantic love are obviously difficult to determine, as are the relative contributions of these factors to any complex social phenomenon. What we claim is the right to hypothesize, in the absence of strong evidence to the contrary, that romantic love has always and everywhere existed as a biological potential whether or not it has been accepted as a basis for marriage and procreation. The same could be said about anger or any other strong emotion over which societies have attempted to exercise control.

This chapter is structured as follows. We begin with a fairly detailed summary of attachment theory, which will be important in our attempt to extend the theory to adult romantic love. We then list some of the observable and theoretical similarities between infant care-giver attachment and adult romantic love. Next, we describe three kinds or styles of attachment identified by Ainsworth and her coworkers (1978) in laboratory studies of mother-infant interaction and report highlights of two empirical studies exploring the possibility that the same three styles characterize adult romantic love. We then assess the limitations of our work to date and suggest how attachment theory might be mined and extended to overcome these limitations. In particular, we discuss the possibility that adult love is an integration of three behavioral systems (discussed by Bowlby): attachment, care giving, and sexuality. These three systems, as Sternberg (1986) and others (for example, Shaver, Hazan, & Bradshaw, 1984) have suggested, operate differently over the course of a relationship, causing the quality of love to change accordingly. Finally, we consider grief, the emotional response to loss of an important attachment figure. One advantage of the attachment-theoretical approach to love is that it helps explain why loss is so painful and why grief involves such strong and irrational-seeming reactions.

ATTACHMENT THEORY SUMMARIZED

Bowlby's purpose, in his three-volume exploration of attachment, separation, and loss (the processes by which affectional bonds are forged and broken), was to describe and explain, within a functionalist, evolutionary framework, how infants become emotionally attached to their primary care givers and emotionally distressed when separated from them. Extending attachment theory to adult love and loss is an enterprise that Bowlby himself has endorsed. In a 1977 paper (reprinted in Bowlby, 1979), he contended that "attachment behavior [characterizes] human beings from the cradle to the grave." In another paper he pointed out the links between attachment processes and familiar emotions, including love:

Affectional [attachment] bonds and subjective states of strong emotion tend to go together, as every novelist and playwright knows. Thus, many of the most intense of all human emotions arise during the formation, the maintenance, the disruption and the renewal of affectional bonds—which, for that reason, are sometimes called emotional bonds. In terms of subjective experience, the formation of a bond is described as falling in love, maintaining a bond as loving someone, and losing a partner as grieving over someone. Similarly, the threat of loss arouses anxiety and actual loss causes sorrow; whilst both situations are likely to arouse anger. Finally, the unchallenged maintenance of a bond is experienced as a source of security, and the renewal of a bond as a source of joy. (Bowlby, 1979, p. 69)

Bowlby's attachment theory grew out of observations of the behavior of infants and young children who were separated from their primary care giver (usually mother) for various lengths of time. Bowlby noticed what primate researchers had also observed in the laboratory and the field: when a human or primate infant is separated from its mother, the infant goes through a predictable series of emotional reactions. The first is *protest*, which involves crying, active searching, and resistance to others' soothing efforts. The second is *despair*, which is a state of passivity and obvious sadness. And the third, discussed only with reference to humans, is *detachment*, an active, seemingly defensive disregard for and avoidance of the mother if she returns.

Because of the remarkable similarities between human infants and other primate infants, Bowlby was led to consider the evolutionary significance of infant care-giver attachment and its maintenance in the face of occasional separations. He hypothesized that the major biological function of this affectional bonding system in humans' "environment of evolutionary adaptedness" was to protect infants from predation and other threats to survival. He adopted from ethology and artificial intelligence theory a control systems approach, according to which attachment is a behavioral system, a set of behaviors (crying, smiling, clinging, locomoting, looking, and so on) that function together to achieve a set-goal, in this case a certain degree of proximity to the primary care giver. The set-goal changes systematically in response to illness, pain, darkness, unfamiliar surroundings, and so on—all conditions associated with potential harm.

The attachment system is just one among a number of behavioral systems (for example, care giving, mating, affiliation, and exploration), each with its own set of distinct behaviors and functions. According to Bowlby, however, the attachment system is central and of critical importance for the smooth functioning of the other systems. He and other observers of both human and primate behavior have noticed that when an infant is healthy, alert, unafraid, and in the presence of its mother, it seems interested in exploring and mastering the environment and in establishing affiliative contact with other family and community members. Researchers call this "using the mother as a secure base." When mother is unavailable, the infant becomes preoccupied with regaining her presence, and exploration and socializing fall off dramatically. Thus, exploratory behavior (the exploration system) can be preempted by activation of the attachment system.

Systematic observation reveals that the typical infant checks back periodically, visually and/or physically, to make sure that mother is available and responsive. If she moves or directs her attention elsewhere, the child attempts to regain that attention by vocalizing or returning to her side. When the attachment system is activated strongly, most children cry and seek physical contact with their primary care giver. When the system is quiescent, they play happily, smile easily, share toys and discoveries (such as rocks and pieces of lint) with their care giver, and display warm interest in other people. In this sense, attachment is the basis of happiness, security, and self-confidence.

Bowlby claimed that infants and children construct mental models of themselves and their major social-interaction partners, and that these models regulate a person's social behaviors and feelings throughout life. His entire theory can be summarized in three propositions:

> The first [proposition] is that when an individual is confident that an attachment figure will be available to him whenever he desires it, that person will be much less prone to either intense or chronic fear than will an individual who for any reason has no such confidence. The second proposition concerns the sensitive period during which such confidence develops. It postulates that confidence in the availability of attachment figures, or a lack of it, is built up slowly during the years of immaturity—infancy, childhood, and adolescence—and that whatever expectations are developed during those years tend to persist relatively unchanged throughout the rest of life. The third proposition concerns the role of actual experience. It postulates that the varied expectations of the accessibility and responsiveness of attachment figures that individuals develop during the years of immaturity are tolerably accurate reflections of the experiences those individuals have actually had. (Bowlby, 1973, p. 235)

According to Bowlby, mental models of self and relationship partners, and the behavior patterns influenced by them, are central components of personality. Personal continuity, in fact, is primarily due to the persistence of mental models, which are themselves sustained by a fairly stable family setting. The two aspects of mental models—representations of self and representations of relationships—are closely interrelated, as Bowlby explains in the following passage:

> Confidence that an attachment figure is, apart from being accessible, likely to be responsive can be seen to turn on at least two variables: (a) whether or not the attachment figure is judged to be the sort of person who in general responds to calls for support and protection; [and] (b) whether or not the self is judged to be the sort of person towards whom anyone, and the attachment figure in particular, is likely to respond in a helpful way. Logically these variables are independent. In practice they are apt to be confounded. As a result, the model of the attachment figure and the model of the self are likely to develop so as to be complementary and mutually confirming. (1973, p. 238)

Bowlby's belief that these mental models play an important part in determining the fate of a person's feelings and relationships across the life span is still the focus of heated controversy, but it is supported by a growing number of longitudinal studies of social behavior from infancy through the early elementary school years (Dontas, Maratos, Fafoutis, & Karangelis, 1985; Erickson, Sroufe, & Egeland, 1985; Main, Kaplan, & Cassidy, 1985; Sroufe, 1983; Waters, Wippman, & Sroufe, 1979). We take these studies as encouragement for exploring longer-range continuity between childhood attachment and adult romantic love.

SIMILARITIES BETWEEN INFANT CARE-GIVER ATTACHMENT AND ADULT ROMANTIC LOVE

Given the foregoing theoretical background, we are ready to suggest more explicitly that all important love relationships—especially the first ones with parents and later ones with lovers and spouses—are attachments in Bowlby's sense. We begin by examining similarities between infant and adult attachments. Table 4.1 lists the key features of mother-infant attachment and adult romantic love. For every documented feature of attachment there is a parallel feature of love, and for most documented features of love there is either a documented or a plausible infant parallel. (References for the documentation are listed in a note beneath the table.) The two sets of features are so remarkably similar that before rejecting the hypothesis that attachment and love are variants of a single underlying process, one should feel compelled to offer another explanation of the parallels.

TABLE 4.1   Comparison of the Features of Attachment
and Adult Romantic Love

Attachment	Romantic Love
Formation and quality of the attachment bond depends on the attachment object's (AO's) sensitivity and responsiveness.	The love feelings are related to an intense desire for the love object's (LO's) (real or imagined) interest and reciprocation.
AO provides a secure base and infant feels competent and safe to explore.	LO's real or imagined reciprocation causes person to feel confident, secure, safe, etc.
When AO is present, infant is happier, has a higher threshold for distress, is less afraid of strangers, etc.	When LO is viewed as reciprocating, the lover is happier, more positive about life in general, more outgoing, and kinder to others.
When AO is not available, not sensitive, etc., infant is anxious, preoccupied, unable to explore freely.	When LO acts uninterested or rejecting, person is anxious, preoccupied, unable to concentrate, etc.
Attachment behaviors include: proximity- and contact-seeking— holding, touching, caressing, kissing, rocking, smiling, crying, following, clinging, etc.	Romantic love is manifest in: wanting to spend time with LO; holding, touching, caressing, kissing, and making love with LO; smiling and laughing; crying; clinging; fearing separation, etc.
When afraid, distressed, sick, threatened, etc., infants seek physical contact with AO.	When afraid, distressed, sick, threatened, etc., lovers would like to be held and comforted by LO.
Distress at separation or loss: crying, calling for AO, trying to find AO, becoming sad and listless if reunion seems impossible.	Distress at separation or loss: crying, calling for LO, trying to find LO, becoming sad and listless if reunion seems impossible.
Upon reunion with AO, infants smile, greet AO with positive vocalization or cry, bounce and jiggle, approach, reach to be picked up, etc.	Upon reunion with LO, or when LO reciprocates after reciprocation was in doubt, the lover feels ecstatic, hugs LO, etc.
Infant shares toys, discoveries, etc. with AO.	Lovers like to share experiences, give gifts, etc., and imagine how LO would react to interesting sights, etc.
Infant and AO frequently engage in prolonged eye contact; infant seems fascinated with AO's physical features and enjoys touching nose, ears, hair, etc.	Lovers frequently engage in prolonged eye contact and seem fascinated with each other's physical features and like to explore noses, ears, hair, etc.

TABLE 4.1 (*Continued*)

Attachment	Romantic Love
Infant feels fused with AO and, with development, becomes ambivalent about the balance of fusion and autonomy.	Lover sometimes feels fused with LO, and the balance of fusion and autonomy is frequently a matter of concern.
Although the infant can be attached to more than one person at a time, there is usually one key relationship (a "hierarchy of attachments").	Although many adults feel they can and do "love" more than one person, intense love tends to occur with only one partner at a time.
Separations, maternal nonresponsiveness, etc., up to a point, increase the intensity of the infant's attachment behaviors (proximity-seeking, clinging, etc.).	Adversity (social disapproval, separations, etc.), up to a point, increases the intensity of the lovers' feelings and commitment to each other.
Infant coos, "sings," talks baby talk, etc.; mother talks a combination of baby talk and "motherese." Much nonverbal communication.	Lovers coo, sing, talk baby talk, use soft maternal tones, etc., and much of their communication is nonverbal.
The responsive mother senses the infant's needs, "reads the infant's mind," etc. Powerful empathy.	The lover feels almost magically understood and sympathized with. Powerful empathy.
Infant experiences AO as powerful, beneficent, all-knowing, etc. In the early stages of development the "good AO" is mentally separate from the "bad AO."	Lover at first ignores or denies LO's negative qualities and perceives LO as powerful, special, all-good, "a miracle," etc.
When relationship is not going well, and infant is anxious, it becomes hypervigilant to cues of AO's approval or disapproval.	Before a love relationship becomes secure, the lover is hypersensitive to cues of LO's reciprocation or nonreciprocation, and feelings (ecstasy to despair) are highly dependent on these cues.
The infant appears to get tremendous pleasure from AO's approval, applause, attention, etc.	At least early in a relationship, the lover's greatest happiness comes from LO's approval, attention, etc.

Sources: Facts about attachment are derived from Ainsworth et al., 1978; Bell & Ainsworth, 1972; Bowlby, 1969, 1973, 1980; Campos et al., 1975; Cohen & Campos, 1974; Haith, Bergman, & Moore, 1977; Heinicke & Westheimer, 1966; Kaye, 1982; Mahler, Pine, & Bergman, 1975; Morgan & Ricciuti, 1969; Robeson, 1967; Schaffer & Emerson, 1964; Stayton & Ainsworth, 1973; Stern, 1977; Tracy, Lamb, & Ainsworth, 1976; Waters et al., 1979. Facts about adult romantic love are from our own data, plus Driscoll, Davis, & Lipetz, 1972; McCready, 1981; Pope et al., 1980; Reedy, Birren, & Schaie, 1981; Reik, 1941; Rubin, 1973; Tennov, 1979; Vaillant, 1977; Walster & Walster, 1978; Weiss, 1979.

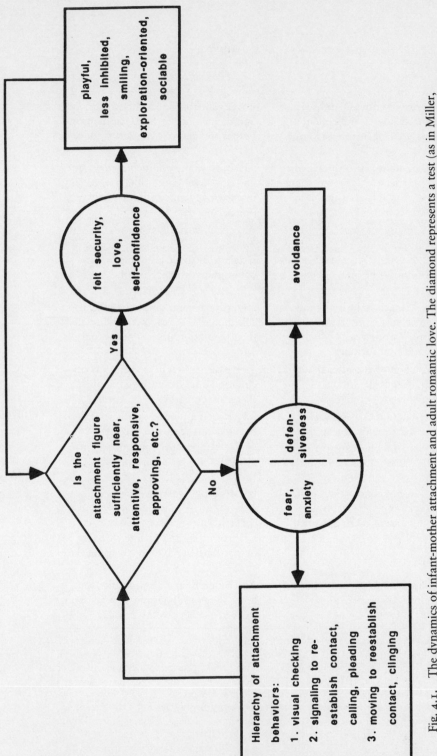

Fig. 4.1. The dynamics of infant-mother attachment and adult romantic love. The diamond represents a test (as in Miller, Galanter, & Pribram's, 1960, test-operate-test-exit model of behavior); circles represent emotions and squares represent behaviors. The term *sufficiently* in the test question implies that the degree of proximity (and emotional closeness, in the case of adult lovers) is influenced by relationship history and current psychological state (including such things as pain, illness, fatigue, stress, and novelty).

In addition to sharing many features, the two kinds of attachment exhibit similar *dynamics*. When the attachment figure (or attachment object, AO) is available and responsive, the infant (or adult lover) feels secure enough to wander off and explore the environment and to interact with others, occasionally checking back with AO. If AO suddenly becomes unavailable, attachment behaviors such as signaling or moving closer are initiated and maintained, until feelings of security are restored (see figure 4.1). The loop in the upper right-hand corner of the figure represents the process experienced most often by secure infants and secure lovers. The loop in the bottom left portion of the figure represents the negative, painful side of love relationships, experienced occasionally by every lover but, as explained below, especially characteristic of insecure infants and insecure lovers.

THREE KINDS OR STYLES OF ATTACHMENT

The formation during early childhood of a smoothly functioning (that is, secure) attachment relationship with a primary care giver, although the norm in American society, is by no means guaranteed. In a test of Bowlby's ideas, Mary Ainsworth found that a mother's sensitivity and responsiveness to her infant's signals and needs during the first year of life are crucial prerequisites for a secure early attachment relationship. Mothers who are slow or inconsistent in responding to their infant's cries or who regularly intrude on or interfere with their infant's desired activities (sometimes to force "affection" on the infant at a particular moment) produce infants who cry more than usual, explore less than usual (even in mother's presence), mingle attachment behaviors with overt expressions of anger, and seem generally anxious. If instead, or in addition, mother frequently rebuffs or rejects the infant's attempts to establish physical contact, the infant may learn to avoid her. On the basis of their observations, Ainsworth and her colleagues delineated three types of attachment, often called *secure* (characterizing 66 percent of the infants tested), *anxious/ambivalent* (19 percent), and *avoidant* (21 percent). The anxious/ambivalent type frequently exhibits the behaviors that Bowlby called protest, whereas the avoidant type seems detached. The following quotations (from Ainsworth et al., 1978) provide brief accounts of the three types:

> *Secure.* Even when [mother] is out of sight, [the secure infant] nevertheless usually [seems to believe] she is accessible to him and would be responsive should he seek her out or signal to her. It is our hypothesis that expectations of her accessibility and responsiveness

have been built up through [the infant's] experience of her generally sensitive responsiveness to his signals and communications. Such experience has been repeatedly confirmed by interactions with her in many different contexts—including feeding, face-to-face [interactions], close bodily contact, and by her response to his crying—throughout the first year. By the end of the first year it is probably only when attachment behavior has already been activated to some extent by conditions such as fatigue, hunger, or illness, or by some unaccustomed and somewhat alarming circumstance, that he protests her departure and/or continuing absence. (p. 312)

Anxious/Ambivalent. There is every reason to believe that [anxious/ambivalent] infants are anxious in their attachment to mother. Both at home and in the [unfamiliar laboratory] situation, they cry more than [secure] babies. They manifest more separation anxiety. They do not seem to have confident expectations of the mother's accessibility and responsiveness. Consequently they are unable to use the mother as a secure base from which to explore an unfamiliar situation—at least not as well as [secure] infants. . . . Because they are chronically anxious in relation to mother, they tend to respond to [her] departures in the separation episodes with immediate and intense distress; their attachment behavior has a low threshold for high-intensity activation. (pp. 314–315)

Avoidant. [In interpreting the avoidant babies' behavior], we began by noting the similarity between avoidance of the mother in the [laboratory] reunion episodes and the "detachment" behavior that has been observed to result from "major" separation experiences. . . . We suggested that both mother avoidance in the [laboratory] situation and detachment during and after longer separations served a defensive function. Our next clue was to note that the mothers of [avoidant] infants were more rejecting than either [secure] or [anxious] mothers. . . . One major way in which they rejected their infants was to rebuff infant desire for close bodily contact. [They were also more frequently angry or irritated than the mothers of secure and anxious/ambivalent infants, and less expressive of positive emotions. They were characterized by observers as more rigid and compulsive.] (pp. 316–317)

Notice that all three kinds of infants are "attached," although in different ways, so it makes little sense to talk about varying degrees or intensities of attachment. Instead, Ainsworth and her followers speak of the quality of attachment. This is one of the major ways in which their approach differs from a focus on unidimensional constructs such as attitude, affection, or dependency. A major goal of our recent work has been to apply Ainsworth et al.'s three-category system to the study of adult romantic love. Another goal has been to pursue Bowlby's idea that continuity in relationship style is a matter of mental models of self and relationships. A third goal has been to explore the possibility that the specific characteristics of parent-child relationships identified by Ainsworth et al. as the probable causes of differences in infant attachment styles are also among the determinants of grown-ups' romantic attachment styles. Details of the studies can be found in Hazan and Shaver (1987); here we summarize the major results.

TWO STUDIES OF LOVE AS ATTACHMENT

Our first study was based on a questionnaire that appeared in the *Rocky Mountain News*, Denver's largest circulation newspaper, in the summer of 1985. More than twelve hundred people responded, and we analyzed questionnaires from about half of them (N=620). The survey included a "Love Quiz" comprising fourteen a priori subscales (for example, trust, jealousy, desire for reciprocation, emotional extremes), based on previous adult love measures and extrapolations from the literature on infant caregiver attachment. Subjects described their "most important" love relationship. We also included questions concerning relationships with parents (attachment history), and mental models of self and relationships. Respondents were grouped according to a single-item measure of attachment type designed by translating Ainsworth et al.'s descriptions of their infant forms into terms appropriate to adult love.

Possible limitations of the first study, especially respondents' self-selection, made it desirable to conduct a conceptual replication. We therefore tested a "captive" university student group (N=108) and included all measures from the first study plus some new ones. Because of space limitations imposed by newspaper editors, the *Rocky Mountain News* study neglected the self side of mental models, so in the university student study we emphasized that. We also added a single classification item for the caregiving style of each parent, based on Ainsworth et al.'s descriptions of the three major kinds of mothers.

The proportions of each of the three attachment types were highly stable across studies. Table 4.2 shows how the alternatives were worded and provides the percentage of people endorsing each description. In both samples, just over half classified themselves as secure, whereas the other half split fairly evenly between the avoidant and anxious/ambivalent cate-

TABLE 4.2   Adult Attachment Types and Their Frequencies

Question:
Which of the following best describes your feelings?

Answers and Percentages:	Newspaper Sample	University Sample
Secure: I find it relatively easy to get close to others and am comfortable depending on them and having them depend on me. I don't often worry about being abandoned or about someone getting too close to me.	56%	56%
Avoidant: I am somewhat uncomfortable being close to others; I find it difficult to trust them completely, difficult to allow myself to depend on them. I am nervous when anyone gets too close, and often, love partners want me to be more intimate than I feel comfortable being.	25%	23%
Anxious/Ambivalent: I find that others are reluctant to get as close as I would like. I often worry that my partner doesn't really love me or won't want to stay with me. I want to merge completely with another person, and this desire sometimes scares people away.	19%	20%

gories. These figures are not terribly different from the proportions reported in Ainsworth et al.'s (1978) study of infant-mother attachment. Interestingly, there were no significant sex differences, which is another parallel between our results and those from infant studies.

People with different self-designated attachment styles also differed in the way they characterized their most important love relationship. (See table 4.3, which displays means from the *Rocky Mountain News* study.) Secure lovers described love as especially happy, friendly, and trusting, and emphasized being able to accept and support their partner despite the partner's faults. Moreover, their relationships tended to endure longer (10.02 years, on the average, compared with 4.86 years for the anxious/ambivalent and 5.97 years for the avoidant lovers), even though all three groups were the same age, on the average (36 years). Avoidant lovers were characterized by fear of intimacy, emotional highs and lows, and jealousy. They never produced the highest mean on a positive (desirable)

TABLE 4.3   Attachment Style and the Experience of Love

	Attachment Type		
	Avoidant	*Anxious/ Ambivalent*	*Secure*
Happiness	3.19	3.31	**3.51**
Friendship	3.18	3.19	**3.50**
Trust	3.11	3.13	**3.43**
Fear of closeness	**2.30**	2.15	**1.88**
Acceptance	**2.86**	3.03	3.01
Emotional extremes	**2.75**	**3.05**	**2.36**
Jealousy	**2.57**	**2.88**	**2.17**
Obsessive preoccupation	3.01	**3.29**	3.01
Sexual attraction	3.27	**3.43**	3.27
Desire for union	2.81	**3.25**	2.69
Desire for reciprocation	3.24	**3.55**	3.22
Love at first sight	2.91	**3.17**	2.97

Note: Statistically significant differences between means within a row are indicated by bold-face type. Where one mean differs from the other two, which do not significantly differ from each other, that one appears in boldface type. Where one mean differs significantly from one other, those two appear in boldface type. Where all three differ significantly from each other, all three are boldfaced.

feature of love. The anxious/ambivalent lovers experienced love as involving obsession, desire for reciprocation and union, emotional highs and lows, and extreme sexual attraction and jealousy (a pattern of emotions similar to what Tennov, 1979, called "limerence"). These effects of attachment style on love experiences were very similar in the university student study, although not all the subscales yielded significant mean differences with the smaller sample. Once again, there were no important sex differences (see Hazan & Shaver, 1987, for details).

We attempted to assess a generalized version of what Bowlby called working models of relationships using the items shown in table 4.4. Each was either checked or not checked as describing how a respondent generally "view[s] the course of romantic love over time," and how he or she views self and others. Secure lovers more often said that romantic feelings wax and wane but at times reach the intensity experienced at the start of the relationship, and that in some relationships romantic love never fades. Avoidant lovers said that the kind of head-over-heels romantic love depicted in novels and movies doesn't exist in real life, that romantic love rarely lasts, and that it is rare to find a person one can *really* fall in love with.

Anxious/ambivalent respondents claimed it is easy to fall in love and said they frequently feel themselves beginning to do so, although (like the avoidant lovers) they rarely find what they would call "real" love. Once again, the results were similar across our two studies and held for both sexes, although there were fewer significant differences for the smaller university sample.

Table 4.4 also includes the self-model items used only in the university student study. Secure respondents described themselves as easy to get to know and as liked by most people, and endorsed the claim that other people

TABLE 4.4   Attachment Style and Mental Models

	Avoidant	Anxious/ Ambivalent	Secure
1. The kind of head-over-heels romantic love depicted in novels and movies doesn't exist in real life.	.25	.28	**.13**
2. Intense romantic love is common at the beginning of a relationship, but it rarely lasts forever.	**.41**	.34	.28
3. Romantic feelings wax and wane over the course of a relationship, but at times they can be as intense as they were at the start.	**.60**	.75	.79
4. In some relationships, romantic love really lasts; it doesn't fade with time.	.41	.46	**.59**
5. It's easy to fall in love. I feel myself beginning to fall in love often.	.04	**.20**	.09
6. It's rare to find someone you can really fall in love with.	.66	.56	**.43**
7. I am easier to get to know than most people.	.32	.32	**.60**
8. I have more self-doubts than most people.	.48	.64	**.18**
9. People almost always like me.	.36	.41	**.68**
10. People often misunderstand me or fail to appreciate me.	.36	.50	**.18**
11. Few people are as willing and able as I am to commit themselves to a long-term relationship.	.24	**.59**	.23
12. People are generally well intentioned and good-hearted.	.44	.32	**.72**

Note: Results for the first six items are from the newspaper sample and were replicated in the university sample; results for the last six items are from the university sample only. The system of boldfacing is explained in the note beneath table 4.3.

are generally well intentioned and good-hearted. Anxious/ambivalent lovers reported having more self-doubts, being misunderstood and under-appreciated, and finding others less willing and able than they are to commit themselves to a relationship. The avoidant group generally fell between the extremes set by their secure and anxious/ambivalent counter-parts, and in most cases were closer to the anxious than to the secure lovers.

Attachment history was assessed by asking respondents to describe how each parent had generally behaved toward them during childhood and how the parents had gotten along with each other. Respondents indicated their answers by checking or not checking adjectives such as *caring*, *critical*, *intrusive*, and *responsive*. Stepwise multiple regression procedures were used to determine which adjectives discriminated between attachment types considered in pairs (secure versus avoidant, and so on).

In the newspaper sample, mothers of avoidant respondents were characterized as more demanding, more disrespectful, and more critical, when compared with mothers of secure respondents. Fathers of avoidant respondents were characterized as more forceful and uncaring. The relationship between mother and father was described as not affectionate. These results fit well with Ainsworth et al.'s (1978) observations, indicating that mothers of avoidant infants are relatively cold and rejecting. When anxious/ambivalent respondents were compared with secure respondents, their mothers were portrayed as more intrusive and unfair, the fathers were described as more unfair and threatening, and the parental relationship was characterized as unhappy. The term *intrusive* was the main one used by Ainsworth et al. in their description of mothers of anxious/ambivalent infants. "Unfair" may be a child's way of characterizing that kind of parent's inconsistent and unreliable care giving. Finally, when anxious/ambivalent lovers were compared with avoidant lovers, mothers of the former were described as more responsive and funny, and their fathers were portrayed as relatively unfair but affectionate. Nothing about the parental relationship predicted differences between these two groups. This last set of results parallels Ainsworth et al.'s characterization of the mothers of avoidant infants as more uniformly negative than the mothers of anxious/ambivalent infants. In general, the results fit remarkably well with attachment theory and suggest that both mothers and fathers are important in determining their children's long-term attachment styles and that both have the same kinds of effects.

In the university student study, perceptions of relationships with parents also predicted attachment type. The specific adjectives were not identical across studies, but their meanings with respect to attachment theory were similar. The statistical results were stronger for the university students, who averaged eighteen years of age, than for the newspaper readers (who averaged thirty-six years of age), suggesting that the younger the sample, the easier it is to predict their adult attachment styles from descriptions of relationships with parents. In line with this interpretation, when the newspaper readers were divided into younger and older age groups, the connections between love styles and relationships with parents were stronger for the younger group. As distance from parents increases and adult love experiences accumulate, the effect of childhood relationships on adult mental models and behavior patterns decreases. (For more complex analyses of the parent data, see Hazan & Shaver, 1987.)

LIMITATIONS OF OUR INITIAL STUDIES

The results of our first two studies provide encouraging support for an attachment-theory perspective on adult romantic love. Their major shortcomings have to do with the preliminary measures of attachment constructs. First, because both questionnaires had to be brief, we were able to inquire about only a single romantic relationship. To increase the chances of detecting features of love experiences that are due to subjects' attachment styles, it might be better to ask about more than one relationship (as, for example, Hindy & Schwarz, 1984, have done). It might also be useful to assess both partners in the relationship, employing a multimethod approach (see Kobak & Sceery, in press). Roger Kobak, in conjunction with us, is currently beginning such a study, assessing adult attachments via observational coding, intensive interviews, and self-report questionnaires.

Second, our measures were limited in terms of number of items and number of answer alternatives provided for each item. The love subscales contained only a few items each, and the questions about mental models and attachment history received either yes or no answers. In future studies it should be possible to develop highly reliable assessment scales for each of the domains and dimensions we have identified.

Finally, there are reasons to suspect that no amount of psychometric improvement will solve all the problems associated with self-report assessment of attachment-related variables. First of all, people may be unable to articulate exactly how they feel in love relationships. Second, they are unlikely to have anything like perfect recall of past love experiences or of the nature of their relationships with parents, especially during preschool years. Third, they are likely to be defensive and self-serving when recalling and describing some of the events we wish to inquire about. (See George, Kaplan, & Main, 1984, and Kobak & Sceery, in press, for more probing and complexly scored interview procedures that may solve some of these problems.)

Another important issue has to do with continuity and change in attachment style. For theoretical reasons, we have been interested in exploring continuity between childhood and adulthood, and we consider it important that there is good evidence for some continuity between ages one and six. Nevertheless, it would be overly pessimistic from the perspective of insecurely attached people to conclude that simple continuity between early childhood and adulthood is the rule rather than the exception. The correlations we obtained between parent variables and current attachment type were statistically significant but not terribly strong, especially for older respondents.

There is evidence that thinking about and working through unpleasant childhood experiences helps people change their mental models of relationships (Main et al., 1985). This kind of insight can break the chain of cross-generational continuity, allowing once-insecure parents to respond appropriately to their young children, who then go on to become secure adults. The process by which an insecure person becomes increasingly secure, probably by participating in relationships that disconfirm negative features of experience-based mental models and/or gaining insight into the workings of one's mental models, offers an extremely important topic for future research. Obviously, the results will be especially interesting to research-guided psychotherapists.

Because some critics have called our approach Freudian, we should mention the important differences between familiar Freudian conceptions of infant-to-adult continuity, on the one hand, and the conception offered by attachment theory, on the other. Unlike the Freudian conception, according to which the supposed irrationalities of adult love indicate regression to infancy or fixation at some earlier stage of psychosexual development, attachment theory asserts that social development involves a continuing need for secure attachments and the continual construction, revision, integration, and abstraction of mental models. This latter idea, which is similar to the notion of scripts and schemas in cognitive and social psychology (for example, Fiske & Taylor, 1984), is compatible with the possibility of change based on new information and experiences, although change may become more difficult with repeated, uncorrected use of habitual models or scripts.

Freud argued his case beautifully, if not persuasively, by likening the unconscious mind to the city of Rome, which has been ravaged, revised, and rebuilt many times over the centuries. In the case of the unconscious, according to Freud, it is as if all the previous cities still exist in their original form and on the same site. Bowlby's conception is more in line with actual archaeology. The foundations and present shapes of mental models of self and social life still bear similarities and connections to their predecessors— some of the important historical landmarks, bridges, and crooked streets are still there. But few of the ancient structures exist unaltered or in mental isolation, so simple regression and fixation are unlikely. There is continuity in attachment behavior, but there can also be significant change.

THREE BEHAVIORAL SYSTEMS: ATTACHMENT, CARE GIVING, AND SEXUALITY

Aside from measurement problems, our attachment-theoretical approach to romantic love must overcome some sizable conceptual obstacles. In our preliminary studies, we chose largely to overlook the fact that child-parent relationships differ in important ways from adult romantic relationships. One of the most striking differences is that romantic love is usually a two-way street between people with approximately equal power and status; both partners are sometimes anxious and security seeking and at other times able providers of security and care. A second important difference is that romantic love almost always involves sexual attraction (Berscheid, this volume, chap. 16; Tennov, 1979), whereas only the most speculative psychoanalysts have claimed that infants' attachments to parents are sexual in nature.

Bowlby (1969) and Ainsworth (for example, 1982, 1985) have already provided the conceptual tools with which to attack this problem. In the same way that exploration and foraging are behavioral systems that differ from attachment, Bowlby and Ainsworth have argued that care giving and mating (or sexual reproduction) are behavioral systems distinct from attachment.

The care-giving system is the one activated in a parent when his or her child displays attachment behaviors. In its optimal form it includes sensitivity and responsiveness, behaviors aimed at soothing the child (holding, patting, rocking), and attempts at problem solution. Like attachment behaviors on the part of infants, care-giving responses on the part of parents can easily be observed among nonhuman primates (and other mammals). In the case of parents and infants, the care-giving and attachment systems are naturally complementary. When the infant's attachment system is active, it elicits care-giving behavior from the parent; when the parent's care-giving system is active, it produces behaviors that ease the child's distress. In the same way that attachment reactions can be distorted by faulty care giving, the care-giving system can be distorted by nonoptimal social-learning experiences. In fact, the various forms of deficient parenting observed by Ainsworth et al. (1978)—including rejection, intrusiveness, and inconsistency—can be viewed as distortions in the parents' care-giving systems that are due to faulty socialization experiences.

The sexual system requires less comment. Animals, including humans, have been constructed by evolution to place a high priority on sexual reproduction. Sexual desires are among the strongest motivators of human behavior, and sexual gratification is one of the greatest human pleasures. The cycle of desire and arousal followed by sexual behavior and orgasm can easily be viewed as an innate system with an important biological function. Perhaps less obvious but nevertheless well documented is the vulnerability of the sexual system to deviations and distortions caused by nonoptimal socialization and sexual experiences. (Consider, for example, the "perversions" that captured Freud's attention and the sexual "dysfunctions" studied by Masters and Johnson, among others.)

Of the three biologically based behavioral systems—attachment, care giving, and sexuality—attachment would seem to be the preeminent system, developmentally speaking. It arises first and adapts itself to whatever care-giving environment happens to be encountered. It seems reasonable to suppose that care giving is learned, at least in its rudimentary forms, by modeling the behavior of primary attachment figures or, less commonly, by responding to an attachment figure's need for care. If so, people should grow up exhibiting the same kinds of care-giving deficiencies evident in their own care givers' behavior, or at least with deficiencies related to those care givers' needs and behaviors, a sad conclusion for which there is growing evidence (for example, Hazan & Shaver, 1987; Main et al., 1985; Ricks, 1985).

Because the attachment system is the first social-behavioral system to develop, it plays an important role in the creation of cognitive models of social life. During the first months and years of life everyone learns what to expect from others, especially attachment figures, and reaches some important conclusions about the self, perhaps both as a care giver and as a love object. Later, when the care-giving system and the sexual system become more fully developed, mental models of the social world constructed during infancy and early childhood are likely to be invoked. Thus, the functioning of all social-behavioral systems is, to a certain degree, influenced by what happens when attachment is first attempted.

Given the division of love into three somewhat independent behavioral systems—attachment, care giving, and sexuality—how might we expect love to develop over time? Clearly, the three systems need not follow the same time course, a fact that allows us to account for the many conceptual schemes developed over the years to explain differences in types of love and changes over time in the form of love. Table 4.5 summarizes some of these schemes.

The first one, a tripartite division proposed by Wilson (1981), is very similar to Bowlby's, which is not surprising given their mutual reliance on evolutionary biology. The second scheme is based on a factor analysis of Rubin's (1973) well-known love scale by Steck, Levitan, McLane, and Kelley (1982). The scale, especially as elaborated by Steck et al., contains three components very similar to Bowlby's, although to the best of our knowledge the similarities have not been noted before. The remaining three schemes are representative of much of the social psychological literature. Tennov (1979) distinguished between "limerence," on the one hand, a neologism for what Berscheid and Walster (1974; Walster & Walster, 1978) called passionate love, and "love," on the other hand, which the latter authors called companionate love. It is common to claim, as Walster

TABLE 4.5 Previous Conceptions of Love Components
Compared with Attachment Theory's Attachment, Care-giving,
and Sexuality Components

Authors	Attachment	Care giving	Sexuality
Wilson (1981)	attachment	parental protection	sex
Rubin (1973); Steck et al. (1982)	trust	caring	need
Berscheid & Walster (1974); Walster & Walster (1978)	companionate love		passionate love
Sternberg (1986)	intimacy and commitment		passion
Tennov (1979)	limerence		limerence
	love		

and Walster did, that passionate love precedes and somehow becomes transformed into companionate love, but the reasons for the transformation are usually left vague.

Sternberg's (1986) scheme is a bit different. It includes three rather than two components: passion, intimacy, and commitment, each of which follows its own time course. Passion rises quickly and then typically drops off; commitment gradually rises and then levels off, in a step-function fashion; intimacy grows slowly and steadily over a long period of time. The unique feature of this scheme is the inclusion of commitment, which Sternberg seems to view more as a decision than as an emotional process. Whether all aspects of commitment can be so viewed (for example, the gradual commitment of time and resources to a relationship; the gradual constraints a couple experiences as family and friends begin to view them as a unit) is still a matter of debate (for example, Stanley, 1986).

The advantage of the attachment approach is that the three systems it highlights—attachment, care giving, and sexuality—all make biological sense and have the status of behavioral systems. Whether commitment makes similar sense remains to be seen. Sternberg's (1986) time-course analysis of love, according to which different components of love (passion, commitment, and intimacy) increase (and in some cases decline) at different rates, also applies to the three behavioral systems. Sexual attraction can increase very quickly and pull people into a relationship. Attachment and care giving, both perhaps aspects of what Sternberg calls intimacy, develop more slowly. In a secure relationship, attachment and care giving probably develop in tandem, each person providing responsive kindness and support which the other person comfortably relies upon.

In the various kinds of insecure relationships, the attachment and care-giving components take distorted forms (Bowlby, 1979), three of which are compulsive self-reliance (common among avoidant types), compulsive care giving (another, less common strategy of vulnerability avoidance), and premature attachment (common among anxious/ambivalent lovers, who, as our results indicate, are eager for union and commitment). The exact nature of such relationships and the reasons for their early demise (as revealed by our newspaper sample, in which secure people's relationships lasted twice as long, on the average, as those of insecure people) are high-priority topics for future research. We suspect that the distinction between attachment and care giving will prove important, since a lover can be attached to someone (be dependent for emotional security on that person) without also being an adequate care giver.

It is important to understand, while considering the time course of love, that by calling romantic love an attachment process we do not mean to imply that the early phases of romance are equivalent to *being attached*. Our idea, which needs further development, is that romantic love is a biological process designed by evolution to facilitate attachment between adult sexual partners who, at the time love evolved, were likely to become parents of an infant who would need their reliable care. Romantic love and infant care-giver attachment thus both contribute to reproduction and survival. As Bowlby said in a passage quoted earlier, "The formation of [an attachment] bond is described as falling in love, maintaining a bond as loving someone." The early phases of romance are, when all goes well, the processes of bond formation (and, before the invention of birth control, of sexual reproduction); the long-term result—again, if all goes well—is attachment among members of a nuclear family.

Why does romantic love seem to wane after a period of months or years? The usual reason offered is that sexual attraction just naturally declines, especially among males for whom it supposedly makes evolutionary sense to seek new sexual partners (Wilson, 1981). Another reason may have to do with the dynamics of attachment. If one's lover repeatedly proves to be available and responsive, the fear component of the attachment system (refer back to figure 4.1) becomes quiescent, and a feeling of security reigns. In childhood, the process of establishing such taken-for-granted security occupies about three years. According to Bowlby (1969), "By most children attachment behavior is exhibited strongly and regularly until almost the end of the third year. Then a change occurs. . . . In many children the change seems to take place almost abruptly, suggesting that at this age some maturational threshold is passed" (pp. 204–205). Surprisingly, and perhaps only coincidentally, the time period most often mentioned in connection with the duration of romantic love is also three years (for example, Tennov, 1979).

When romantic passion wanes, problems in care giving are likely to arise. We suspect that this, rather than the decline of passion per se (which most marital relationships survive), largely accounts for the fact, mentioned earlier, that the relationships of avoidant and anxious/ambivalent respondents to our newspaper survey lasted little more than a few years, on the average. When two lovers are no longer preoccupied by sexual attraction, they can more easily see each other's care-giving deficiencies and will perhaps weigh those more heavily in deciding whether the relationship is rewarding and equitable (Hatfield, Traupmann, Sprecher, Utne, & Hay, 1985).

BROKEN ATTACHMENTS: GRIEVING FOR LOST LOVE

An advantage of the attachment-theoretical approach to adult love is that it helps explain the powerful emotional reactions that accompany broken relationships, whether they come about through separation, divorce, or death. It is hard to see how love-as-an-attitude theorists or love-as-labeled-arousal theorists could say very much about this, whereas attachment theory was designed from the start to deal with separation and loss as well as with love. When loss of a spouse occurs, for example, especially if it occurs abruptly, the typical reaction is similar to separation distress in infancy, including uncontrollable restlessness, difficulty in concentrating, disturbed sleep, anxiety, tension, and anger. These are deep and uncontrollable reactions, which Bowlby argues are biologically designed to regain the lost attachment figure. They therefore seem irrational in situations where contact with the lost figure is temporarily or permanently impossible. Consider the following examples, one involving a three-year-old child whose mother left him in a residential nursery, the other involving a young wife whose husband was killed in a car accident.

> Patrick tried to keep his promise and was not seen crying. [His mother had told him to be a good boy and not to cry; otherwise she would not visit him.] Instead he would nod his head whenever anyone looked at him and assured himself and anybody who cared to listen that his mother would come for him, she would put on his overcoat and would take him home with her again. Whenever a listener seemed to believe him he was satisfied; when anybody contradicted him, he would burst into violent tears. . . .
>
> Later an ever-growing list of clothes that his mother was supposed to put on him was added: She will put on my overcoat and my leggings, she will zip up the zipper, she will put on my pixie hat.
>
> When the repetitions of this formula became monotonous and endless, somebody asked him whether he could not stop saying it all over again. Again Patrick tried to be the good boy that his mother wanted him to be. He stopped repeating the formula aloud, but his moving lips showed that he was saying it over and over to himself.
>
> At the same time he substituted for the spoken words gestures that showed the position of his pixie hat, the putting on of an imaginary coat, the zipping of the zipper, etc. . . . While the other children were mostly busy with their toys, playing games, making music, etc., Patrick, totally uninterested, would stand somewhere in a corner, moving his hands and lips with an absolutely tragic expression on his face. (Freud & Burlingham, 1943, p. 89)

Obviously, the attachment system does not relax in response to simple environmental demands that it do so. The same holds for adult attachment. The following passages are taken from an interview with a woman who was notified that her husband had been injured in an accident. When she arrived at the hospital emergency room, they directed her to the morgue, which, if rationality had prevailed, would have indicated that her husband was dead and that calling him was futile.

> We went in and told them what we were looking for and that we wanted to identify him. But he was already identified. They had his name down, just like it was on the cards in his wallet. The man finally came up and took us down. You know, you have to go down, walk down the steps. And I knew he was dead. . . .
>
> I walked in and felt his skin. It was just as warm as mine. He was lying there just like he's in bed some nights, with his eyes half opened. And I closed them, and I rubbed his face, and I called him for twenty minutes. And the man told me, "Lady, your husband didn't even go to the accident room. Your husband came right here, because he was dead when he left the scene."
>
> I didn't believe it. I stayed for twenty minutes. I rubbed him, I rubbed his face, I patted him, I rubbed his head. I called him, but he didn't answer. And I knew if I called him he'd answer because he's used to my voice. But he didn't answer me. They said he was dead, but his skin was just as warm as mine. . . . I thought, well, maybe if I stay here and call him, maybe he'll answer me, because he didn't look like he was dead. (Parkes & Weiss, 1983, pp. 83–84)

Weeks later, the young widow was still having what she recognized to be a mysteriously difficult time accepting her husband's death: "It's been like that ever since he died. I listen for the key in that bottom door. . . . I went over and saw him and identified him and still I said, 'Well, he'll be home.' I know he's there, buried, but right now I don't believe it. I have it in my mind that he'll come home. It's a mystery how a grown-up would say that. But I really have it in my mind that he'll come home around 5:00" (Parkes & Weiss, 1983, p. 85). As anyone knows who has been through such an experience, yearning for the lost person can continue for months or years and can be mingled with anger at the person for leaving—even though that, too, is recognized as "irrational." We would say that the attachment system is more primitive than rationality, which is why both intense romantic love and intense grieving for a lost love seem uncontrollable and hence a bit "crazy." The system as a whole, however, does not seem crazy at all, given its important biological functions in both infancy and adulthood. It only looks crazy when its goals are unattainable.

The same thing might be said with respect to irrational-seeming religious experiences of the kind discussed by Brehm in chapter 11 of this volume. Widows and widowers, as well as children like little Patrick, can think so intently of their absent primary attachment figure that he or she seems actually to be present. In fact, it is normal for adults to hallucinate the presence of their dead spouse, to plead with him or her for help (in making important life decisions, for example), and to try to live in ways that would please the person. The attachment figure need not be physically present for such an "interaction" to take place, which makes it more understandable that people have imaginary but very convincing and affecting interactions with rock singers, dead philosophers, and religious figures of all kinds. Attachment, separation distress, and grieving are primarily psychological processes; they require psychological, not physical, interaction partners. Since adult attachment often involves three interwoven behavioral systems—attachment, care giving, and sexuality—it is natural that relations, say, between mystics and their image of Jesus can involve soothing his wounds, drying his tears, and expressing intense feelings that border on sexual passion.

CONCLUSION

What lessons can be drawn from our comparison of love and attachment? One implication is that love is a complex dynamic system involving cognitions, emotions, and behaviors. It is not a unidimensional phenomenon, not an attitude, not a simple state of labeled physiological arousal. Consider how impoverished the psychology of infant care-giver bonding would be if the concept of attachment were replaced by the idea that infants have a positive attitude toward their mothers or get physiologically aroused in the presence of their mothers and interpret this as love. These conceptions seem almost facetious until one realizes that they are taken directly from the social psychology of romantic love. If anything, adult love should be more, not less, complicated than infant care-giver attachment, involving as it does a much more differentiated understanding of self, others, and both real and ideal relationships; a much longer history of relationship experiences; more mature feelings of empathy; and adult sexuality.

Another implication, although one that needs further conceptual and empirical analysis, is that love, like early attachment, has biological bases and functions. According to Bowlby (1969), infants emerge from the womb ready for attachment because, in evolutionary history, physical proximity to a care giver greatly increased infants' chances of survival. Subsequent theorists have added that more than immediate biological survival is at stake. The relationship between infant and care giver is the infant's ticket to emotional self-regulation, education about the environment, and training in social skills. Does romantic love have similarly consequential functions? One obvious possibility is that love encourages sexual reproduction; but, as sociobiologists have pointed out, sexual attraction in itself, and hence reproduction, would not require attachment. Thus, the function of attachment between adult lovers may be primarily to increase the likelihood of parental health, stability, and investment in offspring. More speculative is the possibility that the happiness, openness, and care giving associated with adult love fosters good parenting behavior.

A third implication is that romantic love, although perhaps based on a single, general biological system or an interrelated set of systems, takes on somewhat different forms depending on a person's attachment history. Tennov's (1979) well-known distinction between "limerence," a passionate, painful sort of romantic love, and "love," a calmer state of friendship and support, may be similar to our distinction between anxious/ambivalent and secure love. The same distinction may help explain individual differences in religious experiences of the kind discussed by Brehm in this volume. Perhaps some of the most florid religious experiences, like some of the great human love affairs, depend on the existence of people who are desperately seeking a form of security never attainable in previous relationships.

There are many research-worthy mysteries in the domain of romantic love. We will close by mentioning three. First, what is the role of perceptual and cognitive model building during the early phases of attachment and love? The fact that infants stare with intense interest at their mother for much of the first few months of life, gradually achieving an integrated picture of her that allows for quick recognition (and perhaps contributes to feelings of pleasure and reassurance in her absence), has seemed natural enough to researchers. After all, the infant's nervous system is physically immature and has had no previous experience with visual perception. But what about the seemingly parallel phase of adult love: gazing intently at the partner, being fascinated with his or her physical features, mannerisms, personal history, and so on? What about the dreaming, daydreaming, and cognitive preoccupation with the new love object? Could it be that here, too, the mind seeks a particularly complete representation of the lover, perhaps because, once enshrined at the center of the subject's social network, this person is destined to play a highly significant role in the subject's emotional life?

Second, what role, if any, is played by successive love relationships in childhood? Presumably there is never a direct mental leap from infant attachment to adult love, but instead a long series of infatuations and crushes about which psychologists seem to know almost nothing (for an exception, see Easton, Hatfield & Synodinos, 1984). While writing this chapter, the three of us found that we could easily recall such infatuations, running back at least to kindergarten, and the memories included vivid imagery and still-significant feelings. These memorable relationships, however fragmentary and short-lived they may have been, seem to have left an indelible mark on us. In a forthcoming book about love, sociologist Jack Douglas (personal communication) argues, mostly on the basis of personal experience, that childhood crush partners form a psychological bridge between parents and subsequent adult romantic partners, and that the kind of people a particular individual finds attractive and lovable can be traced back to parents only through a history of infatuations. This would seem to create problems for our analysis of adult love in terms of three behavioral systems—attachment, care giving, and sexuality. Do all three of these exist in rudimentary forms in childhood crushes? If not, which is primary? Why do memories of crushes seem to involve all the components of romantic love: pleasure, yearning, desire to touch and be near, attempts to be generous and kind, and so on?

Finally, the attachment literature is alive with controversy concerning the role of temperament and care-giver continuity in the determination of temporal stability of attachment styles (Campos, Barrett, Lamb, Goldsmith, & Stenberg, 1983; Lamb, Thompson, Bardner, Charnov, & Estes, 1984; Waters, 1983). These controversies are relevant to our attempt to find connections between early attachment experiences and adult love. If infant temperament is, say, even half as important as parental responsiveness in determining whether the attachment bond will be anxious, secure, or avoidant, and if temperament persists throughout life, part of the continuity in attachment style from infancy to adulthood may be temperamental. And if the stability of attachment behavior between infancy and the early school years is due largely not just to intrapsychic continuity in the child but to stability in the parent-child relationship which is supplied mainly by the parents, then the degree of continuity between infancy and adulthood may vary widely depending on the continuity or discontinuity of a person's actual relationships over time.

Clearly, there is still a great deal to be learned about romantic love. It seems likely that attachment theory will be helpful in mapping the terrain.

REFERENCES

Ainsworth, M. D. S. (1982). Attachment: Retrospect and prospect. In C. M. Parkes & J. Stevenson-Hinde (Eds.), *The place of attachment in human behavior* (pp. 3–30). New York: Basic Books.

———. (1985). Attachments across the life span. *Bulletin of the New York Academy of Medicine, 61,* 792–811.

Ainsworth, M. D. S., Blehar, M. C., Waters, E., & Wall, S. (1978). *Patterns of attachment: A psychological study of the strange situation.* Hillsdale, NJ: Erlbaum.

Averill, J. R. (1985). The social construction of emotion: With special reference to love. In K. J. Gergen & K. E. Davis (Eds.), *The social construction of the person* (pp. 89–109). New York: Springer-Verlag.

Bell, S. M., & Ainsworth, M. D. S. (1972). Infant crying and maternal responsiveness. *Child Development, 43,* 1171–1190.

Berscheid, E., & Walster, E. (1974). A little bit about love. In T. L. Huston (Ed.), *Foundations of interpersonal attraction* (pp. 355–381). New York: Academic Press.

Bowlby, J. (1969). *Attachment and loss: Vol. 1. Attachment.* New York: Basic Books.

———. (1973). *Attachment and loss: Vol. 2. Separation: Anxiety and anger.* New York: Basic Books.

———. (1979). *The making and breaking of affectional bonds.* London: Tavistock.

———. (1980). *Attachment and loss: Vol. 3. Loss.* New York: Basic Books.

Bretherton, I. (1985). Attachment theory: Retrospect and prospect. *Monographs of the Society for Research in Child Development, 50*(1–2), 3–35.

Campos, J. J., Barrett, K. C., Lamb, M. E., Goldsmith, H. H., & Stenberg, C. (1983). Socioemotional development. In M. M. Haith & J. J. Campos (Eds.), *Handbook of child psychology: Vol. 2. Infancy and psychobiology* (pp. 783–915). New York: Wiley.

Campos, J. J., Emde, R. N., Gaensbauer, T. J., & Henderson, C. (1975). Cardiac and behavioral interrelationships in the reactions of infants to strangers. *Developmental Psychology, 11,* 589–601.

Cohen, L., & Campos, J. (1974). Father, mother, and stranger as elicitors of attachment behaviors in infancy. *Developmental Psychology, 10,* 146–154.

de Rougement, D. (1940). *Love in the Western world.* New York: Harcourt.

Dontas, C., Maratos, O., Fafoutis, M., & Karangelis, A. (1985). Early social development in institutionally reared Greek infants: Attachment and peer interaction. *Monographs of the Society for Research in Child Development, 50*(1–2), 136–146.

Driscoll, R., Davis, K. E., & Lipetz, M. E. (1972). Parental influence and romantic love: The Romeo and Juliet effect. *Journal of Personality and Social Psychology, 24,* 1–10.

Easton, M., Hatfield, E., & Synodinos, N. (1984). *Development of the Juvenile Love Scale*. Unpublished manuscript, University of Hawaii at Manoa.

Erickson, M. F., Sroufe, L. A., & Egeland, B. (1985). The relationship between quality of attachment and behavior problems in preschool in a high-risk sample. *Monographs of the Society for Research in Child Development, 50*(1–2), 147–166.

Fiske, S. T., & Taylor, S. E. (1984). *Social cognition*. Reading, MA: Addison-Wesley.

Freud, A., & Burlingham, D. (1943). *War and children*. New York: International Universities Press.

George, C., Kaplan, N., & Main, M. (1984). *Attachment interview for adults*. Unpublished manuscript, University of California at Berkeley.

Haith, M. M., Bergman, T., & Moore, M. J. (1977). Eye contact and face scanning in early infancy. *Science, 198,* 853–855.

Hatfield, E., Traupmann, J., Sprecher, S., Utne, M., & Hay, J. (1985). Equity and intimate relations: Recent research. In W. Ickes (Ed.), *Compatible and incompatible relationships* (pp. 91–117). New York: Springer-Verlag.

Hazan, C., & Shaver, P. (1987). Romantic love conceptualized as an attachment process. *Journal of Personality and Social Psychology, 52,* 511–524.

Heinicke, C., & Westheimer, I. (1966). *Brief separations*. New York: International Universities Press.

Hindy, C. G., & Schwarz, J. C. (1984). *Individual differences in the tendency toward anxious romantic attachments*. Paper presented at the Second International Conference on Personal Relationships, Madison, WI.

Kaye, K. (1982). *The mental and social life of babies: How parents create persons*. Chicago: University of Chicago Press.

Kobak, R. R., & Sceery, A. (in press). The transition to college: Working models of attachment, affect regulation, and perceptions of self and others. *Child Development*.

Konner, M. (1982). *The tangled wing: Biological constraints on the human spirit*. New York: Holt, Rinehart, & Winston.

Lamb, M. E., Thompson, R. A., Bardner, W. P., Charnov, E. L., & Estes, D. (1984). Security of infantile attachment as assessed in the "strange situation": Its study and biological interpretation. *Behavioral and Brain Sciences, 7,* 157–181.

Mahler, M. S., Pine, F., & Bergman, A. (1975). *The psychological birth of the human infant*. New York: Basic Books.

Main, M., Kaplan, N., & Cassidy, J. (1985). Security in infancy, childhood, and adulthood: A move to the level of representation. *Monographs of the Society for Research in Child Development, 50*(1–2), 66–104.

McCready, L. E. (1981). *Experiences of being in love: An interview study describing peak times in reciprocal love relationships*. Unpublished doctoral dissertation, New York University.

Mellen, S. L. W. (1981). *The evolution of love*. San Francisco: W. H. Freeman.

Miller, G. A., Galanter, E., & Pribram, K. H. (1960). *Plans and the structure of behavior*. New York: Holt.

Morgan, S., & Ricciuti, H. (1969). Infants' responses to strangers during the first year. In B. Foss (Ed.), *Determinants of infant behavior* (Vol. 4, pp. 253–272). London: Methuen.

Parkes, C. M., & Weiss, R. S. (1983). *Recovery from bereavement*. New York: Basic Books.

Pope, K. S., & Associates. (1980). *On love and loving: Psychological perspectives on the nature and experience of romantic love*. San Francisco: Jossey-Bass.

Reedy, M. N., Birren, J. E., & Schaie, K. W. (1981). Age and sex differences in satisfying love relationships across the adult life span. *Human Development*, 24, 52–66.

Reik, T. (1941). *Of love and lust*. New York: Farrar, Straus, & Cudahy.

Ricks, M. H. (1985). The social transmission of parental behavior: Attachment across generations. *Monographs of the Society for Research in Child Development*, 50(1–2), 211–227.

Robeson, K. S. (1967). The role of eye contact in maternal-infant attachment. *Journal of Child Psychology and Psychiatry*, 8, 13–25.

Rubin, Z. (1973). *Liking and loving: An invitation to social psychology*. New York: Holt, Rinehart, & Winston.

Sappho. (6th C. B.C./1958). *Sappho: A new translation* (M. Barnard, Trans.). Chicago: University of Chicago Press.

Schachter, S. (1964). The interaction of cognitive and physiological determinants of emotional state. In L. Berkowitz (Ed.), *Advances in experimental social psychology* (Vol. 1). New York: Academic Press.

Schaffer, H. R., & Emerson, P. (1964). The development of social attachments in infancy. *Monographs of the Society for Research in Child Development*, 29 (3, serial no. 94).

Shaver, P., Hazan, C., & Bradshaw, D. (1984). *Infant-caretaker attachment and adult romantic love: Similarities and differences, continuities and discontinuities*. Paper presented at the Second International Conference on Personal Relationships, Madison, WI.

Sroufe, L. A. (1983). Infant-caregiver attachment and patterns of adaptation in preschool: The roots of maladaptation and competence. In M. Perlmutter (Ed.), *Minnesota Symposium on Child Psychology* (Vol. 16, pp. 41–83). Hillsdale, NJ: Erlbaum.

Sroufe, L. A., & Waters, E. (1977). Attachment as an organizational construct. *Child Development*, 48, 1184–1199.

Stanley, S. M. (1986). *Commitment and the maintenance and enhancement of relationships*. Unpublished doctoral dissertation, University of Denver.

Stayton, D., & Ainsworth, M. D. S. (1973). Development of separation behavior in the first year of life: Protest, following, and greeting. *Developmental Psychology*, 9, 213–225.

Steck, L., Levitan, D., McLane, D., & Kelley, H. H. (1982). Care, need, and conceptions of love. *Journal of Personality and Social Psychology*, 43, 481–491.

Stern, D. (1977). *The first relationship: Infant and mother*. Cambridge, MA: Harvard University Press.

Sternberg, R. J. (1986). A triangular theory of love. *Psychological Review*, 93, 119–135.

Sternberg, R. J., & Grajek, S. (1984). The nature of love. *Journal of Personality and Social Psychology, 47*, 312–329.

Tennov, D. (1979). *Love and limerence: The experience of being in love.* New York: Stein & Day.

Tracy, R. L., Lamb, M. E., & Ainsworth, M. D. S. (1976). Infant approach behavior as related to attachment. *Child Development, 47*, 571–578.

Vaillant, G. E. (1977). *Adaptation to life: How the best and the brightest came of age.* Boston: Little, Brown.

Walster, E., & Walster, G. W. (1978). *A new look at love.* Reading, MA: Addison-Wesley.

Waters, E. (1983). The stability of individual differences in infant attachment: Comments on the Thompson, Lamb, and Estes contribution. *Child Development, 54*, 516–520.

Waters, E., Wippman, J., & Sroufe, L. A. (1979). Attachment, positive affect, and competence in the peer group: Two studies in construct validation. *Child Development, 50*, 821–829.

Weiss, R. S. (1979). The emotional impact of marital separation. In G. Levinger & O. C. Moles (Eds.), *Divorce and separation: Context, causes, and consequences.* New York: Basic Books.

Wilson, G. (1981). *The Coolidge effect: An evolutionary account of human sexuality.* New York: Morrow.

CHAPTER FIVE

Love Acts

The Evolutionary Biology of Love

BY DAVID M. BUSS

A song by the Doobie Brothers asks where we would be now, without love. This question captures two key themes of this chapter. The first is that love does not reside solely in our subjective thoughts, feelings, and drives. Instead, love involves overt manifestations or actions that have tangible consequences. Love is not simply a state; love *acts*. The second theme is that the key consequences of the phenomena of love center around reproduction. Thus, love acts owe their existence and urgency to prior evolutionary forces. These two themes are closely linked: evolution requires tangible manifestations on which selection can operate.

This chapter presents an evolutionary approach to love based on these themes. I outline a conceptual framework that depicts love as a natural category of acts. These acts are hypothesized to be products of evolution by natural selection. The basic idea is that acts of love occur primarily in the context of mating relationships, parent-child relationships, and other kin relationships. For humans, these relationships are crucial for reproducing. Thus, acts that fall in the category of "love" are hypothesized to have evolved to serve functions, accomplish tasks, or achieve goals that are linked with reproductive success. These proximate goals include resource display, exclusivity (fidelity and guarding), commitment and marriage, sexual intimacy, reproduction, resource sharing, and parental investment. I

This work was partly supported by NIMH Grant No. MH–41593–02. Special thanks go to Randy Nesse and Carolyn Phinney for insightful comments on an earlier draft of this chapter. Correspondence pertaining to this chapter should be addressed to David M. Buss, Department of Psychology, University of Michigan, 580 Union Drive, Ann Arbor, MI 48109–1346.

present data from two studies of love acts that support several tenets of the evolutionary framework. Subsequently, I compare this evolutionary account with other approaches to the study of love. The final section draws out key implications and outlines a research agenda.

AN EVOLUTIONARY APPROACH TO LOVE

The evolutionary approach starts with the fundamental premise that love represents a category of naturally occurring actions. Acts of love exist in the present because in the past they have served several proximate goals in the generation of offspring who will in turn be reproductively successful. Perhaps the most central of these goals are mate selection and having children. The most striking evidence that love is centrally involved in mate selection comes directly from research on the criteria people say they use to select their mates. In a series of studies using the same eighteen-item instrument, "mutual love" consistently emerged as one of the most important prerequisites of selecting a mate (Hill, 1945; Hudson & Henze, 1969; McGinnis, 1958). If acts of love exist because they accomplish certain goals related to reproductive success, what, precisely, are those goals? The following set of goals represents a first approximation of an evolutionary theory of love. These goals result from a conceptual analysis of the tasks that usually must be accomplished in order to produce children who themselves become reproductively successful.

These tasks are ordered by the time sequence in which they typically occur. They function to (1) attract a mate, (2) retain that mate, (3) reproduce with the mate, and (4) invest parentally in the resulting offspring. In order to attract a reproductively valuable mate, it is often necessary to display certain resources that are desired by members of the opposite sex. Thus, the first goal of acts of love is resource display.

Resource Display

Display of key resources is typically crucial for attracting a desirable mate. Examples of love acts of resource display are "he bought her a necklace," "she made him a fantastic dinner," "he bought her an engagement ring," and "she made herself attractive for him." The purpose of such displays is to alert potential mates to reproductively relevant resources they could acquire by choosing this particular mate.

Major sex differences are predicted for the sorts of resources that will be displayed through love acts. These differences are based on the resources that are differentially scarce for males and females. Specifically, because females have sharper constraints on the potential number of offspring they can produce, they should select mates most capable and willing to invest tangible resources in their offspring. Trivers's (1972) theory predicts that potential parental investment by males will be used by females as a basis for sexual selection: they will more frequently choose males who display resources. Thus, characteristics that lead to male resource acquisition and the signaling of the resources he can invest in a female and her offspring will be selected over generations. This leads to the prediction that male love acts will indicate willingness and ability to invest monetary and other tangible resources.

In contrast, the major reproductive limitation imposed on human males is access to reproductively valuable or fertile females. Thus such females become the resource that is in scarce supply for males. Males who select as mates reproductively valuable females will have relatively greater reproductive success than males who choose females less capable of producing offspring. Therefore, females who display love acts that signal high reproductive capability will be at a selective advantage over females who do not.

Reproductive capability, however, is not something that can be evaluated directly. Instead, males have been selected to respond to external cues that are correlated with reproductive capability. In human females, perhaps the two strongest cues are *age* and *health* (Buss, in press; Symons, 1979). That is, females who are between the ages of fifteen and twenty are more reproductively valuable than are females between thirty-five and forty. But age and health themselves are not characteristics that can be evaluated directly. Instead, physical appearance must be used to evaluate them and hence the woman's reproductive capability (Buss, 1987; Buss & Barnes, 1986; Symons, 1979). This leads to the hypothesis that female love acts, more than male love acts, will center around enhancing physical appearance. These relations are depicted in figure 5.1

To summarize, both males and females have been selected to maximize gene replication. Characteristics that lead to greater gene replication will be favored over characteristics that do not or that are simply neutral. Males and females, however, have different limitations imposed on maximizing reproductive success. Females are constrained by the resources that are available for investment in their relatively few offspring. Males, in contrast, are constrained primarily by access to reproductively valuable females.

These fundamental differences lead to sex differences in the criteria people use to select their mates. Males should value characteristics in females that indicate their reproductive capability. Females should be se-

Fig. 5.1.   Hypothesized Sequence Leading to Sex Differences in Love Acts

Sex Differences in:	*For Females*	*For Males*
Scarce resources and reproductive constraints	Resources and protection for offspring	Access to reproductively capable females
Mate selection criteria	Male possession or likely acquisition of resources	Female age and health cues that signal reproductive capability
Cues for evaluation	Earning capacity, ambition, industry, status, possessions	Youth, health, beauty, clear skin, smooth skin, lustrous hair, full lips, white teeth, lively gait
Love acts	Female selection for male love acts that involve resource display	Male selection for female love acts that signal reproductive capability

lected to value characteristics in males that indicate their ability and willingness to invest resources. Female reproductive value, then, will turn on physical attractiveness, age, and health, as well as the physical and behavioral characteristics (for example, smooth skin, spritely gait) that are correlated with them. In contrast, the cues to male resource potential are signs of money, possessions, status, and the behavioral characteristics that lead to their acquisition, such as ambition and industry.

Thus, male and female love acts should signal different sorts of resources. Male love acts should involve gift giving and other signs of willingness and ability to invest resources. Female love acts should involve appearing youthful, attractive, healthy, and reproductively valuable.

This conceptual framework leads to a set of testable predictions: (1) that female attractiveness, more than male, will be determined by the physical cues that vary with youth and health (for example, smooth skin, firm muscle tone, clear eyes, lustrous hair, full lips, white teeth, lively gait); (2) that males, more than females, will value physical appearance (attractiveness) in potential mates because it covaries more with reproductive capability than does male appearance; (3) that females will compete with one another in terms of physical characteristics that signal their ability to have children; (4) that males will compete among themselves for access to the resources that females value; (5) that where female deception of males occurs, it will be in the direction of appearing young and healthy; (6) that male deception of females, when it occurs, will involve dissembling about their actual or potential resources; (7) that love acts performed by females will provide indications of their reproductive capability (attractiveness, age, and health) because that is the resource important to males; and (8) that love acts performed by males will indicate their willingness and ability to invest resources in the woman and her potential offspring.

Thus far, there is empirical support for hypotheses 1 (Cunningham, 1986) and 2 (Buss, 1985, 1987; Buss & Barnes, 1986), but only anecdotal support for the remaining hypotheses. An example of the latter would be the booming cosmetic industry for women (hypothesis 3) and female dissembling about age in the youthful direction (hypothesis 5).

Attracting a mate by a display of resources, however, is just the first step in the sequence of love. Once a mate is obtained, she or he must be retained and guarded to ensure fulfillment of the reproductive promise. Thus, exclusivity is the second task that is accomplished through acts of love.

Exclusivity: Fidelity and Guarding

Love acts that promote exclusivity also have an evolutionary biological basis. The purposes of exclusivity are (1) to ensure high confidence in paternity (maternity rarely being in doubt), and (2) to ensure mutual commitment to the reproducing pair. Love acts in this category include "she gave up going out with other guys," "he resisted the sexual opportunity he had with another woman," "she remained faithful to him when he was away," and "he became jealous when she talked to another guy."

Although there are undoubtedly many manifestations of exclusivity, two important forms are *fidelity* and *mate guarding*, which are hypothesized to occur for both sexes because each has an investment to protect. Female infidelity threatens male confidence in paternity; male infidelity threatens redirection of his resources to another female and her potential offspring. Males and females failing to ensure the fidelity of their partner will be at a selective disadvantage. Similarly, males and females failing to display love acts of fidelity will be at a selective disadvantage because they risk losing the reproductively relevant resources provided by their selected partner. Displays of fidelity as well as mate-guarding behaviors should evolve to protect resources for each sex.

Males and females should differ, however, in the importance attached to fidelity and to mate guarding. Specifically, the hazards for a male of one-time female infidelity are far worse than the analogous hazards for females of one-time male infidelity. Female philandering directly decreases her partner's confidence in paternity, thus decreasing her reproductive value to him and exposing him to the possibility of raising other men's children. In contrast, male infidelity is threatening to his partner only if it redirects his resources away from her and to another. This would be likely to occur in the case of a serious affair, but less likely in the case of a casual sexual liaison. In sum, the different nature of male and female reproductive resources leads to sex differences in the importance of fidelity.

This reasoning leads to three testable predictions about fidelity and guarding. The first is that female love acts displaying fidelity should be much more frequent than male love acts of fidelity. Second, females should be more forgiving than males of infidelity, especially if it involves casual sex and not serious involvement. And third, acts of mate guarding should be more frequently displayed by males than by females.

In addition to *behavioral* manifestations that ensure fulfillment of reproductive promise, most societies have developed *cultural institutions* for similar purposes. The most obvious one is the institution of marriage.

Commitment and Marriage

According to this evolutionary approach, love is central to the process of commitment, marriage, and mate selection. Data confirming this basic premise come from numerous studies in which mutual love is rated consistently high as the reason for choosing a mate (Hill, 1945; Hudson & Henze, 1969; McGinnis, 1958). One of the goals of love acts is marriage. Love acts included in this category are "he talked to her about marriage," "they discussed their future plans together," "she told him she wanted to marry him," "he agreed to marry her," and "they were wed."

Marriage serves to enforce exclusivity (including fidelity), to ensure commitment of resources, and to provide a context for bearing and raising children. Marriage is public commitment enforced by kin—those who have a genetic stake in ensuring that the resources promised are delivered. It is probably not chance that male failures surrounding work and female failures surrounding willingness and ability to bear children are treated with great concern in many cultures (Ford & Beach, 1951).

Sexual Intimacy

The fourth major goal of love acts is sexual intimacy, although this may often occur prior to, as well as after, marriage. Although emotional intimacy may be involved, sexual intimacy may be regarded as the sine qua non of heterosexual love, at least in its mature stages. Sexual intimacy serves to seal the bond and results sometimes in conception. Love acts of sexual intimacy include "she gave up her virginity to him," "she was sexually open to him," "they had sexual intercourse," and "he made love to her."

There is some evidence that among humans sexual intercourse more frequently preoccupies males than females (Symons, 1979). This sex difference might be expected on the basis of our earlier discussion. Because males are limited in their reproductive success by sexual access to reproductively valuable females, they should be selected to initiate sex more often and to be more generally concerned about sex in the context of heterosexual relations, including those involving love. Females, in contrast, are not limited reproductively by sexual access to males. Indeed, only a trivial amount of sexual access is needed for a female to achieve full reproductive potential. Therefore, female concerns and activity initiation should involve sexual intercourse considerably less.

In sum, sexual intimacy, for the purposes of sealing a bond and for producing offspring is an important and necessary goal of love acts. Love acts of sexual intimacy sometimes produce tangible consequences—the conception of offspring.

Reproduction

There is a crucial sense in which the four previous functions of love lead up to and would be evolutionarily bankrupt without reproduction of children. Thus, reproduction represents a fifth goal of love acts. Love acts central to this category are "she got pregnant by him," and "she gave birth to his child."

It should be noted, however, that love acts surrounding reproduction need not be limited to direct conception and birth. Indeed, love acts by both sexes in the nine-month interval between conception and birth are critical to the survival of the coming child. Such acts might involve protection and provisioning by the male so that the female and her fetus thrive and do not succumb to aggressors or the hostile forces of nature.

Resource Sharing

While sexual intimacy and reproduction can be viewed as a female delivering the reproductive value she promised, resource sharing (such as financial support, protection) by the male can be viewed as a delivery of his reproductive promise. The purposes served by sharing such resources as money, food, shelter, and territory are to provide security and organismic viability for the female and to provide materials to be invested in the offspring; sharing resources is important for both the survival and reproductive success of the male's mate and children. The families of males who *fail* to provide these resources are more susceptible to disease, poor nutrition, parasites, predation, aggression by others, and, for offspring, poor opportunities for learning and handicaps in their future lives.

Parental Investment

Once children are produced, they must be fed, nurtured, protected, taught, and loved. Among the varieties of love, that for a mate and parental love are probably the most intense and profound. Most theories of love, however, omit parental love or find it puzzling. For example, one prominent theorist recently noted, "The needs that lead many of us to feel unconditioned love for our children also seem to be remarkably persistent, for reasons that are not at present altogether clear" (Sternberg, 1986, p. 133).

From an evolutionary perspective, however, it would be baffling if parental love for children were not a powerful force in social animals such as ourselves. Indeed, the successful accomplishment of the first six tasks of love would be evolutionarily bankrupt if the children produced by lovers did not themselves mature to reproductive age, find a mate, and reproduce in turn.

Acts of parental love are many and extremely varied. They include affection (for example, "she gave her daughter a hug"), commitment of resources ("she paid for her son's college education"), commitment of time ("he spent Saturday afternoon teaching his son to play baseball"), and self-sacrifice ("she gave up her own dinner so that her daughter could have more food"). The function served by parental love acts is to produce healthy, reproductively valuable offspring who will, in time, invest in their children.

In sum, there are seven broad goals toward which love acts are directed: resource display, exclusivity (fidelity and guarding), commitment and marriage, sexual intimacy, reproduction, resource sharing, and parental investment. This evolutionary approach to love posits that love acts have evolved to serve these goals because of their consequences for reproductive success. This approach should not be regarded as final or exhaustive. Additional goals will undoubtedly be added as the specific functions served by love acts are explored empirically.

Nonetheless, the evolutionary approach is powerful because it offers

Fig. 5.2. Proximate and Ultimate Goals of Love Acts

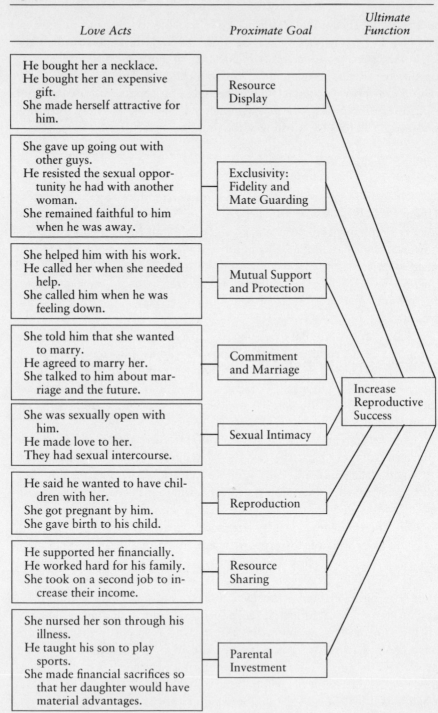

Love Acts	Proximate Goal	Ultimate Function
He bought her a necklace. He bought her an expensive gift. She made herself attractive for him.	Resource Display	
She gave up going out with other guys. He resisted the sexual opportunity he had with another woman. She remained faithful to him when he was away.	Exclusivity: Fidelity and Mate Guarding	
She helped him with his work. He called her when she needed help. She called him when he was feeling down.	Mutual Support and Protection	
She told him that she wanted to marry. He agreed to marry her. She talked to him about marriage and the future.	Commitment and Marriage	Increase Reproductive Success
She was sexually open with him. He made love to her. They had sexual intercourse.	Sexual Intimacy	
He said he wanted to have children with her. She got pregnant by him. She gave birth to his child.	Reproduction	
He supported her financially. He worked hard for his family. She took on a second job to increase their income.	Resource Sharing	
She nursed her son through his illness. He taught his son to play sports. She made financial sacrifices so that her daughter would have material advantages.	Parental Investment	

testable empirical predictions. These include the following: (1) specific love acts should emerge from the nominations of acts that fit the category of love, (2) there should be reasonable consensus about which acts are central and which are peripheral members of the category of love, (3) these love acts should be categorized by agreement into the seven categories identified above, and (4) males and females should differ in the frequency of displaying acts within these categories such that (a) males should display more love acts of tangible resource display, (b) females should display more love acts signaling reproductive value, (c) females should display more love acts of fidelity, (d) males should display more love acts of mate guarding, (e) males should be more concerned about love acts surrounding sexual intimacy, and (f) males should display more love acts of resource sharing.

The links between love acts, their immediate goals, and the ultimate goal of reproductive success are depicted in figure 5.2. The following studies were designed to provide the first empirical tests of this evolutionary approach to love.

LOVE AS A NATURAL COGNITIVE CATEGORY

A basic premise of the evolutionary view is that love is not simply an internal state of feelings, drives, and thoughts. Love has tangible manifestations in everyday conduct, and these manifestations have clear goals and ultimate reproductive consequences. Therefore, it is crucial to demonstrate that love does have a behavioral medium consisting of acts forming the natural social category of love.

In this view, acts are the basic constituents of the behavioral world, as objects are of the inanimate world (Buss & Craik, 1983, 1984). Naturally occurring social categories such as love offer a system for categorizing acts by partitioning and granting conceptual order to the everyday stream of behavior. As natural constructs emerging from and subsuming temporally dispersed arrays of acts, social categories such as love can be analyzed in terms of their cognitive properties.

Two features warrant emphasis. First, social categories are treated as "fuzzy sets": category members are not sharply demarcated and each category blends into adjacent ones. Thus, the category of love may blend into the categories of liking, lust, friendship, affection, or passion. Empirical work is needed to identify the fuzzy boundaries of each category, their relations to each other, and the transition zones between them. In this view, category membership is continuous or probabilistic rather than discrete.

Second, not all members within a given social category possess equivalent status within it. Rosch and her colleagues (Rosch, 1975; Rosch & Mervis, 1975; Rosch, Simpson, & Miller, 1976) have conceptualized the differing status of category members in terms of their prototypicality (clearest cases, best examples, instances par excellence). Thus, social categories are composed of acts that differ in their status from highly central or prototypical to progressively more peripheral until the fuzzy borders are reached and the adjoining categories are entered. The following studies were conducted to explore categories of love acts based on this framework.

Study 1: Obtaining Examples of Love Acts

The purpose of this study was to identify the range of acts that belong within the category of love. Love is thought of as a natural category with specific acts, feelings, and thoughts as members. In order to identify the range and diversity of love acts, the following procedure was administered to a sample of one hundred subjects:

> Please think of people you know of your own gender (sex) who have been or are currently in love. With these individuals in mind, write down five acts or behaviors that they have performed (or might perform) that reflect or exemplify their love. Be sure to write down acts or behaviors. An act is something that a person does or did, not something that they are. Do not say "he is infatuated" or "she is love-struck." These are not behaviors. You should describe acts or behaviors that someone could read and answer the questions: "Did you ever do this?" and "How often have you done this?"

After five acts were listed, subjects were instructed to name love acts performed by members of the opposite sex.

MOST AND LEAST FREQUENTLY MENTIONED CATEGORIES. Simple tallies were made of how many subjects mentioned a love act falling into each of the five categories. Acts involving exchange of resources (as giving gifts and providing financial support) were nominated by 44 percent of the sample. Acts of fidelity were nominated by 14 percent, although acts representing the guarding aspect of exclusivity were absent. Marriage was nominated by 17 percent of the sample in one form or another ("he proposed marriage to her," "she agreed to be his wife," "they were betrothed"). Sex was mentioned by 19 percent of the sample, and having children, by 8 percent.

Two other themes that received relatively high frequencies were not anticipated by the evolutionary framework. One concerned acts of sacrifice such as "she changed her career plans to be with him" and "he canceled his important engagement in order to be with her." Such acts were nominated by 15 percent of the sample. The second theme concerned acts involving the parents of the lovers. These included such acts as "she introduced him to her parents," and "she made a special effort to get along with his parents even though they were bitchy." Acts involving parents were mentioned by 12 percent of the sample. Interestingly, most of these acts involved the female's parents.

SEX DIFFERENCES IN ACTOR NOMINATIONS. Preliminary tests were made of several of the sex differences that are hypothesized by the evolutionary account. These tests should be regarded as tentative, awaiting further replication. The first concerned sex differences in resource display and sharing. Such acts were mentioned by 43 percent of the sample for male actors, but by only 15 percent for female actors. This large sex difference confirms the prediction that males, more than females, will display love acts signaling tangible resources.

Second, having children was nominated as a love act by 8 percent of the sample for female actors, but by only a single subject for males. In contrast, no sex differences occurred with respect to marriage or commitment.

Love acts involving fidelity were nominated by 12 percent of the sample for female actors, but by only 6 percent for males. Interestingly, several love acts involved forgiveness for a partner's infidelity. When this occurred, it was exclusively female forgiveness for her male partner's infidelity.

Finally, there were no major sex differences between male and female actors in nominations of love acts surrounding sex. Sex acts were nominated for male actors by 15 percent of the subjects, and for females by 13 percent. However, an interesting sex difference occurred in *who* nominated sex acts as love acts. Whereas only 8 percent of the female sample mentioned sex as a love act, a full 32 percent of the male subjects nominated sexual love acts. These preliminary data suggest that sex may be more integral to love in the minds of men than in the minds of women.

Study 2: Prototypicality Judgments of Love

The acts were then prepared for the second study. Acts judged to be duplicates were eliminated, as were general tendency statements, single adjectives, or descriptions too vague to constitute an observable act. After these elimination procedures, 115 clear and reasonably distinct acts remained. For the purposes of the next stage of the study, 15 acts were randomly eliminated to obtain a more manageable number. Thus, 100 love acts formed the final product of this nomination stage. Examples of love acts were "he ignored his friends to spend time with her," "he bought her flowers," "she dressed up more than he usually did," "he tried to befriend all of her friends," "he took her out to dinner," and "she made love to him."

This study was designed to identify the relative centrality or prototypicality of each act within the love category. The following instructional set was adapted from Rosch and Mervis (1975) and Buss and Craik (1980):

> This study has to do with what we have in mind when we use words that refer to categories. Let's take the word *red* as an example. Close your eyes and imagine a true red. Now imagine an orangish red . . . imagine a purple red. Although you might still name the orange-red or the purple-red with the term *red*, they are not as good examples of red (as clear cases of what red refers to) as the clear "true" red. In short, some reds are "redder" than others.
>
> In this specific study you are asked to judge how good an example of a category various instances of the category are. The category is LOVE. Below are listed 100 acts. You are to rate how good an example of that category each act is on a 7-point scale. A "7" means that you feel the act is a very good example of your idea of what LOVE is; a "1" means you feel the act fits very poorly with your idea of what LOVE is (or is not a member of the category at all). A "4" means that you feel the act fits moderately well. Use the other numbers to indicate intermediate judgments.

Participating in this stage of the study were forty subjects, none of whom had been involved in the act-selection stage. Twenty subjects were males and twenty were females. Half of the males and females rated the prototypicality of love acts involving a male as actor; the remaining half of the males and females rated the prototypicality of love acts involving a female as actor.

RELIABILITY OF PROTOTYPICALITY JUDGMENTS. Alpha reliability coefficients were computed for male raters, female raters, acts with male as actor, acts with female as actor, and all judges and actor forms combined. Male and female raters achieved composite reliabilities of .89 and .88, respectively. Male as actor and female as actor achieved alpha reliabilities of .88 and .90, respectively. Across all forty judges, the alpha reliability was .94. These results suggest a moderate consensus among judges concerning which acts are more and less prototypical for the category of love.

MOST PROTOTYPICAL LOVE ACTS. Table 5.1 shows the forty acts judged by the forty subjects to be the most prototypical of the category of love, along with their mean ratings and standard deviations. It is clear from perusal of these acts that several of the goals identified earlier are present. The acts "he surprised her with a gift" (twenty-five) and "he brought her a special present" (thirty-four) suggest *resource display*. The act "she remained faithful to him when they were separated for more than a month" (two) implies *fidelity* and *exclusivity*. The act "she agreed to marry him" (one) suggests *commitment*. The acts "she spent the night with him" (thirty-seven) and "he made love to her" (thirty-nine) imply *sexual intimacy*. The act "he told her that he wanted to have children with her" (twelve) points to the importance of *reproduction* in love.

It is equally clear that a theme of mutual support emerged that was not anticipated by the evolutionary framework. This included acts such as "called her/him when she/he was feeling down," "canceled his/her plans to be with her/him when she/he was upset," and "listened devotedly to his/her problems." Although love acts involving mutual support are not incompatible with the evolutionary approach, they highlight the point that not all facets of human love can be predicted by this theory. They also illustrate the value of the act-selection and prototypicality judgment procedures in the context of discovery.

Acts of parental love did not emerge in these studies. It seems likely that most of the undergraduate subjects were thinking of romantic love rather than parental love when they suggested love acts. Future research could directly request acts for the categories of mother love, father love, brother love, and so on. In addition, future research could profitably use a larger age range of subjects to elicit love acts at different stages of life.

In sum, these results suggest that love can be viewed as a natural social category, with specific love acts as members. Furthermore, the category of love is structured so that some acts are more central and others are more peripheral. Subjects can readily recall acts of love, as well as making consensual judgments about the relative centrality of these acts.

Preliminary support was found for several evolutionary predictions surrounding sex differences in love acts. Male love acts more frequently involved resources. Female love acts more frequently involved fidelity and having children. Males nominated sex acts as love acts about four times as

TABLE 5.1   Love Acts Ordered by Prototypicality: Top Forty Love Acts

No.	Mean	SD	Love Acts[1]
1	6.05	1.08	She agreed to marry him.
2	5.95	0.90	She remained faithful to him when they were separated for more than a month.
3	5.83	1.11	He called her when she was feeling down.
4	5.80	1.20	He canceled his plans in order to be with her when she was upset.
5	5.75	1.03	She gave up going out with other men for him.
6	5.75	1.03	She listened devotedly to his problems.
7	5.70	1.38	He resisted the sexual opportunity he had with someone else.
8	5.68	1.53	He told her that he wanted to marry her.
9	5.60	1.19	She stuck up for him when someone tried to put him down.
10	5.78	1.39	She told him "I love you."
11	5.58	1.41	He put up with her "bad days."
12	5.58	1.47	He told her that he wanted to have children with her.
13	5.55	1.24	He talked to her about marriage and the future.
14	5.38	1.50	She took care of him when he was sick.
15	5.30	1.26	She talked to him about her personal problems.
16	5.25	1.51	He ignored the other attractive females at the party.
17	5.23	1.10	He traveled a long distance to be with her.
18	5.11	1.41	He gave her verbal support for her tough decision.
19	5.10	1.63	She told him a very private secret about her past.
20	5.05	1.36	She gave him a symbolic ring.
21	5.00	1.59	He told his friends that he was madly in love with her.
22	5.00	1.28	He gave her a prolonged hug.
23	4.90	1.37	She became distraught after she had a fight with him.
24	4.85	1.41	She said "I miss you" when she hadn't seen him for a day.
25	4.83	1.20	He surprised her with a gift.
26	4.82	1.26	He cooked a special meal for her.
27	4.80	1.68	He called her up when he needed help.
28	4.78	1.23	She dropped by unexpectedly just to see him.
29	4.75	1.53	She lost sleep thinking about him.
30	4.75	1.39	He went for a walk with her at night.
31	4.75	1.43	He gazed into her eyes.
32	4.73	1.55	She nuzzled him.
33	4.73	1.28	She wrote him a poem.
34	4.70	1.34	He bought her a special present.
35	4.70	1.29	He wrote her a love note.
36	4.68	1.56	She worked to keep in shape for him.
37	4.65	1.31	She spent the night with him.
38	4.65	1.69	He held her hands.
39	4.65	1.82	He made love to her.
40	4.63	1.73	She cried when he had to go away for a time.

[1]These means and standard deviations represent the statistics for the entire sample of 40 raters, including those who rated the "he . . ." and "she . . ." acts. The male and female pronouns are alternated for expositional clarity. The rating scale used was 1–7, with 7 being the most prototypical love act, and 1 being the least prototypical love act. This table shows only the most prototypical 40 love acts out of the 100 acts that were rated.

often as did females. These results, however, should be regarded as tentative, awaiting replication in other samples and with other methods. Nevertheless, they suggest that this evolutionary approach may bear much empirical fruit.

COMPARISON WITH OTHER MODELS OF LOVE

Several features of the evolutionary framework bring it into sharp contrast with other approaches to love and are worth enumerating. One central feature of this framework is that, unlike earlier ones, it posits an *ultimate* (evolutionary) *causal account*. Other approaches, if they propose causal explanations at all, deal exclusively with immediate ones (see Mellon, 1981, for an exception). Natural and sexual selection favored in the past those individuals who engaged in the actions that now fall within the category of love. The existence of love acts may be traced ultimately to the reproductive advantages conferred on those performing such acts effectively. Thus current love acts may be traced to their ultimate selective advantage.

The second feature of this evolutionary model that sets it apart from others concerns its emphasis on *action*. Rubin (1970) considers love to be an "attitude," whereas Sternberg (1986) considers love to consist of the conjunction of certain cognitions, emotions, and drives. Acts of love are derivative and subsidiary in these approaches; in contrast, they are central to the evolutionary model. Evolution requires overt phenotypic manifestations on which selection can operate.

The third unique feature of this model concerns its emphasis on *tangible consequences*. Thoughts, feelings, and drives may exist within the organism without, in principle, exerting any impact on the surrounding social world. In contrast, acts of love have tangible consequences whose effects extend into the social and biological world.

The fourth feature is that these consequences can be categorized by the *proximate functions* they serve. Among these, as we have seen, are resource display, exclusivity, mate selection and marriage, sexual intimacy, reproduction, resource sharing, and parental investment. These functions can be reduced conceptually to effective means of resource acquisition and allocation as strategies of achieving reproductive success (Alexander, 1979).

CONCLUDING COMMENTS

I have proposed an evolutionary approach to love in which love is manifested in tangible actions or love acts. These acts serve several immediate goals such as mate selection, exclusivity, copulation, conception, and resource sharing. Achieving these goals is hypothesized to have been linked in the past, and perhaps in the present, with reproductive success. According to this approach, love cannot be understood without identifying (1) specific acts of love, (2) the functions they serve, and (3) their links with natural and sexual selection. As noted in the opening quote, "Without love, where would you be now?"

Sex differences in the manifestation of love are central to the evolutionary approach. As depicted in figure 5.1, there are sex differences in the biological constraints on reproductive success. For females, the major constraint is access to resources for her offspring; for males, it is access to reproductively valuable females. These sex differences lead to differences in criteria for choosing a mate: females value males with resources and males value females who appear to be able to have children. The cues for these attributes reduce to wealth, ambition, industriousness, status, and expensive possessions in males, and youth, health, beauty, clear skin, full lips, lustrous hair, lively gait, and white teeth in females (Buss, 1987; Symons, 1979). These differences lead to differences in the love acts that will have evolved in males and females. Males should be selected to display love acts surrounding resource display; females should be selected to display love acts surrounding the signaling of reproductive capability. Preliminary empirical support for these predictions has been found here and elsewhere (Buss, 1987; Symons, 1979).

One intriguing issue concerns cultural influences on love. Some theorists would argue, for example, that romantic love is a relatively recent phenomenon, occurring mainly in Western societies, and that thus it is anchored in culture, not in biology. The evolutionary perspective on love offered here suggests that acts of love have existed among humans long before the linguistic category of *love* was invented to describe those acts. That is, males and females have long used various resources to attract each other (for example, large game, protection, shelter, mating opportunities, implied parental investment). Males and females have long formed couples, guarded the mates they acquired, and attempted to ensure their fidelity. Males and females have long engaged in sexual relations with each other, usually in private and suffused with a "special feeling." Males and females have long borne children and then protected, cared for, nurtured, fed, clothed, and taught them. The fact that linguistic categories lag behind the performance of clusters of acts for which they were named does not imply that the *phenomena* in act form did not exist prior to the cultural invention of the label "love."

More generally, it is a common misunderstanding of evolutionary perspectives on human behavior that they are somehow opposed to, or in competition with, cultural perspectives. The misunderstanding stems from a confusion of two levels of analysis: proximate and ultimate. To say that a cluster of acts exists because it has been linked with reproductive success in our evolutionary past (ultimate explanation) does not negate the fact that there are *simultaneously* many proximate causes of those acts in culture, immediate situations, or even physiology (promixate explanations). It is clear, for example, that the sorts of resources that males choose to display will vary tremendously across cultures—from goats and cows to prestigious plots of land to money to fast cars. Both ultimate and proximate explanations are needed for a complete account of the phenomena of love.

Much empirical work remains to be done. Identification and assessment of specific love acts, the functions they serve, and their links with current reproductive success are challenging enterprises. It is anticipated that other immediate functions of love acts will emerge as these links are examined more closely. Thus, the present approach to love represents only a beginning. But perhaps like conception, it is a beginning whose promise reaches beyond the narrow confines of its current proximate boundaries.

REFERENCES

Alexander, R. D. (1979). *Darwinism and human affairs.* Seattle: University of Washington Press.

Buss, D. M. (1985). Human mate selection. *American Scientist, 73,* 47–51.

———. (1987). Sex differences in human mate selection criteria: An evolutionary perspective. In C. Crawford, M. Smith, & D. Krebs (Eds.), *Sociobiology and psychology: Issues, ideas, and findings.* Hillsdale, NJ: Erlbaum.

Buss, D. M., & Barnes, M. (1986). Preferences in human mate selection. *Journal of Personality and Social Psychology, 50,* 559–570.

Buss, D. M., & Craik, K. H. (1980). The frequency concept of disposition: Dominance and prototypically dominant acts. *Journal of Personality, 48,* 379–392.

———. (1983). The act frequency approach to personality. *Psychological Review, 90,* 105–126.

———. (1984). Acts, dispositions, and personality. In B. A. Maher & W. B. Maher (Eds.), *Progress in experimental personality research* (Vol. 13, pp. 241–301). New York: Academic Press.

Cunningham, M. R. (1986). Measuring the physical in physical attractiveness: Quasi-experiments on the sociobiology of facial beauty. *Journal of Personality and Social Psychology, 50,* 925–935.

Ford, C. S., & Beach, F. A. (1951). *Patterns of sexual behavior.* New York: Harper & Brothers.

Hendrick, C., & Hendrick, S. (1986). A theory and method of love. *Journal of Personality and Social Psychology, 50,* 392–402.

Hill, R. (1945). Campus values in mate selection. *Journal of Home Economics, 37,* 554–558.

Hudson, J. W., & Henze, L. P. (1969). Campus values in mate selection: A replication. *Journal of Marriage and the Family, 31,* 772–775.

McGinnis, R. (1958). Campus values in mate selection. *Social Forces, 36,* 368–373.

Mellon, L. W. (1981). *The evolution of love.* San Francisco: W. H. Freeman.

Rosch, E. (1975). Cognitive reference points. *Cognitive Psychology, 7,* 532–547.

Rosch, E., & Mervis, C. B. (1975). Family resemblances: Studies in the internal structure of categories. *Cognitive Psychology, 7,* 573–605.

Rosch, E., Simpson, C., & Miller, R. S. (1976). Structural bases of typicality effects. *Journal of Experimental Psychology: Human Perception and Performance, 2,* 491–502.

Rubin, Z. (1970). The measurement of romantic love. *Journal of Personality and Social Psychology, 16,* 265–273.

Sternberg, R. J. (1986). A triangular theory of love. *Psychological Review, 93,* 119–135.

Symons, D. (1979). *The evolution of human sexuality.* New York: Oxford University Press.

Trivers, R. L. (1972). Parental investment and sexual selection. In B. Campbell (Ed.), *Sexual selection and the descent of man: 1871–1971* (pp. 136–179). Chicago: Aldine.

CHAPTER SIX

Triangulating Love

BY ROBERT J. STERNBERG

The cool ocean breeze brushed gently against them. It was midnight, and the beach was deserted. He had been waiting for a moment like this to make his solemn pronouncement. A large wave crested, spraying them lightly with cold ocean water. They laughed and gazed in each other's eyes. The moment was right. He said it: "I love you, honey." It came out as a whisper.

"And I love you, too, dearest."

That night, he gave her the ring he had brought with him, saving it for just the right moment. She accepted. Three months later they were married.

Five years and countless battles later, they were ready to throw in the towel. The marriage was not working at all.

"If you loved me, you would listen to me, and spend time with me, and support me when I get down in the dumps," she said to him, bitterness in her voice.

"But I do love you. If you loved me, you wouldn't be complaining about me all the time, and besides, you'd make love when I get horny, instead of always finding reasons to do something else."

"I can't make love to a man who doesn't have much use for me except as a sex object. The only time you want to spend with me is when we're in bed."

"At least you don't complain then."

A year later they were divorced, both convinced that their love was one-sided.

What went wrong in this relationship? What goes wrong in the close to half of all marriages that end in divorce—and in the many other marriages that ought to? Of course, many things can go wrong. But one of the most important—and frequent—is disagreement as to just what it means to love one another. Each partner loves the other, but in his or her own way, and not necessarily in the way the other partner loves back and expects to be loved. At least some of the distress in close relationships might be avoidable if each partner understood what the other meant by love and how the interpretations were related.

What are the kinds of love one can experience in a close relationship? How are these kinds of love related to each other? Many different classifications of love have been proposed (see Berscheid & Walster, 1978; Brehm, 1985; Hatfield & Walster, 1981; Hendrick & Hendrick, 1983, for descriptions of various classifications of love). The classification described below is one I have found particularly useful in understanding love in close relationships. Before presenting it, however, I will briefly describe the triangular theory of love, upon which this classification is based.

THE TRIANGULAR THEORY OF LOVE: AN OVERVIEW

The triangular theory of love is so called because it holds that love can be understood in terms of three components that together can be viewed as forming the vertices of a triangle. I present here only a brief overview of the theory. For more details, see Sternberg (1986). The three components of love, according to the triangular theory, are an intimacy component, a passion component, and a decision/commitment component (see figure 6.1).

THE INTIMACY COMPONENT. Intimacy refers to close, connected, and bonded feelings in loving relationships. It thus includes feelings that create the experience of warmth in a loving relationship. Sternberg and Grajek (1984) identified ten signs of intimacy in a close relationship: (1) desiring to promote the welfare of the loved one, (2) experiencing happiness with the loved one, (3) having high regard for the loved one, (4) being able to count on the loved one in times of need, (5) mutual understanding with the loved one, (6) sharing one's self and one's possessions with the loved one, (7) receiving emotional support from the loved one, (8) giving emotional support to the loved one, (9) having intimate communication with the loved one, and (10) valuing the loved one in one's life.

THE PASSION COMPONENT. The passion component refers to the drives that lead to romance, physical attraction, sexual consummation, and the like in a loving relationship. Although sexual needs may form the main part

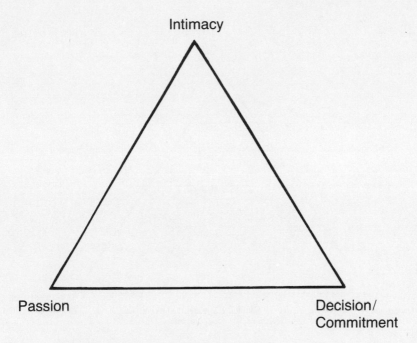

Fig. 6.1. The Three Components of Love

of passion in many relationships, other needs—such as those for self-esteem, affiliation with others, dominance over others, submission to others, and self-actualization—may also contribute to the experience of passion.

THE DECISION/COMMITMENT COMPONENT. The decision/commitment component of love consists of two aspects, one short term and one long term. The short-term one is the decision that one loves someone. The long-term aspect is the commitment to maintain that love. These two aspects of the decision/commitment component of love do not necessarily go together, for the decision to love does not necessarily imply a commitment to that love. Nor does commitment necessarily imply decision, oddly enough. Many people are committed to the love of another person without necessarily even admitting that they love or are in love with that person. Most often, however, decision will precede commitment.

Combining the Components

If one takes all possible combinations of the three components of love, one obtains eight subsets, which form the basis for the classification of love

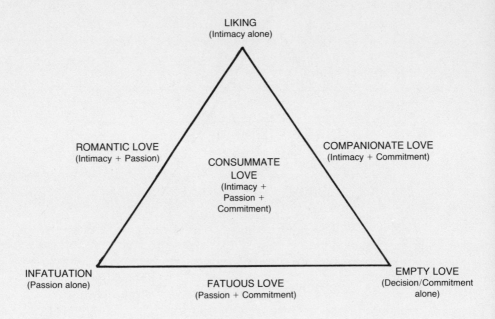

Fig. 6.2.   The Kinds of Loving as Different Combinations of the Three Components of Love

described in this chapter. These eight types represent extremes, of course. In actuality, one would only occasionally obtain an instance in which there is passion with no intimacy at all (perhaps in relations with prostitutes), or commitment with absolutely no intimacy at all (perhaps in marriages held together only by the thread of religious sanction against divorce). Consider now the eight possible types of love generated by the triangular theory (see figure 6.2).

KINDS OF LOVING: A CLASSIFICATION

The Intimacy Component Alone: Liking

Joe was intensely jealous. He had thought he and Stephanie were "an item." But Stephanie seemed to be spending almost as much time with Alex as she was spending with Joe. To make matters worse, he was afraid she was two-timing him. Finally, he confronted her.

"I just can't stand this anymore."

"Huh? What can't you stand?"

"Your relationship with Alex. If you prefer him to me, that's fine. Just say the word, and I'll be on my way. But you seem to want us both, and I just won't stand for it any longer."

"I don't know what you're talking about. Alex is no competition for you. None at all. What in the world makes you think he is?"

"But you're spending as much time with him as you are with me, not to mention what you all may be doing with that time."

"Joe, you're off, you're way off. Alex is a good friend. I do like his company. I like doing things with him. I like talking to him. But I don't love him, and I never will. I don't plan to spend my life with him. He's a friend, and nothing more, but nothing less either."

"Oh, I see." Joe didn't really see.

Liking results when one experiences only the intimacy component of love in the absence of the passion and decision/commitment components. The term *liking* is used here in a nontrivial sense, not merely to describe feelings one has toward casual acquaintances and passers-by in one's life. Rather, it refers to the set of feelings and experiences in relationships that are true friendships. One feels closeness, bondedness, and warmth toward the other, without intense passion or long-term commitment.

The Passion Component Alone: Infatuated Love

Tom sat behind Lisa in physics class. Tom hated physics, but he could not say the same for Lisa. One look at her was enough to change his life: he had fallen madly in love with her. Instead of listening to the teacher or looking at the blackboard, he would gaze at Lisa throughout the class. Lisa was aware of this and was not happy about it. She did not much care for Tom, and when he tried to start a conversation with her, she moved on as quickly as possible. Tom's staring and his awkwardness in talking to her made her feel uncomfortable. Tom, on the other hand, could think of little else besides Lisa, and his grades began to suffer as he spent the time he should have been devoting to his homework thinking about her. He was a man obsessed. The obsession might have gone on for quite some time had not both Tom and Lisa graduated that June and gone to different colleges. Tom never saw Lisa again, and after several unanswered love letters, he finally gave up on her.

Infatuated love is "love at first sight," or, in general, love that turns toward obsession with the partner being loved as an idealized object rather than as him- or herself. Infatuated love, or simply, infatuation, results from passionate arousal in the absence of the intimacy and decision/commitment components of love. Infatuations are usually easy to spot, at least for people other than the individual who is infatuated. They can arise almost instantaneously and dissipate as quickly under the right circumstances. They tend to be characterized by a high degree of mental and physical arousal. Tennov (1979) has referred to infatuation as "limerence," and her book is an excellent guide on the nature and course of infatuations.

Several major problems tend to be associated with infatuated love. The first is that it is based upon an idealization of an individual rather than upon the individual as he or she exists in reality. It is thus not surprising that infatuations tend to last only if a relationship is not consummated, or at least is frustrated in various ways. The best cure for infatuation is the opportunity to get to know the object of one's infatuation very well, so that reality has a chance to compete with ideality. The other cure, as Tennov (1979) points out, is to become convinced that one has absolutely no hope of attaining the object of one's infatuation.

The second problem is that infatuations tend to be obsessive. One can be devoured or consumed by the love, so that it ends up taking time, energy, and motivation from other things in one's life. The obsessive character of the infatuation also can make the object of the infatuation uncomfortable, as he or she realizes that the love is more a projection of the lover's needs than a true interest in the loved one.

The third problem is that infatuated love relationships are usually asymmetrical. Our research (Sternberg & Barnes, 1985) indicates that the greater the degree of asymmetry, the more a relationship is subject to distress. Because infatuation is usually based upon an idealization of a person, such relationships are particularly susceptible to distress.

The Decision/Commitment Component Alone: Empty Love

John and Mary had been married for twenty-eight years. For twenty of them, Mary had been thinking about getting a divorce, but was never able to go through with it. Because she did not work outside the home, she was afraid she would be unable to make a living, and besides, life alone might be worse than with John. And life with John was not that bad: basically, he left her alone. He was almost never home, and when he was, he pretty much stuck to doing his work. Whatever passion they might once have had was long since gone— Mary had long had the feeling that John had found others—and although the relationship had never been a very intimate one, even the little intimacy they had once had had vanished. At this point, they hardly ever even talked. Mary often wondered whether John would leave and sometimes hoped he would. But John seemed content to have Mary wash his clothes, prepare his meals, keep house, and do all the things that Mary had long ago been taught a wife should do. Mary often felt that her life would be completely empty were it not for her children.

Empty love results from someone's making a decision that he or she loves another (a commitment to love) when neither intimacy nor passion is present. It is the kind of love one sometimes finds in stagnant relationships that have been going on for years but that have lost the mutual emotional involvement and physical attraction that once characterized them. Unless the commitment to love is strong, such love can melt away because commitment is relatively susceptible to conscious modification.

Although, in our society, empty love most often occurs as the final or near-final stage of a long-term relationship, in other societies, empty love may occur as the first stage of a long-term relationship. For example, in societies where marriages are arranged, the marital partners may start with the commitment to love each other and have to take things from there. Thus, empty love need not be terminal in relationships.

As Lazarus (1985) points out, however, when all that is left in a marriage is the commitment, and the other elements have died away, it is very difficult to restore those other elements in order to renew the marriage. Often, people wait years for the magic to return, only to be disappointed to find that it is gone forever: the couple never again is able to feel either intimate or passionate toward each other.

Empty love, like any other kind of love, can be one-sided. One of the partners may retain genuine feelings of closeness and bondedness to the other, while the other feels only commitment to the first. Such asymmetrical relationships can be particularly difficult because of the added guilt felt by the less involved spouse at not being able to reciprocate the more involved spouse's feelings.

The Intimacy + Passion Components: Romantic Love

Susan and Ralph met their senior year in high school. Their relationship started off as a good friendship, but rapidly turned into a deeply involved romantic love affair. Susan and Ralph spent as much time together as they could and enjoyed practically every minute. But both were unready to commit themselves permanently to the relationship. They felt they were too young to make any final decisions, and that until they knew what college they would be attending, they couldn't know even how much they could be together. Ralph was admitted to Boston University and decided to go there. Susan had applied to nearby Massachusetts Institute of Technology and was accepted, but was not offered financial aid. She was also accepted by the California Institute of Technology and was awarded a large scholarship. The difference in financial packages left her with little choice but to go to California. When she left the East, neither she nor Ralph had much confidence that their relationship would survive the distance, and in fact, after a year of occasional commutes and not so occasional strains, it ended.

Romantic love derives from a combination of the intimacy and passion components of love. In essence, it is liking with an added element of physical or other attraction. In this view, then, romantic lovers are drawn to one another both physically and emotionally. Commitment is not a necessary part of romantic love, however. The lovers may realize that permanence is unlikely, impossible, or simply an issue to be dealt with at some future time. A summer love affair, for example, may be highly romantic, but without any real chance of lasting beyond the summer.

This view of romantic love seems to be similar to that found in classic works of literature, such as *Romeo and Juliet*. Two lovers feel strongly passionate toward one another and feel that they can bare their souls to one another as well. This view of romantic love differs, however, from that of Hatfield and Walster (1981), who argue that romantic love does not differ from infatuation. I think it is important to distinguish between the two. Some infatuations never proceed beyond that stage, but others do. Two partners initially attracted to each other for sheerly physical reasons may come to realize they have much more in common than just the physical attraction; or conversely, they may come to realize they do not. Moreover, romantic love need not start off as infatuation. Sometimes, what starts as liking in a friendship becomes romantic love, as when a couple who admire each other become drawn to each other passionately.

The Intimacy + Commitment Components: Companionate Love

Sam and Sara had been married for twenty years. They had been through some rough times together in those years. They had seen most of their friends through divorces, Sam through several jobs, and Sara through an illness that at one point had seemed as though it might be fatal. Both had a number of friends, but there was no doubt in either of their minds that they were each other's best friend. When the going had been rough, the one person each knew he could count on was the other. Neither Sam nor Sara felt any great passion in their relationship, but they had never sought out others because they both believed they had what mattered most to them: the ability to say or do anything they might want without fear of attack or reprisal. Although they each knew there were probably limits to their regard for each other, they had never sought to test those limits because they were happy to live within them.

Companionate love results from a combination of the intimacy and decision/commitment components of love. It is essentially a long-term committed friendship, the kind that frequently occurs in marriages in which the physical attraction (as a major source of passion) has waned. Companionate love seems to be what Duck (1983) was talking about when he entitled his book on close relationships *Friends for Life*. This view of companionate love is also much the same as that put forth by Berscheid and Walster (1978).

Most romantic love relationships that do, in fact, survive eventually turn into companionate love relationships: the passion begins to melt, but the intimacy remains. Passion may be replaced over time by long-term and deeply felt commitment. Individuals and couples differ in the extent to which they are satisfied with love that is primarily companionate. Some people wish no more and perhaps never did. Others cannot be happy unless they have some kind of romance going on in their lives. Such persons will be unhappy or seek outside affairs "to keep the marriage together" or eventually leave the marriage in order to start anew, with a fresh romance, the cycle of love. Of course, their new relationship, too, may eventually become companionate, in which case they will be back to where they started when they dissolved the former relationship.

The Passion + Commitment Components: Fatuous Love

Tim and Diana met on a cruise to the Bahamas. Both were on the rebound. Tim's fiancée had abruptly broken off their engagement and eloped with Tim's best friend. Moreover, Tim had just lost his job (again—he was getting used to it). Diana was recently divorced, the victim of "the other woman." Each felt desperate for love, and when they met each other, they immediately saw themselves as a match made in heaven. Indeed, it was as though someone had watched over them, seen their plight, and brought them together in their time of need. The company sponsoring the cruise was always looking for shipboard romances, which were good publicity for the cruise line. The company offered to marry them on board and to throw a lavish reception at no charge at all, asking only their cooperation in promotional materials. After thinking it over, Tim and Diana agreed. They knew they were right for each other, and because neither was particularly well off at the moment, the possibility of a free wedding appealed to both of them. Regrettably, the marriage proved to be a disaster once Tim and Diana got off the ship. Although he was great fun to be with, Tim was never one for taking employment seriously, whereas Diana expected Tim to get a job and support her. Tim, in turn, was shocked to learn that Diana did not expect to work, as his aspirations to be a poet could never be fulfilled unless he received at least some financial support from her.

Fatuous love results from the combination of the passion and decision/commitment components of love in the absence of the intimacy component. It is the kind of love we sometimes associate with Hollywood or with whirlwind courtships: a couple meet one day, become engaged shortly thereafter, and marry very shortly after that. It is fatuous in the sense that a commitment is made on the basis of passion without the stabilizing element of intimate involvement—which takes time to develop.

Fatuous love is highly susceptible to distress. When the passion fades— as it almost inevitably does—all that is left is the commitment, but it is not likely to be a commitment that has grown and deepened over a long period of time. Rather, it is a commitment that is still young and possibly shallow. Occasionally, there is a chance that intimacy will grow. But the expectations with which the couple enter into the relationship can hinder rather than help the development of intimacy. They expect a marriage made in heaven, but do not realize what they must do truly to maintain such a marriage. They base the relationship on passion and are disappointed when the passion starts to fade. They feel shortchanged—they have gotten much less than they bargained for. The problem, of course, is that they bargained for too much of one thing (passion) and not enough of another (intimacy).

The Intimacy + Passion + Commitment Components: Consummate Love

Harry and Edith seemed to all their friends to be the perfect couple. And what made them distinctive from most such "perfect couples" was that they very nearly were. They felt close to each other, they continued to have great sex after fifteen years, and they could not imagine themselves happy over the long term with anyone else. Harry had had a few flings, none of them serious, and had eventually told Edith about them, unaware of the fact that she had already known because Harry was about as transparent as glass. But they had weathered what few storms they had had, and each was delighted with the relationship and with the other.

Consummate, or complete love, results when all three components are present. It is a kind of love toward which many of us strive, especially in romantic relationships. Attaining consummate love can be difficult, but keeping it is even harder. We do not seek consummate love in all our loving relationships or even in most of them. Rather, we tend to reserve it for those loves that mean the most to us and that we want to make as nearly complete as possible.

The Absence of the Components: Nonlove

Jack saw Myra, his secretary, almost every day. Jack and Myra interacted well within their professional relationship, but neither was fond of the other. Neither felt comfortable talking to the other about personal matters, and after a few tries, they tacitly decided to limit their conversations to business. Although neither Jack nor Myra especially liked the other or sought the other as a friend, their interactions were generally smooth and conducive to getting business matters accomplished.

Nonlove is simply the absence of all three components of love. Nonlove characterizes the majority of our interpersonal relationships, which are casual interactions that do not partake of love, or even of friendship, in any meaningful way. We usually do not expect much more of our acquaintanceships.

TIME COURSES OF THE COMPONENTS OF LOVE

The course of each of the components of love over time is different. Details of these time courses—and their theoretical underpinnings—are described in Sternberg (1986). I will only sketch the time courses here, without giving details of the underlying theory.

Intimacy

Bill and Brenda had what for both of them was an ideal courtship. They shared the same interests and values, and felt that they could confide in each other. When they married, they had every reason to expect a successful marriage. And it wasn't bad. But as time went on, they found they had less and less to say to each other and sometimes found themselves manufacturing small talk to keep themselves occupied. Bill worked hard, but because he didn't believe in bringing his work home with him, he didn't talk to Brenda about it. Brenda was involved in various clubs and group activities, but Bill didn't seem very interested in hearing about them. Their sexual relationship continued to be good, but they felt themselves drifting away from each other. It wasn't any one thing—just a slow, seemingly imperturbable drift. What had started as an intimate relationship became a rather distant one, and eventually Brenda remarked that she felt they were living in parallel courses rather than together. At that point, they sought marital counseling, which succeeded in bringing them back together again. They realized that their lack of communication and mutual support had become, essentially, a bad habit, but one that could be broken with effort on both their parts.

The development of intimacy follows a course prescribed by Berscheid (1983) for emotions in close relationships. Berscheid's view is in turn based upon Mandler's (1980) more general theory of emotion. Intimacy tends to increase steadily at first, then grows at a slower rate, and finally levels off. To understand what happens next, it is necessary to distinguish between manifest, or observable intimacy and latent, or nonobservable intimacy.

As two people come to know each other better, each becomes more predictable to the other, and they are no longer aware of feeling as close to each other as they once did. But, as Berscheid points out, one of two things may actually be happening. On the one hand, the relationship may truly be dying—the two may be evolving separately and growing apart. On the other hand, the relationship may be thriving, with the two growing closer, but because of the smoothness of the growth, they are hardly aware of their interdependence. Thus, in a successful relationship, there will be continuing development of latent intimacy, even though the level of observable intimacy is decreasing. In an unsuccessful relationship, both latent and observable intimacy will be declining. But unfortunately, it is often difficult for a couple to know which kind of relationship they have; in each case, the experience of observable intimacy is the same. Usually, it will take some kind of interruption—time away from each other, a loss in the family, even a separation or divorce—for the couple to find out how they actually feel about each other. Is it any wonder, then, that some couples realize only after their divorce that they were in fact close to and dependent on each other?

Passion

When Rick met Sally, he felt passionate love for the first time. He had had other relationships and a string of casual affairs, but the relationship with Sally was different. He had never felt truly passionate toward and engrossed by a woman as he did now. Sally, in turn, viewed the relationship as her salvation. She had just finished the second of two disastrous relationships, and this one was as different as could be. Rick and Sally saw each other every day and made love every time they got together. Although the relationship continued to be a rewarding one, both of them felt the passion dwindling. And both of them worried: what had happened to what for both of them was the passion of their lives? Where had it gone, and how could it be restored? They both tried, and tried even harder. But it wouldn't come back, and they felt keen disappointment that they had lost what had once seemed so valuable to each of them.

The time course of passion in romantic relationships follows a standard pattern (see Solomon, 1980). Rapid development of passion is followed by habituation, so that a partner is no longer as stimulating as he or she used to be. Addictions to certain substances—coffee, alcohol, cigarettes, or whatever—follow the same pattern. Once habituation sets in, even more time with the person (or increased amounts of the substance) can no longer stimulate the arousal that was once possible. However, should one lose the person (or should the substance be withdrawn), one experiences symptoms of withdrawal—depression, agitation, fatigue, and the like. In other words, one does not simply go back to the baseline—where one was before the person or substance entered one's life. Rather, one falls well below it, feeling strongly the effects of the withdrawal. Gradually, however, one starts returning to baseline.

Decision/Commitment

They were nothing if not committed to each other: for Jeanne and Jim, nothing took priority over their relationship. They married after a six-year-long engagement. Their marriage had the usual ups and downs, and there were some really rocky times because Jim's job required frequent moves to enable him to climb the corporate ladder. But they got through it all, and when they turned fifty within a week of each other, they decided they were ready for their second honeymoon. While on the honeymoon, they realized that even when they had married, they were unaware how committed they could be to each other. Commitment was no longer declarations of everlasting love or assurances that their relationship was forever. It was being together and staying together through the hard times as well as the easy ones, and reaffirming to each other and to themselves that through it all, their relationship always had come first and always would.

The course of the decision/commitment component of love over the duration of a close relationship depends in large part upon the success of that relationship (and vice versa). Generally, this level starts at a zero baseline before one meets or gets to know the individual and then starts increasing. Usually, if the relationship is to become a long-term one, the increase in level of commitment in the decision/commitment component will be gradual at first and then speed up. If the relationship continues over the long term, the amount of commitment will usually level off. If the relationship begins to flag, the level of commitment will begin a period of descent, and if the relationship fails, in the sense of approaching an end, the level of commitment may return to zero.

Since the respective time courses for intimacy, passion, and decision/commitment are somewhat different, relationships will change over time. How can one understand these changes in terms of the theory? This issue is discussed below.

THE GEOMETRY OF THE LOVE TRIANGLE

Allen and Wendy knew they loved each other. They also knew they had a problem. For Allen, a true love was based on physical passion. After a series of unsatisfactory relationships, he had come to the conclusion that if a couple were good in bed, they could get through pretty much everything. For Wendy, closeness had to come first. She just couldn't go to bed with Allen if they were having an argument or feeling distant from each other. But Wendy's attitude frustrated Allen because he believed there was scarcely a problem a couple couldn't work out in bed, if only given the chance. At the same time, Wendy felt frustrated with Allen. Solutions to problems couldn't come out of going to bed because then they weren't really solutions at all, but rather avoidance of the problems. Eventually, Allen and Wendy split up, unable to resolve what had become a fundamental difference between them.

The geometry of the love triangle depends upon two factors: intensity of love and balance of love.

Basically, the greater the intensity of love one experiences toward another, the larger (greater in area) will be one's love triangle for that other. The greater a given component of love, the further that vertex lies from the center of the triangle.

The balance of love in the relationship determines the shape of the triangle. A completely balanced relationship (in terms of the three components of the theory) would be represented by an equilateral triangle. Unbal-

BALANCED TRIANGLE

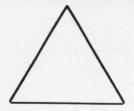

UNBALANCED TRIANGLES

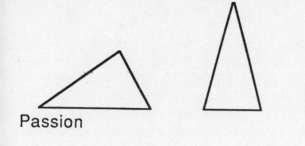

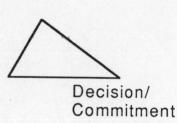

Fig. 6.3. Balanced and Unbalanced Relationships

anced relationships are represented by triangles that point in the direction of the largest component. Thus, a relationship emphasizing the intimacy component would be represented by an elongated, upward-pointing triangle; one emphasizing the passion component would point to the lower left; and one emphasizing the decision/commitment component would point to the lower right (see figure 6.3).

Because relationships vary both in intensity and in balance, triangles of love vary in both size and shape. Knowing the size and shape of a given individual's love triangle for another gives one a good sense of how that person feels about the other.

THE MULTIPLE TRIANGLES OF LOVE

Geoff was thirty-six, reasonably happy, but eager to get married. But although he had met a number of women over the years, he did not feel that any of them was quite right for him. He viewed himself as having very high standards, and none of them had met those standards. He couldn't see himself entering into a permanent relationship with a woman he felt was not what he really wanted. Early on in some of the relationships, he had thought he had found what he was looking for, only to become disappointed once he got to know the women better. He was discouraged, wondering whether he would ever find the woman of his dreams. Friends suggested that he set more reasonable standards for the women he met, but he did not view his standards as unreasonable. A marriage that represented a compromise could hardly be a marriage at all for him: he would always wonder whether if he had waited just a little bit longer, might not he have found the woman he had always been looking for?

Love does not involve only a single triangle, but rather a number of triangles, only some of which are of interest. The main triangles will be considered here.

REAL VERSUS IDEAL TRIANGLES.   One has not only a triangle representing one's love for the other in a close relationship but also a triangle representing an ideal other for that relationship. This ideal may or may not be grounded in reality. Underinvolvement occurs when the real triangle is of lesser area than the ideal triangle, whereas overinvolvement occurs when the real triangle is of greater area than the ideal triangle. Misinvolvement occurs when the real triangle differs substantially in shape from the ideal triangle. In other words, the amount of love may be right, but the kind of love is not. Of course, it is possible to have mismatches between the real and the ideal in both area and shape. The research of Sternberg and Barnes (1985), described earlier, suggests that the greater the mismatch between real and ideal triangles, the lesser the experienced satisfaction is likely to be in a given love relationship.

SELF VERSUS OTHER TRIANGLES.   There are always at least two people involved in a love relationship, and each of them experiences a triangle of love. Hence, one can visualize the degree of match or mismatch by comparing the triangles of the partners in the loving relationship. Again, the Sternberg-Barnes research suggests that greater mismatch in triangles tends to be associated with lesser satisfaction.

SELF-PERCEIVED VERSUS OTHER-PERCEIVED TRIANGLES.   It is possible, also, to distinguish between self-perceived and other-perceived triangles. In a loving relationship, one has a triangle that represents one's love for another. There is no guarantee, however, that this triangle will be experienced by the other in the same way. One partner in a loving relationship may not feel loved as he or she loves the other. Hence, there can be discrepancies between an individual's triangle as experienced by the self and as experienced by the other.

THOUGHT VERSUS ACTION TRIANGLES. It was noted above that the triangle representing the way an individual feels toward another may differ from the triangle perceived by the other. There can be any number of sources of this discrepancy in perceptions, but one of the most powerful is the failure of many individuals to express their love fully in action. It is one thing to feel a certain way, but another to express these feelings; often the feelings fail to be communicated because of the inability or unwillingness of the individual to translate the three components of love into actions. Hence, it is necessary to think in terms of an "action triangle" that represents the three components of love as translated into action.

> Craig had assured Lucy that she was everything to him—that his life would mean nothing without her. At first, Lucy was very pleased with Craig's assurances. She wanted a man who put her as his top priority in his life. But over time, the assurances began to wear thin. Because although Craig said that Lucy was the most important thing in his life, Lucy did not feel that Craig acted that way. He traveled a great deal, and when he was around, he always seemed to have things to do that took precedence over Lucy. Craig and Lucy talked about her perception, and Craig told her he understood why she felt the way she did; but he also assured her that she was misconstruing his actions because it was she who came first. At the same time, though, he did have other responsibilities and could not very well let them go unfulfilled. Eventually, Lucy decided to leave the relationship: she couldn't reconcile Craig's actions with his words, and she decided that actions speak louder than words.

The actions that convey each of the three components of love differ. For example, intimacy might be expressed through communication or doing something concrete to support the other person. Passion might be expressed through hugging or making love. Commitment might be expressed through fidelity or some tangible symbol, such as a ring. However the three components are expressed, the actions will have tangible effects on the relationship, because the partner's experience of the three components will affect his or her actions, which will then affect the components themselves. Feelings of intimacy, for example, lead to intimate actions, which lead in turn to more feelings of intimacy. But if the feelings are not expressed in action, then often destruction of the feelings will ensue, especially if lack of follow-through leads to lack of trust on the part of one of the two partners.

Neither love nor a theory of love should get "lost" within the individuals involved in the relationship. It is necessary to take into account the ways in which individuals express their love. Without expression, even the greatest of loves can die.

Interactions among the Love Triangles

The important thing to remember is that the triangles are not independent, but interactive. Something that affects one can affect another, and the triangles themselves can affect each other. Hence, although one can understand love in terms of its components and the triangles they generate, one must always be sensitive to the interactions among the components and triangles that make love such a complex entity.

A Word of Caution

The triangle serves as a useful metaphor for visualizing how the three components of love are related and for understanding how they are manifested in different types of love relationships. In the triangular theory, the location of each vertex represents the extent of one of the three components of love, but there is no intention for the distances between vertices to represent, in any sense, the "distances" between the various components, or for the cosines of the angles at the vertices to represent correlations between the three components. In other words, the triangle is meant as a helpful metaphor, not as a full-fledged geometric model partaking of all the properties of analytic geometry. Obviously, metaphors other than the triangle could serve the same purpose. It is important to distinguish between the theory itself (which presents and defines the three components) and the triangular metaphor used to make the theory easier to visualize and reflect upon.

CONCLUSIONS

I have proposed in this chapter a triangular theory of love that seems to help us understand many, although certainly not all, love-related phenomena. According to the theory, love can be understood as comprising three components: intimacy, passion, and commitment. Different kinds of loves are represented by subsets of the three components. The three components have different time courses, practically guaranteeing that relationships will change over time. Part of the success of these relationships depends upon the adaptability of the people involved to these changes.

The three aspects of love can be visualized as three vertices of a triangle. When one does so, the amount or intensity of love in a relationship can be understood in terms of the area (size) of the triangle, and the balance of love in the relationship can be understood in terms of the shape of the triangle. Moreover, not only one triangle is involved in a given relationship but rather multiple triangles. For example, each member of a couple has a triangle representing his or her view of the relationship, and each has both a real and an ideal triangle for the other's behavior. Greater discrepancies in size or shape of the various triangles tend to be associated with lesser satisfaction in relationships. Corresponding to each of the three elements of the triangle is a set of actions: in order for love to thrive, the actions in the loving relationship should reflect the size and shape of the lover's triangle. Often, however, the actions do not reflect the feelings, in which case problems may arise as the other partner tries to ascertain the true state of the lover's feelings, and why it is not reflected in actions.

Many previous theories of love seem to concentrate upon just one or two of the seven kinds of love postulated by the triangular theory. Freud (1922), for example, seems to have concentrated upon what was called in this chapter infatuated love; Hatfield and Walster (1981) deal primarily with infatuated and companionate love, and possibly with romantic love; Peele and Brodsky (1976), in dealing with the addictive aspect of love, seem to concentrate upon infatuated love, as does Tennov (1979). The theory of love most akin in spirit to this one is possibly that of Lee (1977), which also generates a classification of different kinds of love. I believe a classification is important so that love can be understood in its multiplicity rather than as a unitary phenomenon.

The triangular theory of love has at least two practical applications. The first is diagnostic. I am currently developing a scale to measure each of the three components. With this scale, it should become possible for therapists and couples to have a better sense of where each partner in a loving relationship stands. The second application is therapeutic. By pointing out the specific differences between the loves of two members of a couple, the measuring instrument based on the triangular theory should help pinpoint the areas in which change is necessary and suggest the kinds of actions (from the action triangle) that might effect change. Thus the couple might be brought more closely together or at least helped to understand and respect their differences.

Perhaps the most important use of the triangular theory is to help people recognize that relationships are, almost inevitably, dynamic. "Living happily ever after" need not be a myth, but if it is to be a reality, the happiness must be based upon different configurations of mutual feelings at various times in a relationship. Couples who expect their passion to last forever, or their intimacy to remain unchallenged, are in for disappointment. The theory suggests we must constantly work at understanding, building, and rebuilding our loving relationships. Relationships are constructions, and they decay over time if they are not maintained and improved. We cannot expect a relationship simply to take care of itself, any more than we can expect that of a building. Rather, we must take responsibility for making our relationships the best they can be.

REFERENCES

Berscheid, E. (1983). Emotion. In H. H. Kelley, E. Berscheid, A. Christensen, J. H. Harvey, T. L. Huston, G. Levinger, E. McClintock, L. A. Peplau, & D. R. Peterson (Eds.), *Close relationships* (pp. 110–168). New York: Freeman.

Berscheid, E., & Walster, E. H. (1978). *Interpersonal attraction* (2nd ed.). Reading, MA: Addison-Wesley.

Brehm, S. S. (1985). *Intimate relationships*. New York: Random House.

Duck, S. (1983). *Friends for life*. New York: St. Martin's.

Freud, S. (1922). Certain neurotic mechanisms in jealousy, paranoia, and homosexuality. In *Collected Papers* (Vol. 2, pp. 235, 240, 323). London: Hogarth.

Hatfield, E., & Walster, G. W. (1981). *A new look at love*. Reading, MA: Addison-Wesley.

Hendrick, C., & Hendrick, S. (1983). *Liking, loving, and relating*. Monterey, CA: Brooks/Cole.

Lazarus, A. A. (1985). *Marital myths*. San Luis Obispo, CA: Impact.

Lee, J. A. (1977). A typology of styles of loving. *Personality and Social Psychology Bulletin*, 3, 173–182.

Mandler, G. (1980). The generation of emotion: A psychological theory. In R. Plutchik & H. Kellerman (Eds.), *Emotion: Theory, research and experience: Vol. 1. Theories of emotion*. New York: Academic Press.

Peele, S., & Brodsky, A. (1976). *Love and addiction*. New York: New American Library.

Solomon, R. L. (1980). The opponent-process of acquired motivation: The costs of pleasure and the benefits of pain. *American Psychologist*, 35, 691–712.

Sternberg, R. J. (1986). A triangular theory of love. *Psychological Review*, 93, 119–135.

Sternberg, R. J., & Barnes, M. (1985). Real and ideal others in romantic relationships: Is four a crowd? *Journal of Personality and Social Psychology*, 49, 1589–1596.

Sternberg, R. J., & Grajek, S. (1984). The nature of love. *Journal of Personality and Social Psychology*, 47, 312–329.

Tennov, D. (1979). *Love and limerence*. New York: Stein & Day.

CHAPTER SEVEN

Can We Picture "Love"?

BY GEORGE LEVINGER

Love is "a many-splendored thing"; the title of Han Suyin's (1952) book sticks in my mind. Love has many forms and guises. It may be reciprocated or not, satisfying or unfulfilled. Its object may be a peer, a parent, a child, a group, a nation, or an impersonal being such as God or Nature. As indicated by the variety of chapters in this volume, social scientists have considered love phenomena both widely and deeply, but love continues to retain its mystery. Furthermore, poets, novelists, playwrights, and others have written many millions of lines on the topic. In fact, *love* has far more entries in *Bartlett's Familiar Quotations* than does any other word except *man*.

Thus I doubt that my words can add much that is novel. My emphasis here, therefore, will be on pictures, on diagramming contrasting love phenomena in terms of the life spaces of the members of a relationship. My approach, influenced especially by Sternberg's (1986) triangular theory of love, draws attention to *relational* aspects of love. By doing so, it aims to put Sternberg's components of love in a somewhat different light.

SOME EARLIER PICTORIAL IMAGES

Before presenting my images, I will introduce two earlier pictorial models of love phenomena: Kelley's comparison of conditions that affect love and commitment, and Sternberg's three-component theory of love.

Kelley's Distinction between Love and Commitment

In his recent analysis of the concepts of love and commitment, Kelley (1983) proposes that *love* refers to positive feelings and behaviors, and

For their helpful comments on a previous version of this chapter, I thank Ann Levinger, Susan Fiske, and Ronnie Janoff-Bulman.

commitment to the stability of the forces that affect an ongoing relationship. Figure 7.1 conveys his image of the conditions that promote either or both via a two-by-two diagram: factors that affect a relationship may be (1) either positive or not, and (2) either stable or not. His diagram implies that all sorts of "stable" conditions promote continued commitment, but not all "positive" conditions promote love. Not every kiss nor every gift leads us to love another, and many reasons for interacting with another person have little to do with love.

Kelley's analysis discusses the kinds of positive factors that may constitute love between two people—caring for the other, needing, trusting, and tolerance, as well as various behaviors and feelings associated with it—but it does not clarify the connections among those factors. It is necessary to specify further the nature of the positive factors that determine different kinds of love phenomena. Sternberg has recently proposed a more differentiated triangular model that distinguishes among varying forms of love. Since this chapter builds on Sternberg's ideas, let us consider his model in somewhat more detail.

Sternberg's Three-Component Theory of Love

Sternberg (1986) suggests that love has three main components, which he represents as vertices of a hypothetical triangle (see figure 7.2). His three components are intimacy, passion, and decision/commitment. Whereas intimacy is said to connote the warmth of one's feeling toward a partner and passion its heat, the third component suggests cooler feelings of obligation and conscience. Sternberg's intimacy component derives largely from "emotional investment," the passion component from "motivational involvement," and the decision/commitment component from "cognitive decision in and commitment to the relationship" (1986, p. 119). The meaning of each term will be elaborated later, but a Freudian might link the three contrasting aspects to a lover's ego, libido, and superego, respectively.

In Sternberg's model, different forms of love or lack of love can be represented by various combinations of these three ingredients. He suggests the following eight types as "limiting cases," characterized by the presence or absence of the various components: (1) *nonlove* would mean the absence of all three components; (2) *liking*, the presence of intimacy without either passion or commitment; (3) *infatuated love*, the existence of passion alone; (4) *empty love*, a commitment in the absence of either intimacy or passion; (5) *romantic love*, the presence of both intimacy and passion, but without commitment; (6) *companionate love*, the feeling of intimacy and commit-

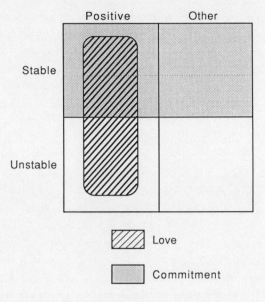

Positive   Other

Stable

Unstable

Love

Commitment

Fig. 7.1.   Kelley's Conception of Factors That Promote Love and Commitment
in a Pair Relationship (adapted from Kelley, 1983, p. 266)

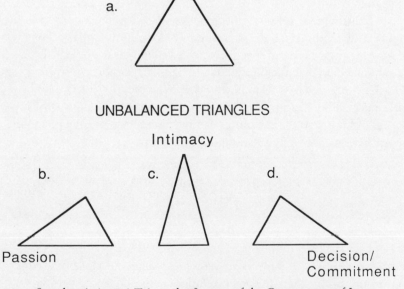

BALANCED TRIANGLE

a.

UNBALANCED TRIANGLES

Intimacy

b.   c.   d.

Passion   Decision/
                              Commitment

Fig. 7.2.   Sternberg's (1986) Triangular Images of the Components of Love

ment, but without passion; (7) *fatuous love*, passion and commitment but without intimacy (as in a shallow Hollywood-type marriage); and (8) *consummate love*, the presence of large amounts of all three ingredients.

These eight cases are ideal types. They convey extremes rather than the gradations and fluctuations likely to occur in real relationships. They are useful, though, for illustrating systematically how varying combinations of the three components lead to differing meanings of love.

Nevertheless, Sternberg's triangle image is only a starting point for trying to convey differing meanings of love. For one thing, his triangle metaphor does not distinguish among intimacy, passion, and commitment pictorially. For instance, in figure 7.2, triangles b, c, and d represent Sternberg's images of "liking," "infatuated love," and "empty love," respectively, but the shapes of his triangles are arbitrary. There is no reason intimacy *must* be located at the top, passion at the left, and decision/commitment at the right vertices of these triangles. In other words, his triangle image does not encourage analytical comparisons of the different components or their combinations.

Furthermore, the image does not lend itself to comparisons between one person (the lover) and the other (the loved). Although "love" is essentially one individual's personal feeling about another or a relationship, it has crucial interpersonal aspects that ought also to be represented in efforts to picture it. In actual cases, it matters a great deal whether a person (P) believes the other (O) reciprocates P's love. And it also matters what O's own perception is.

This chapter explores another set of images to encourage such further analysis. It employs contrasting symbols for representing intimacy, commitment, and passion, respectively. It first reviews each of Sternberg's three components in detail and suggests visual analogues drawn from my earlier thinking about pair relatedness (for example, Levinger, 1976, 1977; Levinger & Snoek, 1972). Later it offers pictorial analogues of his eight types of love, and then explores the representation of love phenomena in pairs before examining them in other contexts.

PICTURING THE INTIMACY, COMMITMENT, AND PASSION COMPONENTS

Intimacy

"The intimacy component refers to feelings of closeness, connectedness, and bondedness in loving relationships" (Sternberg, 1986, p. 119).

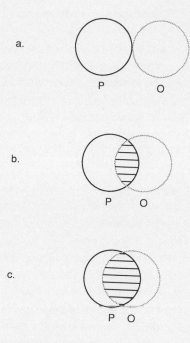

Fig. 7.3. Differing Degrees of Intimacy (as Perceived by P)

This component, more than either of the others, is at the core of all loving relationships. Citing his own research, Sternberg says that intimacy includes

(a) desire to promote the welfare of the loved one, (b) experienced happiness with the loved one, (c) high regard for the loved one, (d) being able to count on the loved one in times of need, (e) mutual understanding with the loved one, (f) sharing of one's self and one's possessions with the loved one, (g) receipt of emotional support from the loved one, (h) giving emotional support to the loved one, (i) intimate communication with the loved one, and (j) valuing the loved one in one's life. (1986, pp. 120–121)

In other words, the intimacy component of love refers to affective involvement and behavioral interdependence. This involvement aspect can be depicted by two intersecting person and other circles, to represent varying degrees of relatedness (Levinger & Snoek, 1972). In figure 7.3 — which depicts three pairs of (a) zero, (b) moderate, and (c) high degrees of intimacy—such involvement is shown by both the amount of overlap and the darkness of its shading. The solid circumference of P's circle, as against the broken circumference of O's, indicates that this picture reports only P's view of the relationship.

Picturing intimacy in this way points to a hitherto unnoticed complexity. There seem to be two empirically correlated, but theoretically distinct aspects of intimacy that should be depicted separately. One aspect of pair intimacy pertains to the partners' past and current sense of interdependence or investment—such as the amount of sharing or communication either has experienced with the partner (for example, Rusbult, 1980). A second aspect pertains to the partners' present feelings of warmth, support, and understanding for each other.

Although interdependence and warmth are highly correlated in many relationships, they are not identical. Interdependence refers to "cumulative intimacy": the amount of P's past disclosures and investments in the relationship; this aspect can be depicted by the *area* of the horizontal lines in P's connection with O. Warmth refers to "current intimacy": P's current good feeling about O; this aspect can be modeled by the *density* of the lines in the P-O intersection. A large area of P-O overlap would signify that a pair has built up many connections, many unique interchanges; high density would mean that P feels very warm and positive toward O.

For example, Pamela may feel that her relationship with Olga is highly intimate in any of several ways: (1) she may feel both that she has previously shared a great deal with Olga and that she feels closer to her than to any other friend; or (2) she recognizes her high past involvement but currently feels a lack of closeness; or (3) she has known Olga only briefly and has so far shared little with her, but she feels extremely warm, trusting, and attracted toward her.

This distinction between cumulative interdependence and current warmth becomes important when we turn to the commitment component of love. That is, it is possible to feel commitment without feeling warmth, but not without a minimal amount of investment in the relationship. Even in extreme cases where commitment occurs in the total absence of intimacy—in instances of empty love or of fatuous love—P must have been somewhat invested in the relationship at the time of the earlier commitment, and some of that earlier investment will still be evident in the current P-O relationship.

Commitment

The second component to be pictured here is commitment to a relationship—Sternberg's decision/commitment component. Sternberg suggests that this component is divisible into a short-term and a long-term aspect—"the *decision* that one loves a certain other" and "the *commitment* to maintain that love" (1986, p. 122). Each of these aspects implies a cognitive appraisal of one's connection with the partner.

Although the two aspects are not identical, I prefer to subsume both under the single rubric of commitment: in this usage, the decision that we love another is considered a form of short-term commitment. With no long-term maintenance of the love, though, a mere short-term decision remains superficial and could just as well be subsumed under passion (as the cognitive label one attaches to one's physiological arousal) or under intimacy (as the labeling of one's warmth).

This component can be said to be important for the following reason: "Loving relationships almost inevitably have their ups and downs, and there may be times in such relationships when the [commitment] component is all or almost all that keeps the relationship going" (Sternberg, 1986, p. 123). Although most definitions of love have deemphasized such a cognitive, stable aspect, our feeling of commitment does color our sense of love and appreciation.

In my own earlier analyses of marital cohesiveness (Levinger, 1965, 1976) I conceived of commitment-related aspects of the marital bond in terms of psychological "barrier forces." Such forces were said to derive from internally experienced obligations and from externally generated constraints around a marriage. Barriers inhibit one's leaving a relationship; they make it costly to terminate interpersonal connections. Commitment— that is, the intention to stay in a relationship regardless of its pleasures or pains—is a form of internally generated barrier forces. A legal contract is an example of an external barrier, whereas joint ownership of a home or other possessions is probably a mixture of internal and external pressures.

Externally derived constraints can be imagined as brackets around the entire P-O field, but personal commitment is here depicted by the solidity of the boundary around the P-O intersection. Figure 7.4 shows three contrasting relationships in which P experiences either (a) minimal, (b) moderate, or (c) strong degrees of commitment. Minimal commitment is shown as a weak, permeable boundary, moderate commitment as a solid line around the intersection, and strong commitment as a heavily accentuated boundary. P's own commitment is here symbolized by only the left boundary of the P-O intersection; the right boundary would refer to O's commitment as perceived by P.

In pair 7.4a, P may feel rather close to the partner, but feel no sense of permanence or bars against leaving the relationship. In pair 7.4b, P senses

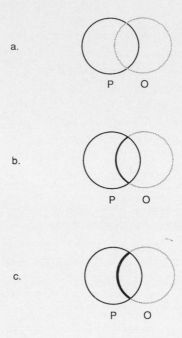

Fig. 7.4.   Differing Degrees of Commitment (as Perceived by P)

an obligation to maintain the bond. And, in pair 7.4c, P feels a strong commitment to protect the relationship against possible incursions.

Although the term *commitment* may have varying meanings, all indicate the stability of an interpersonal tie in the face of fluctuating personal, relational, and environmental circumstances. One's continuing high commitment to a bond—despite the absence of warmth, or even the presence of hostility—derives from one's feeling of cumulative investment or interdependence. Thus the loss that long-time spouses feel after the breakup of a lengthy but no longer intimate marriage reflects their feeling of having to abandon a long-term emotional investment, even if it has gone sour (Berscheid, 1983; Weiss, 1975). Holding on to a commitment after the destruction of intimacy often reflects apathy or the lack of any more attractive alternative; but it may also come from the hope that the bottom has been reached and that things in the future will get better.

Passion

Strong psychological and physiological arousal marked by an "intense longing for union with the other" (Hatfield & Walster, 1981, p. 9) characterizes the passion aspect of love. In romantic relationships such passion

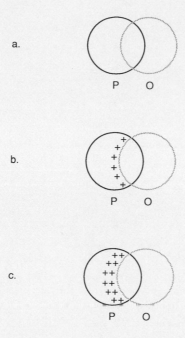

Fig. 7.5. Differing Degrees of Passion (as Perceived by P)

usually includes a powerful sexual aspect, the desire to embrace the other bodily and to merge biologically. In nonromantic relationships—for example, in parental love or in religious devotion—the sexual aspect is suppressed and psychological arousal takes other forms.

Passion is difficult to represent pictorially. Figure 7.5 does so in terms of the density of the plus signs in the P circle at the periphery of the P-O intersection. Three pair relationships, differing in P's feeling of passion for O, are depicted: (a) no passion, (b) some, and (c) extremely high passion. The stronger the arousal is, the denser the array of pluses. P's bodily arousal is directed specifically toward O—hence the location of the pluses inside the P circle, at the periphery of the O circle.

Passion need not, of course, be only positive. Some forms of interpersonal arousal can be extremely negative, as indicated by the phrase "I hate you with a passion!" Intense hate would be symbolized by a heavy sprinkling of minus signs. And ambivalence, surely not foreign to love relationships, can be depicted by a mixture of plus and minus symbols within one or both partners' circles. The study of ambivalence, incidentally, has been neglected in theory and research on interpersonal relationships (Berscheid, 1983).

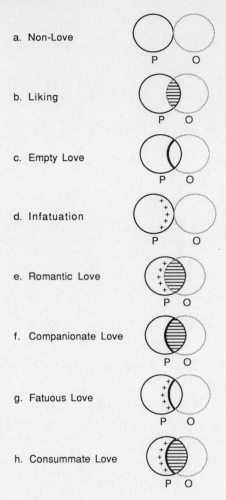

a. Non-Love

b. Liking

c. Empty Love

d. Infatuation

e. Romantic Love

f. Companionate Love

g. Fatuous Love

h. Consummate Love

Fig. 7.6. Eight Types of Love

Picturing the Three-Component Taxonomy

So far I have depicted each of the three components singly. The proper test of the pictorial schema, however, is picturing the components jointly. How can different types of love be viewed differently with the use of our circles? Figure 7.6 graphically depicts Sternberg's previously mentioned eight types of love. The eight ideal types are shown as P may perceive his or her love relationship to O. Let us consider each in turn.

a. *Nonlove.* Nonlove is indicated by zero P-O intersection, no boundary around the relationship, and no plus or minus signs. This condition is typical of the large majority of interpersonal contacts.

b. *Liking*. This is implied by P's warm regard for O, but unaccompanied by either long-term commitment or passionate arousal.

c. *Empty love*. A commitment to the relationship without any feeling of intimacy or passion is represented by figure 7.6c. The solid boundary around an unshaded intersection indicates some investment but an absence of current warmth.

d. *Infatuation*. This concept is depicted by P's arousal (pluses inside the P circle) with little of either intimacy or commitment.

e. *Romantic love*. Romantic love is depicted by the presence of both passion and intimacy, but with no boundaries around the P-O relationship.

f. *Companionate love*. Here a heavily shaded intersection together with a solid commitment, but no discernible passion, imply permanence but little evident arousal.

g. *Fatuous love*. Here passion and commitment coexist, but they are unsupported by intimacy.

h. *Consummate love*. Finally, we have the ideal of love; it is implied by a large, heavily shaded P-O intersection, a strong boundary locking P into the bond, and a large dash of passion.

In principle, it is possible to depict many other gradations of love by varying the ingredients appropriately. In practice, the limits of visual depiction and the complexities of actual human pairs make our pictures only crude approximations of the multiple forms and degrees of love. Furthermore, as is true of Lewin's (1951) life spaces, any given picture pertains to the psychological field at only a single time point; the P-O relation can be rather different another time.

THE PROBLEM OF RECIPROCATION

Until now we have concentrated on one person's feelings toward the other to the neglect of the second partner's amount of reciprocation. But, of course, it is most unlikely that we would find a precise equality between two partners' feelings toward each other. Although partners often tolerate substantial differences between them, and for substantial lengths of time, the three components of love are likely to vary considerably between the two partners. How should those differences be represented pictorially?

Two perspectives will be employed here. First, I will consider P's view of the P-O relationship: to what extent does he or she believe that the two partners' feelings of love are similar or different? Second, I will take the viewpoint of an outside observer: to what degree is there a match between P's and O's separate images when they are contrasted?

P's Perception of the Pair Relationship

To consider symmetry and asymmetry in love, I will consider each of the three components in turn. That is, I will compare P's and O's relative feelings of intimacy, commitment, and passion, as well as the psychological significance of each example.

RELATIVE INTIMACY. Figure 7.7 refers to three different P-O pairs. In pair 7.7a, P believes that O's feeling of intimacy is the same as P's own. Both the density and the area of the shading in the two circles are identical. In other words, P perceives the two partners' feelings of warmth and investment as approximately equal. This pair's intimacy, then, is seen as entirely symmetrical—as when a lover believes that the beloved fully reciprocates his or her own feeling of closeness.

In contrast, pairs 7.7b and 7.7c are instances of perceived asymmetry. In case 7.7b, P's feeling of warmth is noticeably greater than O's (as indicated by the greater density of the horizontal as compared with the vertical lines), but the area of perceived overlap is the same. For example, Paul feels that his current attraction to Olive is not fully shared by her, although they have each in the past invested themselves considerably in their relationship.

In pair 7.7c, not only the density but also the area of the horizontal lines exceed that of the vertical ones. Here P's investment in the relationship—for example, dependency on the partner, amount of past and present self-disclosure, or nurturance toward the other—is perceived as significantly higher. For example, Pat believes she has put far more of herself into the marriage than has her husband Owen (greater area of horizontal than of vertical shading), who currently seems rather cool and preoccupied (widely spaced vertical lines).

Partners do, of course, perceive many other sorts of discrepancies between their own and the other's sense of intimacy. In each such instance, there are noticeable differences between one or more aspects of the partners' feelings (for example, their need, caring, trust), of their self-expression (openness of disclosure), or of other intimate behavior. The possibilities are numerous. In accord with Simmel's (1908/1950) discussion of pair intimacy, however, I propose that an intimate partner tends to believe that the other's feelings are similar to his or her own. The very notion that the other

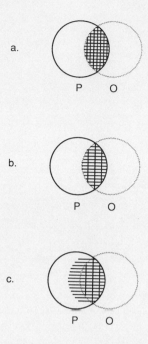

Fig. 7.7. Symmetry and Asymmetry in Perceived Intimacy

fails to reciprocate one's own positive feelings tends to violate the spirit of intimacy.

COMMITMENT. Figure 7.8 pertains to differences in perceived commitment. Again, the first case is one of complete symmetry. In pair 7.8a, the boundaries on both sides of the intersection are equally solid; this indicates that P assumes both have an equal commitment to maintain their bond. Given a pressure toward symmetry in interpersonal relations, P's assumption is probably fairly common among members of close relationships.

Pairs 7.8b and 7.8c are instances of inequality. In pair 7.8b, P believes that his own commitment is somewhat stronger than O's; in pair 7.8c, it is *far* stronger. Such differences usually reflect a variety of other differences between the partners: one person may take the pair's pledge more seriously than the other, may define the relationship itself as more permanent, or may be more influenced by disruptive pulls from outside the relationship—see Levinger's (1976) conception of "barrier forces." Whatever the situation, one partner is inclined to try harder than the other to maintain the stability of the relationship.

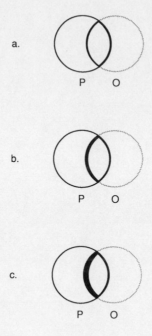

a.

P   O

b.

P   O

c.

P   O

Fig. 7.8.   Symmetry and Asymmetry in Perceived Commitment

PASSION. Figure 7.9 shows three contrasting cases. In pair 7.9a, P believes that both partners find the other equally arousing. In pair 7.9b, P feels passionate but perceives little reciprocity. In pair 7.9c, P believes that O reciprocates his feelings to some extent but feels less intense about their relationship. Examples can be easily imagined.

An Outside Observer's Perception

Until now we have considered the love relationship from the viewpoint of only one member. Yet P's perspective is only one part of the story. Quite possibly, P's perception fails to properly represent O's own feelings and thoughts. How, then, can we illustrate a more dyadic perspective on the person-other relationship?

Figure 7.10 shows how this may be done with regard to the intimacy component of love. The left half of figure 7.10 shows P's conception of the pair's intimacy, conveyed to a hypothetical interviewer. According to P, the P-O bond is highly intimate and symmetric; that is, P believes that his own considerable warmth toward O (horizontal lines) and investment in the relationship (area of those lines) are equal to O's.

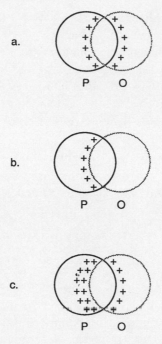

Fig. 7.9. Symmetry and Asymmetry in Perceived Passion

The right side of figure 7.10, however, reveals that O has a very different perception. She acknowledges that P has been involved in the relationship (as indicated by the area of the horizontal lines), but she believes that her own past investment has been much larger (area of vertical lines). Currently, however, she sees P's attraction to the relationship as far

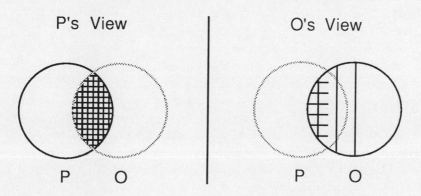

Fig. 7.10. P's and O's Contrasting Views of the P-O Relationship

greater than her own (note the greater density of the horizontal compared to the vertical lines). In other words, O has become disenchanted with the relationship and has withdrawn emotionally. Figure 7.10 could picture a marriage that the husband believes is satisfying and intimate—about the same as it has always been. His wife, on the other hand, has fallen out of love; she now focuses mainly on the interdependence aspects of her "intimacy," but she has cooled greatly in her respect for and attraction toward him.

The interpersonal meaning of the relationship displayed in figure 7.10 can be interpreted in a variety of ways. I will here consider only the distinction between temporary and lasting person-other discrepancies.

TEMPORARY DISCREPANCIES. It is possible that O is physically exhausted or temporarily depressed. She thus focuses on no longer loving or being loved and on being exploited by her husband. She is indeed "out of love," but she is also out of energy and out of patience with people in general. In such a case, O's personal recuperation may promote relational recuperation.

This interpretation recognizes that relationships have ups and downs and that one member's downs are often not shared by the other. Given continued commitment, such downs can well be followed by ups that restore the relationship to its former highly intimate level.

Nonetheless, repeated personal downs—especially if they are not understood by the partner—are likely to have destructive long-term effects. Unshared or uncommunicated downs are likely to erode the continuity of a pair's love.

LASTING DISCREPANCIES. An alternative possibility is that the discrepancy between P and O reflects long-standing, serious interpersonal difficulties. Rather than being due to mood swings, it may derive from the partners' long-term private changes in opposite directions.

In the example of figure 7.10, the wife would have given up on the marriage months or years ago. Publicly, she has continued to adjust politely and to give an impression of little change in her feelings. Privately, though, she has given much thought to alternative possibilities; if such thoughts continue, they will lead to a further erosion in her long-term commitment. This situation is not uncommon in long-term marriages, where one partner may start to withdraw emotionally long before the other notices anything is amiss (Hagestad & Smyer, 1983); if the more involved member then tries to repair the rift, the difficulty is compounded by the partners being out of phase with each other.

Dyadic versus Monadic Analyses

Most analyses of love are highly individualistic. They focus on one person's feeling for another, without considering the extent of reciprocity. Nevertheless, whereas the emotion of love can be aroused regardless of the feelings of the beloved, love's longevity depends on its mutuality. If that is true, we need images for describing similarities and differences between P's and O's perspectives.

Figure 7.10 is but one example of how to depict such differing perspectives. It displays the considerable discrepancy between P's and O's views. I will not present any further examples of person-other differences—for instance, in perceptions of commitment or passion, or in combinations of various elements. Other such instances can undoubtedly be imagined. Suffice it to say, although reciprocity in love is desirable, in actual relationships it is often lacking. I have merely made a start toward diagramming some of the possible discrepancies between partners in love relationships.

THIRD-PARTY INFLUENCES

Until now I have considered love from the standpoint only of an isolated pair. Intimate relationships, however, exist within a wider social context. For any given individual, the pair relationship is only part of his or her life. Both partners existed separately before their relationship began, and both continue to have separate relations with their families, friends, and work partners. Both individuals continue to have their own thoughts and dreams, as well as daily activities that are separate from those of the other. In other words, even in the most intense love relationship, each member relates and responds to other people and objects aside from the partner.

Such third-party relations often have minimal effect on the P-O relationship, but their influence can range from highly positive to highly negative. According to Heider's (1958) theory of cognitive balance and to Newcomb's (1953) theory on systems of co-orientation, relations to third parties (X) have positive effects on the person-other bond if they contribute to balance in the P-O-X system. Assuming that P and O are fond of each other (+), their fondness is supported if both of them have the same positive or negative feelings about object X; in contrast, it may be strained if P and O disagree about X.

Let us consider contrasting cases in which P and O are (1) both related positively to X, (2) both related negatively to X, and (3) have opposite relations with X.

1. P's and O's positive co-orientation to X is the most congenial. Examples include having mutual friendships or holding similar attitudes. The more relevant the friendship or the attitude similarity is to their relationship, the more facilitative it will be.

Love, especially its intimacy component, is sustained by the partners' harmony about important people or ideas. It is far easier to communicate about topics on which both agree than to discuss differences. Mutual friendships also help support an interpersonal tie in other ways (Ridley & Avery, 1979).

2. According to Heider (1958), the P-O-X system is also balanced if both partners have a negative relation to X. As one woman told us only partly in jest, "We love each other because we both hate dogs." Agreement about evil politicians or their wicked policies may also have beneficial effects on maintaining a relationship.

What is the implication of a negative X who is personally connected to the members of the love pair? Premarital couples, especially, sometimes find that their love relationship is the object of parental pressure or interference. What is the effect of such pressure? Recalling the experience of Romeo and Juliet, Driscoll, Davis, and Lipetz (1972) hypothesized that parental interference is more likely to increase than to decrease a couple's love, and they found that the subjective reports of intimate partners tended to confirm their hypothesis. Nevertheless, such predictions should probably be qualified: the effect would depend on each partner's relation to the other and to the parents and other kin, and on the timing of parental interference.

3. If the P-X and O-X relations are opposites, their influence on the pair's love will be detrimental. The most extreme example would be if X is another lover—Xavier competing with Palladio in trying to win the affection of Olivia. Under certain circumstances—say, violent quarrels or debilitating jealousy shown by one or both lovers—the relationship will be in severe danger.

Milder examples pertain to lesser sorts of disagreements or tensions. But unless they are resolved constructively, they often will strain the relationship.

Other Network Effects

During the development of an intimate relationship, the partners' separate social networks are likely to shrink and their joint networks are likely to grow. Previously separate friends are likely either to become mutual friends or to be seen less frequently by the respective partners. Evidence for such effects was recently obtained in a longitudinal study by

Milardo, Johnson, and Huston (1983); they found that couples at more advanced stages of courtship saw their friends and acquaintances less often and for a shorter duration than pairs at an earlier stage. The only exceptions to that trend were members of the partners' kin network, who became increasingly relevant to the couple's relational progress. On the other hand, intimate partners are likely to report a far larger proportion of jointly held friendships than partners at an early stage of courtship.

Johnson and Leslie (1982) have suggested that pair members do not withdraw from all parts of their social network equally, but only from those that they believe may interfere with their development of a highly committed relationship. To the extent that Western norms concerning romantic pairings require a monogamous exclusivity, network ties that partners consider incompatible will be weakened or terminated.

These considerations are strongly related to the intimacy and commitment components of love. Both are strengthened by interpersonal balance and by mutual co-orientation toward third parties.

CONCLUSION

This chapter has focused primarily on how the intimacy, commitment, and passion components of love (Sternberg, 1986) can be translated into visual images of a love relationship. In constructing a set of diagrams for picturing these aspects, several heretofore neglected issues have been noted.

One issue concerns the intimacy component. In modeling this component, it appears that there is a significant difference between current feelings of warmth or closeness and cumulative feelings of past and present investment in a relationship. Sternberg's concept encompasses both. Are there advantages in distinguishing between these two aspects?

A second issue pertains to commitment. To begin with, I here replaced Sternberg's (1986) term of *decision/commitment* with the simpler term of *commitment* alone. I did so initially in order to describe the commitment component pictorially, but in doing so realized that "decisions" per se are no more pertinent to the commitment component of love than to either intimacy or passion. Beyond that, I would ask the following question: if commitment is conceived as an internally generated set of restraints against leaving a relationship, what is its conceptual connection to externally generated restraints that derive from one's cultural or economic environment?

A final issue pertains to the influence of third parties on the love relationship. Assuming that few lovers live totally isolated lives, it is important to ask about the impact of their social networks. To what extent can we understand the growth and decline of love by learning about the partners' association with other people who are significant in their lives?

REFERENCES

Berscheid, E. (1983). Emotion. In H. H. Kelley et al., *Close relationships* (pp. 110–168). New York: Freeman.

Driscoll, R., Davis, K. E., & Lipetz, M. E. (1972). Parental interference and romantic love: The Romeo and Juliet effect. *Journal of Personality and Social Psychology, 24*, 1–10.

Hagestad, G. O., & Smyer, M. A. (1983). In S. Duck (Ed.), *Personal relationships. 4: Dissolving personal relationships* (pp. 155–188). New York: Academic Press.

Hatfield, E., & Walster, G. W. (1981). *A new look at love*. Reading, MA: Addison-Wesley.

Heider, F. (1958). *The psychology of interpersonal relations*. New York: Wiley.

Johnson, M. P., & Leslie, L. (1982). Couple involvement and network structure: A test of the dyadic withdrawal hypothesis. *Social Psychology Quarterly, 45*, 34–43.

Kelley, H. H. (1983). Love and commitment. In H. H. Kelley et al., *Close relationships* (pp. 265–314). New York: Freeman.

Levinger, G. (1965). Marital cohesiveness and dissolution: An integrative review. *Journal of Marriage and the Family, 27*, 19–28.

———. (1976). A social psychological perspective on marital dissolution. *Journal of Social Issues, 32*(1), 21–47.

———. (1977). The embrace of lives: Changing and unchanging. In G. Levinger & H. L. Raush (Eds.), *Close relationships: New perspectives on the meaning of intimacy* (pp. 1–16). Amherst: University of Massachusetts Press.

Levinger, G., & Snoek, J. D. (1972). *Attraction in relationship: A new look at interpersonal attraction*. Morristown, NJ: General Learning Press.

Lewin, K. (1951). *Field theory in social science*. New York: Harper.

Milardo, R. M., Johnson, M. P., & Huston, T. L. (1983). Developing close relationships: Changing patterns of interaction between pair members and social networks. *Journal of Personality and Social Psychology, 44*, 964–976.

Newcomb, T. M. (1953). An approach to the study of communicative acts. *Psychological Review, 60*, 393–404.

Ridley, C. A., & Avery, A. W. (1979). The influence of the social network on dyadic interaction. In R. L. Burgess & T. L. Huston (Eds.), *Social exchange in developing relationships* (pp. 223–246). New York: Academic Press.

Rusbult, C. E. (1980). Commitment and satisfaction in romantic associations: A test of the investment model. *Journal of Experimental Social Psychology, 16*, 172–186.

Simmel, G. (1908/1950). *The sociology of Georg Simmel*. (K. H. Wolff, Ed.). New York: Free Press.

Sternberg, R. J. (1986). A triangular theory of love. *Psychological Review, 93*, 119–135.

Suyin, H. (1952). *A many-splendored thing*. Boston: Little, Brown.

Weiss, R. S. (1975). *Marital separation*. New York: Basic Books.

CHAPTER EIGHT

Fools for Love

The Romantic Ideal, Psychological Theory, and Addictive Love

BY STANTON PEELE

PROLOGUE

"It seems likely to have been a desirable match for Jane," said she. "I am sorry it went off. But these things happen so often! A young man, such as you describe Mr. Bingley, so easily falls in love with a pretty girl for a few weeks, and when accident separates them so easily forgets her, that these sort of inconstancies are very frequent."

"An excellent consolation in its way," said Elizabeth, "but it will not do for us. We do not suffer by accident. It does not often happen that the interference of friends will persuade a young man of independent fortune to think no more of a girl, whom he was violently in love with only a few days before."

"But the expression of 'violently in love' is so hackneyed, so doubtful, so indefinite, that it gives me very little idea. It is as often applied to feelings which arise from an half-hour's acquaintance, as to a real, strong attachment. Pray, how violent was Mr. Bingley's love?"

"I never saw a more promising inclination. He was growing quite inattentive to other people, and wholly engrossed by her. Every time they met, it was more decided and remarkable. At his own ball he offended two or three young ladies, by not asking them to dance, and I spoke to him twice myself, without receiving an answer. Could there be finer symptoms? Is not general incivility the very essence of love?"

"Oh, yes!—of that kind of love which I suppose him to have felt. Poor Jane! I am sorry for her, because, with her disposition, she may not get over it immediately. It had better have happened to you, Lizzy; you would have laughed yourself out of it sooner."

—JANE AUSTEN, *Pride and Prejudice*

I am indebted to Keith Davis for his unstinting help, including providing me with both published and unpublished materials of his own and by other writers. I also thank my old friends—Stan Morse, Archie Brodsky, and Mary Arnold—for their ideas, critiques, and continuing discussions about love. Mary Arnold provided the financial support needed to complete this chapter.

The above description of love makes the following points:

1. The most violent experience of love may be the most superficial and short-lived and may be that most readily influenced by accident and whim.
2. People have different perceptions of love and these perceptions have important consequences for behavior and feelings.
3. One popular view of love is of an obsessive attachment that exists solely in the experience of two lovers; love is best indicated in this view by the intensity of the lovers' feelings and their mutual preoccupation, their incapacity in the absence of their loved one, and their disregard for ordinary standards of conduct.
4. Attachments that may be described both by those involved in them and by outside observers as love can have negative consequences—sometimes quite severe ones.
5. People differ in their abilities to resist and extricate themselves from destructive love relationships; some seem practically immune to them while others seem able to form *only* this type of relationship.
6. Allegiance to one view of love versus another—along with how the person in love behaves—is related to the person's personality and worldview (what Austen here calls "disposition").

Jane Austen's discussion of love was written early in the nineteenth century. We may detect cultural variations in attitudes toward love as well as individual variations—in particular, Austen's sensibilities about this topic may now be rarer than they were in her time. Alternately, although her views may be shared by many contemporary Americans and others, they may be less frequently expressed by love philosophers.

My chapter is devoted to exploring psychological approaches to love in connection with the dimensions of love Jane Austen addressed. The essential dimension is that of love as a heedless involvement whose genuineness is measured by its intensity and perhaps its very destructiveness to the lovers and others. In this connection, I discuss (1) the acceptance by psychologists of the dominant contemporary love ethos, one based on mutual absorption by two lovers, (2) psychologically reductionist methods that fail to examine the natural contexts of intimate relationships, (3) the particular failure of social psychologists to be aware of the destructive consequences of addictive love, (4) the tendency for clinicians who do observe such consequences to describe them as disease states whose sources are inbred and biochemical, and (5) an overall failure to examine the cultural moorings and consequences of current views of love.

Rubin (1984) remarked that "the most illuminating writing about close relationships has come from storytellers and playwrights, not from psychologists and sociologists" (p. 856). That this is so reveals a deficiency in the social sciences worth examining in itself. This chapter aims to improve psychological theorizing by opening it to insights into love that have been regularly presented by fiction writers and that continue to appear in literature, movies, and—occasionally—psychological writing, including Fromm's *The Art of Loving* and my own *Love and Addiction*. Among its other failures, psychological theory has come perilously close to labeling social and individual pathology as love. It is to identifying an opposite model of love that I dedicate this chapter.

ERICH FROMM'S SOCIAL PSYCHOLOGY OF LOVE

Erich Fromm (1956) emphasized that love is an active expression of a person's outlook and abilities. The ability to love chiefly engages a person's concern for others; for Fromm, love is not a separation of two people from the rest of humanity but rather requires two people to be alive to others and to the world at large. The most extreme failure of love is an overwhelming urge to be one with another person—an égoïsme à deux or "fusion without integrity." This state demonstrated to Fromm the immaturity of the lovers. The intensity of feeling in an égoïsme à deux comes, Fromm believed, from the desperate effort by two people to overcome their prior aloneness through dominating or submitting to another person. Fromm felt modern capitalistic society objectifies and reduces all relationships—even while packaging and glorifying the image of romantic love—into purely materialistic terms.

Fromm was a pioneer in relating both clinical syndromes and ordinary behavior to the social and economic milieu (which caused him to break with orthodox Freudian theory). Although today Fromm's socialistic analyses seem overdrawn and slightly doctrinaire, he clearly grasped some emergent characteristics of the modern love relationship that were less evident in other epochs, including the Europe in which Fromm himself grew up. At the same time, Fromm perceived an intimate connection between the outlook of the individual and the type of relationship the person was likely to form, especially the destructive kind of dependency that has come to be a major concern for modern clinicians. Thus, although it relied on politically stereotyped categories, Fromm's work gave an important emphasis to the personal and social meanings of love.

Because he was concerned with the nexus of social and individual feelings and action, Fromm was a social psychologist. The kind of social psychology that came to dominate American universities was, however, very different from Fromm's. This academic social psychology was strictly empirical and relied almost entirely on laboratory experimentation (see Peele, 1983). Love examined in a laboratory context took on quite a different form from anything that Fromm espoused. In order to reduce love to laboratory dimensions, for example, Berscheid and Walster (1974) examined love as a self-labeling of sexual excitation or of any stimulation that might be interpreted sexually. In research based on this theory, people who were scared or otherwise excited felt more attracted to a nearby person of the opposite sex; by deciding they were "in love" with this person, they could conveniently account for their abnormal palpitations.

Some commentators have described Berscheid and Walster's deductions about intimate relationships to be the reductio ad absurdum of a misguided paradigm of scientific psychology (see Solomon, 1981). Yet another example of psychological impenetrability is offered by Rubin's (1974) experimental effort to test a Frommian hypothesis. Rubin categorized people's relationships in terms of love and liking scales, the former focusing on a preoccupation with a lover (to be discussed below). Rubin found that couples who measured high on this love scale stared at each other more while they were unobtrusively observed in an experimental waiting room. Rubin also tested Fromm's idea that love reflects "an *orientation of character* which determines the relatedness of a person to the world as a whole, not toward one 'object' of love." He did so by assessing whether two unacquainted people who had measured high on his love scale made more eye contact than did low love scorers.

High love scorers did not look at strangers more, prompting Rubin (1974) to conclude "that when two people are in love with one another they have fewer emotional resources left for others" (p. 393). This would be exactly the characterization Fromm would apply to his immature lovers. Exactly where do these theorists diverge? Clearly, Fromm would disagree with a love scale whose items indicated a completely uncritical attitude toward a lover ("I would forgive ———— for practically anything"), an inability to function without the person ("It would be hard for me to get along without ————"), strong elements of submission and control ("I would do almost anything for ————" and "I feel very possessive toward ————"), and a general tendency to moon over the other person ("When I am with ————, I spend a good deal of time just looking at him or her").

Rubin's criteria for love seem to operationalize the kind of immature love that Fromm contrasted with mature love, which Fromm saw as the more outward looking, independent, and connected with other people and larger social networks. By misinterpreting Fromm's view of love, Rubin reached an opposite conclusion from Fromm. That the two theorists have different conceptions of love is evident, and understandable. That Rubin has not comprehended the essential differences in these conceptions, however, does not bode well for his ability—or that of the social psychology he represents—to deal with what some see to be a key dimension of love and its "stronger" and "weaker" variations. Jane Austen, for example, would not be well-disposed toward or impressed with lovers who demonstrated their affection by ignoring others.

SOCIAL PSYCHOLOGICAL VERSUS CLINICAL PERSPECTIVES ON LOVE

Davis and his coworkers have also set out systematically to characterize love and friendship. For Davis and Todd (1982), friendship was marked by equality, enjoyment, trust, mutual assistance, acceptance, respect, spontaneity, understanding, and intimacy. Love added to friendship the cluster of passion—as indicated by fascination (paying "attention to that person even when one should be engaged in other activities," Davis & Todd, p. 89), exclusivity ("What we have is different than I've ever had with anyone else," Davis, 1985, p. 24), and a special kind of enjoyment. Davis (1985) later listed sexual desire as a third trait of passion and also added another cluster to the love prototype, this one called caring. Its elements were giving the utmost ("sometimes to the point of self-sacrifice," p. 24) and being a champion/advocate ("I realized that whatever my parents said that was critical of him just made me all the more determined to defend him," p. 25).

Whereas Rubin conceived of separate scales for love and friendship, in this sense diametrically opposing them, Davis and Todd conceived love to be a state added to friendship, incorporating and expanding on friendship's elements. At the same time, Davis and Todd viewed love as an unstable and potentially explosive admixture, and they offered warnings with each component of their passion cluster. Fascination can become obsession, as it did for *The Collector* in John Fowles's novel: "To see another as worthy of devotion and yet not be allowed to express that devotion is to be liable to extreme despair; indeed one is likely to be lovesick" (Davis & Todd, 1982, p. 90). Exclusivity also has "its dark side. . . . When one becomes preoccupied with the possibility of losing the loved one—either to death or to a rival, one then has the condition for . . . jealousy . . . possessiveness or overdependency" (p. 91). These authors also explored "the implications for a relationship when one or more members no longer finds any joy in it" (p. 92), even though the relationship continues.

Rubin was unconcerned with these dark sides of love, and Davis and Todd mentioned them only in passing. Their love research typifies social-psychological approaches that have been more concerned with mutual attraction and with the formation of love relationships (Berscheid & Walster, 1978; Murstein, 1976) than with the evolution, struggles, and consequences of intimate relationships, in good part because these are harder to study. However, researchers have been busy lately studying relationships over time, examining the work and mutual adjustments that intimacy requires (Braiker & Kelley, 1979; Gottman, 1979; Hahlweg & Jacobson, 1984) and the success of relationships, especially whether they last (Levinger & Moles, 1979). Still, contemporary psychology is reluctant to evaluate the quality of relationships, given that they endure. Psychologists seem unwilling to scrutinize private visions of love or to examine the larger emotional and practical implications of an ongoing relationship.

In a startling paper, Shaver, Hazan, and Bradshaw (1984) likened adult love (as represented by what Tennov, 1979, called "limerence") to the infant-caretaker attachment. They found the process common to both was underlaid by "the cognitive obsession with the loved object, the emotional intensity that makes all other matters seem unimportant" (p. 9). Elements shared by infant attachment and love are a fear of rejection, distress at separation, the prior needfulness of the lover (or infant), and the reliance on the loved one to fulfill basic emotional and security needs. Shaver et al. noted in addition some very negative-seeming aspects of limerence, including "dependency of mood (all the way from agony to ecstasy) on the loved object's actions; the central role of . . . fantasy; the aching of the heart; intensification through adversity; and the inability to react limerently to more than one person at a time. Most of these features have at least plausible analogs in infant-caretaker attachment" (pp. 9–10).

Shaver et al. draw these comparisons while mentioning only in passing that "Tennov's description of limerence, with its heavy emphasis on anxiety, fantasy, and frightening obsession, does normal love an injustice. . . . [In a study conducted by the authors] most . . . subjects emphasized the joy, security, and reciprocity of love, whereas Tennov's examples highlighted the uncontrollability and psychological suffering of limerence" (pp. 22–23). Indeed, Tennov's concern is with a severe emotional disability, one that leads people (primarily women) desperately to pursue often inappropriate love objects, frequently to fail at relationships, and to be incapable of learning from such experiences so that their ardor and desperation are often increased by their failures at love. Overall, they experience love as painful and futile, a clinical condition whose nature Shaver et al. neglected in drawing parallels with infant attachment.

Thus Shaver et al. project a claustrophobic picture of infant attachment (one that does not hold for the majority of infants; cf. Ainsworth, Blehar, Waters, & Wall, 1978) while slighting the crucial growth in adult cognition, self-control, and moral and personal responsibility that ought to characterize mature attachments. "Narcissistic pleasure is our term for the exalted feeling that infants seem to experience and adults report experiencing when . . . [loved ones] shower affection and approval upon them. . . . It seems likely that unencumbered fusion [recall Fromm's use of this term] or merger with the loved one is a form of pleasure and security in both infancy and adulthood" (Shaver et al., 1984, pp. 13, 15). It is this uncritical urge to fuse that means "infants can become strongly attached even to severely abusive parents" and that leads "Tennov [to] offer many examples of unrequited love in which the loved object doesn't look very objectively lovable" but to whom the person nonetheless remains compulsively attracted (p. 14).

Fromm's normative view that love should reach toward certain standards along with the notable lack of success and satisfaction for the limerent lovers Tennov described suggest that we go beyond the parallels to infant attachment in describing adult love relationships. At the very least the growth in the capacity to form mature intimacy would seemingly include a healthy growth in (1) self-protective mechanisms and an ability to judge appropriate love objects (for example, those not motivated by a desire to control or harm one), (2) an ability to learn from experience and to extricate oneself from repetitive, self-destructive patterns, (3) an expanded awareness of life opportunities and of the potential for intimacy beyond that provided by one core emotional attachment, and (4) a recognition of one's obligations both to lovers and to others so that "being in love" is not an all-purpose excuse for rudeness, self-preoccupation, and—strangely— spiteful or harmful behavior toward the supposed object of one's affection. Even popular mythology provides counterpoints to immature love with images of the foolhardiness of teen love, the formerly-oppressed-now-liberated woman who devoted herself to her husband because she married too young to know better, and the persistently wrongheaded lover who always "picks the wrong man [or woman]." The failure to make these moral and psychological distinctions is a serious deficiency in modern social psychology.

WHAT IS LOVESICKNESS AND HOW DO PEOPLE GET IT?

The love described by social psychologists can take on the romantic glow of love as seen in cheap novels. In Berscheid and Walster's (1974) approach, love is a matter of sharing a special emotional—at times druglike—state. The primary issues are finding the right love match and experiencing an otherworldly, untrammeled passion. Such love may sour or dissipate; it may not even constitute a suitable basis for a long-term relationship. Rarely does it appear to be harmful or ugly, however, so that even love's failures seem mainly a prod to seek greater love elsewhere.

Meanwhile, since *Love and Addiction* appeared in 1975, a series of books has highlighted the painful and negative potential of so-called love relationships (cf. Carnes, 1983; Halpern, 1982; Tennov, 1979). By the mid-eighties, books with these themes appeared regularly on the best-seller lists (cf. Cowan & Kinder, 1985; Norwood, 1985). All these books found that love could take unsatisfactory forms—up to and including full-blown pathologies—that stemmed from deficiencies in the individual lovers. Tennov (1979) developed the proposition that the deficiency was an inbred, biochemical trait that made women "limerent"—or unusually predisposed to form desperate, unrequited attachments to inappropriate men. Liebowitz (1983) explicated the biochemistry of the phenomenon as an inadequate regulation of neurotransmitters (again one that strikes women almost exclusively) which leads to an affective disorder (as per DSM III) requiring antidepressant drug treatment.

Why have social psychologists emphasized romance where some clinicians see mainly sickness? Perhaps negative consequences of intimacy are rare events that social-psychological surveys would not pick up, even though clinicians might encounter them regularly. Yet the appearance of best-sellers on the topic suggests that negative love experiences are relatively common. Alternately, social psychologists or their methods may be blind to these negative aspects of love relationships. For example, Rubin (1974) examined love primarily as an idealized conception of intimacy among college undergraduates—a group overrepresented in the social-psychological study of love. The same dichotomy in perspectives is present in the drug addiction and alcoholism fields: epidemiological surveys rarely uncover the type of full-blown alcoholism or drug addiction that addiction-as-disease proponents find to be typical (Peele, 1985a).

Clinicians approach love with their own biases, of the type that typify DSM III, third-party payment schedules, and medical models of mental illness and health. For example, Carnes (1983)—relying on the model of

Alcoholics Anonymous—identified sexual addiction as an inescapable in-herent trait that can only be arrested for the individual but not cured. This view and the views of Tennov (1979) and Liebowitz (1983) do not make sense of, among other evidence, social variations in the behaviors in ques-tion. For example, psychodynamic views hold that socialization accounts for women's relationship styles more than do special biochemical abnor-malities (cf. Arieti & Bemporad, 1978) and that men express similar addic-tive impulses to women only in role-typical male fashion (Peele with Brodsky, 1976). Irrational love is influenced not only by gender but by age—for example, addictive attachments often seem more or less typical events in adolescence. Young love often expresses—in addition to imma-turity and youth—a reaction against parental restraint (Driscoll, Davis, & Lipetz, 1972).

Is it plausible that the tendency to teen love that many or most people experience is a permanent biological susceptibility for some people? Rather, the intense and often unhappy approach to love that teens ex-emplify seems more likely to be a learned or developmental process. From this perspective, contrary to Shaver et al.'s (1984) model, adults who form childlike or adolescent-style affairs demonstrate retarded relationship skills. In his late fifties, Peter Lawford married an eighteen-year-old girl whom he claimed to love (à la Davis and Todd's definition of love) like none of his previous wives or lovers. In a few weeks the woman left him and filed for divorce, claiming Lawford mistreated her. Such a series of events is acceptable and to some extent normal in adolescence or young adulthood, but it represents a psychological dysfunction with serious practical conse-quences (the woman claimed half of Lawford's property) for an adult of Lawford's age.

Sternberg (1986) attempted to account for addictive love by referring to Solomon's (1980) opponent-process model as applied to addictive states generally. Solomon's conditioning model holds that intensely pleasurable stimulation initially weds a person to an involvement. Over time, however, the avoidance of an antithetical—or dysphoric—state replaces the initial stimulation as the primary reinforcement in the addictive behavioral se-quence. Solomon's model is based on the homeostatic functioning of the nervous system, as exemplified by the appearance of a complementary-colored afterimage following direct initial exposure to a color. Solomon has successfully demonstrated the conditioning of the opponent process in animals for seconds or hours, or at the most several days. Why this motiva-tion should determine persistent behaviors with drugs—or love affairs—that may last for years is not clear.

In fact, I have argued that the opponent-process model does not begin to explain the most obvious or fundamental aspects of addictive behavior (Peele, 1985b, 1985c). Most people do not experience narcotic effects as pleasurable—for example, when receiving pain medication. Rather narcotic addicts are often notable for the atypical appeal drugs and narcosis have for them (cf. Chein, Gerard, Lee, & Rosenfeld, 1964). Ordinary subjects with full lives, on the other hand, report tiring of drug effects that they initially described as pleasurable (Johanson & Uhlenhuth, 1981). In the case of hypersexuality (Orford, 1978), although most people do experience orgasm as intensely pleasurable, only a few pursue it without restraint (and fewer women still than men). We are left then with the essential questions of why some people report narcosis or other sensations as pleasurable in the first place and why—having found a given involvement pleasurable—some are consumed by it to the exclusion of all other environmental cues and rewards.

Solomon's model maintains that it is the strength and repetition of an initial stimulus that determines the strength of its opponent reaction as a motivating force. Consider in this light the case of Romeo and Juliet, lovers who kill themselves rather than live without each other (a rather strong sign of withdrawal reaction). Yet they have met only a handful of times, most being at arm's—or balcony's—distance. Apparently the need for each other and the intolerance for separation they feel, rather than resulting from repeated conditioning, is actually a *precondition* of their love. Romeo and Juliet's attraction—which Shakespeare depicted as the result of their very specific personalities, family situations, and cultural milieu—indicates how personal and social forces give both addiction and love experiences their essential meanings (cf. Peele, 1985a).

ADDICTIVE LOVE: INDIVIDUAL FACTORS

Romeo and Juliet stand as a summary of individual and environmental forces in love addiction. Juliet, a teenager, is unhappy at home and rebels against her parents' domination. Romeo, slightly older than his lover, is on the rebound from another love affair when he encounters Juliet. Throughout the play, Romeo demonstrates a headstrong and heedless disposition. And, of course, the lovers come from feuding families who will never allow them to marry. We must remember that the idea of prearranged or socially dictated marriage—or prohibition of marriage—was not so alien to Shakespeare and his readers as it is to us. While Shakespeare could understand and depict the effect of such a prohibition on impassioned youth, he and his audience did not automatically assume the lovers were right to reject social dictates: Hamlet drives Ophelia to suicide (and goes to his own death) when he rejects their betrothal, which had been brought about through family connection.

The play commences with Romeo depressed and listless, since he has just broken up with his previous lover, Roselyn. Do some individual dispositions, as embodied by Romeo, predispose people to love addiction? It is, after all, the persistent tendency for some people to engage in frantic and unsatisfactory relationships that has convinced some theorists there must be a biological basis to love addiction. Romeo has no apparent occupation, or diversion, other than falling in love. He is also a rather superheated young man. He is impatient and jumps to conclusions (as when he decides, prematurely, that Juliet is dead, prompting his own suicide), and he angers quickly and acts out his aggression: he kills two people during the course of the play, including Juliet's other suitor. Indeed, Romeo and Juliet's courtship is marked throughout by the lovers' frequent references to death as an ultimate consummation of their relationship. This low tolerance for frustration, lack of positive activity, history of dependent relationships, and antisocial misbehavior smack of the teenage heroin addicts' outlooks revealed by Chein et al. (1964).

What does it mean to maintain that relationships and drug addiction can assume the same forms? Unlike the highly schematic, laboratory formulation of addiction proposed by Solomon (1980), a model faithful to the behavior of human drug addicts must relate individual outlook, setting, and drug experience (Peele, 1985a; Zinberg, 1984). This model replaces the opponent-process vision of pleasure as a Platonic ideal and avoidance of withdrawal as an all-purpose reinforcer with the idea that drug effects mediate the individual's experience of his or her environment. That is, the person utilizes specific psychoactive effects as a form of coping or adaptation. Reliance on the drug's effects creates a self-exacerbating cycle by creating a further need for these effects, since they depreciate the user's capacity for functional coping. Hence the person must rely with increasing urgency on the drug involvement for emotional sustenance the person has lost all other means to obtain.

For a relationship to define the same type of self-feeding addictive cycle, it must also fulfill essential needs while making other forms of emotional gratification less obtainable. Like other addictions, such a relationship is necessary to the person's functioning and is *not* necessarily pleasurable; addictive relationships are marked by their endurance *in the face* of decreasing pleasure and even intense painfulness. At the same time, an addictive relationship lessens the person's sensitivity to, involvement with, and capacity to deal with other people, activities, and emotional demands. All in all, an addictive relationship is marked by its exclusively inward focus, its absorption of the lovers' attention, the lovers' loss of concern for other involvements and people, the depreciated coping and enjoyment of outside activity by the lovers, and the negative impact of the relationship—including often quite destructive consequences—for the lovers.

These elements of addictive love bear a striking resemblance to some of the notable elements in the definitions of love put forward by Berscheid and Walster (1974), Davis and Todd (1982), Rubin (1974), and Shaver et al. (1984). Evaluating a love relationship in the larger framework of a couple's psychological functioning and connection to their environment often yields a picture different from that of an idyllic love affair. What is most lacking in ostensibly social-psychological perspectives is this sense of context, so that the research focus on the intensity of the lovers' experience of each other itself supports the notion that love can be isolated from the rest of the lovers' lives. Thus, more serious than the criticism of simplemindedness that has been leveled against social-psychological perspectives on love (Solomon, 1981) is that they are positively wrongheaded and potentially harmful.

Limiting the assessment of love to measuring the strength of two people's mutual attraction fails to distinguish variations in the love experience. Love—even romantic love—has its varieties. In the clinical setting, we are most struck by this when people label abusive relationships as love, as in the statement "I can't leave my husband even though he abuses me because I love him (he loves me)." The repetitive nature of such problems not only within a given relationship but in the *type* of relationships some people repeatedly form (as in the case of the woman who is attracted to alcoholics or the man who is drawn to women who won't have him) suggests there is something in a person's basic outlook, both toward love and toward the world at large, that determines the kind of relationship he or she seeks. It is an inescapable observation that people differ in their availability to harmful or beneficial relationships. It is fundamental for some people, for example, that a lover treat him or her well.

How do people guarantee that a lover is good for them? Love theories have not generally included the idea that people judge the contribution to their lives a lover will make. Psychoanalytic theories have emphasized hidden or infantile needs as the sources of attraction between lovers. Social psychologists have been concerned primarily with attractiveness, and secondarily with other sorts of social "assets" (such as status or wealth), as providing the glue for relationships (cf. Walster, Walster, & Berscheid, 1978). Sternberg (1986) described three components to love relationships—commitment, intimacy, and passion—which vary in different ways over time. Although passion is foremost in the early stages, this feeling fades and intimacy and then commitment take over as the primary motivators in love relationships. Yet how are some people able correctly to judge their long-term prospects for intimacy and commitment while others misjudge badly how durable their feelings for another person will be? In other words, Sternberg's formulation begs the question of which people and relationships achieve intimacy and commitment.

Some personal and social characteristics that are implicated in the differences in the success with which people form relationships are the person's sense of self, the models of relationships the person has had, and the alternate opportunities the individual perceives both for gaining love and for finding satisfaction of all types. Chein et al.'s (1964) heroin addicts were marked by their narrowly limited views of themselves and intensely negative expectations about the world. For these ghetto adolescents, the trade-off between accepting the state of narcosis and giving up the potential benefits of a full involvement in life was readily resolved in favor of narcosis. Yet even in ghetto environments that seemingly offer little opportunity for nonaddictive satisfactions, the majority of such adolescent heroin addicts outgrow their addictions as they develop a mature sense of themselves and their possibilities (Winick, 1962). It is this changing behavior with changed personal circumstance and outlook that most belies the idea that addiction is a static, permanent trait.

Addicted or abused lovers are more often found in deprived circumstances, although some people not obviously deprived feel and act as though they have few options. For example, some people believe they can't attract a lover who will be good to them. Alternately, because they feel that life is too bleak when they are alone, they search desperately for lovers without taking the time critically to evaluate potential mates. But addicted love can be more insidious even than selecting inappropriate or deleterious love matches. The *relationship itself* can enervate the participants or attack their self-esteem. People who have been abused in a relationship are ashamed and become *less* capable of asserting themselves. Murstein (1967) discovered that people choose and maintain relationships with people who are about as emotionally healthy as they are. In relationships in which one party is more clearly emotionally debilitated—as when he or she is a drug addict—the less obviously addicted mate can use the other's debilitated state as a way to guarantee the security of the relationship.

Security is a primary focus for addictive relationships, even when they are at their most volatile. Addiction is a constancy of stimulation, an inability to be sated. In order to maintain this security, then, lovers may insist on increasingly cutting each other off from other potential satisfactions, which the lovers perceive as challenges to the continuity of the relationship. This kind of exclusivity takes its most recognizable form in extravagant jealousy (again a trait some see as a hallmark of genuine love). Adams (1980), summarizing research by Elliot Aronson and Ayala Pines and by Gregory White, noted that "jealousy goes along with both a sense of dependence on a relationship and with a person's feeling that he or she is in some way lacking" (p. 43). As Adams quoted Theodore Isaac Rubin, "Jealousy is born of feeling that we have so little to give compared to someone else" (p. 106).

Although differences in the healthiness/destructiveness, expansiveness/constrictiveness, openness/possessiveness of relationships have not been sounded by researchers, they are primary issues for novelists and other artists. In *Love and Addiction*, my co-author, Archie Brodsky, and I presented an analysis of D. H. Lawrence's *Women in Love* contrasting the pivotal couple Ursula and Birkin with their foils Gudrun and Gerald. The first couple question their relationship while remaining open to other possibilities both within and outside the relationship. Gudrun and Gerald, while ostensibly more attached in the early going of the novel, enter a destructive phase that ends with Gerald's death. Ursula and Birkin, still unsettled at the end of the novel, present the question of whether a relationship that is never fully defined can exceed the love offered by relationships that quickly reach their limits, accept them, and proceed indefinitely as closed systems.

In a study of Alfred Hitchcock's treatment of love relationships (Peele, 1986b), I argue that Hitchcock is the preeminent psychological portrayer of love in the cinema, and especially of the male-female battle over possessiveness and independence (see his films *Vertigo* and *Marnie*). In *Notorious*, Hitchcock described an insecure relationship between a U.S. government agent (Cary Grant) and his lover (Ingrid Bergman). Bergman, whose father was a Nazi, proves her loyalty to the United States by agreeing to marry a German agent (Claude Rains) so as to spy on his group's activities. She waits vainly for Grant to ask her not to, but never stops loving him. Grant nevertheless turns on his former lover and at the same time is intensely jealous of Rains. When Grant has the chance to save Rains's life at the end of the film, he instead seals Rains's doom by literally shutting the door on this weak and pitiable figure. The lingering smile on Grant's face is not from duty well done but from his revenge for a rivalry of his own creation.

Why is great literature—as represented by the work of Shakespeare, Austen, Lawrence, and Hitchcock—so much more skeptical than contemporary social psychology of the attachments people form and give the name love to? Austen used the word *penetration* to describe a critical consciousness of human motivation and action. The term conveys more than what we would call psychological insight, adding to it a moral dimension in which behavior may be evaluated against critical standards of conduct. By training and disposition, experimental psychologists repress their critical faculties. Psychology as a value-free science strives against any conception of the superiority or preferability of one kind of consciousness or set of behaviors over any other. If a person feels something deeply, in one view, the feeling deserves evenhanded scientific attention and is no better or worse than any other feelings.

ADDICTIVE LOVE: CULTURAL MEANINGS

Psychologists themselves may be part of a culturewide shift in attitudes, one less critical and evaluative and at the same time more responsive to the romantic ideal of love. The view of love conveyed in some social-psychological treatises—while perhaps overemphasizing the sophomoric vision typified by college undergraduates—may simply reflect a near-unanimous cultural value. From this perspective, the unhealthy extremes of love depicted by clinicians may represent a failed or otherwise pathologically extreme version of what is generally held to be true, correct, and healthy by most members of the culture. Love addiction is then a primary manifestation of individual aberrance in a society whose values "hold out the possibility of falling in love as a life solution, where love is seen as a transcendent experience and as a rite of passage into adulthood, and where social life is organized almost entirely around being with the one you love" (Peele, 1977, pp. 120–121).

In some societies passionate love is unknown. Tahitians and other South Pacific peoples cannot conceptualize our idea of falling head over heels in love (Levy, 1973). Hupka (1981) surveyed two centuries of anthropological reports and found cultures varied greatly in their jealousy quotient; jealousy was rare in societies that did not emphasize private ownership, had relatively unrestricted sexual practices, and did not base social recognition on marriage and heading a household. Cultural variability, as always, must restrain our current impulse to find biological imperatives in every strongly felt need or emotion in twentieth-century America. The kind of love Tennov (1979) discussed as a biological condition marked by loss of reason, coping skills, and self- and social-consciousness does not seem to exist in a fixed proportion of people in every society. Nor does the kind of enraptured, possessive crush most notably found among adolescents in our culture seem to be hard-wired in the species.

Averill (1985) argued that "love . . . is a complex syndrome composed of . . . biological, psychological, and social factors, but no component by itself is a necessary or sufficient condition for the entire syndrome. Moreover, the way the components are organized into a coherent whole is determined to a large extent by paradigms, of which the romantic ideal is one illustration" (p. 88). Averill reviewed evidence that the Greeks did not have this romantic ideal. Rather, it was introduced by Dante's presentation of the sublimity of love or else through the medieval idea of courtly love. Whatever the origins of this concept, its basis as the fundamental foundation for intimate relationships is far more recent. Rothman (1984) studied changes in courtship patterns in the United States between the colonial period and the twentieth century. In colonial America, romantic love as the basis for courtship and marriage was just beginning to be an internalized value. "Friendship was still an essential element in conjugal love" (p. 36) until "after 1800 . . . [when] romantic love gradually reduced the value placed on friendship" within a marriage (p. 37). Romance nonetheless conveyed the idea of irrationality and was often depicted in negative terms and as something to be guarded against.

"After about 1860," falling in love "was increasingly regarded as desirable, even compulsory" (p. 105). "Where the state of one's body and . . . one's soul dominated [the] eighteenth-century . . . , the state of one's heart became a central theme in the nineteenth" (p. 11). These developments took place within a social context. Eighteenth- and nineteenth-century courtship and marriage were cushioned and supported by a rich social fabric of family, friends, and community. Around the turn of the twentieth century, Rothman showed, wooing became a more socially isolated act. City life created anonymous entertainments for couples, a trend accelerated by the automobile. Solomon (1981) described the impact of modern social organization and values on the romantic ideal: "Only in a society with an enormously powerful ideology of the individual, in which the 'alienation' of the individual from the larger society is not only tolerated but even encouraged and celebrated, can the phenomenon of romantic love be conceivable" (p. 136). (This may be an overstatement, however, since the romantic ideal was *conceived* in the thirteenth century.)

In an increasingly urbanized society, marriage came completely to dominate all other emotional attachments. The modern focus on one love relationship as the major—perhaps the sole—source of emotional sustenance for a person is a new idea in human society. Ariès (1962) traced the appearance of the nuclear family as a recent historical development. His seminal work on childhood indicated that the connection between parents and children gradually became closer in the last centuries and much more rapidly so in the twentieth century when the family became a refuge from the world. The tightening confinement of the family dictated the emotional closeness and envelopment of the husband-wife relationship. In Ariès's historical perspective, the family is "now turned inward and demanding too much of each other" and "has become intolerably confining" (Mousseau, 1975, p. 53). Thus, although the romantic and conjugal ideals have been with us for some time, their pervasiveness as the glue of social life has never been so great as it is today.

Rothman (1984) noted an increase in the percentage of people marrying and a lower median age of marriage in the United States through the middle of this century; since the 1940s, the percentage of Americans who are married has declined and their age at marriage has risen. More recently, the number of unmarried people has been fed by a high divorce rate, while we have also returned to later marriage ages and significant numbers of people who remain single. With marriage a less reliable and unquestioned social force, we see that a cultural allegiance to the romantic ideal can coexist with more fragmented and less stable romantic partnerships. The belief that another person can fulfill the majority of our emotional needs, a social structure organized strictly around the nuclear coupling of husband and wife, and the readiness to quit a relationship when it does not live up to high romantic standards all work against stable social and romantic involvements.

In this milieu, a devotion to romantic ideals can be dysfunctional and pathologic. Sam Shepard has epitomized the modern, socially disconnected lovers in the play *Fool for Love* (made into a film by Robert Altman). Shepard's lovers, who spend most of their time apart and when together engage in orgies of mutual destruction, are completely adrift and alienated from all other relationships. Drawn to each other like moths to a flame in a caricature of romance, they can never separate. Yet they remain eerily susceptible to the idea of love as a salvation; they are in fact incurable romantics. Clinical theorizing about aberrant love behavior like this that fails to consider its social context cannot deal adequately with addictive love.

Take, for instance, a case in which a grade school invited its sixth-graders to a dance to which they could bring dates. One twelve-year-old boy came unattached (after failing to find a date) but soon met a little girl whom he danced with throughout the night. He returned home to tell his parents that "I'm in love, just like you; I want to be with her for the rest of my life." While the girl felt she needed a companion that night, however, she lost interest in the boy afterward. He was devastated and told his parents, "I'll never be happy again." In his despair he clenched his jaws and banged his head against the walls; later he threatened suicide and ran away from home for a few hours.

This boy seemingly demonstrated good school and social adjustment and appeared for the most part a happy and successful child (although he had had some conflict with his very demanding father). Perhaps, then, his lovesickness arose as an entirely independent syndrome. The opposite view is that he learned a model of overclose attachment at home and from other typical relationships he observed, at the same time that he rankled at this stifling attachment and suffered some of its negative consequences. Thrust into the role of suitor and spurned lover at an alarmingly early age, he became overwrought. In this analysis, we should examine the school policy in setting up a dance in which pre-teens were encouraged to pair off. We can be concerned by the boy's emotional overreaction but also be optimistic because his basic life structure is secure and happy. He should outgrow a severe case of puppy love that has been exacerbated by its prematurity into addictive love.

Other helpful changes in the situation would include the father's becoming less harsh with the boy and also the boy's becoming more critical of a romantic ideology he is too young to support. Mothers and other older relatives historically have offered this type of therapeutic folk wisdom: "Go out and have fun. You're too young to worry about love and marriage. All that will come in good time." Either the biomedical approach to lovesickness (Liebowitz, 1983) or a psychological approach emphasizing early attachment experiences in overdependence (cf. Shaver et al., 1984) could be interpreted in line with current disease treatments of young people's substance abuse (Peele, 1986a). These treatments insist the teenager has an inbred, permanent malady that demands total abstinence and lifetime vigilance lest the child succumb to his or her inherently addictive nature. Rather, love addiction can be considered a societal malady or an individual problem resulting from an oversubscription to an unrealistic cultural image.

The costs of our society's heavy investment in romantic love are not limited to those who cannot realize this difficult ideal or to those who are obviously harmed by their relationships. Even those who successfully fulfill an exaggerated love ideal, as measured by maintaining such a relationship for a long time, may sacrifice a good deal of themselves for love. If the price of love is loss of other interests and intimate friendships (for example, parents so committed to each other they cannot respond to their children), suppression of a full range of feelings and behavior (the woman who must assume a subordinate, "total woman" role to perpetuate a marriage), or a stultifying mutual entanglement even the two partners do not consider enjoyable, then the game may not be worth the candle.

The reification of romantic love is a particular concern for societies like ours that incur so many individual and social costs by favoring nuclear attachment so greatly over a commitment to community. Paradoxically, one of the costs of this couple-and-romance-oriented society is a high incidence of compulsive aloneness (Bellah, Madsen, Sullivan, Swidler, & Tipton, 1985; Slater, 1970). Psychologists have not questioned the relativity of modern social norms. Yet some such critical detachment is called for in evaluating a pervasive notion of love that has grown up serendipitously and has strongly negative elements. Describing an opposite view of love is useful to the individual and the culture because of the costs of the prevailing current image of what it means to love someone.

A NOTE ON SEXUAL EXCLUSIVENESS

For the sociobiologist, sexual possessiveness is a species imperative (Dawkins, 1976). Human behavior is typically more complicated: most of the societies Ford and Beach (1951) studied had some form of "wife swapping." Even in the United States, where the romantic ideal demands absolute fidelity, Kinsey, Pomeroy, Martin, and Gebhard (1953) found as many men who reported that they would not be troubled if their wife had an affair as those who said they would be extremely troubled by such an affair. In terms of actual behavior, a survey of 100,000 readers of a popular woman's magazine revealed that 38 percent of the married respondents aged thirty-five to thirty-nine had had an extramarital affair (and 47 percent of the wage-earning women of this age). The majority of all the women who had had extramarital sex said they were happily married and sexually satisfied with their husbands. The main difference between satisfied wives who had had sex with someone other than their husbands and those who had not was that the former did not see exclusiveness as an essential marital commitment (Levin, 1975).

This diversity in views of marriage is not well reflected in psychological advice giving. In a *Playboy* interview (1986), the popular and liberal media sex counselor Dr. Ruth Westheimer declared extramarital sex was taboo (while okaying such practices as threesomes and sex with inflatable dolls). One wonders why actual sexual practices seem so out of kilter with psychological models of marital health. Dr. Ruth reported that she had been married three times, suggesting that she might herself practice a serial monogamy in which partners are faithful to each other just as long as they are together. In this approach, partners may break up with each other—perhaps never to have any more contact—because they love each other too much to tolerate a single infidelity of their own or their partner's.

A modern American is liable to be perplexed by the passionate love affair Mabel Todd maintained with her next-door neighbor Austin Dickinson (Emily's brother) for thirteen years until Dickinson's death at the end of the nineteenth century (Longsworth, 1984). The lovers' spouses knew of the affair, as did everyone in Amherst. Nevertheless, Mabel recounted in her diary that she had an active sex life with her husband as well as her lover—in the average month in 1884 she had intercourse with the former eight times and the latter twelve times (Dickinson was in his fifties when the affair commenced). Making love with her husband twice a week in itself qualifies as a solid sexual performance by today's standards (cf. Levin & Levin, 1975). Opinions of the affair differed in the community. The principal complaints lodged against the lovers (as relayed to them by Mabel's parents) were that Mabel was a poor housekeeper and that Austin stayed late at the Todds'.

In our contemporary milieu, the primary concern would hardly be these violations of social form. Instead, we are horrified to think of the violation of her exclusive intimacy with either her lover or her husband of which Mabel was guilty. Could the modern focus on total sharing and commitment between husband and wife (or lovers) be more emotionally constricting than was the concern for community standards that prevailed in earlier centuries? Mabel and Austin were able to conduct their affair successfully for more than a decade because they did not flout social customs, as they would have if they had run off together. While people today often accept divorce and desertion, they find it hard to imagine being able to share oneself with more than one person. Mabel Todd seemingly lacked this sense of limitation. Besides being passionately devoted to Austin

Dickinson (and a good friend of Emily's), she was a caring and affectionate wife, mother, and friend.

Mabel and Austin were also tremendously involved with their community. Austin was Amherst's leading citizen, and Mabel was a talented writer, painter, musician, and lecturer. Their personal and social schedules were remarkable (especially in the year Mabel was having sex—frequently orgasmic sex—two days out of three). These energetic lovers strongly contradict Rubin's assertion "that when two people are in love with one another they have fewer emotional resources left for others." Rather, for them, a full life and engagement in the community appears to have been an aphrodisiac. They certainly had more enjoyable—and more frequent— passionate sex than many people with a more limited focus, such as Shepard's thoroughly modern "fools for love." Shepard's characters have no other consistent personal involvements to interfere with their concentration on each other. But their love is a sickness.

WHAT IS LOVE AND HOW DO PEOPLE GET IT?

Love and Addiction begins with the words " 'Love' and 'addiction': the juxtaposition seems strange. . . . Ideally, love and addiction do not have anything at all to do with one another. They are polar opposites. Nothing could be further removed from genuine love . . . than the desperate self-seeking dependency which . . . we call addiction." Nonetheless, it has been difficult to overcome the idea that the book proposes that love *is* an addiction, the summary sentence normally accorded to *Love and Addiction*. Instead, by referring to an appropriate person-setting-involvement model of addiction, I aim to define love in opposition to addiction. The resulting model of love strikes strong chords in some key visions of love, clarifies some pivotal issues in other descriptions of love, and outlines important ways in which love is best approached both individually and culturally. Key dimensions of this definition of love follow.

1. Love as absorption in another person versus love as an expansive experience: The idea that lovers cannot look beyond each other strongly suggests the total focus on a drug in substance addiction. In its place, love should open the individual to other opportunities in the world and facets of the self that were not previously available to the person. Love is an awakening, expansive experience that makes the person more alive, daring, and exposed.

2. Love as idealization and total acceptance of another versus love as a helping relationship: A notion of love predicated on a blindness to a lover's

flaws or a willingness to ignore them describes the kind of defensive system addicts employ to convince themselves their drug-induced state is superior to ordinary reality. Love instead is a helping relationship in which people trust each other enough to offer and accept criticism without feeling that their basic worth is being undermined. Loving a person is to wish another person will be all that person can be.

3. Love as internal adjustment and a private world versus love as an enhanced capacity and outward growth: Addiction is a preoccupation with personal needs; in the case of love addiction, this means a concern solely that another person fulfill one's demands and fantasies. Adjustments required by the addicted lover are designed only to create a more suitable partner; such adjustments actually make the person *less* capable and appealing to others by creating a world whose private standards are incompatible with those of the outer world. These addicted lovers are notable for their dominance or their malleability or, in Fromm's terms, their sadism and masochism.

Love means valuing a relationship and a lover because they are successful in the outer world. It is this feeling that one is a valuable person and that a lover is likewise worthy of admiration, and love, that creates a secure basis for love. Relationships lacking such existential *and* worldly validity flounder in uncertainty, mutual distrust, and jealousy. Certainly everyone is capable of being jealous; but jealousy is not the *hallmark* of a relationship in which each partner is confident of himself or herself and of a lover. Neither partner in such a relationship must direct or be directed by the other, since each is already capable and worthy.

4. Love as painful or as a refuge from a painful world versus love as an intensification of the pleasure in life: Tennov's lovers report their relationships to be terribly painful, and songs about teenage love describe the experience as an incessant ache. Other lovers claim that they find peace only when they are with their loved one, and that time spent on their own is unbearable. The literature and music of romantic love is, on the balance, more about pain than pleasure. The pain in the addicted love is present from the start. People who are susceptible to addictive love are characterized by a pained sense of the world. To say one cannot endure without a lover is to say one cannot tolerate one's life.

Not only should love be pleasurable, but it should inspire and benefit from the joy lovers feel toward life. The passion of genuine love is not an escape from personal desperation, but instead expresses—and intensifies—the passion that a person brings to all he or she does. Love cannot "save" a miserable person; no external experience has such power. Only a person in love with life can love other people.

5. Love as an incapacitating experience versus love as a productive and beneficial experience: Addiction harms and depreciates those engaged in it. Addicted lovers like those in *Fool for Love* are constantly hurting each other; Tennov's limerent lovers are incapacitated by their love. Even addicted lovers (unlike Tennov's) who succeed in bonding with another person are unable to function outside their lover's presence. Yet they hardly seem concerned about this diminution; indeed, it signals for them that their feelings are real. Neither are their lovers concerned that the person has been diminished. Each partner, out of his or her insecurity, welcomes the incapacity of the other as a better guarantee of fidelity, as a way of making sure a lover cannot escape.

Love is rather an enhancing experience, one that improves its participants. It rewards those in the relationship and the lovers appreciate its rewarding nature. These rewards are concrete—they endure beyond the time spent in each other's presence. No, it is not like a chain letter where those who send the letter along magically find $50,000. The benefits of love are as varied as the things people have to offer and gain from one another. But the benefits are real.

6. Love as accidental and volatile versus love as a natural outgrowth of one's life and a secure part of oneself: Addicted lovers are forever doubting that their love has a substantial existence both because they feel unworthy of love and because they believe the emotion is not an expression of them or of the conduct of the rest of their lives. This accidental thing that has happened to them can disappear in a moment; it cannot be counted on and cannot be planned for. This is why addicted lovers are so desperate and grasping of the experience.

The love Fromm described is not accidental but purposeful; it is the fullest and most crystallized expression of a person. To be a good lover requires one to strive to be a good person. To be valuable to another is to lead a worthwhile life. To love another requires knowing another person (as Romeo and Juliet were not able to do) and having a belief in that person's value and goodness. Linking one's life to another person's is certainly a risky and perilous enterprise. But people get better at relationships as they understand who they are and know what they value in others.

7. Love as an incommensurable experience versus love as an experience continuous with friendship and affection: When the addicted love relationship is over, no relationship between the lovers is possible. In some

cases, one partner may have killed the other. Generally, if one lover finds a better version of addicted love ("I found someone I love more"), he or she simply abandons the first lover. After these breakups, there is no basis for further contact between the two, since the "love they had is gone." That is, the relationship was defined as a total, all-or-nothing experience that leaves no trace once a person emerges from it. Like the religious convert or the recovered alcoholic, this lover rejects all that went before.

An opposite view is that love is not different from—although it may be more intense than—ordinary affection. This love is practiced and seasoned by friendship. It may vary gradually: lovers can improve or suffer setbacks in the relationship without being pushed to a brink (while successfully understanding that they need to work to enable the relationship to continue and improve). If their love ceases to be the primary relationship for two people, they are still capable of respecting, appreciating, and dealing with each other.

8. Love as an uncontrollable urge and unconscious motivation versus love as a state of heightened awareness and responsibility: For addicted lovers, love is something that possesses them and determines their actions. They don't know why they love, and they believe they can as easily (it often seems *more* easily) love an undeserving person. Love is a justification for misbehavior including often hurting their lover. In this view, loving a person too much is a logical defense for killing the lover. The epitome of this approach is love as a biological or unconscious state inadvertently activated by the irrational appeal of some casual object.

Love should stand for a fully aware state of being, one that kindles the most elements of feeling and moral awakening. It is this responsibility for selecting and nurturing a love relationship that actually *defines* our humanity and the special human ability to love. Psychology is not in danger (as it is so often accused) of removing the mystery of love, but rather it faces the danger of defeating the best human qualities that love *should* elicit.

The polar opposites outlined in each point above represent ideals that are never fully realized in human behavior. The resolution to the dispute between social investigators who rarely encounter addiction and clinicians who see only the patient who is totally out of control of an involvement is that they are examining different aspects of the same person. The alcoholic patient describes never being able to control his or her drinking, when away from the therapy setting he or she has drunk moderately for weeks and months between binges. The hand-wringing, despairing love addict goes out with his or her friends and is in all respects one of the boys or girls. All people have within them a range of addictive and nonaddictive behavior, and all display this range at different times.

Despite my emphasis on the dominance of the romantic ideal in America, it is remarkable how much diversity exists amid the constant promotion of this ideal (especially when those questioned include other than college students). Averill and Boothroyd (1977) determined that as many people claimed not to have had idyllic love affairs as claimed they had. Actually, only a tiny minority of 5 to 10 percent had had the full complement of experiences characteristic of romantic love—whether they claimed to have or not was shaped by their acceptance or rejection of the romantic ideal. Some people appeared almost guilty about not having had this experience, whereas others apparently distrusted head-over-heels love experiences. What is more, these different conceptions of love have been found to have implications for people's actual experience of love, including their sexual fantasies (Roberts, 1982). There is thus room for an individual to maneuver within a pluralistic culture like ours; there are competing views of loving one may adopt and different sets of behaviors people consider appropriate to love.

While addictive relationships are manifestations of personal needs and social settings, they also reflect personal and social values (Peele, 1987). In some sense, the addicted lover is the most gullible consumer of the romantic ideal—the person least able to apply a critical perspective to his or her personal life and to the model of romantic love. In part, the work of creating a strong relationship seems to involve dispelling the myth of romantic love, and studies regularly find a lessening of concern for it over the life of a marriage (Driscoll et al., 1972). In one study, people who were married longer had lower "love" scores on Rubin's scale, although "friendship" scores remained high throughout the years of marriage (Cimbalo, Faling, & Mousaw, 1976). It is important, therefore, to teach people early on about the varieties of the love experience and the costs of the romantic ideal.

Our society creates attitudes and values that encourage addiction rather than love. The ability to love can be enhanced—especially for children—by teaching them (1) to value friendship, other people, community, (2) to develop broader purposes and goals in life (for example, health, intellect, accomplishment), (3) to examine their relationships and the impact of their behavior on other people (that is, social mindfulness), (4) to accept responsibility for their actions and to insist on responsible treatment from others, and (5) to recognize and reject addictive entanglements. To identify and to disapprove of some ways of relating to others is a legitimate and age-old form of education. That we don't know how to do so or what to encourage or discourage is a symbol of our uncertainty and confusion about basic social values. The parents of that twelve-year-old—and of all the other children in his class—should have had the awareness and courage to inform their children's school that adolescents and preadolescents already feel enough pressure to couple up without the school adding to this pressure.

To reverse our culture's deification of privatistic motivation and emotion as the absolute standard of personal and social good, we shall need better to develop a sense of community value in the society as a whole. Discussions of love and standard treatments for love addiction for the most part take place within a remarkably uniform framework. The dominant psychological and clinical view presents love as a personal feeling that cannot be scrutinized or critiqued (a view that Shakespeare, Austen, and Fromm would all in their own way reject) and that even when people's interpersonal behavior based on their urge to love is terribly aberrant and destructive, they may not be held accountable for their attitudes about love. Instead, disease approaches to addictive relationships insist these people are suffering from a clinical malady that requires quasi-medical treatment.

Addictive love is an extension of normal attitudes toward love that emphasizes the romantic ideal's unconscious, irresponsible, and uncontrollable aspects. Treating it as an isolated clinical condition simply reinforces the elements that generate the problem. For example, a woman sought help in extricating herself from a series of relationships in which she had placed herself completely at the beck and call of her boyfriends. By defining her problem as an emotional malady that demanded a therapist's attention, she expressed her view that she should operate solely in terms of her emotional needs, without regard for such questions as her obligations to her work or her friends (whom she regularly ignored whenever she ran off to do her boyfriends' bidding). If we see this instead as a problem of social values, then she might benefit most from learning that it is wrong not to make good on your commitments and impolite to ignore your long-time friends for a new one (in this case, her latest lover).

Dunne (1984) described the murder of his young actress daughter by a boyfriend who claimed as a legal defense that he loved the girl too passionately to allow her to leave him. Meanwhile, in court the murderer vilified his victim to justify killing her. Although my sympathy was entirely for the murdered girl and her father in this case, I couldn't help but deplore an incident before the murder in which the boyfriend attacked a professional acquaintance of the girl's at a discotheque (in a mistaken jealous rage). What advice might one give to a young woman so she could avoid dating someone who would kill her if she thwarts him? I believe a sounder education in good manners would be helpful ("it is incorrect to allow a friend to throttle one's acquaintances; the more closely associated one is with this friend, the more serious a reflection his or her misconduct is on you"). Although her action (or inaction) is a world away from the murder she fell victim to and cannot begin to justify her death, the girl would have better armed herself by a mindfulness of her murderous boyfriend's incivility.

People resist addictions, including love addictions, when they have the most emotional and other life ballast operating. So my therapy for long-suffering love addicts emphasizes that they remove their focus from their emotional neediness, which I see to be the root of their malady. In place of this self-concentration, I advise them to become involved in something they are proud of, to be loyal to their friends, and to read a daily newspaper. For the advanced therapy client, I recommend the works of Jane Austen. As a society we face the difficult goal of accepting the advances and benefits that have occurred since Jane Austen's time (for instance, Austen's women characters devoted their genius entirely to the goal of a suitable marriage, from which they derived their chief status and satisfaction), while recognizing what it is we have lost in our cultural consciousness from that time and others, when to love meant to be at one with ourselves and our worlds.

REFERENCES

Adams, V. (1980, May). Getting at the heart of jealous love. *Psychology Today*, pp. 38–47, 102–106.

Ainsworth, M. D. S., Blehar, M. C., Waters, E., and Wall, S. (1978). *Patterns of attachment: A psychological study of the strange situation*. Hillsdale, NJ: Erlbaum.

Ariès, P. (1962). *Centuries of childhood: A social history of family life*. New York: Random House.

Arieti, S., and Bemporad, J. (1978). *Severe and mild depression*. New York: Basic Books.

Averill, J. R. (1985). The social construction of emotion: With special reference to love. In K. J. Gergen and K. E. Davis (Eds.), *The social construction of the person*. New York: Springer-Verlag.

Averill, J. R., and Boothroyd, P. (1977). On falling in love in conformance with the romantic ideal. *Motivation and Emotion*, 1, 235–247.

Bellah, R. N., Madsen, R., Sullivan, W. M., Swidler, A., and Tipton, S. (1985). *Habits of the heart: Individualism and commitment in American life*. Berkeley: University of California Press.

Berscheid, E., and Walster, E. (1974). A little bit about love. In T. L. Huston (Ed.), *Foundations of interpersonal attraction*. New York: Academic Press.

——. (1978). *Interpersonal attraction* (2nd ed.). Reading, MA: Addison-Wesley.

Braiker, H. B., and Kelley, H. H. (1979). Conflict in the development of close relationships. In R. L. Burgess and T. L. Huston (Eds.), *Social exchange in developing relationships*. New York: Academic Press.

Carnes, P. (1983). *The sexual addiction*. Minneapolis: CompCare.

Chein, I., Gerard, D. L., Lee, R. S., and Rosenfeld, E. (1964). *The road to H*. New York: Basic Books.

Cimbalo, R. S., Faling, V., and Mousaw, P. (1976). The course of love: A cross-sectional design. *Psychological Reports, 38*, 1292–1294.

Cowan, C., and Kinder, M. (1985). *Smart women/foolish choices*. New York: Clarkson N. Potter.

Davis, K. E. (1985, February). Near and dear: Friendship and love compared. *Psychology Today*, pp. 22–30.

Davis, K. E., and Todd, M. J. (1982). Friendship and love relationships. In K. E. Davis and T. O. Mitchell (Eds.), *Advances in descriptive psychology* (Vol. 2). Greenwich, CT: JAI.

Dawkins, R. (1976). *The selfish gene*. New York: Oxford University Press.

Driscoll, R., Davis, K. E., and Lipetz, M. E. (1972). Parental interference and romantic love: The Romeo and Juliet effect. *Journal of Personality and Social Psychology, 24*, 1–10.

Dunne, D. (1984, March). Justice: A father's account of the trial of his daughter's killer. *Vanity Fair*, pp. 86–106.

Ford, C. S., and Beach, F. A. (1951). *Patterns of sexual behavior*. New York: Harper & Row.

Fromm, E. (1956). *The art of loving*. New York: Harper.

Gottman, J. M. (1979). *Marital interactions: Experimental investigations*. New York: Academy.

Hahlweg, K., and Jacobson, N. S. (Eds.). (1984). *Marital interactions: Analysis and modification*. New York: Guilford.

Halpern, H. M. (1982). *How to break your addiction to a person*. New York: McGraw-Hill.

Hupka, R. B. (1981). Cultural determinants of jealousy. *Alternative Lifestyles, 4*, 310–356.

Johanson, C. E., and Uhlenhuth, E. H. (1981). Drug preference and mood in humans: Repeated assessment of d-amphetamine. *Pharmacology, Biochemistry & Behavior, 14*, 159–163.

Kinsey, A. C., Pomeroy, W. C., Martin, C. E., and Gebhard, P. H. (1953). *Sexual behavior in the human female*. Philadelphia: W. B. Saunders.

Levin, R. J. (1975, October). The Redbook report on premarital and extramarital sex: The end of the double standard? *Redbook*, pp. 38–44, 190–192.

Levin, R. J., and Levin, A. (1975, September). Sexual pleasure: The surprising preferences of 100,000 women. *Redbook*, pp. 51–58.

Levinger, G., and Moles, O. C. (Eds.). (1979). *Divorce and separation: Contexts, causes, and consequences*. New York: Basic Books.

Levy, R. I. (1973). *The Tahitians*. Chicago: University of Chicago Press.

Liebowitz, M. R. (1983). *The chemistry of love*. Boston: Little, Brown.

Longsworth, P. (1984). *Austin and Mabel: The Amherst affair & love letters of Austin Dickinson and Mabel Loomis Todd*. New York: Farrar, Straus & Giroux.

Mousseau, J. (1975, August). The family, prison of love. *Psychology Today*, pp. 53–58.

Murstein, B. I. (1967). The relationship of mental health to marital choice and courtship progress. *Journal of Marriage and the Family, 29*, 689–696.

———. (1976). *Who will marry whom? Theories and research in marital choice*. New York: Springer.

Norwood, R. (1985). *Women who love too much*. Los Angeles: Tarcher/St. Martin's.

Orford, J. (1978). Hypersexuality: Implications for a theory of dependence. *British Journal of Addiction, 73*, 299–310.

Peele, S. (1977). Redefining addiction: I: Making addiction a scientifically and socially useful concept. *International Journal of Health Services, 7*, 103–124.

———. (1983). *The science of experience*. Lexington, MA: Lexington.

———. (1985a). *The meaning of addiction*. Lexington, MA: Lexington.

———. (1985b). The pleasure principle in addiction. *Journal of Drug Issues, 15*, 193–201.

———. (1985c). What I would most like to know: How can addiction occur with other than drug involvements? *British Journal of Addiction, 80*, 23–25.

———. (1986a). The "cure" for adolescent drug abuse: Worse than the problem? *Journal of Counseling and Development, 65*, 23–24.

———. (1986b). Personality, pathology, and the act of creation: The case of Alfred Hitchcock. *Biography: An Interdisciplinary Quarterly, 9*, 202–218.

———. (1987). A moral vision of addiction: How people's values determine whether they become and remain addicts. *Journal of Drug Issues, 17*, 187–215.

Peele, S., and Brodsky, A. (1976). *Love and addiction*. New York: NAL.

Playboy interview: Dr. Ruth Westheimer. (1986, January). *Playboy*, pp. 61–76.

Roberts, M. K. (1982). Men and women: Partners, lovers, and friends. In K. E. Davis and T. O. Mitchell (Eds.), *Advances in descriptive psychology* (Vol. 2). Greenwich, CT: JAI.

Rothman, E. K. (1984). *Hands and hearts: A history of courtship in America*. New York: Basic Books.

Rubin, Z. (1974). From liking to loving: Patterns of attraction in dating relationships. In T. L. Huston (Ed.), *Foundations of interpersonal attraction*. New York: Academic Press.

———. (1984). Toward a science of relationships. *Contemporary Psychology, 29*, 856–858.

Shaver, P., Hazan, C., and Bradshaw, D. (1984, July). *Infant-caretaker attachment and adult romantic love: Similarities and differences, continuities and discontinuities*. Paper presented at the Second International Conference on Personal Relationships, Madison, WI.

Slater, P. E. (1970). *The pursuit of loneliness: American culture at the breaking point*. Boston: Beacon Press.

Solomon, R. C. (1981). *Love: Emotion, myth, and metaphor*. Garden City, NY: Anchor/Doubleday.

Solomon, R. L. (1980). The opponent-process theory of acquired motivation: The costs of pleasure and the benefits of pain. *American Psychologist, 35*, 691–712.

Sternberg, R. J. (1986). A triangular theory of love. *Psychological Review, 93*, 119–135.

Tennov, D. (1979). *Love and limerence*. New York: Stein & Day.

Walster, E., Walster, G. W., and Berscheid, E. (1978). *Equity: Theory and research*. New York: Allyn & Bacon.

Winick, C. (1962). Maturing out of narcotic addiction. *Social Problems, 9*, 174–186.

Zinberg, N. E. (1984). *Drug, set, and setting: The basis for controlled intoxicant use*. New Haven, CT: Yale University Press.

PART III

Theories of Romantic Love

CHAPTER NINE

Passionate and Companionate Love

BY ELAINE HATFIELD

For most people, love is the sine qua non of an intimate relationship (Berscheid & Peplau, 1983). It comes, however, in a variety of forms. In the literature, a recurring distinction is made between two types of love—passionate love (sometimes termed "puppy love," "a crush," "lovesickness," "obsessive love," "infatuation," or "being in love") versus companionate love (sometimes termed "true love") (see Cunningham & Antill, 1981; Kelley, 1979; Kelley et al., 1983). Researchers have labeled these two basic types of love in various ways—passionate versus companionate love (Hatfield & Walster, 1978), romantic versus conjugal love (Burgess, 1926), eros/mania versus storge/pragma (Lee, 1977), unreasonable versus reasonable love (Lilar, 1965), and deficiency love versus being love (Maslow, 1954).

In this chapter, we will use the terms *passionate love* and *companionate love* to designate the two basic types. Hatfield and Walster (1978) define passionate love this way: "*A state of intense longing for union with another. Reciprocated love (union with the other) is associated with fulfillment and ecstasy. Unrequited love (separation) with emptiness, anxiety, or despair. A state of profound physiological arousal*" (p. 9). Companionate love is defined as "*the affection we feel for those with whom our lives are deeply entwined*" (p. 9). Companionate love has been described as involving friendship, understanding, and a concern for the welfare of the other (Safilios-Rothschild, 1977).

THE GENESIS OF LOVE

What is the origin of passionate and companionate love? Love seems to be a primitive phenomenon. Rosenblum (1985), a primatologist, has observed that even nonhuman primates seem to experience something very much like passionate/companionate love. The ability to love seems to be wired into all primates. In infancy, primates cling to their mothers, and as long as mother and child are in close proximity, all goes well. If a brief separation occurs, however, the young primate becomes desperate. He howls and rushes frantically about, searching for her. When the mother returns, the young primate is joyous; he clasps her and then bounds about in excitement. If the mother does not return and his frantic efforts to find her fail, the infant abandons all hope, and eventually dies (see Bowlby, 1973). The passionate experiences Rosenblum describes certainly sound much like passionate love's "desire for union"—and its accompanying lows and highs. The contentment infants feel in the secure company of their mothers sounds much like companionate love. Our primate wiring, I thought, provides the basis for passionate/companionate attachments.

Ainsworth, Blehar, Waters, and Wall (1978) and Bowlby (1973) describe an identical process of attachment, separation, and loss in children. Here, for example, is Bowlby's description of the way the desire for security and the desire for freedom alternate in a toddler:

> James Anderson describes watching two-year-olds whilst their mothers sit quietly on a seat in a London park. Slipping free from the mother, a two-year-old would typically move away from her in short bursts punctuated by halts. Then, after a more prolonged halt, he would return to her—usually in faster and longer bursts. Once returned, however, he would proceed again on another foray, only to return once more. It was as though he were tied to his mother by some invisible elastic that stretches so far and then brings him back to base. (pp. 44–45)

When a child's mother is around, he's usually not overly interested in her. He glances at her, sees that everything is all right, and sallies forth. Now and then he sneaks a quick glance to make sure she's still there or to check whether she still approves of what he's doing, but then he's off again. But should his mother disappear for a moment, it is a different story. The child becomes distressed and agitated. He devotes all his energy to searching for her. New adventures lose all allure. Of course, once she returns, he's off again. Should she disappear permanently, the child eventually despairs. Children, then, seem to be prewired to "long for union," to take pleasure at its attainment, and to worry or despair when love is absent. Shaver, Hazan, and Bradshaw (1984) attempt to spell out the way these childhood experiences may be reflected in adult love reactions. They observe that the child who has grown up with a secure mother may be prone to experience companionate love, and the child who experiences "anxious attachment" may be especially susceptible to the drama of passionate love in adulthood. But children who have given up on love tend to be relatively immune to love in adulthood.

There is some evidence that all people—regardless of age (see Hatfield, Easton, Synodinos, & Schmitz, 1985; Traupmann & Hatfield, 1981), gender (see Hatfield & Rapson, 1985), ethnic group (see Easton, 1985), intelligence, mental health, or the historical era in which they live (see Hatfield & Rapson, 1985)—are *capable* of passionate/companionate love and are likely to experience such feelings intermittently throughout their lives. How frequently they experience such feelings is probably shaped by the extent to which society rewards or punishes such expressive displays.

In the first major section of this chapter, I will focus at length on what is known about passionate love (passionate emotions are the subject of the chapter). In the second section I will briefly sketch what is known about companionate love (other chapters in this book will focus on this form of love). In the last section, I will discuss the practical implications of recent research into passionate love.

WHAT IS PASSIONATE LOVE?

To repeat my definition of passionate love: it is "*a state of intense longing for union with another. Reciprocated love (union with the other) is associated with fulfillment and ecstasy. Unrequited love (separation) with emptiness, anxiety, or despair. A state of profound physiological arousal*" (p. 9).

The Passionate Love Scale (PLS) was recently developed to measure this emotion (see table 9.1). The PLS contains cognitive, emotional, and behavior indicants of "longing for union."

Cognitive components:

1. Intrusive thinking or preoccupation with the partner (in table 9.1, items 5, 19, and 21 tap this component).
2. Idealization of the other or of the relationship (items 7, 9, and 15 measure this component).
3. Desire to know the other and be known (item 10 measures the desire to know; item 22 measures the desire to be known).

Emotional components:

1. Attraction to other, especially sexual attraction; positive feelings when things go well (see items 16, 18, and 29).

2. Negative feelings when things go awry (see items 1, 2, 8, 20, 28, and 30).
3. Longing for reciprocity; passionate lovers not only love but want to be loved in return (item 14).
4. Desire for complete and permanent union (items 11, 12, 23, and 27).
5. Physiological arousal (items 3, 13, 17, and 26).

Behavioral components—a passionate lover's desire for union may be reflected in a variety of behaviors:

1. Actions toward determining the other's feelings (item 24).
2. Studying the other person (item 4).
3. Service to the other (items 6 and 25).
4. Maintaining physical closeness (the authors of the PLS had hoped to include some items designed to measure lovers' efforts to get physically close to the other, but lovers did not endorse such items, and they were dropped from the final version of the scale).

In sum, passionate love comprises cognitive, emotional, and behavioral components. (See Hatfield & Sprecher, 1985; Easton, 1985; Hatfield et al., 1985; and Sullivan, 1985; for information on the reliability and validity of the PLS.)

Scientists have long been aware that both mind and body shape emotional experience. The semiconscious assumptions people carry in their minds about what they *should* be feeling have a profound impact on what they *do* feel. People learn from society, parents, friends, and their own personal experiences who is appealing, what passion feels like, and how lovers behave. Thus cognitive factors influence how men and women interpret their feelings. But people can experience an emotion only if they experience the neurochemical and autonomic nervous system reactions appropriate to a given emotion. Thus, both mind and body make indispensable contributions to emotion. Cognitive factors determine how people will perceive, interpret, and encode emotional experiences. Physiological factors determine both what emotion they feel and how intensely they feel that emotion (see Hatfield & Walster, 1978).

The Nature of Passionate Love

For centuries, theorists have bitterly disagreed over the nature of love. Is it an intensely pleasurable experience, a painful one, or both? Early

TABLE 9.1 Passionate Love Scale

In this section of the questionnaire you will be asked to describe how you feel when you are passionately in love. Some common terms for this feeling are passionate love, infatuation, love sickness, or obsessive love.

Please think of the person whom you love most passionately *right now*. If you are not in love right now, please think of the last person you loved passionately. If you have never been in love, think of the person whom you came closest to caring for in that way. Keep this person in mind as you complete this section of the questionnaire. (The person you choose should be of the opposite sex if you are heterosexual or of the same sex if you are homosexual.) Try to tell us how you felt at the time when your feelings were the most intense.

All of your answers will be strictly confidential.

1. Since I've been involved with _____, my emotions have been on a roller coaster.
*2. I would feel deep despair if _____ left me.
3. Sometimes my body trembles with excitement at the sight of_____.
4. I take delight in studying the movements and angles of _____'s body.
*5. Sometimes I feel I can't control my thoughts; they are obsessively on_____.
*6. I feel happy when I am doing something to make _____ happy.
*7. I would rather be with _____ than anyone else.
*8. I'd get jealous if I thought _____ were falling in love with someone else.
9. No one else could love _____ like I do.
*10. I yearn to know all about _____.
*11. I want _____—physically, emotionally, mentally. .
12. I will love _____ forever.
13. I melt when looking deeply into _____'s eyes.
*14. I have an endless appetite for affection from _____.
*15. For me, _____ is the perfect romantic partner.
16. _____ is the person who can make me feel the happiest.
*17. I sense my body responding when _____ touches me.
18. I feel tender toward _____.
*19. _____ always seems to be on my mind.
20. If I were separated from _____ for a long time, I would feel intensely lonely.
21. I sometimes find it difficult to concentrate on work because thoughts of _____ occupy my mind.
*22. I want _____ to know me—my thoughts, my fears, and my hopes.
23. Knowing that _____ cares about me makes me feel complete.
*24. I eagerly look for signs indicating _____'s desire for me.
25. If _____ were going through a difficult time, I would put away my own concerns to help him/her out.
26. _____ can make me feel effervescent and bubbly.
27. In the presence of _____, I yearn to touch and be touched.
28. An existence without _____ would be dark and dismal.
*29. I possess a powerful attraction for _____.
*30. I get extremely depressed when things don't go right in my relationship with _____.

Possible responses to each item range from:

1	2	3	4	5	6	7	8	9
Not at all true				Moderately true				Definitely true

*Indicates items selected for a short version of the PLS.

researchers took the position that passionate love was a thoroughly positive experience. Such a vision is often depicted in contemporary films. For example, in Diane Kurys's *Cocktail Molotov*, seventeen-year-old Anne falls head over heels in love with Frederic after he declares his love for her. Scenes of their wild, exuberant, coltish love remind us of the delights of passion.

Theorists such as Kendrick and Cialdini (1977) once argued that passionate love could easily be explained by reinforcement principles—passionate feelings were fueled by positive reinforcements and dampened by negative ones. Byrne (1971) reported a series of carefully crafted studies to demonstrate that people love/like those who reward them and hate/dislike those who punish them. (See Berscheid & Hatfield [1969] for a review of this research.)

By the 1960s, however, social psychologists had begun to develop a far more complicated concept of love. Sometimes passionate love *is* a joyously exciting experience, sparked by exciting fantasies and rewarding encounters with the loved one. But that is only part of the story. Passionate love is like any other form of excitement. By its very nature, excitement involves a continuous interplay between elation and despair, thrills and terror. Think, for example, of the mixed and rushed feelings that novice skiers experience. Their hearts begin to pound as they wait to catch the ski lift. When they realize they have made it, they are relieved. On the easy ride to the top, they are still a bit unnerved; their hands shake and their knees tremble, but they begin to relax. Moments later they look ahead and realize it is time to jump off the lift. The landing looks icy. Their rush quickly turns to panic. They can't turn back. They struggle to get their feelings under control. They jump off the lift, elated and panicky—it is hard to tell which emotion predominates. Then they start to ski downhill, experiencing as they go a wild jumble of powerful emotions. Eventually, they arrive at the bottom of the hill, elated, relieved. Perhaps they feel like crying. Sometimes they are so tired they are flooded with a wave of depression, but usually they get up, ready to try again. Passionate lovers experience the same roller coaster of feelings— euphoria, happiness, calm tranquillity, vulnerability, anxiety, panic, despair. The risks of love merely add fuel to the fire.

Sometimes men and women become entangled in love affairs in which the delight is brief, and pain, uncertainty, jealousy, misery, anxiety, and despair are abundant. Reviewer Blake Lucas (1984) describes just such a passionate relationship in his review of Rainer Werner Fassbinder's fifteen-and-a-half-hour film *Berlin Alexanderplatz*:

From his first low-angle close-up in a bar in the opening minute of the episode, Reinhold . . . the man who will become the key individual in Franz's destiny, is a mesmerizing figure. Lean and intense, with features that are a cross between the reptilian and the hawklike, [Reinhold] immediately becomes a figure who arouses contradictory emotions. Fassbinder suggests through camera placement and dramatic emphasis that there is something dangerous, perhaps evil, about him; but John's skillful projection of vulnerability by means of a subtly underplayed stutter . . . makes the character strangely pitiable, often in the moments that his behavior is most unpredictable and frightening. Franz and Reinhold are drawn to each other almost immediately. (pp. 61–62)

Often, passionate love seems to be fueled by a sprinkling of hope and a large dollop of loneliness, mourning, jealousy, and terror. In fact, in a few cases, it seems as if these men and women love others not *in spite of* the pain they experience, but *because* of it.

Recent social psychological research makes it clear why passionate love, which thrives on excitement, might be linked to a variety of strong related emotions—both positive and negative (see Hatfield & Walster, 1978).

Cognitive Factors

Society describes love in mixed ways.

Tennov (1979) interviewed more than five hundred passionate lovers. Almost all lovers took it for granted that passionate love (which Tennov labels "limerence") is a bittersweet experience. Liebowitz (1983) provides an almost lyrical description of the mixed nature of passionate love:

Love and romance seems [*sic*] to be one, if not the most powerful activator of our pleasure centers. . . . Both tend to be very exciting emotionally. Being with the person or even just thinking of him or her is highly stimulating. . . . Love is, by definition, the strongest positive feeling we can have. Other things—stimulant drugs, passionate causes, manic states—can induce powerful changes in our brains, but none so reliably, so enduringly, or so delightfully as that "right" other person. . . . If the relationship is not established or is uncertain, anxiety or other displeasure centers may be quite active as well, producing a situation of great emotional turmoil as the lover swings between hope and torment. (pp. 48–49)

It is clear, then, that people assume it is appropriate to use the term *passionate love* to label any "intense longing for union with another," regardless of whether that longing is reciprocated (and thus a source of fulfillment and ecstasy) or is thwarted (and thus a source of emptiness, anxiety, or despair).

The Physiological Component of Love

Recently, psychologists have assembled information from neuroanatomical and neurophysiological investigations, ablation experiments, pharmacologic explorations, clinical investigations, and behavioral research as to the nature of love. This research, too, documents the contention that passionate love is a far more complicated phenomenon that it had at first seemed. (See Kaplan's [1979] discussion of the neuroanatomy and neurophysiology of sexual desire and Liebowitz's [1983] discussion of the chemistry of passionate love, for lengthy reviews of this research.)

The Anatomy of Love

According to Kaplan (1979), the anatomy of passionate love/sexual desire is relatively well understood. The brain's sex center consists of a network of neural centers and circuits. These are centered within the limbic system—with nuclei in the hypothalamus and in the preoptic region. The limbic system is located in the limbus, or rim of the brain. In primitive vertebrates, this system controls emotion and motivation; it ensures that animals will act so as to secure their own survival and that of their species. In man, this archaic system remains essentially unchanged. It is here that men's and women's most powerful emotions are generated, their behavior most powerfully driven. In the sex centers, scientists have identified both activating and inhibitory centers.

The sexual system has extensive neural connections with other parts of the brain. For example, it has significant connections, both neural and chemical, with the brain's pleasure and pain centers. All behavior is shaped by the seeking of pleasure (seeking stimulation of the pleasure center) and the avoidance of pain (avoiding stimulation of the pain center).

Chemical receptor sites located on the neurons of the pleasure centers respond to a chemical that is produced by the brain cells. This has been tagged an "endorphin" because it resembles morphine chemically and physiologically—it causes euphoria and alleviates pain. Kaplan observes, "It may be speculated that eating and sex and being in love, *i.e.*, behaviors which are experienced as pleasurable, produce this sensation by stimulation of the pleasure centers, electrically, or by causing the release of endorphins, or by both mechanisms" (p. 11).

Sexual desire is also anatomically and/or chemically connected with the pain centers. If sexual partners or experiences are associated with pain, they will cease to evoke sexual desire. A chemical mediator for pain, analogous to endorphin, may exist. Our brains are organized so that pain takes priority over pleasure. This, of course, makes sense from an evolutionary point of view.

Kaplan acknowledges that cognitive factors have a profound impact on sexual desire. Thus, the cortex—that part of the brain that analyzes complex perceptions and stores and retrieves memories—must have extensive neural connections with the sex center.

The Chemistry of Love

Psychologists are beginning to learn more about the chemistry of passionate love and a potpourri of related emotions. They are also learning more about the way that various emotions, positive and negative, interact.

Liebowitz (1983) has been the most willing to speculate about the chemistry of love. He argues that passionate love brings on a giddy feeling comparable to an amphetamine high. It is phenylethylamine (PEA), an amphetamine-related compound, that produces the mood-lifting and energizing effects of romantic love. He observes that "love addicts" and drug addicts have a lot in common: the craving for romance is merely the craving for a particular kind of high. The fact that most romances lose some of their intensity with time may well be due to normal biological processes.

The crash that follows a breakup is much like amphetamine withdrawal. Liebowitz speculates that there may be a chemical counteractant to lovesickness: MAO (monoamine oxidase) inhibitors may inhibit the breakdown of PEA, thereby "stabilizing" the lovesick.

Liebowitz also offers some speculations about the chemistry of the emotions that crisscross lovers' consciousness as they plunge from the highs to the lows of love. The highs include euphoria, excitement, relaxation, spiritual feelings, and relief. The lows include anxiety, terrifying panic attacks, the pain of separation, and the fear of punishment. His speculations are based on the assumption that nondrug and drug highs and lows operate via similar changes in brain chemistry.

To account for lovers' feelings of *excitement*, Liebowitz proposes that naturally occurring brain chemicals, similar to such stimulants as amphetamine and cocaine, produce the rush they feel. Passionate love is surely most tightly tied to these chemical reactions. A variety of other emotions, and a variety of other chemical reactions, may contribute to the subtle shadings of passionate love, however. Liebowitz articulates some of the chemical reactions that may be threaded through the passionate experience. Inducing *relaxation* are chemicals related to the narcotics (such as heroin, opium, and morphine), tranquilizers (such as Librium and Valium), seda- tives (such as barbiturates, Quaaludes, and other "downers"), alcohol (which acts chemically much like the sedatives), and marijuana and other cannabis derivatives. They produce a mellow state and wipe out anxiety, loneliness, panic attacks, and depression. Chemicals similar to the psyche- delics (such as LSD, mescaline, and psilocybin) produce a sense of beauty, meaningfulness, and timelessness—all *spiritual peak experiences*.

Physiologists do not usually try to produce *separation anxiety*, *panic attacks*, or *depression*. Such painful feelings may arise from two sources, however: (1) withdrawal from the chemicals that produce the highs and (2) chemicals that in and of themselves produce anxiety, pain, or depression. Research has not yet established whether Liebowitz's speculations as to the chemistry of love are correct.

Kaplan (1978) provides some information as to the chemistry of *sexual desire*. In both men and women, testosterone (and perhaps LH-RF) are the libido hormones. Dopamine may act as a stimulant, serotonin or 5-HT as inhibitors, to the sexual centers of the brain. Kaplan observes:

> When we are in love, libido is high. Every contact is sensuous, thoughts turn to Eros, and the sexual reflexes work rapidly and well. The presence of the beloved is an aphrodisiac; the smell, sight, sound, and touch of the lover—especially when he/she is excited—are powerful stimuli to sexual desire. In physiologic terms, this may exert a direct physical effect on the neurophysiologic system in the brain which regulates sexual desire. . . . But again, there is no sexual stimulant so powerful, even love, that it cannot be inhibited by fear and pain. (p. 14)

Kaplan ends by observing that a wide array of cognitive and phys- iological factors shape desire.

Finally, although passionate love and the related emotions we have described may be associated with specific chemical neurotransmitters (or with chemicals that increase/decrease the receptors' sensitivity), *most emo- tions have more similarities than differences*. Finck (1891) made an inter- esting observation. He observed that "love can only be excited by strong and vivid emotion, and it is almost immaterial whether these emotions are agreeable or disagreeable" (p. 240). Negative emotions, he thought, could enhance, if not incite, the positive emotion of love. Chemically, intense emotions do have much in common. Kaplan reminds us that chemically, love, joy, sexual desire, and excitement, as well as anger, fear, jealousy, and hate, have much in common: they are all intensely arousing. They all produce a sympathetic response in the nervous system. This is evidenced by the symptoms associated with all these emotions—a flushed face, sweaty palms, weak knees, butterflies in the stomach, dizziness, a pounding heart, trembling hands, and accelerated breathing. (The exact *pattern* of reaction varies from person to person; see Lacey [1967].)

Recent neuroanatomical/neurophysiological research suggests that the various emotions probably have tighter links than psychologists once thought. This is consistent with the recognition that in a passionately exciting encounter, people can move from elation through terror to the depths of despair and back again in a matter of seconds. Excitement may be confusing, but at least it's arousing. Such observations led Hatfield and Walster (1978) to conclude that passion can be ignited by pleasure and/or by pain—by delight in the other's presence or pain at the other's loss.

Recently, other researchers have begun to examine the exact nature of these interlinkages (see, for example, Zillman, 1984).

Behavioral Evidence that Both Pleasure and Pain May Fuel Emotion

Passionate love is such a risky business. Success sparks delight; failure invites despair. We get some indication of the strength of our passion by the intensity of our delight/despair. Of course, trying to calibrate our emotions is an elusive business. Sometimes it is difficult to tell to what extent your lover is responsible for the delight you feel versus the extent to which the highs you are experiencing are due to the fact that, say, you are ready for romance, or that the day is a glorious one, or that you are simply feeling good. It is difficult to tell to what extent your lover's coolness is responsible for your misery. To what extent is it due to the fact that you are lonely, or that you are afraid to go off on your own, or that your period is about to begin, or that you're simply "low"? Often it is hard to tell. In any case, there is an abundance of evidence to support the contention that, under the right conditions, a variety of intensely positive experiences, intensely negative ones, or neutral but energizing experiences can add to the passion of passion. Hatfield and Walster (1978) have labeled this process the "cross-magnification" or "chemical spill-over" effect.

PASSION AND THE POSITIVE EMOTIONS. In our definition of love we stated, "*Reciprocated love (union with the other) is associated with fulfillment and ecstasy.*" No one has doubted that love is a delightful experience in its own right—it is such a high that the joys of love generally spill over and add sparkle to everything else in life. What has been of interest to psychologists, however, is the converse of this proposition: that the central and peripheral activation associated with a wide variety of highs can spill over and make passion more passionate (a sort of "better loving through chemistry" phenomenon).

A number of carefully crafted studies makes it clear that a variety of positive activities or emotions—listening to a comedy routine, such as Steve Martin's "a wild and crazy guy" (White, Fishbein, & Rutstein, 1982), sexual fantasizing (Stephan, Berscheid, & Hatfield, 1971), erotic excitement (Istvan & Griffitt, 1978), or general excitement (Zuckerman, 1979)—can intensify passion.

In one investigation, for example, Istvan, Griffitt, and Weider (1983) aroused some men by showing them pictures of men and women engaged in sexual activities. Other men were shown nonarousing neutral fare. Then they asked the men to evaluate the appeal of beautiful and unattractive women. When the woman was pretty, the aroused men rated her as more attractive than they normally would; when the woman was unattractive, the aroused men rated her as less attractive than they normally would. Apparently the men's sexual arousal spilled over and intensified whatever they would normally have felt for the woman—for good or ill. Similar results have been secured with women. Sexually aroused women find handsome men more appealing, and homely men less appealing, than usual.

PASSION AND THE NEGATIVE EMOTIONS. In defining passionate love we also observed, "*Unrequited love (separation) is associated with emptiness, anxiety, or despair.*" Psychologists have long observed that the failure to acquire or sustain love is an extraordinarily painful experience. Theorists such as Bowlby (1973), Peplau and Perlman (1982), and Weiss (1973) describe the panic, despair, and eventual detachment that both children and adults feel at the loss of someone they love.

By now, psychologists have amassed considerable evidence that people are especially vulnerable to love when their lives are turbulent. Passion *can* be intensified by the spillover of feeling from one realm to another. A variety of negative experiences has been found to deepen desire. For example, Dutton and Aron (1974), in two studies, discovered a close link between fear and sexual attraction.

In one experiment, the researchers invited men and women to participate in a learning experiment. When the men showed up, they found that their "partner" was a strikingly beautiful woman. They also discovered that, by signing up for the experiment, they had gotten more than they had bargained for. The experimenter was studying the effects of electric shock on learning. Sometimes the experimenter quickly went on to reassure the men that they'd been assigned to a control group and would be receiving only a barely perceptible tingle of a shock. At other times, the experimenter tried to terrify the men: he warned them that they'd be getting some pretty painful electric shocks.

Before the supposed experiment was to begin, the experimenter approached each man privately and asked how he felt about the beautiful coed who "happened" to be his partner. He asked the men to tell him, in confidence, how attracted he was to her ("How much would you like to ask her out for a date?" "How much would you like to kiss her?"). The investigators had predicted that fear would facilitate attraction, and it did. The terrified men found the women a lot sexier than did the calmer men.

In another study, the investigators compared reactions of young men crossing two bridges in North Vancouver. The first, the Capilano Canyon Suspension Bridge, is a 450-foot-long, 5-foot-wide span that tilts, sways, and wobbles over a 230-foot drop to rocks and shallow rapids below. The other bridge, a bit farther upstream, is a solid, safe structure. As each young man crossed the bridge, a good-looking college woman approached him. She explained that she was doing a class project and asked if he would fill out a questionnaire for her. When the man had finished, the woman offered to explain her project in greater detail. She wrote her telephone number on a piece of paper so the man could call her if he wanted more information. Which men called? Nine of the thirty-three men on the suspension bridge called her; only two of the men on the solid bridge called.

This study, of course, can be interpreted several ways. Perhaps the men who called really were interested in her project. Perhaps the adventurous men were more likely both to cross dangerous bridges and to call dangerous women. Perhaps it was not fear but relief at having survived the crossing that stimulated desire. It is always possible to find alternative explanations for any given study.

But by now there is a great deal of experimental and correlational evidence for the more intriguing contention that, under the right conditions, passion can be deepened by a variety of awkward and painful experiences—anxiety and fear (Aron, 1970; J. W. Brehm et al., 1978; Dienstbier, 1979; Dutton & Aron, 1974; Hoon, Wincze, & Hoon, 1977; Riordan & Tedeschi, 1983), embarrassment (Byrne, Przybyla, & Infantino, 1981), the discomfort of seeing others involved in conflict (Dutton, 1979), jealousy (Clanton & Smith, 1977), loneliness (Peplau & Perlman, 1982), anger

(Barclay, 1969), anger at parental attempts to break up an affair (Driscoll, Davis, & Lipetz, 1972), hearing grisly stories of a mob mutilating and killing a missionary while his family watched (White et al., 1981), or even grief.

PASSION AND EMOTIONALLY NEUTRAL AROUSAL. In fact, recent laboratory research indicates that passion can be stirred by excitation transfer from such emotionally neutral, but arousing experiences as riding an exercise bicycle (Cantor, Zillman, & Bryant, 1975) or jogging (White, Fishbein, & Rutstein, 1981).

White, Fishbein, and Rutstein (1981) conducted a series of elegant studies to demonstrate that passion can be intensified by any intense experience. In one experiment, some men (those in the high-arousal group) were required to engage in strenuous physical exercise (they ran in place for 120 seconds). Other men (those in the low-arousal group) ran in place for only 15 seconds. The men's mood was not effected by exertion. A variety of self-report questions and heart-rate measures established that these two groups varied greatly in arousal.

Men then watched a videotaped interview with a woman they expected soon to meet. Half of the time the woman was attractive, half of the time unattractive. After the interview, the men gave their first impression of the woman; they estimated her attractiveness and sexiness. They also indicated how attracted they felt to her, how much they wanted to kiss and date her.

The authors proposed that exertion-induced arousal would intensify men's reactions to the woman—for good or ill. Aroused subjects would be more attracted to the attractive confederate and more repulsed by the unattractive confederate than would subjects with lower levels of arousal. The authors found just that. If the woman was beautiful, the men who were aroused via exertion judged her to be unusually appealing. If the woman was unattractive, the men who were aroused via exertion judged her to be unusually unappealing. The effect of arousal, then, was to intensify a person's initial "intrinsic" attractiveness. Arousal enhanced the appeal of the pretty woman as much as it impaired the appeal of the homely one. (See Zillman [1984] for a review of this research on excitation transfer.)

The evidence suggests, then, that adrenalin makes the heart grow fonder. Delight is one stimulant of passionate love, yet anxiety and fear, or simply high arousal, can often play a part.

Each new discovery, of course, generates more questions. When do powerful emotions such as anxiety, anger, and fear stimulate passionate attraction? When do they destroy it? Answers to this question are obviously critically important. In my University of Hawaii human sexuality class I often find myself explaining in my lecture in week 1 that excitement, fear, and anxiety are important stimulants to passionate love—and explaining in week 10 that anxiety causes disorders of sexual desire and sexual dysfunction. Obviously, what we need now is a theoretical framework to guide us in predicting when powerful emotions will stimulate passion and when they will destroy it. As yet, no one has begun to answer this important question.

WHAT IS COMPANIONATE LOVE? INTIMACY?

Although the focus of this chapter is passionate love, I would like to devote a few paragraphs outlining how passionate love is similar to and different from companionate love. Earlier, we defined companionate love this way: *"The affection we feel for those with whom our lives are deeply entwined."*

What is intimacy? The word itself is derived from the Latin *intimus*, meaning "inner" or "inmost." In a wide variety of languages, the word *intimate* refers to a person's innermost qualities. For example, the French *intime* signifies "secret, deep, fervent, ardent." The Italian *intimo* conveys "internal, close in friendship." In Spanish, *intimo* means "private, close, innermost." To be intimate, then, means to be close to another. Hatfield (1984) defined intimacy as: *"A process in which people attempt to get close to another; to explore similarities (and differences) in the way they think, feel, and behave."*

Intimate relationships have a number of characteristics:

COGNITIVE. Intimates are willing to reveal themselves to one another. They disclose information about themselves and listen to their partners' confidences. In deeply intimate relationships, friends and lovers feel free to reveal most facets of themselves in all their complexities and contradictions. As a result, intimates share profound information about one another's histories, values, strengths, weaknesses, idiosyncrasies, hopes, and fears (Altman & Taylor, 1973; Huesmann & Levinger, 1976; Jourard, 1964).

EMOTIONAL. Intimates care deeply about one another. In passionate love, people usually long for intimacy; in companionate love people usually have it. It is in intimate relationships that people feel most intensely; they love their intimates more than anyone else. Yet, exactly because intimates care so much about one another, they have the power to elicit intense pain. The dark side of love is jealousy, loneliness, depression, and anger. It is this powerful interplay of conflicting emotions that gives vibrancy to the most intimate of relationships (see Berscheid, 1979, 1983; Hatfield & Walster, 1978).

BEHAVIORAL. Intimates are comfortable in close physical proximity. They gaze at one another (Argyle, 1967), lean on one another (Galton, 1884; Hatfield, Roberts & Schmidt, 1980), stand close to one another (Allgeier & Byrne, 1973), and perhaps touch.

These are the definitions of companionate love and intimacy that I will use in the remainder of this chapter.

I began this chapter by discussing the genesis of love, speculating that in primates, passionate and companionate love might be complementary forms of attachment. Passionate love seems to be a state of ecstasy/misery. The infant primate appears to feel most passionately when he first realizes that his mother is gone or when his mother returns after a short, painful absence. Companionate love seems to be an appropriate description for the gentle feelings of affection and attachment that primates feel for others when things are going well. The experience of companionate love seems much the same in human adults and children (see Hatfield et al., 1985; Berscheid & Hatfield, 1978).

Rubin (1970) argues that this type of love (which he terms "romantic love") includes such elements as responsibility for the other, tenderness, self-disclosure, and exclusivity. He has developed an excellent scale to measure what I would consider to be predominantly companionate love. It includes such items as "I feel that I can confide in ——— about virtually everything"; "I would do almost anything for ———"; and "If I could never be with ———, I would feel miserable."

Reinforcement theorists are generally agreed upon the conditions that foster companionate love—they argue that men and women come to love those who reward them and dislike those who punish them. Byrne (1971) has fashioned a rather elegant reinforcement model of interpersonal attraction from this commonsense observation. Byrne's "law of attraction" looks like this:

$$Y = m\left[\frac{\Sigma PR}{(\Sigma PR + \Sigma NR)}\right] + k$$

In Byrne's formula, Y stands for attraction, PR for positive reinforcement, and NR for negative reinforcement; k is a constant.

Byrne points out that we come to companionately love/like people who are merely *associated* with pleasure and to dislike those who are associated with pain. How much companionate love we feel for others, then, should be a direct function of how secure, pleasant, and reinforcing we find their company to be. Insecurity, unpleasantness, and punishment should only detract from this form of love. (For research in support of this contention, and a review of the wide array of things men and women generally find to be reinforcing, see Berscheid & Hatfield, 1978; Byrne, 1971; Hatfield et al., 1984; Duck & Gilmour, 1981–1984.)

Superficially, it would seem that a theoretical principle differentiates passionate love from companionate love: passionate love seems to be fueled by ecstasy or misery, whereas companionate love is intensified only by pleasure; any sprinkling of pain *decreases* companionate feelings. In the main this formulation holds. There is, however, one bit of untidiness in this neat formulation.

In the past, reinforcement theorists could justly be criticized for being simplistic about the things that couples would find reinforcing/nonreinforcing/punishing in their most intimate affairs. Somehow the "maximally rewarding relationship" scientists described always sounded rather boring. Ideally, couples would be locked in total agreement, smiling and nodding at one another, avoiding all stress. Of course, in real relationships, the rewards men and women long for are diverse. Some like partners who will agree with them, but others long for a little spirited debate. Some of us prefer saintly partners, but many of us like others who are no better than ourselves. It is rather a relief when both partners know in their bones that they will be able to make a thousand mistakes and the relationship will still hold together. For most couples, in the long run, an intimate encounter is the ultimate reward, and intimate relationships are a mixed bag of rewards and frustrations.

In sum, it seems that passionate love is fueled by passionate experiences, good and bad, whereas companionate love is fueled by positive experiences and dampened by painful ones. In general, this statement seems to be true. But companionate love and intimacy exist in the real world, and real-world relationships involve both rewards and punishments. The difference, then, between passionate love and companionate love seems to be one of emphasis rather than absolute differences. Passionate love involves ecstasy/misery. Companionate love flourishes in a mixture of pleasure sprinkled occasionally with real-life frustrations.

Most people, of course, hope to combine the delights of passionate love with the security of companionate love in their intimate relationships—and this, of course, takes some doing. Recently, no end of clinicians have come forward to tell them how to do the impossible.

IMPLICATIONS FOR INTIMATE RELATIONSHIPS

In the first section I traced the history of social psychological research on passionate love, and in the second section I reviewed what psychologists know about companionate love. At the same time this basic research was being conducted, clinical psychologists, too, were conducting studies on love and intimate relationships. Their research, however, leaned heavily on clinical observation. They, too, by a very different route, have come to recognize that passionate, intimate love relationships are far more complicated than they had originally believed. Clinicians started out thinking of family relationships as relatively straightforward, capable of rigorous control. They ended up recognizing that relationships are as muddy and mixed as life itself. This recognition has caused marital and family therapists to devise somewhat different strategies for dealing with intimate encounters.

Thus, in the 1940s to the 1960s, clinicians, especially those with a behaviorist bent, tended to think of passionate love and intimate relationships in fairly simple ways. Love and intimacy would thrive best on a steady diet of pleasant interactions; unpleasantness was to be avoided at all costs. This vision shaped the advice early behaviorists gave couples.

In social situations, men and women have a choice as to which of two very different strategies they will adopt—they can act as performers or as intimates.

THE PERFORMING MODE. In some situations—when one is acting in a theater company, interviewing for a job as a salesman, or dealing with people whom one has little reason to trust—one must give a performance. The individual tries to look one's best (or worst), act confidently (or shyly), be rewarding (or punishing). Scales such as Christie's Mach II (Christie & Geis, 1970) or Snyder's Self-Monitoring Scale (Snyder, 1974; Lennox & Wolfe, 1984; Gangestad & Snyder, 1985) measure such manipulative abilities.

THE INTIMATE MODE. In some situations, such as dealing with intimate lovers, family members, and friends, one wants to be as relaxed and honest as possible. Scales such as Schaefer & Olson's Intimacy Scale (1984) or Miller's Intimacy Measure (Miller & Lefocurt, 1982) measure such intimacy skills. In most real-life encounters, men and women engage in a balancing act between performing and intimacy.

In the 1950s, behavioristically oriented clinicians concentrated on teaching men and women how to reward their mates for acting as they wished them to (see Patterson, 1971, Jacobson & Margolin, 1949, or

Berscheid & Hatfield, 1969). Popular authors such as Andelin (1971) advised women to be at the door with a cold martini when their husbands came home. They should have the house spotlessly clean and the children snugly tucked in. Such advice was fine, but it had two shortcomings: (1) the husband might be delighted with all the positive reinforcements he was receiving, but women were getting madder and madder at the inequity, and (2) such relationships were singularly lacking in intimacy—couples were giving a performance. (It is interesting in this regard that the reward Andelin promised wives in return for all their work was not intimacy, but a new stove and refrigerator.)

Sometimes putting on a show is necessary. It can be useful to be able to hold your tongue, to slow things down when that's what's called for. But a relationship that is all acting is no relationship at all.

Recently, the pendulum has begun to shift. Cognitive psychologists (Tavris, 1982; Paolino & McCrady, 1978), family therapists (Guerin, 1976; Napier & Whitaker, 1978), existential humanists (Yalom, 1980), gestalt therapists (Polster & Polster, 1973), eclectic therapists (Offit, 1977; Pope & Associates, 1980), and social psychologists (Brehm, 1985; Duck & Gilmour, 1981–1984) have begun to shape the way people think about relationships. Clinicians now take it for granted that love and intimate relationships are extraordinarily complex phenomena. One person, the performer, just cannot manipulate a relationship into perfection. It takes two, and even then the matter is difficult. In relationships, there are rarely blacks and whites; real existence inhabits the area between, in many shades of gray. One simply has to recognize that life is muddy and to try to enjoy, as best as possible, sloshing around in it. Increasingly, clinicians are involved in teaching their clients intimacy skills, which are fundamental to a relationship. Manipulation is a more limited talent, to be used when a special intractable problem arises.

In sum, in a few situations in life, the only thing one can do is to play out a stereotyped role. In most situations, one has to be at least tactful; in a few situations, downright manipulation may be called for if one is to survive. But on those occasions when real intimacy is possible, independent men and women can recognize its promise, seize the opportunities, and take chances.

A Prescription for Intimacy

Nearly everyone needs a warm intimate relationship. At the same time, one must recognize that in every social encounter there are some risks.

What, then, is the solution? Social psychological research and clinical experience gives us some hints.

A basic theoretical assumption provides the framework we use in teaching people how to be intimate with others. To acquire this ability, people must be capable of independence. Independence and intimacy are not opposing personality traits, but interrelated skills. People who lack the ability to be independent can never really be intimate. Lovers who are dependent on their mates, who cannot get along in life without the other, are precisely those least likely to reveal their fears, irritations, and anxieties to the other lest the partner leave the relationship. They are walking on eggshells, anxious not to upset or anger their mate with their darker interior concerns. They dare not risk intimacy. Independent persons, on the other hand, who know they can make it on their own are in a position to be brave about insisting on intimacy. They're not willing to settle for mates who don't care and can't listen. They can afford to be unusually brave about sharing their innermost lives with their mates.

Dr. Richard Rapson and I have worked as marital and family therapists at King Kalakaua Center for Psychotherapy in Honolulu. Most of the couples who come to see us have trouble initiating, maintaining, and terminating relationships. During the course of therapy, we often set out to teach these people intimacy skills. We try to make couples comfortable with the notion that they are separate people, with separate ideas and feelings, who can nevertheless sometimes come profoundly close to others.

According to theorists, one of the most difficult tasks people face is to learn how to maintain their own identity and integrity while yet engaging in deeply intimate relationships with others (for a fuller discussion of this point, see Hatfield, 1984).

Argyle (1967) and Hatfield (1985) have attempted to provide detailed information on teaching people to be more intimate in their love relationships. The advice they and we give is as follows:

Developing Intimacy Skills

1. *Encouraging people to accept themselves as they are*: It is a great temptation to dwell in the realm of absolutes. One is either a saint or a sinner. Many people are determined to be perfect (at least); they can't settle for less.

Yet saintliness/evil are the least interesting of human conditions. Real life is lived in the middle zone. Real people inevitably have strengths, yet everybody possesses small quirks that make them what they are. One trick to enjoying life is not just to accept diversity but to learn to take pleasure in it.

The first step in learning to be independent/intimate, then, is for people to come to accept the fact that they are entitled to be what they are, that their ideas and their feelings are legitimate. Doing the best they can do is good enough.

In therapy, we try to move people from the notion that one should come into the world perfect and continue that way to a realization that one can gain wisdom only in small steps. People must pick one small goal and work to accomplish it. When that is accomplished, they can move on to another. That way change is manageable, possible (Watson & Tharp, 1981). One can never attain perfection; one can only work toward it.

2. *Encouraging people to recognize their intimates for what they are*: People may be hard on themselves, but they can be even harder on their partners. Most people have the idea that everyone is entitled to a perfect partner, or at least one a little bit better than the one available (see Hatfield et al., 1981). If people are going to have an intimate relationship, they have to learn to enjoy others as they are without hoping to "fix them."

It is extraordinarily difficult for people to accept that their friends are entitled to be the people they are. From our own point of view, it seems so clear that things would be far better if our mates were only the people we wanted them to be. It would take so little for them to change their whole character structure. Why are they so stubborn?

When men and women come to the realization that their lovers or friends are the people who exist right now—not the mates they wish them to be, not the mates they could be—intimacy becomes possible.

3. *Encouraging people to express themselves*: Next, intimates have to learn to be more comfortable about expressing their ideas and feelings. This is harder than one might think.

People's intimate relationships are usually their most important ones. When passions are so intense, consequences so momentous, people are often hesitant to speak the truth. From moment to moment, they are tempted to present a consistent picture. If they're in love, they are hesitant to admit to any niggling doubts. (What if the person they love is hurt? What if their revelations destroy the relationship?) When they are angry, they don't want to speak about their love or their self-doubts; they want to lash out.

To be intimate, people have to push toward a more honest, graceful, complete, and patient communication; to understand that a person's ideas and feelings are necessarily complex, with many nuances, shadings, and inconsistencies. In love there is time to clear things up.

One interesting thing that people often discover is that their affection increases when they begin to admit their irritations. People are often surprised to discover that sometimes, when they think they have fallen out of love and are bored with their affair, if they begin to express their anger and ambivalence, they feel their love come back in a rush.

In *The Family Crucible* Napier and Whitaker (1978) describe just such a confrontation:

> What followed was a classic confrontation. If John's affair was a kind of reawakening, so now was this marital encounter, though of a very different sort. Eleanor was enraged, hurt, confused, and racked with a sense of failure. John was guilty, also confused, but not apologetic. The two partners fought and cried, talked and searched for an entire night. The next evening, more exhausting encounters. Feelings that had been hidden for years emerged; doubts and accusations that they had never expected to admit articulated.
>
> Eleanor had to find out everything, and the more she discovered, the more insatiable her curiosity became. The more she heard, the guiltier her husband became and the angrier she grew, until he finally cried for a halt. It was his cry for mercy that finally led to a temporary reconciliation of the couple. They cried together for the first time either of them could remember.
>
> For a while they were elated; they had achieved a breakthrough in their silent and dreary marriage. They felt alive together for the first time in years. Somewhat mysteriously, they found themselves going to bed together in the midst of a great tangle of emotions—continuing anger, and hurt, and guilt, and this new quality: abandon. The love-making was, they were to admit to each other, "the best it had ever been." How could they have moved through hatred into caring so quickly? (p. 153)

Love and hate tend to flow together (Hatfield & Walster, 1978; Kaplan, 1979).

4. *Teaching people to deal with their intimate's reactions*: To say that people *should* communicate their ideas and feelings, that they *must* communicate if they are to have an intimate affair, does not mean their partners are going to like it. People must expect that it will hurt when they try to express their deepest feelings. Lovers and friends may tell them frankly how deeply they have hurt them and that will make them feel extremely guilty. Or they may react with intense anger.

Intimates have to learn to stop responding in automatic fashion to such emotional outbursts—to quit backing up, apologizing for what they have said, measuring their words. They have to learn to stay calm, remind themselves that they are entitled to say what they think, feel what they feel, listen to what their partners think and feel, and to keep on trying.

Only then is there a chance of an intimate encounter.

REFERENCES

Ainsworth, M. D. S., Blehar, M. C., Waters, E., & Wall, S. (1978). *Patterns of attachment: Assessed in the strange situation and at home.* Hillsdale, NJ: Lawrence Erlbaum.

Allgeier, A. R., & Byrne, D. (1973). Attraction toward the opposite sex as a determinant of physical proximity. *Journal of Social Psychology, 90,* 213–219.

Altman, I., & Taylor, D. A. (1973). *Social penetration: The development of interpersonal relationships.* New York: Holt.

Andelin, H. B. (1971). *Fascinating womanhood.* Santa Barbara, CA: Pacific Press.

Argyle, M. (1967). *The psychology of interpersonal behavior.* Baltimore: Penguin Books.

Aron, A. (1970). *Relationship variables in human heterosexual attraction.* Unpublished doctoral dissertation, University of Toronto, Toronto, Canada.

Aron, A., & Dutton, D. G. (1985). *Arousal, attraction and strong attractions.* Unpublished manuscript. Maharishi International University.

Averill, J. R. (1969). Autonomic response patterns during sadness and mirth. *Psychophysiology, 5,* 399–414.

Barclay, A. M. (1969). The effect of hostility on physiological and fantasy responses. *Journal of Personality, 37,* 651–667.

Berscheid, E. (1979). *Affect in close relationships.* Unpublished manuscript.

———. (1983). Emotion. In H. H. Kelley, E. Berscheid, A. Christensen, J. H. Harvey, T. Huston, G. Levinger, E. McClintock, L. A. Peplau, & D. R. Peterson (Eds.), *Close relationships* (pp. 110–168). New York: Freeman.

Berscheid, E. & Hatfield (Walster), E. (1969 and 1978). *Interpersonal attraction. Eds. 1 and 2.* Reading, MA: Addison-Wesley.

Berscheid, E., & Peplau, L. A. (1983). The emerging science of relationships. In H. H. Kelley, E. Berscheid, A. Christensen, J. H. Harvey, T. L. Huston, G. Levinger, E. McClintock, L. A. Peplau, & D. R. Peterson (Eds.), *Close relationships* (pp. 1–19). New York: Freeman.

Bowlby, J. (1973). Affectional bonds: Their nature and origin. In R. W. Weiss (Ed.), *Loneliness: The experience of emotional and social isolation.* Cambridge, MA: MIT Press.

Brehm, J. W., Gatz, M., Goethals, G., McCrimmon, J., & Ward, L. (1978). Psychological arousal and interpersonal attraction. *JSAS Catalogue of Selected Documents in Psychology, 8,* 63 (ms. 1724).

Brehm, S. (1985). *Intimate relationships.* New York: Random House.

Burgess, E. W. (1926). The romantic impulse and family disorganization. *Survey, 57,* 290–294.

Byrne, D. (1971). *The attraction paradigm*. New York: Academic Press.

Byrne, D., Przybyla, D. P. J., & Infantino, A. (1981, April). *The influence of social threat on subsequent romantic attraction*. Paper presented at the meeting of the Eastern Psychological Association, New York City.

Cantor, J., Zillman, D., & Bryant, J. (1975). Enhancement of experienced sexual arousal in response to erotic stimuli through misattribution of unrelated residual excitation. *Journal of Personality and Social Psychology, 32,* 69–75.

Christie, R., & Geis, F. L. (1970). *Studies in Machiavellianism*. New York: Academic Press.

Clanton, G., & Smith, L. G. (Eds.). (1977). *Jealousy*. Englewood Cliffs, NJ: Prentice-Hall.

Cunningham, J. D., & Antill, J. K. (1981). Love in developing romantic relationships. In S. Duck and R. Gilmour (Eds.), *Personal relationships 2: Developing personal relationships* (pp. 27–52). New York: Academic Press.

Dienstbier, R. A. (1979). Emotion-attribution theory: Establishing roots and exploring future perspectives. In H. E. Howe & R. A. Dienstbier (Eds.), *Nebraska symposium on motivation, 26*. Lincoln: University of Nebraska Press.

Driscoll, R., Davis, K. E., & Lipetz, M. E. (1972). Parental interference and romantic love: The Romeo and Juliet effect. *Journal of Personality and Social Psychology, 24,* 1–10.

Duck, S., & Gilmour, R. (Eds.). (1981–1984). *Personal relationships*. 5 vols. New York: Academic Press.

Dutton, D. (1979). *The arousal-attraction link in the absence of negative reinforcement*. Meetings of the Canadian Psychological Association, Toronto, Canada.

Dutton, D., & Aron, A. (1974). Some evidence for heightened sexual attraction under conditions of high anxiety. *Journal of Personality and Social Psychology, 30,* 510–517.

Easton, M. (1985). *Love and intimacy in a multi-ethnic setting*. Unpublished doctoral dissertation, University of Hawaii at Manoa, Honolulu.

Easton, M. J., Hatfield, E., & Synodinos, N. (1984). *Development of the juvenile love scale*. Unpublished manuscript, University of Hawaii, Honolulu.

Finck, H. T. (1891). *Romantic love and personal beauty: Their development, causal relations, historic and national peculiarities*. London: Macmillan.

Galton, F. (1884). Measurement of character. *Fortnightly Review, 36,* 179–185.

Gangestad, S., & Snyder, M. (1985). To carve nature at its joints: On the existence of discrete classes in personality. *Psychological Review, 92*(3), 1–90.

Guerin, P. J. (Ed.). (1976). *Family therapy: Theory and practice*. New York: Gardner Press.

Hatfield, E. (1984). The dangers of intimacy. In V. Derlaga (Ed.), *Communication, intimacy, and close relationships* (pp. 207–220). New York: Academic Press.

Hatfield, E., Easton, M., Synodinos, N., & Schmitz, E. (1985). *The development of the Juvenile Love Scale*. Paper presented at the meetings of the American Psychological Association, Los Angeles.

Hatfield, E., & Rapson, R. L. (1985). Gender differences in love and intimacy: The fantasy vs. the reality. In H. Gochros and W. Ricketts (Eds.), *Social work and love*. New York: Hayworth Press.

———. (1987). Passionate love: New directions in research. In D. Perlman & W.

Jones (Eds.), *Perspectives in interpersonal behavior and relationships*. New York: JAI Press.

Hatfield, E., Roberts, D., & Schmidt, L. (1980). The impact of sex and physical attractiveness on an initial social encounter. *Recherches de psychologie sociale*, 2, 27–40.

Hatfield, E., & Sprecher, S. (1986). Measuring passionate love in intimate relations. *Journal of Adolescence*, 9, 383–410.

Hatfield, E., Traupmann, J., Sprecher, S., Utne, M., & Hay, J. (1984). Equity and intimate relations: Recent research. In W. Ickes (Ed.), *Compatible and incompatible relationships* (pp. 1–27). New York: Springer-Verlag.

Hatfield, E., & Walster, G. W. (1978). *A new look at love*. Lantham, MA: University Press of America.

Hoon, P. W., Wincze, J. P., & Hoon, E. F. (1977). A test of reciprocal inhibition: Are anxiety and sexual arousal in women mutually inhibitory? *Journal of Abnormal Psychology*, 86(1), 65–74.

Huesmann, L. R., & Levinger, G. (1976). Incremental exchange theory: A formal model for progression in dyadic social interaction. In L. Berkowitz and E. Hatfield (Eds.), *Equity theory: Toward a general theory of social interaction* (pp. 192–230). New York: Academic Press.

Istvan, J., & Griffitt, W. (1978). *Emotional arousal and sexual attraction*. Unpublished manuscript, Kansas State University, Manhattan.

Istvan, S., Griffitt, W., & Weidner, G. (1983). Sexual arousal and the polarization of perceived sexual attractiveness. *Basic and Applied Social Psychology*, 4, 307–318.

Izard, C. (1972). *Patterns of emotions*. New York: Academic Press.

Jacobson, N. S., & Margolin, G. (1949). *Marital therapy: Strategies based on social learning and behavior exchange principles*. New York: Brunner/Mazel.

Jourard, S. M. (1964). *The transparent self*. Princeton: Van Nostrand.

Kaplan, H. S. (1979). *Disorders of sexual desire*. New York: Simón & Schuster.

Kelley, H. H. (1979). *Personal relationships: Their structures and processes*. Hillsdale, NJ: Erlbaum Press.

Kelley, H. H., Berscheid, E., Christensen, A., Harvey, J. H., Huston, T., Levinger, G., McClintock, E., Peplau, L. A., & Peterson, D. (1983). *Close relationships*. New York: Freeman.

Kendrick, D. T., & Cialdini, R. B. (1977). Romantic attraction: Misattribution vs. reinforcement explanations. *Journal of Personality and Social Psychology*, 35, 381–391.

Lacey, J. I. (1967). Somatic response patterning and stress: Some revisions of activation theory. In M. H. Appley & R. Trumbull (Eds.), *Psychological stress*. New York: Appleton.

Lee, J. A. (1977). *The colors of love*. New York: Bantam.

Lennox, R. D., & Wolfe, R. N. (1984). Revision of the self-monitoring scale. *Journal of Personality and Social Psychology*, 46(6):1349–1364.

Liebowitz, M. R. (1983). *The chemistry of love*. Boston: Little, Brown.

Lilar, S. (1965). *Aspects of love in Western society*. New York: McGraw-Hill.

Lucas, B. (1984). Rainer Werner Fassbinder's "Berlin Alexanderplatz." *Magill's Cinema Annual* (New York City), pp. 57–62.

Maslow, A. H. (1954). *Motivation and personality*. New York: Harper & Row.

Miller, R. S., & Lefocurt, H. M. (1982). *The assessment of social intimacy*. Unpublished manuscript, University of Waterloo, Waterloo, Ontario, Canada.

Napier, A., & Whitaker, C. (1978). *The family crucible*. New York: Harper & Row.

Offit, A. K. (1977). *The sexual self*. New York: Congdon & Weed.

Paolino, T. J., & McCrady, B. S. (1978). *Marriage and marital therapy*. New York: Brunner/Mazel.

Patterson, G. R. (1971). *Families: Applications of social learning to family life*. Champaign, IL: Research Press.

Peplau, L. A., & Perlman, D. (1982). *Loneliness*. New York: Wiley-Interscience.

Polster, E., and Polster, M. (1973). *Gestalt therapy integrated*. New York: Vintage.

Pope, K. S., & Associates (Eds.). (1980). *On love and loving*. San Francisco: Jossey-Bass.

Rapson, R. L. (1978). *Denials of doubt*. Washington, DC: University Press of America.

Riordan, C. A., & Tedeschi, J. T. (1983). Attraction in aversive environments: Some evidence for classical conditioning and negative reinforcement. *Journal of Personality and Social Psychology, 44*, 683–692.

Rosenblum, L. (1985, September 18). *Passion and the nonhuman primate*. Observations presented at the International Academy of Sex Research, Seattle.

Rubin, Z. (1970). Measurement of romantic love. *Journal of Personality and Social Psychology, 16*, 265–273.

Safilios-Rothschild, C. (1977). *Love, sex, and sex roles*. Englewood Cliffs, NJ: Prentice-Hall, Spectrum Books.

Schaefer, M. T., & Olson, D. H. (1984). *Diagnosing intimacy: The PAIR inventory*. Family Social Science, 290 McNeal Hall, University of Minnesota, St. Paul, MI 55108.

Shaver, P., Hazen, C., & Bradshaw, D. (1984, July). *Infant-caretaker attachment and adult romantic love*. Paper presented at the Second International Conference on Personal Relationships, Madison.

Snyder, M. (1974). Self-monitoring of expressive behavior. *Journal of Personality and Social Psychology, 30*(4), 526–537.

Stephan, W., Berscheid, E., & Hatfield (Walster), E. (1971). Sexual arousal and heterosexual perception. *Journal of Personality and Social Psychology, 20*, 93–101.

Sternberg, R. J. (1986). A triangular theory of love. *Psychological Review, 93*, 119–135.

Sullivan, B. O. (1985). *Passionate love: A factor analytic study*. Unpublished manuscript, University of Hawaii, Honolulu.

Tavris, C. (1982). *Anger: The misunderstood emotion*. New York: Simon & Schuster.

Tennov, D. (1979). *Love and limerence*. New York: Stein & Day.

Traupmann, J., & Hatfield, E. (1981). Love and its effect on mental and physical health. In R. Fogel, E. Hatfield, S. Kiesler, & E. Shanas (Eds.), *Aging: Stability and change in the family* (pp. 253–274). New York: Academic Press.

Watson, D. L., & Tharp, R. G. (1981). *Self-directed behavior* (3rd Ed.). Monterey, CA: Brooks-Cole.

Weiss, R. S. (1973). *Loneliness: The experience of emotional and social isolation.* Cambridge, MA: MIT Press.

White, G. L., Fishbein, S., & Rutstein, J. (1981). Passionate love and the misattribution of arousal. *Journal of Personality and Social Psychology, 41,* 56–62.

Yalom, I. (1980). *Existential psychotherapy.* New York: Basic Books.

Zillman, D. (1984). *Connections between sex and aggression.* Hillsdale, NJ: Lawrence Erlbaum.

Zuckerman, M. (1979). *Sensation seeking: Beyond the optimal level of arousal.* Hillsdale, NJ: Erlbaum.

CHAPTER TEN

A Vision of Romantic Love

BY NATHANIEL BRANDEN

The passionate attachment between man and woman that is known as romantic love can generate the most profound ecstasy. It can also generate, when frustrated, the most unutterable suffering. Yet for all its intensity, the nature of that attachment is little understood. To some who associate "romantic" with "irrational," romantic love is a temporary neurosis, an emotional storm, inevitably short-lived, which leaves disillusionment and disenchantment in its wake. To others, romantic love is an ideal that, if never reached, leaves one feeling one has somehow missed the secret of life.

Looking at the tragedy and confusion so many experience in romantic relationships, many persons have concluded that the idea of romantic love is somehow fundamentally wrong, a false hope. Romantic love is often attacked today by psychologists, sociologists, and anthropologists, who frequently scorn it as an immature, illusory ideal. To such intellectuals, the idea that an intense emotional attachment could form the basis of a lasting, fulfilling relationship is simply a neurotic product of modern Western culture.

Young people growing up in twentieth-century North America take for granted certain assumptions about their future with the opposite sex, assumptions that are by no means shared by all other cultures. These include that the two people who will share their lives will choose each other, freely and voluntarily, and that no one, not family or friends, church or state, can or should make that choice for them; that they will choose on the basis of love rather than on the basis of social, family, or financial considerations; that it very much matters which human beings they choose and, in this connection, that the differences between one human being and another are immensely important; that they can hope and expect to derive happiness from the relationship with the person of their choice and that the pursuit of such happiness is entirely normal, indeed is a human birthright; and that the person they choose to share their life with and the person they hope and expect to find sexual fulfillment with are one and the same. Throughout most of human history, all these views would have been regarded as extraordinary, even incredible.

Only during the past several decades have some of the educated classes in non-Western cultures rebelled against the tradition of marriage arranged by families and looked to the West and its concept of romantic love as a preferred ideal. Although in Western Europe the idea of romantic love (in some sense) has had a long history, its acceptance as the proper basis of marriage has never been as widespread as it has been in American culture. As Burgess and Locke (1953) write in their historical survey *The Family: From Institution to Companionship*, "It is in the United States that perhaps the only, at any rate the most complete, demonstration of romantic love as the prologue and theme of marriage has been staged."

Why the United States? The answer, at least in part, is philosophical. What was distinctive about the American outlook and represented a radical break with its European past were its unprecedented commitment to political freedom, its individualism, its doctrine of individual rights, and, more specifically, its belief in a person's right to happiness *here on earth*. Both the individualism and the secularism of this country were essential for the ideal of romantic love to take deep cultural root.

Even now, in the midst of the rampant cynicism and despair of the final decades of the twentieth century, and notwithstanding the attacks on romantic love by American intellectuals, people continue to fall in love. The dream dies, only to be reborn. Moved by a passion they do not understand for a goal they seldom reach, men and women are haunted by the vision of a distant possibility that refuses to be extinguished.

What, at its best, is the nature of that vision? And what does its realization depend on? That is the subject I wish to address.

I

Let us begin with a definition. There are, after all, different kinds of love that can unite one human being with another. There is love between parents and children. There is love between siblings. There is love between friends. There is a love made of caring and affection but devoid of sexual feeling. And there is the kind of love we call "romantic."

Romantic love is *a passionate spiritual-emotional-sexual attachment between two people that reflects a high regard for the value of each other's person*. When I write of romantic love, this is the meaning I intend.

I do not describe a relationship as romantic if the couple does not experience their attachment as passionate or intense, at least to some significant extent (allowing, of course, for the normal ebb and flow of feeling that is intrinsic to life). I do not describe a relationship as romantic love if there is not some experience of spiritual affinity, by which I mean some deep mutuality of values and outlook, some sense of being soul mates; if there is not a deep emotional involvement; if there is not a strong sexual attraction (allowing, once more, for normal fluctuations of feeling). And if there is not mutual admiration—if, for example, there is mutual contempt instead (which can certainly coexist with sexual attraction)—again I do not describe the relationship as romantic love.

Let it be acknowledged that almost any statement we make about love, sex, or man/woman relationships entails something of a personal confession. We tend to speak from what we have lived. I have shared some of the life experiences that lie behind my thoughts on love in *The Psychology of Romantic Love* (1980/1981) as well as in *What Love Asks of Us* (written with my wife and colleague, Devers Branden, 1987). But the personal context aside, my writing about love draws on two primary sources. First, it represents an attempt to reason about and understand man/woman relationships on the basis of facts and data more or less available to everyone, the material of history and of culture. Second, as a psychotherapist and marriage counselor, I have had the opportunity to work with thousands of people over the past thirty years and to see something of their struggle to achieve sexual and romantic fulfillment. I have been keenly interested in the question of what people seek from love—as well as the question of why some people succeed in their quest while others fail.

II

Love is our emotional response to that which we value highly. I am speaking now of love in general, love as such, of which romantic love is a special case. Love is the experience of joy in the existence of the loved object, joy in proximity, and joy in interaction or involvement. To love is to delight in the being whom one loves, to experience pleasure in that being's presence, to find gratification or fulfillment in contact with that being. We experience the loved being as a source of fulfillment for profoundly important needs. (Someone we love enters the room; our eyes and heart light up. We look at this person; we experience a rising sense of joy within us. We reach out and touch; we feel happy, fulfilled. Note that this might describe our relationship to a spouse, a lover, a parent, a child, a friend—or a pet).

But love is more than an emotion; it is a judgment or evaluation, and an action tendency. Indeed, all emotions entail evaluations and action tendency. Emotions by their nature are value responses. *They are automatic psychological responses, involving both mental and physiological features, to our subconscious appraisal of what we perceive as the beneficial or harmful relationship of some aspect of reality to ourselves* (Branden, 1984/1985). If we consider any emotional response, from love to fear to rage, we can notice that implicit in every response, is a *dual* value judgment. Every emotion reflects the judgment of "for me" or "against me"—and also "to what extent." Thus, emotions differ according to their content and according to their intensity. Love is the highest, the most intense expression of the assessment "for me," "good for me," "beneficial to my life." In the person of someone we love we see, in extraordinarily high measure, many of those traits and characteristics that we feel are most appropriate to life— life as we understand and experience it—and therefore most desirable for our own well-being and happiness.

Every emotion contains an inherent action tendency. The emotion of fear is a person's response to that which threatens his or her values; it entails the action tendency to avoid or flee from the feared object. The emotion of love entails the action tendency to achieve some form of contact with the loved being, some form of interaction. (Sometimes a lover will complain, "You say you love me, but I could *never tell it from your actions*. You never want to spend time with me, you don't want to talk with me, so how would you *act differently* if you *didn't* love me?")

Finally, and in a sense more fundamentally, we may describe love as representing an *orientation*, an attitude or psychological state with regard to the loved being, deeper and more enduring than any momentary alteration of feeling. As an orientation, *love represents a disposition to experience the loved being as the embodiment of profoundly important (conscious or subconscious) personal values—and, as a consequence, a real or potential source of joy.*

What is unique about romantic love is that it incorporates or draws on more aspects of the self than any other kind of love—our sense of life, our sexuality, our body, our deepest fantasies or longings regarding man or woman, our self-concept, the cardinal values that energize our existence (Branden, 1969/1971, 1980/1981). Our spiritual-emotional-sexual response to our partner is a consequence of seeing him or her as the embodiment of our highest values and as being crucially important to our personal happiness. "Highest," in this context, does not necessarily mean noblest or most exalted; it means most important, in terms of our personal needs and desires and in terms of what we wish to find and experience in life. As an integral part of that response—and this differentiates romantic love from the love for a friend, a parent, or a child—we see the loved object as being crucially important to our *sexual* happiness. The needs of our spirit and body melt into each other; we experience a unique sense of wholeness.

III

In light of the widespread misunderstandings on this subject, I want to say a few words about what romantic love is not.

Many of the commonest criticisms of romantic love are based on observing irrational or immature processes occurring between people who profess to be "in love," and then generalizing to a repudiation of romantic love as such. In such cases, the arguments are not in fact directed against romantic love at all—not if we understand its roots in genuine appreciation and admiration for the person of another. There are, for example, men and women who experience a strong sexual attraction for each other, conclude that they are in love, and proceed to marry, ignoring the fact that they have few values or interests in common, have little or no admiration for each other, are bound to each other predominantly by dependency needs, have incompatible personalities and temperaments, and, in fact, have little or no authentic interest in each other as persons. Of course, such relationships are doomed to failure. But they do not represent romantic love.

To love a human being is to know and love his or her person. This presupposes the ability to see, and with reasonable clarity. It is commonly argued that romantic lovers manifest a strong tendency to idealize or glamorize their partners. Of course, this sometimes occurs. But it is not in the nature of love that it must occur. To argue that love is *necessarily* blind is to maintain that no real and deep affinities of a kind that inspire love can really exist between persons. This argument runs counter to the experience of men and women who do see the partner's shortcomings as well as strengths and who do love passionately.

Infatuation differs from love precisely in that, whereas love embraces the person as a whole, infatuation is the result of focusing on one or two traits or aspects and reacting as if that were the total. I see a beautiful face, for example, and assume it is the image of a beautiful soul. I see how kindly this person treats me and assume we share significant affinities. I discover we share important values in one area and expand this area to include the whole sphere of life.

It is sometimes argued (by Freud, for example) that the experience of romantic love is generated solely by sexual frustrations and, therefore, must perish shortly after consummation. True, frustration can create obsessive want and can foster a tendency to endow a desired object with temporary value. Yet anyone who argues that love cannot survive sexual fulfillment is making an extraordinary *personal* statement and is also revealing extraordinary blindness or indifference to the experience of others.

Since romantic love, in literature, is dramatized through lovers battling obstacles to their love, some writers have concluded that these obstacles are essential to the experience. "Romantic love," writes Arnold Lazarus (1985), "thrives on barriers, frustrations, separations and delays. Remove these obstacles, replace them with the everyday-ness of married life, and ecstatic passion fades." What is one to say, then, to couples who have been married for twenty years and who have preserved their vision of each other as well as their devotion—to say nothing of their sexuality? Such couples exist. Is psychology to have no place for them? "Romantics," says Lazarus, "ignore the fact that people grow weary of each other unless they have cultivated common interests and values." *Do* they ignore this fact? And is such blindness essential to the romantic experience? I do not think so. This is the kind of straw-man version of romantic love that is typical of its critics.

It is sometimes argued, too, that since so many couples do in fact suffer feelings of disenchantment shortly after marriage, the experience of romantic love must be a delusion. Yet many people experience disenchantment somewhere along the line of their careers, and it is not commonly suggested, therefore, that the pursuit of a meaningful and fulfilling career is a mistake. Many people experience some degree of disenchantment in their children, but it is not commonly supposed that the desire to have children and to be happy about them is inherently immature and neurotic. Instead, it is generally recognized that the requirements for achieving happiness in one's career or success in child rearing may be higher and more difficult than is ordinarily supposed.

Romantic love is not omnipotent—and those who believe it is are too immature to be ready for it. Given the multitude of psychological problems that many people bring to a romantic relationship—given their doubts, their fears, their insecurities, their weak and uncertain self-esteem—given the fact that most have never learned that a love relationship, like every other value in life, requires consciousness, courage, knowledge, and wisdom to be sustained—it is not astonishing that most relationships end disappointingly. But to indict romantic love on these grounds is to imply that if *love is not enough*—if love of and by itself cannot indefinitely sustain happiness and fulfillment—then it is somehow in the wrong, is a delusion, even a neurosis. The error lies, not in the *ideal* of romantic love, but in the irrational and impossible demands made of it.

IV

Let us now consider: what are the psychological needs that romantic love satisfies? There are, I believe, a network of complementary needs involved.

1. There is our need for *human companionship*: for someone with whom to share values, feelings, interests, and goals; for someone with whom to share the joys and burdens of existence.

2. There is our need *to love*: to exercise our emotional capacity in the unique way that love makes possible. We need to find persons to admire, to feel stimulated and excited by, persons toward whom we can direct our energies.

3. There is our need *to be loved*: to be valued, cared for, and nurtured by another human being.

4. There is our need to experience *psychological visibility*: to see ourselves in and through the responses of another person, one with whom we have important affinities. This is, in effect, our need for a psychological mirror. (The concept of psychological visibility, developed in considerable detail in *The Psychology of Romantic Love*, is basic to my understanding of man/woman relationships.)

5. There is the need for *sexual fulfillment*: for a counterpart as a source of sexual satisfaction.

6. There is our need for *an emotional support system*: for at least one person who is genuinely devoted to our well-being, an emotional ally who, in the face of life's challenges, is reliably there.

7. There is our need for *self-awareness and self-discovery*: for expanded contact with the self, which happens continually and more or less naturally through the process of intimacy and confrontation with another human being. Self-awareness and self-discovery attend the joys and conflicts, harmonies and dissonances of a relationship.

8. There is our need *to experience ourselves fully as a man or woman*: to explore the potentials of our maleness or femaleness in ways that only romantic love optimally makes possible. Just as we need a sense of identity as human beings, so we need a sense of identity related to gender—of a kind most successfully realized through interaction with the opposite sex.

9. There is our need *to share our excitement in being alive and to enjoy and be nourished by the excitement of another*.

I call these needs, not because we die without them, but because we live with ourselves and in the world so much better with them. They have survival value.

This list does not seem to me to be the slightest bit speculative. I believe common experience, observation, and reason support it. But if I were to be speculative, I might posit a tenth need—the need *to encounter, unite with, and live out vicariously our opposite-gender possibilities*: the need, in males, to find an embodiment in the world of the internal feminine; the need, in females, to find an embodiment in the world of the internal masculine (Sanford, 1980).

V

There are couples who remain deeply in love for many, many years. Even allowing for setbacks, frictions, times of estrangement, and the like, they preserve over time the essential meaning of romantic love. And there are couples for whom romance, whatever that term signifies to them, vanishes almost from the moment of marriage. Psychologists seem to know a good deal more about the failures than the successes, just as they know more about pathology than health. The danger of such one-sided knowledge, of course, is that it may blind us to life's positive possibilities. The temptation is to believe that sickness is normal and health abnormal. Far more attention needs to be paid to those men and women for whom romantic love does *not* end in disenchantment.

My own studies suggest that there are at least some behaviors we can clearly isolate as being far more characteristic of successful couples than the average. Couples who remain happily in love over long periods of time more consistently exhibit these behaviors:

1. *They tend to express love verbally*. This simply means saying "I love you" or some equivalent (in contrast to that attitude best summarized by "What do you mean, do I love you? I married you, didn't I?").

"Saying the words," one married woman remarked, "is a way of touching. Words can nurture feelings, keep love strong and in the forefront of the relationship." Her husband commented, "Saying 'I love you' is a form of self-expression. It's putting a bit of myself out there. So my feelings are in reality, not just inside of me."

2. *They tend to be physically affectionate*. This includes hand-holding,

hugging, kissing, cuddling, and comforting—with a cup of tea, a pillow, or a woolly blanket.

"Aren't we all touch animals?" one husband remarked. "An infant first experiences love through touch. I don't think we ever lose that need." His wife added, "For me, cuddling is as important as talking or making love."

3. *They tend to express their love sexually.* People who are happily in love are inclined to experience sexual intimacy as an important vehicle of contact and expression. Sex remains vital for them long after the excitement of novelty has passed.

This does not mean that they regard sex as the most significant aspect of their relationship. They are far more likely to regard their connection at the level of soul (for want of a better word) as the core of their relationship. And there are great variations in frequency of lovemaking among couples who are happily in love. And yet the expression "With my body I thee worship" is one they understand and relate to. Sex is integrated with, rather than alienated from, their feelings of love and caring. The importance they attach to sex is to be found in the emotions with which they invest the act.

4. *They express their appreciation and admiration.* Happy couples talk about what they like, enjoy, and admire in each other. As a result, they feel visible, appreciated, valued. "My husband has always been my best audience," a woman said to me. "Whether I'm telling him about what I did at work that day, or a remark he liked that I made to someone at a party, or the way I dress, or a meal I've prepared—he seems to notice everything. And he lets me see his pride and delight. I feel like I'm standing in the most marvelous spotlight—his special way of being aware. That kind of awareness—and then talking about it—is what love means to me. I only hope I give as good as I get, because I'll tell you something: being loved may be the second best thing in the world, but loving someone, really being able to appreciate and admire someone—as I do my husband—is the best. And I do let him know that."

5. *They participate in mutual self-disclosure.* This is a willingness to share more of themselves and more of their inner lives with each other than with any other person. They share thoughts, feelings, hopes, dreams, aspirations; hurt, anger, longing, memories of painful or embarrassing experiences. Such couples are far more comfortable with self-disclosure than the average and, as a corollary, more interested in each other's inner life.

Often, of course, one partner is more verbal than the other. One partner may be somewhat awkward at times about verbalizing intimate thoughts and feelings. And yet, on a relative scale, he or she reaches out to the partner as to no other person, and trusts the partner above all others, and listens to the partner above all others.

6. *They offer each other an emotional support system.* They are there for each other in times of illness, difficulty, hardship, and crisis. They are best friends to each other. They are generally helpful, nurturing, devoted to each other's interests and well-being.

In happy marriages, men as well as women tend to understand the importance of nurturing—in contrast to more conventional relationships in which nurturing, at best, is seen as an exclusively female activity. Nurturing is acting to support the life and growth of another person. To nurture another human being is to accept him or her unreservedly, to respect his or her sovereignty, to support his or her growth toward self-actualization, and to care about his or her thoughts, feelings, and wants.

If we can see only our own needs and not the needs of our partner, we relate as a child to a parent, not an equal to an equal. In mature romantic love, independent equals do not drain or exploit each other; they nurture each other. Mutual nurturing is one of the characteristics we tend to find in happy relationships. "I think," a man said to me, "that one of the most important things we look for in love is one person who will be truly devoted to our interests and well-being. And that's what the other person naturally expects in return. Without that, what is love? What is marriage?"

7. *They express love materially.* They express love with gifts (big or small, but given on more than just routine occasions) or tasks performed to lighten the burden of the partner's life, such as sharing work or doing more than agreed-upon chores.

The desire to give pleasure to the partner is powerfully in evidence here. As regards gifts, price and income level are not relevant; what is, is the underlying intention. The reward is to see an expression of joy or satisfaction on the partner's face.

8. *They accept demands or put up with shortcomings* that would be far less acceptable in any other person. Demands and shortcomings are part of every happy relationship. So are the benevolence and grace with which we respond to them.

Another way of thinking about this point is to say that couples who know how to live together happily do not torment themselves or each other over "imperfections." Each knows he or she is not perfect and does not demand perfection of the other. They are clear that, for them, the partner's virtues outweigh the shortcomings—and they choose to enjoy the positives rather than drown the relationship in a preoccupation with the negatives. This does not mean they do not ask for—and sometimes get—changes in behavior they find undesirable. But they do not catastrophize difficulties they know they can live with.

9. *They create time to be alone together*. This time is exclusively devoted to themselves. Enjoying and nurturing their relationship rank very high among their priorities: they understand that love requires attention and leisure.

Such couples tend to regard their relationship as more interesting, more exciting, more fulfilling than any other aspect of social existence. Often they are reluctant to engage in social, political, community, or other activities that would cause them to be separated unless they are convinced there are very good reasons for doing so; they are clearly not looking for excuses to escape from each other, as is evidently the case with many more socially active couples.

"We've been called selfish for wanting to spend so much time alone together," one woman said to me, laughing; she was obviously untouched by the accusation. Her husband added, "But we've never heard that from anyone who's happily married." His wife continued, "I once pointed that out to someone who was trying to give me a hard time. Do you know what she answered? 'Happiness is so middle class.' A loser's consolation prize if ever I heard one."

It can require considerable independence of a couple to treat their relationship as a major priority. But we find that kind of independence among couples who know how to sustain love across many years.

Once, following a lecture in which I was discussing the importance of time and intimacy for a relationship, a young man and woman came over to me, very enthusiastic about the talk, and proceeded to tell me how happily in love they were—which was how they looked. Then the man said to me, "But there's one thing that troubles me. How do you find the time for that intimacy?" I asked him what his profession was and he told me he was a lawyer. I said, "There's one thing that troubles me. Given how much in love you are with your wife, and looking at you both it seems clear that you are, how do you find the time to attend to your law practice?" He looked disoriented and nonplussed. "The question is incomprehensible, isn't it?" I said to him. "I mean, you *have* to attend to your law practice, don't you? That's important." Slowly a light began to dawn on his face. I went on, "Well, when and if you decide that love really matters to you as much as your work, when success in your relationship with this woman becomes as much an imperative as success in your career, you won't ask: *How does one find time*? You'll know how one does it." This, of course, is what happy couples understand perfectly.

In my observation the biggest time threat comes not from our work but from our social relationships or what we tell ourselves are our social obligations. Often it is against these that our love needs to be protected. The time that we and our partner spend in the company of relatives, friends, or colleagues can be a source of pleasure, but it is not a substitute for time spent alone together. Nothing is. Evenings spent with people who do not matter to us, or do not matter nearly as much as the one we love, cannot be reclaimed at a later date, cannot be taken back and relived. *Successful couples seem to know it is now or never.*

Now the characteristics I have outlined are not equally present in every happy marriage or love affair. Even within a relationship each partner does not exhibit them equally at all times. But I strongly doubt that anyone could point to a happy relationship that did not show most of these traits.

VI

I have already suggested that if romantic love is to succeed, it asks far more of us in terms of our personal evolution and maturity than is ordinarily understood.

The first thing it asks is a reasonably good level of self-esteem. If we enjoy healthy self-esteem—if we feel competent, lovable, deserving of happiness—we are very likely to choose a mate who will reflect and support our self-concept. If we feel inadequate, unlovable, undeserving of happiness, again we are likely to become involved with a person who will confirm our deepest vision of ourselves.

If we enjoy good self-esteem, we are likely to treat our partner well and to expect that he or she will treat us well, which tends to become a self-fulfilling prophecy. We will not see ourselves as a martyr or a victim. We will not feel that suffering is our natural destiny, and we will not put up with it in passive resignation—let alone go looking for it. If we lack good self-esteem, we are unlikely to treat our partner well, despite our good intentions, because of our fears and excessive dependency. And if our partner treats us badly, some part of us will feel, "But of course." And if and when our relationship ends and we go looking for a new partner, despair can make us not more thoughtful but more blind—so our self-esteem goes on deteriorating and so does our love life.

If we are to choose a mate wisely, we need to feel that we are deserving of love, admiration, and respect—and that only someone we can truly love, admire, and respect is appropriate for us. If we are to treat our relationship with the care and nurturing it deserves, we need to feel that we are deserving of happiness—that happiness is not a miracle or a mirage but our natural and appropriate birthright.

Our sense of self, the way we perceive and assess ourselves, crucially affects virtually *every* aspect of our existence. That has been the central theme of all my work. As regards love, the first love affair we must consummate successfully is with ourselves. Only then are we ready for other relationships. And how well can we practice "mutual self-disclosure" if we are strangers to ourselves, alienated from our inner life, cut off from feelings and emotions and longings? Self-alienation is the enemy of intimacy and therefore of romantic love (or any other kind of love). Or if we are estranged from our sexuality, or in an adversary relationship to our body, we lack the mind-body integration that romantic love celebrates. If we have not attained a reasonably mature level of individuation and autonomy, chances are we will overburden our relationship with demands that can't be met—such as to create (rather than express) our self-esteem and our happiness or to support the illusion that we are not ultimately responsible for our own existence.

Romantic love requires courage—the courage to stay vulnerable, to stay open to our feelings for our partner, even when we are temporarily in conflict, even when we are frustrated, hurt, angry—the courage to remain connected with our love, rather than shut down emotionally, even when it is terribly difficult to do so. When a couple lacks this courage and seeks "safety" from pain in the refuge of withdrawal, as so commonly happens, it is not romantic love that has failed them but they who have failed romantic love.

VII

I regret there is not space here to develop in more depth the view of love I am presenting or to discuss in detail how it differs from traditional views.

I do not, for example, share the assumption of some champions of romantic love that reason and passion are antithetical. I do not believe that "true love conquers all." Nor that there is only one soul mate for each person on earth. Nor that love necessarily entails marriage or that marriage necessarily entails children. I do not believe it has necessarily failed if it does not last forever. I do not insist that romantic love, under all circumstances and conditions, necessarily and always entails sexual exclusivity. I do not see romantic love as the prerogative of youth. I do not identify it exclusively with the excitement of what is merely its first phase: the phase of novelty.

To say it once more, I see its success over time as a triumph of psychological maturity. I see its essence as the encounter of two selves who see in each other a mirror, an opportunity for the celebration of self and of life, a doorway to our ultimate psychological (including spiritual) home, and a challenge to the best within us.

REFERENCES

Branden, N. (1969/1971). *The psychology of self-esteem.* New York: Bantam Books.
———. (1980/1981). *The psychology of romantic love.* New York: Bantam Books.
———. (1984/1985). *Honoring the self.* New York: Bantam Books.
———. (1987). *What love asks of us.* With D. Branden. New York: Bantam Books.
Burgess, E. W., & Locke, H. T. (1953). *The family: From institution to companionship* (2nd ed.). New York: American Book Co.
Lazarus, A. A. (1985). *Marital myths.* San Luis Obispo, CA: Impact Publishers.
Sanford, J. A. (1980). *The invisible partners.* New York and Ramsey: Paulist Press.

CHAPTER ELEVEN

Passionate Love

BY SHARON S. BREHM

Despite increased interest over the last few years in the topic of emotion (for example, Abelson, 1983; Shaver, 1984; Solomon, 1980), modern psychology's understanding of emotional processes is still both rudimentary and fragmented. Just as we have no commonly accepted general theory of emotion, so we also lack cogent conceptual frameworks for various specific emotional states, including that of passionate love. Perhaps because of this theoretical deficiency, passionate love has become something of the unfavored stepchild in empirical investigations of interpersonal attraction and close relationships (Berscheid, 1985).

The reluctance of many research psychologists to examine the more passionate aspects of our social attachments is paralleled by an explicitly negative evaluation of passionate love on the part of a number of clinically oriented psychologists. Both Dorothy Tennov (1979, see pp. 176–185) and I (1985, see pp. 107–110) have summarized the consistent position taken by most twentieth-century pundits giving advice on love. In their view, passionate love is immature and undesirable, being produced by personal inadequacy/psychopathology and leading to exploitative/destructive behavior toward the partner. These writers argue that the mature, well-adjusted individual should not be tempted by the "romantic demon" (Tennov, p. 184), but should instead strive for dispassionate love based on "true" caring for the other.

This distrust of passionate involvements is, of course, not unique to the

I am grateful to the Intra-University Professorship Program at the University of Kansas for giving me the opportunity to study Christian mysticism, and to Sandra Zimdars-Swartz, Paul Zimdars-Swartz, and Marie Willis for their guidance and encouragement.

modern Western world (see historical accounts by de Rougemont, 1956; Gathorne-Hardy, 1981; Hunt, 1959). The ancient Greeks, for example, may have seen passionate love as providing wonderful material for drama, but they regarded it as madness when it occurred in everyday life. Moreover, every major religion, Eastern as well as Western, has made the control of unruly passions (including but not restricted to the passionate versions of erotic love) a central focus of their theologically justified precepts of desirable human behavior.

Since I happen to believe that one learns more effectively from positive models than from negative ones, my decision to study passionate love immediately threw me into a difficult quandary. Where could I find systematic, detailed accounts of the experience of passionate love that were *not* written for the purpose of condemning it? Tennov's (1979) book, *Love and Limerence*, proved a valuable beginning, although as I will discuss later in this chapter I have some fundamental disagreements with her perspective. Even more helpful was Tennov's own basic source: the works of Marie-Henri Beyle, better known as Stendhal. As Tennov notes, "Stendhal is virtually alone in failing to criticize the lover, the beloved, *or* the experience" (p. 177), and his major treatise on passionate love, *De l'amour* (*On Love*), provided exactly the kind of positive, systematic account I was searching for.

One of the most astonishing things about *De l'amour* is its accessibility 164 years after it was first published (in 1822). Stendhal was a man of modern sensibilities and a first-rate psychologist before the official term was coined. Paradoxically, however, it was precisely this accessibility that began to worry me. Stendhal's perspective on passionate love was so compatible with my own preexisting attitudes toward love that I could not be confident it offered me sufficient psychological distance. I realized that I needed to go further away from home in order to turn around and see it better.

After a few false starts, I discovered what is, in fact, a well-trodden path but one that was entirely new to me: the writings of Christian mystics.[1] These individuals describe their love relationship with God in the most passionate of terms and seemed to me the perfect comparison. What are the similarities and differences between a Stendhalian view of passion-

1. Obviously, Christianity does not provide the only mystical tradition; every religion has its mystics. I have restricted my study to Christian mystical writings for practical reasons: (1) to impose some limits on a field of inquiry that is of enormous size and complexity, and (2) to remain within the Western cultural tradition because of my abysmal ignorance of other cultures.

ate love and the passionate love of God recounted by Christian mystics? Might it be possible by taking each of these perspectives on its own merits (and not derogating one by invidious comparison to the other) to arrive at a more precise and comprehensive understanding of the psychological processes involved in passionate love? This chapter is based on my attempt to use this method of comparison to locate the psychological heart of the experience of passionate love.

STENDHAL'S THEORY OF PASSIONATE LOVE

In *De l'amour*, Stendhal (1783–1842) describes seven stages in the development of passionate love. The first stage is that of ADMIRATION. Here the lover encounters the beloved and is attracted by the beloved's qualities. This first encounter is usually brief, and, by definition, the qualities that elicit the lover's attraction are relatively superficial ones, such as physical appearance, charm, wit, and so on. In the second stage of ANTICIPATION, the lover imagines the pleasures that could come about through association with the beloved. Stendhal does not specify what factors influence whether or not an individual progresses from admiration (which frequently occurs) to the more focused attention of anticipation (which happens less often), although he implies that the situation (such as boredom) and character (such as boldness, imagination) of the lover are important determinants.

Once anticipation takes place, the lover must then consider whether there is sufficient HOPE (the third stage) of being loved in return. Stendhal makes it quite clear that this process of appraisal is not a logical analysis of some objective reality, but depends, again, on the situation and character of the lover. After these three preliminary stages, love is born. For Stendhal, this beginning of passionate love, which might be called ROMANTIC ATTRACTION, is a kind of emotional plateau that sums up what has gone before and, for some lovers, lays the groundwork for what is to follow.

The Stendhalian perspective takes on its greatest interest beginning with the fifth stage of CRYSTALLIZATION. Stendhal defines crystallization as the "deification of a charming object" (p. 29) and describes it as follows:

> I call crystallization that process of mind which discovers fresh perfections in its beloved at every turn of events . . . it is sufficient to think of a perfection in order to see it in the person you love. (p. 6)

> Everything which is beautiful and sublime in the world forms part of the beauty of the person we love, and this unexpected glimpse of happiness suddenly fills our eyes with tears. (p. 38)

In the case of love realities model themselves enthusiastically on one's desires; consequently it is the passion in which violent desire is most completely satisfied. (p. 33)

For Stendhal, then, crystallization is that process by which an ordinary person becomes transformed in the mind of the lover into glittering perfection. The term itself comes from his famous example of salt crystals adhering to the leafless branch of a tree, covering it with sparkling beauty. Crystallization does not occur suddenly nor all at once; it develops over time as each thing of beauty, each joyful feeling, is attached to the lover's image of the beloved. What Stendhal describes is an increasingly tight, closing system in which the world contracts to the beloved and the beloved fills all the world. The beloved becomes joy and beauty incarnate.

One finds this process of contraction and absorption depicted in many novelistic treatments of passionate love. Consider, for example, these passages from the writings of Gustave Flaubert (1821–1880):

[The] world, for him, was all contained within the silky rondure of her skirts. (*Madame Bovary*, p. 45)

[She] was the focal point of light at which the totality of things converged. (*Sentimental Education*, p. 10)

Paris depended on her person, and the great city, with all its voices, resounded like a vast orchestra about her. (*Sentimental Education*, p. 64)

As the beloved increasingly subsumes all joy and beauty, the lover's anticipation of the delight to be gained from being loved by the beloved grows accordingly, as does the lover's fear of being deprived of this love. Thus, Stendhal points to three separate but interactive aspects of the process of crystallization: the perfected image of the beloved, the imagined delights of being loved by this perfect creature, and the terror of being rejected by this unique source of delight. Increase the magnitude of any one of these three factors, and the other two will increase as well; similarly, a decrease in one will decrease the others. In the latter formula, we find the quintessential Stendhalian proposition that passionate love depends on uncertainty and distance. If, for example, the lover becomes less fearful of being rejected, then the imaginative desire, unfettered by reality, that fuels crystallization loses power and lesser real gains take the place of the elaborated, imagined ones. As Flaubert puts it, "We must beware of touching the idol for fear the gilt may come off in our hands" (*Madame Bovary*, p. 310).

So important are uncertainty and distance in Stendhal's perspective that he devotes a separate stage to them: the sixth stage of DOUBT. For Stendhal, it takes a severe crisis of doubt about whether one's love will be reciprocated to transform the moderate passion of one's initial crystallization into the all-consuming obsession of the SECOND CRYSTALLIZATION. In this seventh, and final, stage of passionate love, the tight, closing system of the first crystallization (stage 5) contracts with a vengeance. The ability to judge reality is impaired, and the beloved's behavior is scrutinized minutely for its meaning and implications. In this state, the lover "no longer attributes anything to chance; he loses all sense of probability; anything he imagines becomes actual reality so far as its effect on his happiness is concerned" (De l'amour, p. 34). The lover also interprets everything in terms of the fear of rejection. Thus, a success in life matters only because it provides hope that, impressed by the success itself or the qualities that produced it, the beloved will not scorn the lover's devotion; a failure dashes that hope. Indeed, to love passionately is to be dead to the rest of the world: "One sign of the birth of love is that all the pleasure and all the suffering that all other human passions and all other human needs can give a man, cease at that moment to affect him" (De l'amour, p. 275). But there is no end to the fascination of the beloved: "For [Frederic] each of her fingers was a person, not a thing" (Sentimental Education, p. 253).

Major Psychological Variables in Stendhal's Theory of Passionate Love

IMAGINATION. In general, Stendhal's psychological orientation appears highly cognitive. His theory of passionate love strongly emphasizes the importance of cognitive constructions in eliciting emotional reactions and providing a source of motivation. The term cognitive, however, seems too minimalist to characterize adequately the Stendhalian realm of romantic fantasy. It would be more accurate to say that what Stendhal was concerned with was imagination, that seizing of beauty that Keats believed constituted the apprehension of truth.

In Stendhal's theory, imagination provides the basic fabric from which passionate love is made. First, it is necessary if the process of passionate love is to begin. The individual with a highly developed imagination is more likely, according to Stendhal, to love passionately than someone without this capacity. Imagination is also crucial for the progress of crystallization. The passionate lover is caught up in the image of the beloved, the image of the delights that would be gained from being loved by the beloved, and the image of the loss that would result from being rejected by the beloved. A few quotes from *De l'amour* convey some of Stendhal's ideas about the power of imagination and its role in passionate love:

> Only imagination can avoid satiety for ever. (p. 262)

> Each flight of imagination is rewarded by a moment of delight. It is not surprising that such a method of existence should grow upon one. (p. 117)

> Love is the only passion which pays itself in a coin which it mints itself. (p. 332)

The tenor of Stendhal's remarks on imagination suggests that passionate love is *essentially* an imaginative act. At one point, he states this viewpoint explicitly: "In love one only enjoys the illusion one creates for one's self" (p. 23). It may not be accidental, however, that this statement is attributed to someone else (a woman with whom he discussed love), and elsewhere in *De l'amour* Stendhal harshly criticizes such solipsism:

> Over ardent people with their paroxysms of love . . . throw themselves at the objects of their affections instead of waiting for them. Before any of the sensation which is the consequence of the nature of an object has time to reach them, they endow that object from a distance . . . with that imaginary charm of which they have an inexhaustible supply within themselves. On drawing closer to this object, they see it, not as it really is, but as they have created it, and they take a delight in themselves under the guise of the object, imagining all the time that they are taking a delight in the object itself. (p. 57)

My own reading of Stendhal on this matter is that he is here playing a sort of game with the reader and, more important, with himself. He has developed in considerable detail a theory of love-as-imagination, but then draws back from fully accepting this conclusion. For personal reasons, he needs to continue to believe that when *he* is passionately in love, *he* loves the beloved and not the image of the beloved he has created in his mind. The need for this belief is so strong that he backs away from the conclusion of his own argument. This conclusion, which *we* should not turn away from, is nicely illustrated by an excerpt from a recently published short story:

> It was great to be in love again, particularly so soon after being in despair. I didn't even care whether Wilfredo liked me or not. He had nothing to do with the way I felt in the thirty-one hours before I was to meet him. There I was, there was Wilfredo, and then there was my great love for him. (Janowitz, 1986, p. 40)

The imaginative construction of the beloved takes on a life of its own, free from the constraints of the reality of the individual who is the beloved.

ATTENTION. Imaginative products, of course, do not always become obsessions, and another crucial feature of Stendhal's theory involves the ever-increasing attention the lover devotes to romantic fantasies. As this attention increases, passionate attachment to (the image of) the beloved grows stronger, which in turn focuses attention even more exclusively on the beloved. Not having anything else to do (Stendhal's old enemy, boredom) increases passionate love; distraction decreases it. Indeed, even the beloved may be a distraction, as implied by the following passages from *De l'amour*:

> One of the unfortunate things about life is that the joy of seeing the person we love and of speaking to her does not leave any very distinct impression. (p. 38)

> The thought of the distant town where one once saw her for a moment throws one into a sweeter reverie than even her actual presence does. (p. 39)

> When you are to see the woman you love in the evening, the expectation of such great happiness makes all the moments that separate you from it unbearable. A devouring fever makes you take up and abandon a dozen different occupations. You keep on looking at your watch, and you are delighted when ten minutes have gone by without your having done so; the longed-for hour comes at last, and when you are on her doorstep with the knocker poised you feel that it would be a relief if she were out; this should not worry you unless you brood over it; actually, it is the expectation of seeing her that has produced this unpleasant effect. It is this kind of thing that makes matter-of-fact people say that love is madness. What happens is that the imagination, violently wrenched out of delicious reveries in which every step brings happiness, is dragged back to stern reality. (p. 63)[2]

Stendhal attributes these curious phenomena to the likelihood of "cruel treatment" (p. 39) by the beloved, but there is the clear possibility that it is the "stern reality" (cruel *or* kind) of the beloved that is the problem.

UNCERTAINTY. The reality of the beloved can be problematic because actions by the beloved may break the tension necessary to maintain the

2. Compare Flaubert in *Sentimental Education*: "He made appointments for himself to go and see her; when he reached her door on the second floor he was afraid to ring. Steps approached; the door opened, and at the words, 'Madame's out,' he felt a sense of deliverance, as if there were one less burden on his heart" (p. 52).

crystallization process. This tension is best described as *hope without possession*, the precariously balanced state of uncertainty. If the beloved too readily surrenders, passionate love will not develop fully: "The only way to kill passion-love is to prevent any crystallization from taking place, by making things easy" (p. 214). Only doubts keep one focused on the image instead of the reality: "If one is sure of a woman's love one asks one's self if she is more or less beautiful; if one is in doubt as to her feelings one has not time to think of her appearance" (p. 45). For Stendhal, passionate love inherently involves doubt and fear: "Always some little doubt to calm, that is what keeps one ever eager, that is what keeps alive the spark of happy love. Since it is never devoid of fear, its joys can never pall" (p. 112).

Stendhal draws upon this contrast between assurance and uncertainty in his remarkable novel, *The Red and the Black*. Certainty kills love: "Mathilde, certain of being loved, despised him completely" (p. 160). On the other hand, loss can produce it: "Everything changed rapidly in his heart from the moment when he saw himself parted from her forever. His pitiless memory set to work reminding him of the slightest incidents of that night which in reality had left him so cold. On the second night after their vow of eternal separation, Julien nearly went mad when he found himself forced to admit that he was in love with Mademoiselle de La Mole" (p. 152).

Although the initial response to the threatened loss of the beloved is the intensification of love, the tension required for crystallization will be destroyed if all hope for reciprocation vanishes. It seems probable, however, that putting an end to hope is difficult for the beloved to accomplish. Both hope and doubt are in the mind of the lover-perceiver, and both seem to spring eternal in passionate love. One of the most interesting points made by Tennov (1979) in her consideration of passionate love (which she calls "limerence") is that "the limerent fantasy, intricate as it may be, is satisfying only when it retains fidelity to the possible" (p. 86). Perhaps this verisimilitude (marvelously illustrated in Tennov's book by a teenager's elaborate, detailed, and studiedly plausible romantic fantasies about a rock star) functions as the one way to sustain hope in the face of rational knowledge that there is none.

MOOD STATES. Drawing on both Stendhal's and Tennov's writings, one can identify three mood states that are most prevalent during passionate love. The first is euphoria. Sometimes this occurs in anticipation of gaining the beloved's attention: "With love, I feel that at two paces from me there exists an immense happiness, more than I have ever hoped for, and that it only depends on a word or a smile" (*De l'amour*, p. 97). At other times, there is a more general joie de vivre: "Everything is new, everything is alive, everything breathes the most passionate interest" (De l'amour, p. 263). One's perception of the physical world may be affected: "My perceptions grew stronger. Colors seemed more brilliant" (interview material reported in Tennov, p. 22). Difficulties seem to disappear: "Problems, troubles, inconveniences of living that would normally have occupied my thoughts became unimportant. I looked at them over a huge gulf of sheer happiness" (interview material reported by Tennov, pp. 21–22).

The second mood state that occurs frequently during passionate love is opposite to the first in affective tone, but similarly intense. During this mood, which might be called agitated despair, the individual is overwhelmed with painful yearning for the beloved. Tennov discusses this mood state at some length and provides some striking interview material:

> Fantasy only brings the image of ecstasy, a positive moment amid the pain. But that transitory vision, with its small relief, then stabs me with intensified desire. I am worse. (p. 106)

> All I could think of was that I wanted to stop the feelings; I thought I could distract myself with a bigger pain. (p. 152)

The second individual was trying to explain why he had cut off his little finger during his despair over a deteriorating love affair; he had probably been very close to a serious attempt at suicide. Another person interviewed by Tennov used a similar phrase ("I was trying to stop the pain," p. 153) to explain why he went on a rampage of property destruction during a bout of extreme jealousy. It is possible that his wrecking of things helped him avoid physically attacking his partner or his rival.

Finally, during even the most tumultuous of passionate love affairs, there are likely to be periods of what Stendhal calls the "dead blank": "As passionless as [an acquaintance] on gloomy days, I can see no happiness anywhere, I begin to doubt whether it exists for me and I become bitter" (p. 97). This kind of bleak depression stands in contrast to both the euphoria and the agitated despair of passionate love; it occurs, according to Stendhal, when one stops loving.

CONTROL. Although Tennov's perspective on passionate love is, for the most part, faithfully modeled after Stendhal's views as presented in De l'amour, she places greater emphasis on the involuntary nature of passionate love than he does. Stendhal does remark at one point that "the will has no control over love" (p. 69). He suggests in another passage, however, that one can make oneself sufficiently miserable about the beloved so as to *create* passion: "Two years of misery proved the genuineness of his passion and indeed would have created passion even had it not existed so ardently before" (p. 201). This idea that passions can be created and transformed is even more vividly expressed elsewhere in the book:

> By a great mental effort the utmost wretchedness can immediately be changed into an endurable condition. On the evening of a defeat in battle a man is in headlong retreat upon a jaded horse; he distinctly hears the gallop of the cavalry patrol pursuing him; suddenly he pulls up, dismounts, renews the primings of his carbine and of his pistols, and resolves to defend himself. In a second, instead of seeing death before him, he sees the cross of the Legion of Honor. (p. 283)

Tennov, on the other hand, frequently refers to the "intrusive and inescapable" (p. 40) character of romantic fantasies and constantly under-lines the individual's lack of free choice in the matter. Indeed, she develops an argument that passionate love is a "biologically determined human reaction" (p. 234), genetically transmitted, that strikes some although not all of the human race. The only transformation she discusses involves a change from one beloved to another. Thus, Stendhal takes a relatively flexible view of the emotional state of passionate love and of emotions in general; arousal is necessary and may not be under one's control, but one has some leeway in how one constructs the emotional experience itself. Tennov endorses a more hard-wired theory of emotion, in which passionate love is a specific, innate emotional response to a potential sexual partner and serves the functions of stimulating sexual intercourse and (at least for a time) ensuring a stable attachment between the partners.

ENDURANCE. Stendhal provides no explicit indication of how long passionate love may be expected to last, although it is clear from the events of his own life that he would assume it could endure for years. Basing her estimate on the interview and questionnaire responses she gathered, Ten-nov suggests that the average duration is some two years, but notes that much longer lasting episodes are not rare. Perhaps the best example in her book of its potential duration comes from a man whose passionate love withstood twenty-five years of married life: "I lived in constant fear of divorce. . . . I would do everything I could think of to try and win her affection. . . . She was unpredictable. I could never be sure of how she'd react. . . . From the day I met her until the day she died, she was the most beautiful woman on earth. . . . She was a real queen and she ruled my emotions for a quarter of a century" (pp. 53–54).

THE GOAL OF PASSIONATE LOVE. Despite her emphasis on the reproductive function of passionate love, Tennov denies that sexual intercourse per se is the goal of the lover. Instead, she suggests that what the lover seeks is emotional commitment from the beloved, which she describes as "a kind of merging, a 'oneness,' the ecstatic bliss of mutual reciprocation" (p. 120). Tennov's resort here to the language traditionally associated with mystical (religious) experience is, of course, neither accidental nor unique. It is a commonplace of romantic accounts that the ultimate goal of passionate love is described in exalted religious terminology. For example:

> He was a god. . . . It was not really sexual; it was almost spiritual. (interview material from Tennov, p. 206)

> Do you not feel the yearning of my spirit mounting towards yours? Do you not feel that our souls must mingle, and that I am dying of desire? (*Sentimental Education*, p. 251)

> Often, as he looked at her, it seemed to him as though his soul, freed from the body and seeking to embrace her, broke like a wave about the sleek curves of her head. (*Madame Bovary*, p. 292)

Stendhal—resolute in both his anticlericalism and his distaste for romantic excess—refrains from such language in his essays and novels. When it comes to the ultimate goal of passionate love, this man who suggested "He lived, he wrote, he loved" as his epitaph is silent.

TERESA OF AVILA'S VISION OF LOVE

By any standard, Teresa of Avila (1515–1582) was an extraordinary individual. Canonized shortly after her death (1622) and in 1970 declared a Doctor of the Church, she founded the Discalced[3] Carmelite Order in the face of sometimes fierce clerical opposition during her lifetime. Untutored in Latin, she was forced to write in the vernacular and became one of the greatest of Spanish writers. Teresa's sturdy determination to describe her mystical experiences in the clearest possible terms makes her perhaps the best psychologist among the major Christian mystics and, therefore, particularly valuable for the purposes of this chapter.

Among her writings, the *Interior Castle* provides the most systematic and thorough account of Teresa's mystical experiences. Here she likens the process of loving God to a journey through a great castle containing many

---

3. Literally, without shoes; the term refers to Teresa's reform of the existing Carmelite order to a more austere observance.

rooms (or "mansions"). According to Teresa, there are seven basic stages in the soul's progress toward God:

1. Entering the Castle; this corresponds to an individual's decision to love God.
2. Praying to God.
3. Living an exemplary life of prayer and good works.
4. Coming closer to God through the Prayer of Recollection and the Prayer of Quiet.
5. Being granted by God the promise of union; Teresa calls this the "betrothal."
6. Being granted intimacy with God.
7. Being received by God in permanent union; called by Teresa the "spiritual marriage."

Although by no means perfectly parallel, the first three of Teresa's stages bear some resemblance to the first three stages in Stendhal's theory of passionate love. Both begin with an initial attraction to the beloved, and "anticipation" and "hope" can be assumed to be part of what is generated by prayer during Teresa's second and third mansions. There is, however, one crucial difference between the early stages of passionate love described by Stendhal and the early stages of mystical experience described by Teresa. As noted previously in this chapter, Stendhal does not take (at least, not consistently) an extreme view (of the sort proposed by Tennov) of the involuntary nature of passionate love. He does, however, emphasize the role of one's will much less than does Teresa. Compare, for example, Stendhal's definition of love as "a lucky accident which one cannot procure for oneself" (p. 138) with Teresa's comment that love "is an arrow shot by the will" (*Conceptions of the Love of God*, p. 392). Teresa, strictly orthodox in her theology, was careful to note throughout her writings that God's grace cannot be coerced by human actions; however, she was equally orthodox in her insistence that it is the responsibility of each individual to live the life of devotion that best prepares one to receive grace should God wish to grant it.

The fourth stage represents a kind of plateau in both the Stendhalian and Teresean models, and the last three stages are, for both, the more fully developed instances of passionate love. Even by the fourth stage, however, Teresa is describing complex mystical experiences that are far more difficult to comprehend than the more ordinary psychological processes addressed by Stendhal. One of the most useful guides to an understanding of these experiences is a brief commentary Teresa sent to her confessor in 1576 (Relation V in the *Spiritual Relations*). Written the year before she began the *Interior Castle*, Relation V may have served as a preparatory outline for parts of the larger work; it describes eight types of mystical experience.

1. Presence of God: Teresa notes that this "is in no sense a vision" (p. 333) and states her conviction "that, except perhaps during periods of aridity, anyone who ever desires to commend himself to His Majesty . . . will find Him" (p. 33). It seems likely that this experience is available to individuals in the second and third mansions of the interior castle.

2. Prayer of Recollection (fourth mansion): This is defined as "an interior recollection felt in the soul" where "there is no loss of any of the senses or faculties, which are all fully active: but their activity is concentrated upon God" (p. 327). It is accompanied by "an interior peace and quietude which is full of happiness" and "may last for long periods" (p. 328).

3. Prayer of Quiet (fourth mansion): Here, the "will is wholly concentrated upon God, and the soul sees that it has not the power to engage in any other occupation and activity; but [memory and understanding] are free to act and work in God's service" (p. 328). The Prayer of Quiet seems similar to the Prayer of Recollection, but more intense, with greater concentration, and more removed from all thoughts and concerns other than God.

The remaining five types of mystical experiences recounted in Relation V are variously distributed among mansions 5 and 6 in the *Interior Castle*. It is probably best not to impose any strict linear sequence on these five types, with the one exception that what is called "impulse" (see below) seems restricted to the end of mansion 6, directly prior to entrance into mansion 7.

4. Suspension of the faculties, or union: For a "brief space of time," the will, understanding, and memory are totally concentrated on God and "the senses . . . are no longer awake" (p. 328). This experience results in a "wealth of humility, and of other virtues and desires" (p. 328), but it is itself impossible to describe or understand.

5. Rapture: This lasts longer than suspension of the faculties and "is more readily perceptible from without, for little by little breathing diminishes, so that the subject cannot speak or open the eyes" (p. 328). "When the rapture is deep . . . the hands become as cold as ice and sometimes remain stretched out as though they were made of wood. The body remains standing or kneeling, according to the position it was in when the rapture came on. And the soul is so deeply absorbed in the joy of what the Lord is showing that it seems to forget to animate the body and goes away and abandons it" (p. 329). During rapture, "it is very usual for His Majesty to make . . . certain revelations" (p. 329). The feelings and sweetness pro-

duced by rapture "are so excessive by comparison with anything on earth . . . that, if the memory of them did not pass away, the soul would always feel a loathing for worldly pleasures" (p. 329).

Teresa offers an even more graphic description of rapture in her autobiography (*The Life of the Holy Mother Teresa of Jesus*): "While seeking God in this way, the soul becomes conscious that it is fainting almost completely away, in a kind of swoon, with an exceedingly great and sweet delight. It gradually ceases to breathe and all its bodily strength begins to fail it; it cannot even move its hand without great pain; its eyes involuntarily close, or, if they remain open, they can hardly see" (p. 108). She says that someone in this state cannot read, cannot understand what is said, and cannot speak.

6. Transport: Whereas rapture develops gradually, transport comes "with a swiftness of movement which seems to carry away the higher part of [the soul] and to separate the soul from the body" (*Spiritual Relations*, p. 329). Initially, this causes great fear as "the poor soul does not know . . . what is going to happen to it" (p. 329). This "flight of the spirit" (p. 329) is hard to describe, and Teresa makes use of an extended metaphor: "It is as with a fire which is large and has been prepared for lighting. The soul has been prepared by God, and, like the fire, blazes up quickly and sends up a flame which soars high: yet this is just as much fire as the other which remains below—however high the flame rises, the fire below is still there. So it is here, with the soul: there seems to come out of it something swift and subtle which rises to its higher part and goes whither the Lord wills" (p. 329). In *The Life*, Teresa describes experiences of levitation that occur during what she calls "transport" in Relation V (although in *The Life* itself she calls it a state of rapture). She says that it is "irksome" that she cannot resist the will of God manifested this way and notes the "terrible fear" produced by seeing "one's body being lifted up from the ground" (*The Life*, p. 121).

7. Impulse: This is the name Teresa gives to a desire "caused by a soul's suddenly remembering its absence from God. . . . Sometimes this remembrance is so powerful and so strong that the soul seems in a single moment to have gone out of its mind" (*Spiritual Relations*, p. 330). The soul "feels itself to be in a state of deep loneliness and total abandonment, such as cannot be described, for the world and all worldly things cause it distress, and no created thing can provide it with companionship: it seeks nothing but the Creator, yet sees that without dying it is impossible to have Him. . . . It sees itself suspended between Heaven and earth and has no idea what to do. . . . Though it may last no more than half an hour, it leaves the limbs so

disjointed and the bones so racked that the hands have not power enough to write; it also produces grievous pains" (p. 331). This torment, however, is not felt until the impulse has passed away. During the impulse, the person "is in possession of all his senses; he can speak—he can even observe; walk about, however, he cannot, for the sudden assault of love would fling him to the ground" (p. 331).

8. Wounding of the soul: Teresa describes this as feeling "as if an arrow had pierced the heart, or the soul itself. This causes the soul great affliction, which leads it to complain, but is so delectable that it would like never to be without it" (p. 331). Teresa goes on to distinguish this type of wounding where the "arrow" appears to come from without from a "wound of love [that] seems to spring from the soul's inmost depths" (p. 332). When the soul is so wounded, the desire for God increases as does hatred for the body, which seems "like a great world standing between" (p. 332) the soul and union with God.

The most famous account of an external wounding, now celebrated as the Feast of the Transverberation of the Heart of St. Teresa of Jesus, is found in *The Life*.

> It pleased the Lord that I should sometimes see the following vision. I would see beside me, on my left hand, an angel in bodily form. . . . He was not tall, but short, and very beautiful, his face so aflame that he appeared to be one of the highest types of angels who seem to be all afire. . . . In his hands I saw a golden spear and at the end of the iron tip I seemed to see a point of fire. With this he seemed to pierce my heart several times so that it penetrated to my entrails. When he drew it out, I thought he was drawing them out with it and he left me completely afire with a great love for God. The pain was so sharp that it made me utter several moans; and so excessive was the sweetness caused me by this intense pain that one can never wish to lose it, nor will one's soul be content with anything less than God. It is not bodily pain, but spiritual, though the body has a share in it—indeed, a great share. So sweet are the colloquies of love which pass between the soul and God that if anyone thinks I am lying I beseech God, in His goodness, to give him the same experience. (pp. 192–193)

The seventh mansion (spiritual marriage) of the *Interior Castle* is not mentioned in Relation V, nor does it have a parallel stage in Stendhal's theory of passionate love. This is a state of stability, calm, and resolution of many of the problems encountered earlier in one's spiritual life. Because union with God "cannot be fulfilled perfectly in us during our lifetime" (*Interior Castle*, p. 33), the soul is divided in two. Part of the soul is always in the presence of God and is, therefore, at perfect peace; the other part of the soul, however, remains alert and active in the world, and experiences normal human trials and difficulties. The individual no longer yearns to die as during the periods of impulse; instead, one wants to live in order to serve God. There are few ecstatic or paramystical experiences.

To describe the experiences of that part of the soul that does obtain permanent union, Teresa uses metaphors of water and light: "It is like rain falling from the heavens into a river or a spring; there is nothing but water there and it is impossible to divide or separate the water belonging to the river from that which fell from the heavens. Or it is as if a tiny streamlet enters the sea, from which it will find no way of separating itself, or as if in a room there were two large windows through which the light streamed in: it enters in different places but it all becomes one" (*Interior Castle*, pp. 335–336).

It should be noted that Teresa always carefully avoids the pantheism and antinomianism deemed heretical by the ecclesiastical authorities of her day. The entire soul/person does not unite with God, only a part does. The person in no way *becomes* God. As for being freed from moral law, Teresa strongly emphasizes how awareness of one's sins becomes greater during the seventh mansion than ever before, and that the obligation and desire to obey God's law increase accordingly. She states firmly that from spiritual marriage "are born good works and good works alone" (p. 346).

Major Psychological Variables in Teresa's Vision of Love

IMAGINATION. As a person of faith, Teresa believes that her love is a response to the actual qualities of the beloved, at least as these divine qualities can be made manifest to a human being. She is, however, also convinced that experiences similar to hers can come from sources other than God, and she refers to the need to be on guard against deceptions by the devil and the effects of melancholy. In making the distinction between divinely inspired mystical experiences and diabolical/human ones, Teresa points to the consequences of such experiences. When mystical experiences come from God, the consequences are always good: peace of mind and renewed energy for good works. Teresa assures us that the passionate lover of God is enabled to act for God in the world: "I really think that nothing seems impossible to one who loves" (*Conceptions of the Love of God*, p. 378).

Even though she believes that the essential content of her experiences is real (that is, produced by the actual presence of God), Teresa assumes that God works through the human instrument, and she accepts imagination as a human capacity used by God. She urges people to meditate on the Humanity of Christ and, thereby, to draw upon their imaginative elaborations to become more receptive to God. Teresa also explicitly indicates that imagination is involved in her paramystical experiences by adopting the Augustinian triad of corporeal, imaginative, and intellectual (or spiritual) in classifying her visions and locutions (voices). Corporeal visions/locutions appear to be what modern psychologists would call hallucinations or illusions, believing one sees/hears exteriorly what others do not perceive. Teresa says she never had a corporeal vision and very few corporeal locutions. Imaginative visions/locutions occur in the mind, but have the attributes of things seen or voices heard; many of Teresa's experiences were of this sort. The last type of visions/locutions described by Teresa is regarded as the most satisfying and intimate modality. During intellectual visions/locutions, the individual receives direct contact with God without the mediation of imagery.

In considering the contrast between the more secondary role imagination plays in Teresa's conception of passionate love and the primary role it plays in Stendhal's theory, it should be recognized that the two writers were facing radically differing social contexts. Human lovers, as Stendhal well knew, are not supported by any social consensus for their crystallized, perfected image of the beloved. Indeed, other people often attempt to dissuade them from their "unrealistic" beliefs and hopes. In a religious community, this is not the case. At least in general terms, one's image of God is shared by everyone, and the goal of becoming closer to God is the raison d'être for the community's existence.

One should not, of course, draw this distinction too sharply. On the one hand, some secular societies place positive value on being in love and encourage this behavior through, for example, music and literature. On the other hand, there are religious who deviate from the community's image of God (severe deviations may be condemned as heresy), and there are those who deviate from the community's prescribed methods for coming closer to God. (Teresa's efforts to reform the Carmelite order were seen, and resisted, as just such deviations by some of her sisters in religion and a goodly number of clerics.) Even so, it seems a reasonable proposition that, at least within a certain range of beliefs and practices, the passionate lover of God is far more integrated into and supported by a social network than is the individual whose passionate love is directed toward another human being. Consequently, a mystic's conception of God typically has more social reality and appears (to the faithful) less imaginative than does a passionate lover's image of the beloved.

ATTENTION. Like Stendhal, Teresa describes a process during which attention to the beloved increases while attachment to others declines. At its extreme (during what Teresa called "impulses"), this contrast between the divine beloved and earthly existence becomes a torment. The person yearns to be with God but cannot unite fully with the Godhead; earthly concerns are only a reminder of one's separation from God. Nevertheless, as an orthodox Christian, Teresa never loses sight of the requirement to affirm God's creation and to be lovingly attentive to others. It is of interest that traditional monastic theology (see LeClercq, 1982, for an excellent consideration) worked out over the centuries a conceptual framework and practical discipline to resolve this apparent conflict between detachment and charity. In monastic theology, detachment is seen as facilitating charity; by loving no one person in particular, one can love better all people. The aversive quality of created things is, however, often expressed through loathing of the body and extreme asceticism. Teresa certainly endorsed the first proposition. On the second, she was a moderate, condemning any pampering of one's body but discouraging dramatic mortifications that might impair one's health (and, therefore, interfere with one's ability to serve God).

UNCERTAINTY. The passionate love of God involves a complex interplay between certainty and uncertainty. For those of great faith, like Teresa, there is no uncertainty about God's existence, power, and love. Even in moments of great distress or times when a passionate response to God is not forthcoming (see discussion below on aridity), the will is fixed in faith. Nevertheless, God is beyond human control and human comprehension. God can never be possessed, and God's actions cannot be coerced. Thus, one's faith can be certain, but one's knowledge of God must always be inadequate and, to some degree, tentative. Moreover, as described in the discussion of Teresa's understanding of the role of imagination, the manifestations of God in human lives can be a cause of uncertainty and debate. Teresa endured terrible hardship during the early years after her "second conversion" (at age forty), with many of her confessors telling her that her experiences were of diabolical origin. It took her a long time to convince them and to gain conviction herself that she was in touch with God and not a deluded victim of the devil.[4]

---

4. The result of this struggle between doubt and conviction was that Teresa developed an authority that, although obedient to male ecclesiastics, was also independent from them. "When [my confessors] made me stop prayer [God] seemed to me to have become angry, and He told me to tell them that this was tyranny" (*The Life*, p. 189). As Bynum (1982) discusses in

MOOD STATES. The three mood states described by Stendhal as integral to being passionately in love are also exhibited in Teresa's accounts.

1. Euphoria: The "soul would like to shout praises aloud, for it is in such a state that it cannot contain itself" (*The Life*, p. 97). The love of God is likened to "a glorious folly, a heavenly madness" (*The Life*, p. 97).
2. Agitated despair: During periods of "impulse," Teresa was not afraid she would be rejected by God, but she suffered intense frustration at not being as close to God as she wanted to be.[5]
3. Aridity (Stendhal's "dead blank"): Teresa said that, at times, "I seem to be living simply for the sake of eating and sleeping and avoiding any kind of distress" (*Spiritual Relations*, p. 335).

Three other mood states also figure prominently in Teresa's writings. First, she expresses aggravation with the ordinary trials and tribulations of life: "Oh God help me! What a miserable life is this! There is no happiness that is secure and nothing that does not change" (*The Life*, p. 251). Such statements as these serve as an important corrective to any kind of naive assumptions about Teresa and the life she led. She was no plaster saint, always in ecstasy.

Besides giving us a fuller picture of this more ordinary context than we find in *De l'amour*, Teresa also emphasizes periods of calm and tranquility more than Stendhal does. As noted above, she saw peace of mind as one way to determine whether one has been visited by God or the devil. She also tells us about the seventh mansion, which seems in many ways the calm after the storm. Thus, for Teresa, the mood state brought about by the highest level of closeness to God is not ecstasy, but peace.

Like most Christian mystics, Teresa wrote a great deal about suffering. Of particular relevance to this chapter is her desire to suffer for God. She says that she "would have been glad if she could have been cut to pieces, body and soul, to show what joy this pain caused her" (*The Life*, p. 98). Theologically, the desire to suffer is conceptualized by Teresa as part of (perhaps the most important part of) the Imitation of Christ. God can grant no greater favor than to allow a person to suffer as Christ suffered.

---

her brilliant essay on women mystics in the thirteenth century, mysticism offered women a delicate (one could be condemned as a heretic) but potentially very powerful method for gaining authority in a church that, then as now, barred women from the priesthood.

5. Some mystics recount periods of agonizing alienation, which seem similar in kind to the torment Stendhal describes as resulting from (perceived) rejection by a human beloved. See, for example, Mechthild of Magdeburg's *Flowing Light of the Godhead*. Bynum (1982) describes Mechthild's mystical experiences as the "throbbing alternation of ecstasy and alienation" (p. 230).

Psychologically, the desire to suffer for one's beloved appears to be a common feature of passionate love. Flaubert, for example, writes in *Sentimental Education* about Frederic's "longing for self-sacrifice" (p. 79). This desire to suffer is not the same as the need to use pain to fight pain as described by some of the people Tennov interviewed, nor is it the same as the desire to die described by Teresa as so overwhelming during periods of "impulse." Instead, it is a state of exaltation in which the prospect (and one can assume, for some, the actuality) of suffering in the service of the beloved brings the greatest possible pleasure. Pleasure and pain fuse into one intensity; the self is annihilated in the glory of the beloved.

CONTROL. There is some suggestion in their writings that both Stendhal and Teresa saw individuals as having some control over their emotions during passionate love. Stendhal describes a relatively involuntary alternation of euphoria and despair over the course of passionate love, but (as noted earlier) he implies that to some extent the lover may be able to turn torment into ecstasy through the willful use of the imagination. Teresa also describes an alternation of extreme mood states throughout the prelude to the calm of the seventh mansion. During all of this, however, she is continually willing herself to be more obedient to the will of God and to accept all things without distress.[6]

ENDURANCE. Teresa's life bears witness to the possibility of an enduring passionate love. She had her first mystical experience sometime during the years 1555–1556, when she was around forty and had been a nun for

6. The most remarkable description I have read of the role of one's will in passionate love is found in the writings and conversations of Therese of Lisieux (1873–1897), recently the subject of a popular film. Therese was a French Carmelite who at the age of twenty-three began to suffer from a terminal case of tuberculosis that ended with her death a year and a half later. During that entire period, she was virtually without spiritual consolation: "I must appear to you as a soul filled with consolations and one for whom the veil of faith is almost torn aside; and yet it is no longer a veil for me, it is a wall which reaches right up to the heavens and covers the starry firmament. When I sing of the happiness of heaven and the eternal possession of God, I feel no joy in this, for I sing simply what I WANT TO BELIEVE. It is true that at times a very small ray of sun comes to illumine my darkness, and that the trial ceases for *an instant*, but afterwards the memory of this ray, instead of causing me joy, makes my darkness even more dense" (1975–76, p. 214, written a few months before her death).

Despite the darkness, Therese maintained her faith throughout a brutal dying, and on the day of her death, she called out to God for mercy and in love: "Oh! it's pure suffering because there are no consolations! No, not one!" And later: "Little sisters! . . . Little sisters! . . . My God! My God, have pity on me! I can't take anymore! . . . I can't take any more! . . . And yet I must endure . . . I am . . . I am reduced . . . No, I would never have believed one could suffer so much . . . never! never!" (1977, p. 243). Her last words were: "Oh! I love Him! . . . My God . . . I love you!" (p. 181).

some twenty years. These experiences continued until her death in 1582, despite an extremely busy life of religious duties, administrative work, writing, and counseling others. Even when she was old and sick, and had entered the greater calm of the seventh mansion, she had her visions. Writing in the year before her death, she reported, "The imaginary visions have ceased, but I seem always to be having this intellectual vision of the three Persons and of Christ's Humanity" (*Spiritual Relations*, p. 335).

THE GOAL OF THE PASSIONATE LOVE OF GOD. The goal of the passionate love of God is union with God. As indicated earlier, Teresa's explicit conception of union was the orthodox Christian (and Islamic) one of a maximally intimate relationship between entities that remain distinct in their different natures. In her use of metaphor, however, she sometimes seems to allude to an annihilation of self; this is particularly evident in her use of the classic mystical metaphor of the mixing of fluids—for example, "like rain falling from the heavens into a river . . . there is nothing but water there" (*Interior Castle*, p. 335). It seems reasonable to suggest that although Teresa firmly believed the theology of essential difference and distinctiveness, her own psychological experience may have included the feeling that, at least for brief moments, her being was annihilated and submerged in the Godhead. Such loss of self is, of course, fully acceptable and desirable in some faiths (such as Buddhism and Hinduism), and numerous Christian mystics have been cautioned or condemned by ecclesiastical authority for crossing the fine line between union and unity.[7] It seems possible, then, that there is a persistent inclination toward loss of self during the course of intense devotion to the divine—an inclination that can be reduced but not eliminated by theological constraints.

THE PSYCHOLOGY OF PASSIONATE LOVE

There are two alternative methods than can be followed in using the accounts of Stendhal and Teresa for the purpose of advancing our under-

7. A striking illustration of how fine this line can be is found in the history of Marguerite Porete who in 1310 was burned in Paris as a relapsed heretic. Marguerite was condemned on the basis of a book she had written, which according to the clerics who judged her advocated pantheism and antinomianism. Marguerite's book was also burned, but copies survived. In later years, her authorship was forgotten, but the book itself became widely read, especially by nuns and monks. Lerner (1972) recounts the particular irony of the situation: "Before it was properly identified as the work of a condemned heretic it was even published in modern English under the auspices of the Downside Benedictines with the nihil obstat and imprimatur" (p. 2). Marguerite's authorship of *The Mirror of Simple Souls* was not reestablished until 1946.

standing of the psychology of passionate love. One method is to interpret these writings in terms of existing psychological theory. This approach has much to recommend it, but it also has some serious drawbacks. Among the latter, the most serious is that an adequate integration of these theories with the written material summarized in this chapter would call upon both more page space and greater knowledge than are presently available to me. The alternative method is to work directly from the writings of Stendhal and Teresa to develop a specific, if simplified, model of passionate love. This model is necessarily informed by various theoretical perspectives in psychology, although I mention few of them explicitly in the pages that follow. I have, however, appended at the end of this chapter a partial listing of some possible points of contact between the descriptions taken from Stendhal and Teresa and the conceptual frameworks employed by modern psychologists. As awkward a device as it may be, this appendix gives me an opportunity to make a down payment on some of my debts to other scholars, and it may offer the reader a starting point for the more inclusive integration that, for the moment, I must forgo.

In light of what Stendhal and Teresa have to tell us, I would propose that the core of passionate love lies in the capacity to construct in one's imagination an elaborated vision of a future state of perfect happiness.[8] Not only then is there an essential similarity between the passionate love of another human being and the passionate love of God, but this similarity in process also includes other visionary experiences such as nationalistic enthusiasms, ideological fervor, and even teenage adoration of rock stars. Scientific, artistic, commercial, and political endeavors in which the individual's efforts are directed toward some vision of future perfection would also qualify as varieties of passionate love. This understanding of passionate love is recognizably Platonic. It holds that a passionate attachment to an ideal becomes "a life-transforming miracle, . . . a magical change of perspective that opens up new, enchanted horizons" (Vlastos, 1981, p. 42). The person (or cause or object) is loved because "in him and by him ideal perfection is copied fugitively in the flux" (Vlastos, p. 34).

The capacity to imagine perfection varies widely. Some individuals have more of it than others; some cultures promote it more than others; and some historical periods may foster it more than others. The objects upon which this capacity is exercised also vary as indicated by the range of experiences that can serve as the focus of a passionate devotion. Further-

8. I would emphasize that my position here is without theological implication. One can say of Teresa that she imagined a god who does not exist, or one can say that Teresa's imaginative capacity was the instrument used by God.

more, the inclination to make use of this imaginative capacity is not constant, being enhanced, for example, by discontent with one's present circumstances.

Since the passionate lover is imaginatively constructing a future state of *perfect* happiness, it follows that passionate love can exist only under conditions of uncertainty of goal attainment. Where goal attainment is impossible, there is insufficient incentive for the kind of detailed, elaborate imaginative effort that is the hallmark of passionate love. Where goal attainment occurs, imperfect reality takes the place of imagined perfection and the passionate obsession necessarily dissolves. It is crucial to remember, however, that judgments of impossibility and attainment take place in the mind of the lover and, therefore, bear no simple relation to objective reality. Where we would see impossibility, the lover may hope; where we would see attainment, the lover may despair.

Stendhal called the process by which imagined perfection increases its hold on one's thoughts, feelings, and desires crystallization. It might also be called emotional imperialism. There seem to be two major steps in this process. First, thoughts of the beloved are likely to be elicited whenever one is happy, even when the immediate source of that happiness has nothing to do with the beloved. Second, there is a transfer of emotional experience such that the image of the beloved incorporates the emotion that was elicited initially by another source. Although Stendhal defined crystallization solely in terms of the beloved's gathering in of all the beauty in the world, the same process presumably operates in respect to negative emotions. Fearful thoughts of losing the beloved are likely to occur whenever one is unhappy, even when the immediate source of that unhappiness has nothing to do with the beloved. Emotional experience may then be transferred so that the fear of losing the beloved incorporates the negative emotion initially elicited by another source. Thus, over time, one's affective state (positive and negative) is increasingly ruled by where one stands with the beloved (close or distant).

This notion that arousal (emotional or otherwise) from other sources can serve to increase our romantic attraction to others has also been suggested by a number of psychologists (for example, Hatfield & Walster, 1978). Specifying the exact process by which this might occur, however, has become a matter of dispute (Riordan & Tedeschi, 1983; White & Kight, 1984). One possible paradigm is provided by Zillmann's (1978) work on excitation transfer. According to this model, residual arousal from an initial stimulus A is added to the arousal from a subsequent stimulus B, and the total affective response is then misattributed to B. Although excitation transfer is obviously similar to the emotional transfer explicitly described by Stendhal and implied in much of Teresa's commentary, there are serious discrepancies and unanswered questions.

For instance, the excitation transfer model requires that the individual not be aware that he or she is still responding to the initial stimulus when the subsequent stimulus is presented; an accurate assessment of the causes of one's emotional arousal would prevent interpreting all of it as a response to the second stimulus. In practice, this requirement has meant that excitation transfer effects have been observed only when there is a delay in presentation between the two stimuli (Cantor, Zillmann, & Bryant, 1975; Zillmann, Johnson, & Day, 1974). No such delay seems necessary in the passionate love experiences recounted by Stendhal. Indeed, thoughts of the beloved are especially likely to occur in the midst of one's response to another object/event.

Moreover, Zillmann's model of excitation transfer does not address the long-term effects of, so to speak, taking from Peter and giving to Paul. It is, however, these long-term effects that are of greatest interest to the student of passionate love. The takeover of emotion from other emotion-producing events permits the power of the image of the beloved to expand. Life becomes simplified, both cognitively and emotionally. Happiness *is* coming closer to the beloved; unhappiness *is* falling away from the beloved. As the process continues, one begins to evaluate almost everything that happens in terms of this central schema; one's entire world comes to rest on the fulcrum of the beloved. Clearly, it will take a great deal more research before we understand the precise way in which passionate love comes to hold imperial sway over all the dominions of the heart and mind.

Figure 11.1 outlines my view of the critical components of passionate love. In addition to the joy arising from coming closer to the beloved and frustration from being distant, there are two other essential emotional consequences. First, I would suggest that the experience of aridity is an inevitable part of passionate love and its variations. Feelings of aridity (of being dry, barren, unresponsive) indicate emotional exhaustion on the part of the lover. This depletion may occur after a long period of intense attachment to the beloved or may be brought about by debilitating conditions that are independent of the love affair itself (illness, for example). Often aridity will mark only a pause in passionate love, which can then resume with even greater intensity than before. It is possible, however, for aridity to become a chronic state of depressed, apathetic hopelessness. Perhaps in such instances, the individual has become convinced that perfection does not exist and can no longer either imagine it or strive to obtain it.

Fig. 11.1. The Psychology of Passionate Love

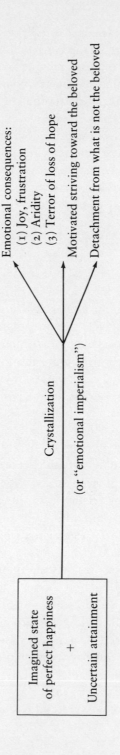

Imagined state
of perfect happiness
+
Uncertain attainment

Crystallization

(or "emotional imperialism")

Emotional consequences:
(1) Joy, frustration
(2) Aridity
(3) Terror of loss of hope

Motivated striving toward the beloved

Detachment from what is not the beloved

The third emotional state included in figure 11.1 is that of terror at the loss of hope. As passionate love intensifies, the beloved becomes not only the source of all delight but the source of all meaning in the lover's life. It is, therefore, not surprising that rejected lovers sometimes kill themselves or their partners (perhaps in a desperate effort to possess the beloved through "taking" his or her life) or their rivals. Nor is it surprising that lovers are highly motivated to maintain their hopes despite what others believe is overwhelming evidence to the contrary.

The lover is also highly motivated to act in ways that promote closeness to the beloved, and this state of motivated striving toward the beloved is indicated in figure 11.1. Conversely, the passionate lover is detached from other people and from all things that are not directly related to the beloved. This detachment, strongly emphasized by religious writers such as Teresa but also noted by secular authors such as Stendhal, is the natural consequence of the relentless emotional imperialism of passionate love. The emotional impact of what is not the beloved is leached out and incorporated into the image of the beloved. The world becomes a pale shadow; love reigns in singular sovereignty.

Related Issues

SEXUALITY. It may seem strange that, in this discussion of passionate love, I have given so little attention to sex. Passionate love does, of course, often focus on a potential or existing sexual partner, and desired or actual sexual activity with that partner can be a major source of heightened emotional experience. I do not, however, regard sexuality as a necessary component of passionate love. Instead, I would suggest that sexual attraction acts to channel the more general process of passionate love into a romantic attachment to another human being. When the cultural context provides models of and encouragement toward romantic sexuality, this too will function to increase the likelihood that one's passionate visions take the form of romantic attachments. But it is a serious mistake to regard all forms of passionate love as essentially sexual in origin or purpose. Just as one can have a highly active sexual life without a trace of passionate love, so one can be passionately in love independent of one's sexual drives.[9]

9. I am aware that this position, although I believe it to be true, is not without its difficulties. One of them concerns the considerable number of mystics who use erotic language in describing their relationship to the divine. If mystical experience is not sublimated sexuality, why then this preference for erotic language? In particular, why a preference that, in Christianity at least, had to overcome strong antisexual attitudes? My guess, and it can be nothing more than a guess at this point, is that sexual activity is such a necessary and constant feature of human life that a language to describe it developed fairly early in human history. Further-

LOSS OF SELF. In the summary of Teresa's writings provided earlier, two types of loss of self were mentioned. One type involved feelings of annihilation of the self in the beloved; the other was the lover's desire for self-sacrifice in the service of the beloved. The question I would like to consider here is whether such experiences should be considered essential components of passionate love.

My view is that they are highly common, but not essential. Instead, I would propose that experiencing a loss of self in the beloved and desiring to sacrifice the self for the beloved are both brought about by the ever-increasing focus on the beloved that takes place during the evolution of passionate love. That is, detachment from the self may be similar to the lover's detachment from whatever is not related to the beloved. Unlike detachment from externals, however, which by and large should steadily increase as passionate love increases, detachment from the self seems harder to sustain. As Flaubert says of Frederic in *Sentimental Education*, "He looked around him for someone to help. No one in need was passing, and his impulse of self-sacrifice faded away" (p. 128). Deeply committed to the value of charity and a life of self-denial, Teresa's impulses toward self-sacrifice were no doubt more robust than Frederic's, but she could not escape awareness of self. In particular, each increment in closeness to God brought with it increased awareness of her own sins and unworthiness. Romantic lovers may not dwell on their sins, but they too are sensitive to what they perceive as their personal inadequacies. This suggests, then, that superimposed on the primary dialectic involving closeness to versus distance from the beloved, there is an alternation between loss of concern about the self and intense awareness of personal shortcomings.

ENDURANCE. It is impossible to stipulate any kind of typical time period for the endurance of passionate love. The state should last as long as the perfected image is maintained, and the image can be maintained so long as attainment of the beloved is uncertain. Extreme life events may destroy concentration on the image for many people, but there are countless instances where individuals suffered unspeakable horrors without losing their visionary fervor.

ETHICS. Passionate love itself is amoral. We call passionate lovers "saints" and refer to their heroic lives if their love serves what we believe to

more, as this language addresses the most intimate human relationship (between adults), it could easily be appropriated as a way to describe an intimate relationship with a personalized God. Finally, physiological sensations of intense delight may be essentially similar, even when produced by different causes. I would still contend, however, that to speak of a final common pathway for physiological sensations is quite different from proposing a single drive state that is expressed directly (through sex) or indirectly (through sublimated activities).

be good. If they serve what we believe to be evil, we judge them "fanatics" and point to their immoral actions.

Unresolved Questions

The present model of the psychology of passionate love suffers from a number of unresolved conceptual issues. Perhaps most glaring is its inability to specify the necessary and sufficient factors for the process to begin. Unfortunately, if we take seriously the wide range I have proposed of the varieties of passionate love, it is possible that such causal precision may be extremely difficult to attain. For the moment, the best I can do is to point to some interaction between the person's reaction to the specific situation (boredom, discontent) and some more general dispositional characteristics (imaginative, persevering).

I am also unable to offer any conclusions about how much the individual can deliberately control the experience of passionate love. I agree with Tennov that passionate romantic love certainly feels involuntary and uncontrollable. Moreover, the orthodox Christian doctrine that God's grace is a free, noncoercible gift may reflect, to some extent, the experientially derived belief that the passionate love of God is also fundamentally involuntary and uncontrollable. On the other hand, religious traditions make great efforts to place passionate love within the context of a disciplined life of devotion, and I have to wonder what passionate romantic love would feel like if there were a cultural tradition encouraging us to work with it rather than be assailed by it.

Some other unanswered questions concern the particulars of the end of passionate love. Tennov believes that passionate love terminates in one of three ways: consummation in which passion turns "into a lasting love or . . . less positive feelings" (p. 255), starvation in which hope dies, and transformation in which passionate love is transferred to a new beloved. On my part, I would argue that it is inappropriate to lump together the serenity and peace of "lasting love" (which, I assume, is akin to Teresa's seventh mansion) and the dullness of faded passion. Uncertainty about how to classify the end states of passionate love is compounded by almost complete ignorance about the specific processes promoting one rather than another outcome.

The Function of Passionate Love

Earlier in this chapter, I mentioned Tennov's suggestion that the function of passionate love is to ensure reproduction and maintain cooperative bonding between the partners. I find this line of reasoning unconvincing. Sexual pleasure seems to me to be fully sufficient to ensure adequate reproductive activity. As for loyalty between partners, I should think that it could be brought about much more effectively by a psychological process that did not depend on uncertainty about the partner's affections.

My own view of the function of passionate love is that this intense combination of imagination and emotion serves to motivate human beings to construct a vision of a better world and to try to bring it about in reality. If there is any truth in this proposition, it may suggest that Mother Nature is not above taking a few evolutionary risks. After all, the better world envisioned by one individual may be disastrous for the rest of us. On the other hand, if no one ever imagined a better world, if no one was ever willing to endure humiliation and pain for a beloved ideal, where would we be?

APPENDIX: STENDHAL, TERESA OF AVILA, AND SOME SELECTED PSYCHOLOGICAL THEORIES

Tesser's (1978; Tesser & Paulhus, 1976) theory of self-generated attitude polarization is consistent with the Stendhalian view of the role of attention: increased attention to the attitudinal object (the beloved) increases the extremity of one's attitude (the intensity of one's love). The process is then likely to double back on itself, with increased extremity of attitude promoting increased attention to the attitudinal object. Over time, one would expect just the kind of obsessive preoccupation and strong attachment characteristic of passionate love.

The importance of imaginative construction for both Stendhal and Teresa (although to different degrees) is strongly echoed in recent theories of emotion (Abelson, 1983; Kahneman & Tversky, 1982) that focus on the ways in which simulation of the past (what might have been) and anticipation of the future (what can be) can generate emotional experience in the present.

The extreme variation in affect described by both Stendhal and Teresa suggests a possible connection between passionate love and Solomon's (1980) opponent-process theory of emotion, which posits that any intense emotional state (pleasure or pain) is followed by its opposite (craving or relief). What is not clear, however, is whether this alternation is best understood in the automatic, mechanistic fashion proposed by Solomon or as mediated by the individual's cognitive constructions about the progress of the love affair.

Theories of emotion that stress interruption (Mandler, 1984) or discrepancy (Abelson, 1983) could account for the negative mood state generated by fears of rejection by the beloved (as emphasized by Stendhal) or by frustrated desires for greater closeness (as emphasized by Teresa). By considering the way in which the reality of the beloved interrupts one's imagined scenarios and is discrepant with one's idealized image, these theories could also provide an explanation for Stendhal's negative reaction to the beloved's actual presence.

The difficulty one has in controlling one's emotional state during passionate love—particularly highlighted by Tennov in her modern rendition of Stendhal's theory—could be cited by Zajonc (1980) as part of his argument for the primacy of affective states over cognitions.

Stendhal's soldier who transformed fear into valor could be said to have performed a self-generated reattribution of arousal, which at least in its broad outlines adheres to the basic principles of Schachter's two-factor theory of emotion (Schachter, 1964; Schachter & Singer, 1962; see also Reisenzein, 1983).

Roseman's (1984) proposal that emotions cannot be understood outside the context of motivation is consistent with the constant striving toward the beloved that characterizes both the Stendhalian and Teresean views of passionate love. Such strivings also fit well with de Rivera's (1984) notion that the function of all emotions is to preserve/enhance relationships.

Stendhal's remark that suffering can lead to committed love and, thus, that it does not necessarily always go the other way round hints at a possible dissonance interpretation (Wicklund & J. Brehm, 1976) for some of the phenomena of passionate love.

The importance of uncertainty explicitly noted by Stendhal and implicitly present in Teresa's account points to theories of motivation that concentrate on how the difficulty of goal attainment increases goal attractiveness (reactance theory, S. Brehm & J. Brehm, 1981; energization theory, J. Brehm et al., 1983).

REFERENCES

Abelson, R. (1983). Whatever became of consistency theory? *Personality and Social Psychology Bulletin, 9*, 37–54.
Berscheid, E. (1985). Interpersonal attraction. In G. Lindzey & E. Aronson (Eds.), *The handbook of social psychology* (3rd ed.). (Vol. 2, pp. 413–484). New York: Random House.
Brehm, J. W., Wright, R. Z., Solomon, S., Silka, L., & Greenberg, J. (1983).

Perceived difficulty, energization, and the magnitude of goal valence. *Journal of Experimental Social Psychology, 19,* 21–48.

Brehm, S. S. (1985). *Intimate relationships.* New York: Random House.

Brehm, S. S., & Brehm, J. W. (1981). *Psychological reactance: A theory of freedom and control.* New York: Academic Press.

Bynum, C. W. (1982). *Jesus as mother: Studies in the spirituality of the High Middle Ages.* Berkeley: University of California Press.

Cantor, J. R., Zillmann, D., & Bryant, J. (1975). Enhancement of experienced sexual arousal in response to erotic stimuli through misattribution of unrelated residual excitation. *Journal of Personality and Social Psychology, 32,* 69–75.

de Rivera, J. (1984). The structure of emotional relationships. In P. Shaver (Ed.), *Review of personality and social psychology: Emotions, relationships, and health* (pp. 116–145). Beverly Hills, CA: Sage.

de Rougemont, D. (1956). *Love in the Western world.* New York: Harper & Row.

Flaubert, G. (1941). *Sentimental education.* (A. Goldsmith, Trans.). Everyman's Library, no. 969. London: J. M. Dent & Sons.

———. (1959). *Madame Bovary.* (G. Hopkins, Trans.). New York: Dell.

Gathorne-Hardy, J. (1981). *Marriage, love, sex and divorce.* New York: Summit Books.

Hatfield, E., & Walster, G. W. (1978). *A new look at love.* Lantham, MA: University Press of America.

Hunt, M. M. (1959). *The natural history of love.* New York: Knopf.

Janowitz, T. (1986, February 3). Patterns. *New Yorker,* pp. 38–46.

Kahneman, D., & Tversky, A. (1982). The simulation heuristic. In D. Kahneman, D. Slovic, & A. Tversky (Eds.), *Judgment under uncertainty: Heuristics and biases* (pp. 201–208). New York: Cambridge University Press.

LeClercq, J. (1982). *The love of learning and the desire for God.* New York: Fordham University Press.

Lerner, R. E. (1972). *The heresy of the free spirit in the later Middle Ages.* Berkeley: University of California Press.

Mandler, G. (1984). *Mind and body: Psychology of emotion and stress.* New York: W. W. Norton.

Mechthild of Magdeburg. (1953). *The revelations of Mechthild of Magdeburg (1210–1297);* Or *The flowing light of the Godhead.* (L. Menzies, Trans.). New York: Longmans, Green.

Reisenzein, R. (1983). The Schachter theory of emotion: Two decades later. *Psychological Bulletin, 94,* 239–264.

Riordan, C. A., & Tedeschi, J. T. (1983). Attraction in aversive environments: Some evidence for classical conditioning and negative reinforcement. *Journal of Personality and Social Psychology, 44,* 683–692.

Roseman, I. J. (1984). Cognitive determinants of emotion: A structural theory. In P. Shaver (Ed.), *Review of personality and social psychology: Emotions, relationships, and health* (pp. 11–36). New York: Academic Press.

Schachter, S. (1964). The interaction of cognitive and physiological determinants of emotional state. In L. Berkowitz (Ed.), *Advances in experimental social psychology.* (Vol. 1, pp. 49–80). New York: Academic Press.

Schachter, S., & Singer, J. E. (1962). Cognitive, social, and physiological determinants of emotional state. *Psychological Review, 69*, 379–399.

Shaver, P. (1984). *Review of personality and social psychology: Emotions, relationships, and health.* Beverly Hills, CA: Sage.

Solomon, R. L. (1980). The opponent-process theory of acquired motivation. *American Psychologist, 35*, 691–712.

Stendhal (Beyle, M.). (1926). *The red and the black.* (C. K. Scott-Moncrieff, Trans.). New York: Liveright.

———. (1927). *On love.* (H. B. V., Trans.). New York: Boni & Liveright.

Tennov, D. (1979). *Love and limerence.* New York: Stein & Day.

Teresa of Avila (1946). *The complete works of St. Teresa of Jesus.* (E. A. Peers, Trans.). London: Sheed & Ward.

Tesser, A. (1978). Self-generated attitude change. In L. Berkowitz (Ed.). *Advances in experimental social psychology.* (Vol. 2, pp. 289–338). New York: Academic Press.

Tesser, A., & Paulhus, D. L. (1976). Toward a causal model of love. *Journal of Personality and Social Psychology, 34*, 1095–1105.

Therese of Lisieux (1975–76). *Story of a soul: The autobiography of St. Therese of Lisieux.* (J. Clarke, Trans.). Washington, DC: Institute of Carmelite Studies.

———. (1977). *Her last conversations.* Washington, DC: Institute of Carmelite Studies.

Vlastos, G. (1981). The individual as an object of love in Plato. In G. Vlastos, *Platonic studies* (2nd printing) (pp. 3–42). Princeton, NJ: Princeton University Press.

White, G. L., & Kight, T. D. (1984). Misattribution of arousal and attraction: Effects of salience of explanations for arousal. *Journal of Experimental Social Psychology, 20*, 55–64.

Wicklund, R. A., & Brehm, J. W. (1976). *Perspectives on cognitive dissonance.* Hillsdale, NJ: Erlbaum.

Zajonc, R. B. (1980). Feeling and thinking: Preferences need no inferences. *American Psychologist, 35*, 151–175.

Zillmann, D. (1978). Attribution and misattribution of excitory reactions. In J. H. Harvey, W. J. Ickes, & R. F. Kidd (Eds.), *New directions in attribution research.* (Vol. 2, pp. 335–368). Hillsdale, NJ: Erlbaum.

Zillmann, D., Johnson, R. C., & Day, K. D. (1974). Attribution of apparent arousal and proficiency of recovery from sympathetic activation affecting excitation transfer to aggressive behavior. *Journal of Experimental Social Psychology, 10*, 503–515.

CHAPTER TWELVE

Romantic Love

Individual and Cultural Perspectives

BY KENNETH L. DION AND KAREN K. DION

In this chapter, we will describe the results of our research program into the role of personality in heterosexual romantic love, which we have pursued for several years. This research has largely concerned such questions as these: Are certain sorts of persons more likely to experience romantic love than others? Are personality and individual differences associated with subjectively different experiences of romantic love? After reviewing and summarizing this work, we shall consider the phenomenon of romantic love from a broader cultural framework, in particular contrasting the Western conception of romantic love with the perspectives of Eastern cultures, especially those of China and Japan. Following that, we shall relate the issues raised by individual and cultural differences in romantic love to the more general theme of individualism versus collectivism, a fundamental value dimension on which individuals and cultures clearly differ and that we believe is important for fully understanding the phenomenon of romantic love.

PERSONALITY CORRELATES OF ROMANTIC LOVE

A Phenomenological Approach

In exploring questions of personality differences in romantic love (who is likely to experience love and with what effect?), we have adopted a phenomenological approach, in the sense of focusing on individuals' descriptions of their romantic love experiences. This approach reflects a tacit assumption on our part, now well justified by our findings and those of other investigators, that romantic love as reportedly experienced by individuals is not a unitary or single phenomenon at all. As we shall see, when asked to describe what love has felt like to them, individuals report very different experiences. We shall argue from such findings that love obviously means different things to different people, and that some insight concerning these subjective differences can be found in terms of key personality differences emphasized by psychological theorists interested in the phenomenon of love.

To elicit individuals' descriptions of their heterosexual romantic love experiences, we have relied upon a Romantic Love Questionnaire, largely of our own construction. Its initial version included items concerning various parameters of love, such as whether or not the respondent had ever been in love, was presently in love or not, and the frequency, duration, and intensity of the person's experiences of romantic love. The questionnaire also contains several classes of measures aimed at exploring the respondents' subjective experience of romantic love. For example, they are asked to describe their love experiences in terms of a series of bipolar, adjectival scales (for example, slow-fast, impulsive-deliberate, sensual-intellectual, mysterious-understandable) and to indicate the extent to which these adjectives applied to their experiences. They are also asked to report the extent to which they have experienced symptoms commonly believed in the Western cultural tradition to be associated with the experience of romantic love (for example, euphoria, difficulty concentrating, sleeplessness). Respondents indicate their attitudes toward love on items aimed mainly at gauging how romantic and idealistic versus pragmatic they are in their orientation toward love. In analyzing the results from these measures, we have relied upon factor analysis, a statistical technique for revealing different dimensions underlying a set of interrelated items. In more recent versions of the Romantic Love Questionnaire, we have also incorporated Rubin's (1970) Love Scale, which defines love as an interpersonal attitude consisting of caring, need, and trust toward another person (Steck, Levitan, McLane & Kelley, 1982), and questions concerning the respondents' experience of unrequited love.

In exploring the role of personality in heterosexual love, one must decide on a strategy for determining which personality dimensions are apt to be important. One can avoid having to deal with the question at all by relying on omnibus personality inventories (such as the Minnesota Multiphasic Personality Inventory) that measure a number of personality dimensions simultaneously and relating individuals' standings on these dimensions to their reported experiences of romantic love. We have avoided this path because of its obvious susceptibility to the criticism of being a "shot-gun" approach or mindless empiricism. Instead, we have preferred to rely upon our own theories and others' concerning personality and love as a guide to selecting personality dimensions to explore as likely correlates of romantic love. In addition to garnering insights from those who have thought a great deal about the phenomenon of love, a reliance upon theory has greater potential for lending coherence, direction, and organization to social-psychological research into romantic love.

Locus of Control

In our first study, we considered a personality dimension identified by clinical and personality psychologist Julian Rotter (1966) as "locus of control." According to Rotter, this dimension consists of opposite expectancies concerning one's personal efficacy as a causal agent. Persons that Rotter characterizes as internally controlled tend to view events that affect them as being under their personal control; they regard themselves as being the captain of their fate. Externally controlled people, on the other hand, are more likely to see events affecting them as being beyond their personal control and due to such forces as luck, fate, powerful others, and so on.

To measure these orientations or "beliefs about the nature of the world," Rotter (1966) has constructed an I-E Scale containing forced-choice items in questionnaire format: for each item respondents are asked to choose between a statement that reflects a belief in the personal control-lability of events and another reflecting a belief in the inevitability of events and their control by powerful external forces. Since the content of items taps a wide variety of domains, including politics, vocational success, scholastic achievement, leadership, and so on, Rotter (1966) characterizes the I-E Scale as gauging *generalized* expectancies concerning one's perceived locus of control.

In our first study of personality and romantic love, then, a sample of 243 undergraduates of both sexes on the Minneapolis campus of the University of Minnesota completed both Rotter's I-E Scale to measure their standing on the locus of control dimension as either internal or external and the initial version of the Romantic Love Questionnaire to assess the nature and quality of their love experiences (Dion & Dion, 1973). For the most part, the respondents in this study (as well as in our other studies to be described subsequently) completed these two questionnaires at different times under different rationales and with different experimenters. This was done so that any associations found between locus of control and romantic love would reflect genuine relationships between the two and not simply either the respondents' perceived pressure for consistency in responding or their attempted compliance to our hypotheses, as they perceived them, that might have resulted if the two questionnaires had been administered together.

The preceding study was conducted to test several of our hypotheses that were based on the Western cultural stereotype of love and the tendencies of internals and externals as reflected in the social-psychological literature. For example, the prevalent stereotype in Western cultures portrays romantic love as an external force that is allegedly intense, mysterious, and volatile, and that engulfs the "fated" individuals in an overwhelming, idealized experience surpassing ordinary pleasures (Schon, 1963). With romantic love defined this way, internals should be less likely than externals to label instances of heterosexual attraction as "love" because of their penchant for interpreting events in terms of personal causes. One would hypothesize, then, that externals would be more likely to report having been in love than would internals. And it would also follow that externals should be more prone than internals to report personal experiences of heterosexual love in terms of the prevalent Western cultural stereotype—as a mysterious, volatile, intense, and idealized experience.

Research by personality and social psychologists on individuals classified as internal or external by means of Rotter's I-E Scale (for example, Phares, 1976) also indicates that internals dislike being personally influenced and that they prefer instead to control others. In a heterosexual relationship, such a manipulative orientation on the part of internals would tend to (1) endow it with a rational, calculated, nonreciprocal quality, (2) undermine feelings of positive attachment between the partners, and (3) result in the pair relationship being perceived in pragmatic rather than idealistic terms.

In general, these expected differences between internals and externals in their romantic love experiences were borne out reasonably well. As predicted, for example, the Minnesota undergraduates categorized as internals from their scores on Rotter's scale differed from those classified as externals in being proportionally less likely to report ever having experienced romantic love on the Romantic Love Questionnaire. Second, among those who reported being or having been in love, internals described qualitatively different experiences than did externals. Specifically, internals depicted their subjective experience of love as being more rational and tending to be less volatile than externals. Furthermore, in terms of their attitudes toward love, internals were more strongly opposed to an idealistic view of romantic love than were externals. Subsequent studies by other investigators with North American samples have similarly found that internals were less idealistic and prone to less romanticism in their attitudes toward love than were externals (see Dion & Dion, 1985, pp. 213–214, for further discussion of this research). To summarize, then, this evidence suggests that the love experiences of externals are indeed more in keeping with the Western cultural stereotype of romantic love.

Self-Esteem and Defensiveness

Several psychological theories of romantic love agree in pointing to dimensions of the individual's self-concept, especially one's level of self-esteem or self-actualization, as likely to be important in deciding "who falls in love and with what effect." There is marked disagreement, however, as regards the *nature* of the relationship between self-concept and one's experiences of romantic love. On one hand, for example, psychological thinkers as diverse as psychoanalyst Erich Fromm (1939), self-actualization theorist and early leader of the human potential movement Abraham Maslow (1970), and Carl Rogers (1959), the originator of client-centered therapy, have all contended that self-accepting and nondefensive individuals should be more capable of loving others and experiencing satisfying and fulfilling heterosexual relationships than others. Underlying these contentions is the notion that one must love oneself before being able to love another person. Fromm (1939), for example, carefully distinguished between selfishness and self-love, viewing the latter as healthy regard and esteem for oneself that is necessary before one can love another.

Advocates of self-esteem theories, on the other hand, have taken an opposite view of the likely relation between self-esteem and romantic love. Illustrative of this stance is social psychologist Elaine Hatfield's proposal (see Walster, 1965) that persons who are low in self-esteem perhaps have a special need for affection, and therefore such individuals would find the experience of romantic love more rewarding and fulfilling than persons with high self-esteem. Another argument consistent with this line of thought is that being the object of another's affection would confirm one's feeling of worthiness—a consequence that should be particularly appreciated by those relatively lacking in self-esteem.

To test these opposing views in a second study of personality and romantic love (Dion & Dion, 1975), we obtained measures of self-esteem and defensiveness from over 150 undergraduate women and men at the University of Toronto (Canada) who, in later sessions, also completed a revised and expanded version of the Romantic Love Questionnaire. A problem known as the social desirability artifact frequently plagues putative measures of self-esteem because respondents often can easily discern the aim of the instruments and present themselves in an especially positive light that does not reflect their *genuine* level of self-esteem. To limit or possibly even eliminate this problem, we employed as our index of self-esteem a measure known as Self-Social Symbols Tasks, which Robert Ziller (1973) contends is less susceptible to the social desirability artifact than traditional self-esteem measures—a fact we validated for ourselves (see Dion & Dion, 1975). As an illustration of Self-Social Symbols Tasks, one item presents the respondent with a horizontal series of circles and asks that the circles be labeled with letters representing self and specified significant others, such as father, spouse or dating partner, friend, physician, and so on. The location of the self symbol relative to the other symbols is assumed to reflect one's level of self-esteem. Specifically, Ziller assumes that the more leftward placement of the self symbol relative to the other symbols reflects greater importance of the self as perceived by the respondent and is therefore taken as indicating higher self-esteem.

Theorists, such as Rogers and Maslow, who have argued that the relationship between self-esteem and romantic love is a positive one have also stressed the need to focus on *nondefensive* high self-esteem. An individual's self-esteem can be high either because it is genuinely so or because the person presents an artificially enhanced or exaggeratedly positive self-image owing to perceived threat or vulnerability on his or her part. For this reason, our respondents also completed the Marlowe-Crowne Social Desirability Scale, which psychologists Douglas Crowne and David Marlowe (1964) have shown can be viewed as reflecting an individual's level of defensiveness—which refers to an individual's sense of weak or vulnerable self-esteem. The Social Desirability Scale contains items concerning one's alleged personal traits and one's hypothetical actions in social situations. Approximately half the items concern culturally acceptable statements about one's self that are untrue of most individuals, whereas the other half depicts common shortcomings with socially undesirable connotations that typify most people. Persons who attribute culturally acceptable statements to themselves while failing to admit typical faults would attain high scores on this scale and would be classified as high in defensiveness. With respondents' scores on defensiveness and self-esteem in hand, we were able to classify them relative to one another as being high or low on each dimension separately as well as jointly.

Consistent with the contentions of self theorists Rogers and Maslow, we found that individuals who were high in self-esteem but also low in defensiveness (nondefensive, self-accepting persons) were indeed the ones who reported experiencing romantic love most frequently. Yet, in other regards, the findings favored the expectations of self-esteem theorists. For example, persons with low self-esteem reported more intense experiences of romantic love and described them as being less rational (that is, character-ized by such adjectives as *superficial*, *predictable*, and *controllable*) than did those high in self-esteem. They also expressed stronger interpersonal atti-tudes of love, liking, and trust for their partners and evaluated their part-ners more favorably than did those with high self-esteem. For their part, highly defensive individuals reported experiencing romantic love less fre-quently, described their love episodes as more guarded, and were more cynical in their attitudes toward love than were less defensive persons.

We have suggested two processes that may help explain why self-esteem and defensiveness together affect a person's openness and respon-siveness to romantic love. First, those low in self-esteem may simply be less successful in engaging love relationships because they are less skilled so-cially and less adept in interpersonal relationships. If individuals low in self-esteem are less capable at inducing others into romantic relationships, they should also experience unrequited love more frequently than those high in self-esteem, which we found to be the case in our study. Second, once a romantic love relationship has been established, those low in self-esteem clearly seem to appreciate the relationship and their partners more than those high in self-esteem—consistent with the contentions of self-esteem theorists.

In the case of the personality dimension of defensiveness, we believe that highly defensive people avoid intimate heterosexual relationships in order to protect their vulnerable self-images, especially because of the threat of self-revelation, which increases in such relationships. Crowne and Marlowe (1964) suggested that defensive individuals actively avoid inter-personal situations, such as psychotherapy, typified by high self-revelation and self-disclosure of intimate details. Consistent with this line of thought, we ourselves provided some experimental evidence suggesting that highly defensive women do indeed respond less positively to another individual who engages in intimate self-disclosure as well as to those of the opposite sex (Dion & Dion, 1978).

Self-Actualization and Romantic Love

Another way to test the predictions of self-actualization theorists such as Maslow is directly to assess personality differences in self-actualization. Useful for this assessment is the Personal Orientation Inventory (POI) devised by Everett Shostrom (in consultation with Maslow) who incorporated ideas of psychologists Maslow, Rollo May, and Fritz Perls as well as sociologist David Riesman's concept of the inner-directed individual. Shostrom's goals in formulating the POI were to create an instrument that would reflect an individual's degree of positive mental health and the extent to which the person was fulfilling his or her potential. Most of the items in the POI are aimed at indexing the respondent's extent of inner-directedness and autonomy from external pressures. A smaller number of items are aimed at gauging the respondent's "time competence": is the person focused on the present rather than the past or future? Psychological evidence to date suggests that the POI is the best available measure of personality differences in self-actualization (see Dion & Dion, 1985, pp. 217–218, for a review of this evidence).

In our study (Dion & Dion, 1985), University of Toronto undergraduates completed the POI, the Romantic Love Questionnaire, and Wessman and Ricks's (1966) Inventory of Affect Scales. Of particular relevance, the last inventory includes a Love and Sex Scale that focuses on love as an emotional experience involving a sense of subjective satisfaction. The respondent is asked to indicate "the extent to which you feel loving and tender, or sexually frustrated and unloving." Several findings were consistent with expectations from self-actualization theorists. For one thing, individuals high in self-actualization reported a richer, more satisfying love experience than did those lower in self-actualization, when describing an ongoing or previous heterosexual relationship. Also, highly self-actualized persons described the subjective experience of love as being less guarded and more intense than those less self-actualized.

On the other hand, not all romantic love experiences of self-actualized individuals were more positive. High self-actualized persons were less idealistic and more pragmatic in their attitudes toward love than their less self-actualized counterparts. Furthermore, on Rubin's (1970) Love Scale mentioned earlier, individuals high in self-actualization expressed *less* need and *less* caring for their romantic partners than those low in self-actualization.

We have concluded from our studies that *both* self-esteem and self-actualization theories are needed to understand how personality and self-concept relate to romantic love. Persons who are genuinely self-accepting and high in self-actualization do seem to be more open to the experience of romantic heterosexual love. On the other hand, individuals lower in these qualities report greater esteem and affection for their partners, perhaps because they have greater needs and appreciation for affection from a member of the opposite sex.

CROSS-CULTURAL PERSPECTIVES ON LOVE

Love and Interdependence

As can be seen from the preceding section, there is considerable evidence that at least among young adults (university students), there are indeed individual differences in the experience of love. What do these findings suggest about the nature of romantic love? First, they support the view that love is multidimensional, that it refers to qualitatively different types of experiences and feelings toward one's partner. This view is compatible with that expressed by other scholars. For example, social psychologist Harold Kelley (1983) argues that "the single word *love* refers to different phenomena" (p. 280), and he proposes conceptual models of different types of love. And sociologist John Lee (1973), too, has presented a typology describing different forms or styles of love. Our view stresses the contribution of personality as a key factor that partially accounts for why people experience the phenomenon of love so differently from one another.

Second, we would argue that since intimacy is integral to love, responses to it underlie individuals' experiences of romantic love (Dion & Dion, 1979, 1985). Our research suggests that certain dimensions of personality are such that they may facilitate the development of the kind of intimacy exemplified by romantic love; in contrast, other personality dimensions may inhibit this process. Moreover, there is evidence that the kinds of experiences people describe as characterizing love are related to their responses to intimacy and dependence on a partner. Our findings are consistent with and extend sociological theorist Peter Blau's (1964) provocative conjectures that (1) personality is the key factor influencing whether an intimate love relationship is likely to develop and (2) attitudes toward dependency are critical to romantic attraction. Our findings suggest that certain dimensions of personality reflect different reactions to interdependence, which in turn are related to the likelihood of experiencing romantic love and to the nature of this experience.

From this perspective, internal control and defensiveness are examples of personality dimensions that seem to inhibit or constrain romantic love. Both these dimensions appear to be characterized by an aversion to, or ambivalence about, dependency on others. As an individual's involvement in a romantic relationship increases, interdependence and emotional vulnerability also increase. For individuals showing a strong need for personal control, the prospect of greater intimacy can heighten conflicts about personal vulnerability. Indeed, that romantic love is regarded as an experience in which one loses control is illustrated by the phrases used to describe it: one "falls in love," one is "swept off one's feet," or one is "head over heels in love." Similarly, defensive individuals will be more likely to feel distress over the loss of control and the close interdependence accompanying romantic love than will nondefensive people. As a result of this ambivalence, it may be harder for the former to involve themselves fully in an intimate relationship.

On the other hand, other dimensions of personality should increase the likelihood that a person will become involved in an intimate relationship. Thus, a greater capacity to experience love should be found among people characterized by greater genuine self-acceptance (namely, a low level of defensiveness and a high level of self-esteem) and among self-actualized individuals. Following this line of argument, one might assume that both groups are more involved with their partners in a romantic relationship and experience greater interdependence. As mentioned earlier, however, we have not found such a pattern. Instead, we found that those with greater self-acceptance seem to be less emotionally dependent on their partner, as reflected in their expressed feelings about their partner. Our most recent research suggests that self-actualized young adults may be more involved in love as a fulfilling personal experience than in love as an intense interdependency with another person.

It appears, therefore, that the issue of interdependence in a love relationship is central to understanding the relation between personality and love. Moreover, this issue is pertinent for understanding not only the personality attributes that may inhibit the experience of romantic love (such as defensiveness) but also those attributes that may enhance the experience (such as self-actualization). We also believe that a comparative analysis of cultural perspectives on dependence, intimacy, and heterosexual love can provide valuable insights on the nature of interdependence in love relationships. We now turn to a consideration of these perspectives.

We begin by noting that to a North American, the term *dependence* has negative connotations or at the very least elicits an ambivalent response. This is understandable in a culture where self-sufficiency and personal autonomy are stressed. Social psychologist and critic Edward Sampson (1977), for example, used the phrase "self-contained individualism" to characterize American values. And Maslow's theory also reflected this type of cultural orientation. In his discussion of deficiency versus growth motivation, Maslow characterized the deficit-motivated individual as more dependent on others than the growth-motivated person. He regarded the former's greater dependency negatively, saying it was a state that "colors and limits interpersonal relations" (1968, p. 36). Needing or dependency in this framework is a form of pathology, as indicated by the terminology employed.

When applied to the experience of love, this same value orientation is apparent. Maslow's account of the love experiences of self-actualized persons portrayed them as freer of dependency on others, and he proposed that there are two types of love (1968, 1970). One, labeled "deficiency love," he saw as based on unfulfilled needs, which the individual tries to satisfy in the context of an intimate relationship. According to Maslow, this type of love would have a possessive, demanding quality since the individual *needed* the relationship. In contrast, the other type, "being love," was presumably based on an appreciation of the partner's qualities and of the experience of love per se. Maslow suggested that this type characterized the love experiences of self-actualized persons since they did not *need* their partner in the usual sense of the term. Implicit in this formulation is the belief that, consistent with North American cultural ideals concerning personal autonomy, a desire to gratify personal needs in a love relationship represents a less psychologically mature type of love. In many respects, then, Maslow's theory of self-actualization is a prototypically Western, or North American, perspective on psychological functioning.

The cultural specificity of Maslow's perspective becomes strikingly apparent when his ideas are contrasted with Japanese psychiatrist L. Takeo Doi's (1962, 1963, 1973) analysis of the motivational basis of personal functioning in Japanese society. According to Doi, the key to understanding the Japanese cultural perspective is the concept of *amae*. A term that derives from a verb meaning "to depend and presume upon another's benevolence," *amae* has no equivalent in Western languages (Doi, 1962). Extending Doi's analysis, American psychologists Lazarus, Averill, and Opton (1970) have suggested that amae and dependency reflect in common a fundamental need for social attachment whose expression is culturally conditioned. Doi (1973) notes that to the Japanese, amae has positive connotations, an orientation he contrasts with the Western emphasis on individual freedom, with the result that the kind of dependency represented by this concept is regarded negatively by Westerners.

Important to our present discussion is Doi's remark that "amae, generally speaking, is an inseparable concomitant of love" (1973, p. 118). The amae concept closely links dependency with the desire to be loved. The psychological state of amae is believed to derive from an infant's relationship with its mother, reflecting the infant's "craving for close contact" with the mother as the child becomes aware of her separate existence (Doi, 1973, p. 74). This feeling is subsequently extended to other relationships. One could argue that developmental continuity in the growth of interpersonal attachment may be stronger in Japanese culture than in North American society, since attachment and dependency needs continue to be accepted as the individual matures. According to Doi, the Japanese acknowledge their needs for dependency on others as an accepted part of intimate relationships throughout their lives. In summary, comparing Doi's concept of amae to Maslow's concept of self-actualized love draws attention to the different motivational dynamics underlying love in a variety of cultures.

Love and Views of Self

Cross-cultural comparison illuminates yet another important aspect of the Western concept of love, which will help us better understand the nature of the relation between personality and love. Western ideals of romantic love portray it as an intense emotional experience that is the basis for an exclusive commitment to one's partner in marriage or a long-lasting relationship. This means that the relationship is of great psychological importance to the individual—thus, the need for understanding how one's orientation toward others influences the likelihood of one's developing an intimate relationship. In North America, the capacity to form an intimate heterosexual relationship is an important aspect of personal well-being in adulthood. Campbell's (1981, p. 226) conclusion, based on survey findings concerning the correlates of subjective well-being among Americans, supports this point, since this evidence indicates that "the basic source of social support among adult Americans is marriage."

As part of his comparative analysis of American and Chinese ways of life, psychological anthropologist Francis L. K. Hsu (1981) compares American and Chinese beliefs and values about love and marriage—a comparison that highlights the differences between the two cultures. Hsu characterizes American culture as "individual-centered," with great importance attached to emotions; in contrast, Chinese culture is "situation-centered" and tends to "underplay all matters of the heart" (p. 12). He speculates that intense affective experiences are more likely to occur among North Americans. Hsu argues that in the Chinese cultural tradition individuals' greater dependency on others mitigates the intensity of their emotional experiences because they are more likely to be shared in a broader social network.

In his discussion of cross-cultural differences, Godwin Chu (1985), a research associate of Hawaii's East-West Center, also compares the North American view of the self with the "traditional Chinese self." Chu contrasts Americans' emphasis on the individual with the traditional Chinese view, in which self was defined in terms of the role relationships individuals had with others. Elaborating this point, he comments: "A male Chinese would consider himself a son, a brother, a husband, a father, but hardly *himself*. It seems as if . . . there was very little independent self left for the Chinese" (1985, p. 258).

These cultural differences are reflected in the relative importance of romantic love in each society. Hsu suggests that the concept of romantic love fits in well with the North American cultural perspective, given its emphasis on the individual, but not the Chinese cultural orientation where one is expected to consider obligations to others, especially one's parents, as well as personal feelings. This contrast is captured in Hsu's depiction of love in North America compared to China: "An American asks, 'How does my heart feel?' A Chinese asks, 'What will other people say?'" (1981, p. 50). Hsu comments that the Western idea of romantic love has not had much of an impact on young adults in China.

Chu (1985) has pointed out that the qualities a person seeks in a mate are as revealing about views of self as of others. He describes a popular depiction of desirable qualities in a prospective mate for contemporary women in China and notes that, in this list, romance is not referred to, consistent with Chinese tradition. Instead what is emphasized is a series of more pragmatic attributes—income earned by the prospective mate, for example, or the type of housing he can provide—as well as a desire to be free of traditional kinship-related obligations.

As Hsu (1981) has pointed out, from the Chinese perspective, the use of the term *love* to describe a relationship between a man and a woman typically connotes an illicit liaison, not a respectable, socially sanctioned relationship. This point is well-illustrated in the following quote in which a Chinese woman describes the development of her relationship with her fiancé: "While our impressions of each other deepened, we remained on the level of platonic friendship. We never talked about the word love when we saw each other; therefore I trust him deeply and respect him very much" (quoted in Hsu, 1981, p. 52). This description reflects a perspective on the concept of love very different from the Western view. Another apparent difference concerns societal approval of public expressions of intimacy and affection. Hsu comments that this type of behavior traditionally has been, and continues to be, regarded negatively in Chinese culture, consistent with the situation-centered orientation he suggests exists in Chinese society.

In view of these differences, several findings from another recent study of styles of love are of interest. American social psychologists Clyde Hendrick and Susan Hendrick (1986) administered a questionnaire that assessed attitudes toward love based on Lee's (1973) typology to a large sample of students at the University of Miami (Florida). As one of several questions about background characteristics, respondents were asked to indicate their "ethnic heritage" using one of five categories designated by the researchers—black, white non-Hispanic, white-Hispanic, Oriental, and other. Of the 807 respondents, 62 described their ethnic background as Oriental. These students, when compared to white non-Hispanic students, were less likely to endorse a style of love characterized by physical attraction and intensity of feeling ("eros") and more likely to endorse practical ("pragma") and friendship-based ("storgic") styles of love. Commenting on these findings for this ethnic group, Hendrick and Hendrick speculate that "Oriental students seemed relatively low in affect (low in Eros, high in Storge and Pragma). It may well be that the six love styles do not capture properly Oriental conceptions of love" (1986, p. 401). Alternatively, however, we would suggest that this pattern of findings is, in fact, consistent with Hsu's characterization of one Asian culture's perspective on love, which from the viewpoint of Western cultural ideals appears to be "low in affect."

In summary, we have discussed some key cultural contrasts in the relation between (1) love and interdependence and (2) love and views of self, particularly in Western versus Asian cultural traditions. This type of cross-cultural conceptual analysis can foster a deeper, more comprehensive understanding of the nature of love. Viewed from this perspective, the theoretical rationale for our program of research and our study of the relation between personality and love is in many respects a quintessentially Western approach. In our theoretical framework, we have hypothesized that the experience of love and feelings toward one's partner is related to one's dispositional attributes, and the evidence discussed in the first part of this chapter indicates that this approach does advance our understanding of love in the United States and Canada.

What other approaches to the study of love are suggested by this kind of analysis? Some social scientists have suggested that the behavioral sciences are heavily influenced by an individualistic orientation and have proposed that different constructs having their origin in Asian cultural traditions should receive more attention. Hsu (1971, 1985), for example, states that the process of "psychosocial homeostasis" is the basic unit of psychological functioning and that this concept should guide research rather than the concept of personality. He suggests using the Chinese term *jen* (meaning "man") to describe aspects of psychological functioning that he argues are not included in the construct of *personality*. In contrast to the intrapsychic focus of personality that reflects an individualistic orientation, jen stresses "the place of the individual in a web of interpersonal relationships" (Hsu, 1985, p. 33). The framework for understanding a person's behavior emphasizes "how it fits or fails to fit the interpersonal standards of the society and culture" (1971, p. 29, italics omitted).

Related to this is Hong Kong psychologist David Y. F. Ho's (1982) examination of several concepts (including jen and amae) from three Asian societies, in which he identifies a common theme. In Ho's analysis, Asian concepts of relevance to the behavioral sciences are "relational" (for example, jen, amae, face), whereas Western concepts tend to be "individualistic" in nature (for example, self, personality, actor). When contrasted with those of the West, Asian psychological constructs stress the "relational, reciprocal aspects of social behavior between individuals, rather than . . . the characteristics of single individuals" (Ho, 1982, p. 233). Ho proposes that these relational constructs may make valuable contributions to the development of theory in the behavioral sciences.

These constructs have the potential to provide insights into the dynamics of love and intimacy. We have already discussed how the concept of amae highlights alternate formulations of the role of dependency in love relationships in Eastern versus Western cultural traditions. To cite another example, Hsu's (1971, 1985) discussion of jen has focused attention on the individual's need for intimacy. He argues that although the need is fundamental, cultural factors may make it easier or harder for the individual to maintain psychological balance by the social structuring of intimate relationships. He suggests that in Chinese society, since the individual's bonds to the family are a major source of intimacy throughout life, the person has little need to search for intimacy in relationships with "unrelated peers." In contrast, Western values discourage dependence on parents in adulthood, encouraging the person to form intimate bonds with others—hence the importance of romantic love and of a marriage partner. Hsu, however, regards relationships with unrelated people as inherently riskier than relationships with one's kin. Thus he speculates that it is harder to maintain one's personal sense of equilibrium in Western society because of this fragmentation and diffusion of intimate relationships.

INDIVIDUALISM-COLLECTIVISM AND ROMANTIC LOVE

The differences between Western and Eastern cultures in the way love is viewed also partly reflects an underlying value difference concerning the relation between the individual and society—individualism-collectivism. In this section, we briefly review cross-cultural research on this value dimension, explore critiques and rejoinders concerning individualism in America, and conclude with an exploration of the relation between individualism and love.

Individualism-Collectivism: Cross-cultural Perspectives

Perhaps the main thrust of modern social science research on individualism-collectivism has come from the work of Dutch behavioral scientist Geert Hofstede (1984). During the late 1960s and 1970s, Hofstede and his colleagues conducted an extensive comparative study of work-related values among members of the subsidiaries of a large multinational corporation in over fifty modern countries. The aim of Hofstede's research was to isolate the basic differences in thinking and action across countries. Through extensive analysis of his survey data concerning values, he found four main dimensions along which the dominant value systems of these countries could be ordered and compared; individualism-collectivism was one of them. Countries that scored highest on individualism included the United States, Australia, Great Britain, Canada, the Netherlands, and New Zealand. Countries that scored lowest on individualism and reflected the alternate pole of collectivism included such countries as Venezuela, Colombia, and Pakistan as well as cities and states with a large representation of Chinese people, such as Taiwan, Singapore, and Hong Kong.

According to Hofstede (1984), the fundamental difference represented on this dimension concerns, of course, the relation between the individual and the group or collectivity. In collective societies, individuals belong to groups that look after their interests in return for loyalty. Other societal norms tied to collectivism include reduced privacy, emotional dependence on organizations and institutions, a belief in the superiority of group over individual decisions, and one's identity being defined by one's place in the social system. Hofstede suggests that the Chinese concept of jen is the best illustration of a collectivistic ethos. For societies characterized by individualism, on the other hand, people look out for their own interest and that of their family only. These societies emphasize rights over duties, personal autonomy, self-realization, individual initiative and achievement, and the superiority of individual decisions; personal identity is defined by the individual's attributes. Psychological traits consistent with individualism, such as internal control and inner-directedness, are seen as desirable and are emphasized in socializing children.

More recently, University of Illinois psychologist Harry Triandis (in press) has extended the work of Hofstede and his colleagues. Triandis believes that the individualism-collectivism dimension is one of the most important sources of cultural differences in social behavior. Accordingly, he has proposed using the dimension as a basic concept in cross-cultural social psychology by (among other things) reconceptualizing it and outlining its likely antecedents and consequences.

To Triandis, the notion of the "in-group"—a group to which one belongs (family, ethnic group, nationality, religion) or wishes to belong (a profession, say)—is the key element of the concept of collectivism. In his words, "*Collectivism* [reflects a] great emphasis on (a) the views, needs, and goals of the ingroup rather than oneself, (b) social norms and duty defined by the ingroup rather than behavior to get pleasure, (c) beliefs shared with the ingroup rather than . . . beliefs that distinguish oneself from [the] ingroup, and (d) great readiness to cooperate with ingroup members." In other words, the more one's needs, goals, beliefs, and behavior are determined by one or more in-groups rather than by one's personal preferences, the more collectivistic the person or the society.

To assess how collectivistic a given society is, Triandis suggests that the number of relevant in-groups, as well as their sphere (the selection of one's spouse, career, place of residence) and the depth or power of their influence must also be taken into account. Greater collectivism is associated with a small number of in-groups having such broad influence over individuals' behavior, it is difficult for them to resist. Since in-groups can also differ in size as well as in the areas of life they influence, it follows from Triandis's argument that there can be different kinds of individualism and collectivism. For example, Triandis characterizes the United States as having a "consultative" form of individualism because there are many relevant and potentially competing in-groups that individuals must "consult" as guides to behavior, and the influence of each is narrow. Mediterranean rural societies of Greece and Italy, on the other hand, are collectivistic within the family but individualistic outside it.

As regards its antecedents, Triandis proposes that collectivism is closely linked to ethnocentrism, usually defined as the tendency to use one's in-group and its values as the standard of comparison and evaluation for oneself and others. Thus, factors that heighten ethnocentrism, such as external threat from other groups (out-groups), should be associated with tendencies toward greater collectivism. On the other hand, such factors as small family size, emphasis on autonomy in child rearing, emphasis on hedonism in the culture, social and geographical mobility, and exposure to multiple viewpoints and sources of information are proposed as antecedents to individualism by Triandis.

Triandis suggests that the consequences of either extreme individualism or extreme collectivism are apt to be undesirable. Many authors, including Triandis (in press) and his colleague Hui (1984) as well as others (as discussed below), basing their argument on the well-documented literature of the therapeutic benefits of social support, have suggested that marked individualism may be associated with a wide variety of physical and mental illnesses as well as social problems, such as divorce, alcoholism, or crime. On the other hand, individualism with its stress on personal competence and success is certainly conducive to economic progress, although the obvious success of some collectivistic Asian economies such as Japan or Hong Kong suggest that the link between individualism and economic progress is not inevitable.

Not surprisingly, given this theoretical work by Hofstede, Triandis, and others, the concept of individualism-collectivism is proving to be a rich one for social scientists. The concept has figured prominently in any number of recent studies. Some are aimed at understanding certain cultures in their own right, especially the United States (Bellah, Madsen, Sullivan, Swidler, & Tipton, 1985) and China (Ho, 1975, 1979; Hsu, 1981). Others examine cultural differences in behavior such as the links between the way persons are perceived and reported behavioral intentions toward them (Bond & Forgas, 1984), responses to verbal insult (Bond, Wan, Leung, & Giacolone, 1985), and the allocation of rewards to individuals in groups (Murphy-Berman, Berman, Singh, Pachauri, & Kumar, 1984; Leung & Bond, 1984).

American Individualism: Critiques and Rejoinders

As we have seen, the United States is the prototypic individualistic society. Of the more than fifty societies in Hofstede's monumental study of values, the United States scored highest in terms of individualism. Indeed, as American sociologist Bellah and his colleagues (1985) point out, the French philosopher and observer Alexis de Tocqueville was the first to use the term *individualism* in its modern sense in his perceptive analysis of early nineteenth-century America. Tocqueville saw a thoroughgoing individualism as the preeminent characteristic of growing America but felt that other indigenous institutions—biblical religion, republican traditions, the influence of women—served to blunt the negative consequences he believed would follow from unrestrained individualism.

Some of the concerns that Tocqueville expressed as well as new ones have emerged among social scientists in the last ten years or so. For example, in a thoughtful and provocative paper, personality and social psychologist Robert Hogan (1975) argues persuasively with ample illustration that much of American psychology could be characterized as "theoretically egocentric," in the sense that its prevalent theories of personality and social and moral development reflect a strong bias in favor of individualism. By individualism, Hogan means the view that distinct individuals compose society and that it is best for each to pursue his or her own self-interest unfettered by social restraints. To illustrate the negative consequences flowing from this bias, Hogan and others (for example, Kanfer, 1979; Sampson, 1977, 1985; Smith, 1978) cite such well-known cases as Hardin's (1968) "tragedy of the commons" and Platt's (1973) "social traps," where the pursuit of individual self-interest threatened community survival.

Sampson (1975, 1977, 1978, 1985) has perhaps been the most persistent critic of individualism in American society and psychology. His arguments were most effectively presented in his 1977 paper "Psychology and the American Ideal." In this paper, Sampson proposed that the dominant cultural ethos in the United States held up as an ideal an extreme individualistic form of self-sufficiency, which he labeled "self-contained individualism." As the label implies, self-contained individualists strive to be complete in themselves, independent of other persons or groups. Such people, Sampson contended, would become alienated and isolated from others, bearing in addition a heavy burden of personal responsibility for success and their psychological well-being. Instead of self-contained individualism, Sampson suggested that interpersonal interdependence offers the better hope for sustaining democratic governance and coping effectively with national problems that require social rather than individual problem solving. Extending this theme, Sampson in 1985 argued that self-contained individualism is ultimately illusory and unattainable.

The psychological anthropologist Hsu has also criticized the ethic of rugged individualism in American society. According to Hsu (1983), its two key attributes are self-reliance and fierce competitiveness. Among the correlates of rugged individualism, he cites a lowering of sexual morality, corruption and dishonesty, pressures toward conformity, racial and religious prejudice, unrealism in interpersonal and international relations, and a tendency to excessive bureaucratic organization. To offset these undesirable aspects, Hsu suggests that the ethic be tied to a "social framework" and a "social frame of reference" that would encourage a broader perspective than the self.

Another interesting critique concerning individualism has been provided by Mordechai Rotenberg (1977), a social and clinical psychologist with the Hebrew University in Israel. He contrasts two forms of individualism that differ in their cultural roots and their effect on the human spirit. "Alienating individualism," defined as a type of independence characterized by separation from and antagonism toward others, is a product of the Protestant (especially Puritan and Calvinistic) religious tradition, which Rotenberg sees as responsible for loneliness and an egoistic, competitive achievement orientation. In contrast, he portrays "reciprocal individualism" as a less alienating form of independence that permits more harmonious and meaningful relations with others and arises from non-Western cultures such as Japan and Israel. For example, Rotenberg describes the amae concept in Japan as a situation wherein dependency upon others is compatible with mental health and economic success. He also cites Buber's Hasidic Judaism and I-Thou philosophy of individuality tied to community with other people as another illustration of a non-Western form of reciprocal individualism, in which one can be different from others without being indifferent to them.

American social psychologist Alan Waterman (1981, 1984), on the other hand, has suggested that critics of individualism have based their analyses on outmoded and undocumented assumptions of individualism. He argues that psychological theorists such as Maslow, Erikson, and Kohlberg reflect a more positive philosophical framework that Waterman terms "normative" or "ethical" individualism and that is characterized by the following qualities: "eudamonism" (being true to oneself and fulfilling one's potentials), freedom of choice and personal responsibility, and "universality" (which involves respect for the integrity of others). Waterman

(1981, 1984) has reviewed a number of areas of psychological research to buttress his claims that espousing individualistic values increases the probability that one will exhibit "productive and satisfying interdependent behavior." In other words, according to Waterman, individualism fosters rather than constrains interdependence.

Individualism and Romantic Love

What, then, is the relationship between individualism and romantic love? Love relationships, of course, provide perhaps the most important crucible for testing the hypothesis of a link between individualism and interdependence. In the area of love, Waterman (1981, 1984) bases his claims for the putatively beneficial effects of individualism mainly on studies (for example, Orlofsky, Marcia, & Lesser, 1973; Hodgson & Fischer, 1979; Kacerguis & Adams, 1980) suggesting that young adults who have resolved an identity crisis will be more likely to be involved in an intimate or committed relationship than those whose identity status is not as fully developed. Moreover, two further studies (Dietch, 1978; Gelbond, 1979) suggesting a positive relationship between self-actualization, as measured by the Personal Orientation Inventory, and measures devised by the authors to assess Maslow's concept of "being love" are also presented by Waterman (1984) as being consistent with his thesis.

Yet, there are several other important sources of evidence that yield a less clear picture of the relationship between individualism and love than Waterman has presented. Perhaps most directly relevant, our own program of research on the personality correlates of romantic love discussed at the outset of this chapter is certainly germane to the issue of whether individualism facilitates or hinders romantic love. The personality dimensions of internal control, high self-esteem, and self-actualization are all ones that Waterman himself employed as reflections of individualism to test his hypotheses in different behavioral domains. Our findings, however, portray a much less positive picture of the "individualist" in love. For example, internals were less likely to report having been in love and those who had been described their love relationships as having a more rational, calculated quality (Dion & Dion, 1973). Our self-esteem and self-actualization studies (the latter with more and better validated measures of love than those of other such studies) suggest that the individualist's love relationships have some narcissistic qualities. Specifically, we found that those high in genuine self-acceptance and self-actualization, respectively, reported more frequent love experiences and derived greater personal satisfaction and enjoyment from their relationships; however, it was the persons lower on these personality dimensions who were fonder of their partners, esteemed them more highly, and had a stronger love for them (Dion & Dion, 1975, 1985).

A similar mixed picture of individualism and love emerges from social-psychological literature on the role of equity in social and intimate relationships. Briefly, the equity principle states that individuals should receive outcomes or payoffs from a relationship in proportion to their investments. Both advocates (such as Waterman, 1981, 1984) and critics (such as Sampson, 1975) of individualism view adherence to the equity principle as a reflection of American individualism. Social psychologist Elaine Hatfield and her colleagues have explored sexual involvement in heterosexual romantic relationships in several studies (for example, Hatfield, Traupmann, & Walster, 1979; Hatfield, Utne, & Traupmann, 1979; Hatfield, Walster, & Traupmann, 1979). They found that perceived equity in a heterosexual relationship is related to greater sexual contentment, earlier sexual involvement before marriage, and less reported indulgence in extramarital sex once the commitment has been made.

Yet other studies of romantic love imply that concern over equity in a relationship or external rewards is counterproductive to the development of deep attachment. James Milord (1979), for example, measured in depth the norms that members of heterosexual couples employed with regard to their partners and categorized them as to whether they subscribed to equity in their relationship or followed some other norm. Equity-oriented individuals indicated less love and trust for their partners than those adhering to alternative norms of equality or communion (the latter meaning "sharing based on need"). In a similar vein, social psychologists Clive Seligman, Russell Fazio, and Mark Zanna (1980) found that members of heterosexual couples for whom the external rewards of dating their partners were salient reported less romantic love for their partner; they also believed marriage to be less likely than those induced to focus on the more intrinsic (personal) aspects of their relationship.

Finally, a team of sociologists and a philosopher (Bellah et al., 1985) made an important analysis of American culture and the contemporary relation between character and society in the United States. Their study raises some serious questions about whether individualism facilitates romantic love. Bellah and his colleagues describe two forms of individualism as characterizing contemporary America: (1) "utilitarian individualism" involving the notion that social welfare is best served by individuals pursuing their own self-interest, which applies in the public sphere of economic and occupational affairs, and (2) "expressive individualism" focusing on the need to realize and explore the self, which applies in the sphere of private life.

Ann Swidler, the member of this team who concentrated on the private sphere of love and marriage, interviewed couples in San Jose, California, for her portion of the analysis. She suggests that the philosophy of individualism that is so deeply ingrained in the American character informs much of what contemporary Americans believe about love. For them, romantic love represents the "quintessential form" of expressive individualism. Love gives them the opportunity to share and expand their "real selves" while leaving them free to express their individuality; their autonomous selves, then, can obtain the psychological gratifications of both mutual exploration and self-enhancement. Americans, she says, call a relationship "love" if it feels right or natural or sufficiently gratifying. In Swidler's words, "Searching for a definition of 'real love' becomes pointless if one 'feels good' enough about one's relationship. After all, what one is looking for is the 'right place' for oneself" (Bellah et al., 1985, p. 91).

Americans confront several problems in reconciling their sense of expressive individualism and self with the ideals of a love relationship. First, one can "lose" one's self and the feeling of personal autonomy in a love relationship, feeling used and exploited as a result. Second, satisfying the autonomous needs of two "separate" individuals in a love relationship obviously becomes a difficult balancing act. Third, the spirit of American individualism makes it difficult for either partner in a relationship to justify sacrificing or giving to the other more than one is receiving. Finally, and inevitably, Americans confront a fundamental conflict trying to reconcile personal freedom and individuality, on the one hand, with obligations and role requirements of marital partner and parent, on the other. The result, Swidler believes, is that often "Love . . . creates a dilemma for Americans" (Bellah et al., 1985, p. 93).

In conclusion, we share with Ann Swidler and her colleagues the view that individualism-collectivism plays a critical role vis-à-vis romantic love in the culture of the United States and elsewhere around the world. We also suggest that individualism makes it difficult for individuals to become intimate and loving with one another. It is likely, for example, that the high divorce rate that characterizes American society is due in good part to the culture's exaggerated sense of individualism. A complete understanding of the relation between individualism and love remains a task for future research that we, for our part, shall continue to pursue.

REFERENCES

Bellah, R. N., Madsen, R., Sullivan, W. M., Swidler, A., & Tipton, S. M. (1985). *Habits of the heart: Individualism and commitment in American life*. Berkeley: University of California Press.

Blau, P. M. (1964). *Exchange and power in social life.* New York: Wiley.

Bond, M. H., & Forgas, J. P. (1984). Linking person perception to behavior intention across cultures: The role of cultural collectivism. *Journal of Cross-Cultural Psychology, 15,* 337–352.

Bond, M. H., Wan, K.-C., Leung, K., & Giacolone, R. A. (1985). How are responses to verbal insult related to cultural collectivism and power distance? *Journal of Cross-Cultural Psychology, 16,* 111–127.

Campbell, A. (1981). *The sense of well-being in America: Recent patterns and trends.* New York: McGraw-Hill.

Chu, G. C. (1985). The changing concept of self in contemporary China. In A. J. Marsella, G. DeVos, & F. L. K. Hsu (Eds.), *Culture and self: Asian and Western perspectives* (pp. 252–277). London, England: Tavistock.

Crowne, D. P., & Marlowe, D. (1964). *The approval motive.* New York: Wiley.

Dietch, J. (1978). Love, sex roles, and psychological health. *Journal of Personality Assessment, 42,* 626–634.

Dion, K. K., & Dion, K. L. (1975). Self-esteem and romantic love. *Journal of Personality, 43,* 39–57.

———. (1978). Defensiveness, intimacy, and heterosexual attraction. *Journal of Research in Personality, 12,* 479–487.

———. (1985). Personality, gender, and the phenomenology of romantic love. In P. R. Shaver (Ed.), *Self, situations and behavior: Review of personality and social psychology* (Vol. 6, pp. 209–239). Beverly Hills, CA: Sage.

Dion, K. L., & Dion, K. K. (1973). Correlates of romantic love. *Journal of Consulting and Clinical Psychology, 41,* 51–56.

———. (1979). Personality and behavioural correlates of romantic love. In M. Cook & G. Wilson (Eds.), *Love and attraction: An international conference* (pp. 213–220). Oxford, England, and New York: Pergamon.

Doi, L. T. (1962). Amae: A key concept for understanding Japanese personality structure. In R. J. Smith & R. K. Beardsley (Eds.), *Japanese culture: Its development and characteristics.* New York: Viking Fund Publications in Anthropology.

———. (1963). Some thoughts on helplessness and the desire to be loved. *Psychiatry, 26,* 266–272.

———. (1973). *The anatomy of dependence.* Tokyo: Kodansha International.

Fromm, E. (1939). Selfishness and self-love. *Psychiatry: Journal for the Study of Interpersonal Processes, 2,* 507–523.

Gelbond, B. (1979). Self-actualization and unselfish love. *Journal of Religious Humanism, 13,* 74–78.

Hardin, G. (1968). The tragedy of the commons. *Science, 162,* 1243–1248.

Hatfield, E., Traupmann, J., & Walster, G. W. (1979). Equity and extramarital sex. In M. Cook & G. Wilson (Eds.), *Love and attraction: An international conference* (pp. 311–321). Oxford, England, and New York: Pergamon.

Hatfield, E., Utne, M. K., & Traupmann, J. (1979). Equity theory and intimate relationships. In R. L. Burgess & T. L. Huston (Eds.), *Social exchange in developing relationships* (pp. 99–133). New York: Academic.

Hatfield, E., Walster, G. W., & Traupmann, J. (1979). Equity and premarital sex. In M. Cook & G. Wilson (Eds.), *Love and attraction: An international conference* (pp. 323–334). Oxford, England, and New York: Pergamon.

Hendrick, C., & Hendrick, S. (1986). A theory and method of love. *Journal of Personality and Social Psychology, 50,* 392–402.

Ho, D. Y. F. (1975). Traditional Chinese approaches to socialization. In J. W. Berry & W. J. Lonner (Eds.), *Applied cross-cultural psychology* (pp. 309–314). Lisse, Holland: Swets & Zeitlinger.

———. (1979). Psychological implications of collectivism: With special reference to the Chinese case and Maoist dialectics. In H. H. Eckensberger, W. J. Lonner, & Y. H. Poortinga (Eds.), *Cross-cultural contributions to psychology* (pp. 143–150). Lisse, Holland: Swets & Zeitlinger.

———. (1982). Asian concepts in behavioral science. *Psychologia, 25,* 228–235.

Hodgson, J. W., & Fischer, J. L. (1979). Sex differences in identity and intimacy development in college youth. *Journal of Youth and Adolescence, 8,* 37–50.

Hofstede, G. (1984). *Culture's consequences: International differences in work-related values* (Abridged ed.). Beverly Hills, CA: Sage.

Hogan, R. (1975). Theoretical egocentrism and the problem of compliance. *American Psychologist, 30,* 533–540.

Hsu, F. L. K. (1971). Psychosocial homeostasis and jen: Conceptual tools for advancing psychological anthropology. *American Anthropologist, 73,* 23–44.

———. (1981). *Americans and Chinese: Passage to difference* (3rd ed.). Honolulu: University Press of Hawaii.

———. (1983). *Rugged individualism reconsidered: Essays in psychological anthropology.* Knoxville: University of Tennessee Press.

———. (1985). The self in cross-cultural perspective. In A. J. Marsella, G. DeVos, & F. L. K. Hsu (Eds.), *Culture and self: Asian and Western perspectives* (pp. 24–55). London, England: Tavistock.

Hui, C. H. (1984). *Development and validation of an individualism-collectivism scale* (Report No. ONR-31). Arlington, VA: Office of Naval Research.

Kacerguis, M. A., & Adams, G. R. (1980). Erikson stage resolution: The relationship between identity and intimacy. *Journal of Youth and Adolescence, 9,* 117–126.

Kanfer, P. H. (1979). Personal control, social control, and altruism: Can society survive the age of individualism? *American Psychologist, 34,* 231–239.

Kelley, H. H. (1983). Love and commitment. In H. H. Kelley, E. Berscheid, A. Christensen, J. H. Harvey, T. L. Huston, G. Levinger, E. McClintock, L. A. Peplau, & D. R. Peterson (Eds.), *Close relationships* (pp. 265–314). New York: W. H. Freeman.

Lazarus, R. S., Averill, J. R., & Opton, E. M., Jr. (1970). Towards a cognitive theory of emotion. In M. Arnold (Ed.), *Third international symposium on feelings and emotions* (pp. 207–232). New York: Academic.

Lee, J. A. (1973). *Colours of love.* Toronto, Canada: New Press.

Leung, K., & Bond, M. H. (1984). The impact of cultural collectivism on reward allocation. *Journal of Personality and Social Psychology, 47,* 793–804.

Maslow, A. H. (1968). *Toward a psychology of being.* Princeton, NJ: Van Nostrand.

———. (1970). *Motivation and personality* (2nd ed.). New York: Harper.

Milord, J. T. (1979). *Norms of exchange and affect in couples.* Unpublished manuscript, Department of Psychology, University of Toronto, Canada.

Murphy-Berman, V., Berman, J. J., Singh, P., Pachauri, A., & Kumar, P. (1984). Factors affecting allocation to needy and meritorious recipients: A cross-cultural comparison. *Journal of Personality and Social Psychology, 46,* 1267–1272.

Orlofsky, J. L., Marcia, J. E., & Lesser, I. M. (1973). Ego identity status and the intimacy versus isolation crisis of young adulthood. *Journal of Personality and Social Psychology, 27,* 211–219.

Phares, E. J. (1976). *Locus of control in personality.* Morristown, NJ: General Learning Press.

Platt, J. (1973). Social traps. *American Psychologist, 29,* 641–651.

Rogers, C. R. (1959). A theory of therapy, personality, and interpersonal relationships, as developed in the client-centered framework. In S. Koch (Ed.), *Psychology: A study of a science* (Vol. 3, pp. 184–256). New York: McGraw-Hill.

Rotenberg, M. (1977). Alienating individualism and reciprocal individualism: A cross-cultural conceptualization. *Journal of Humanistic Psychology, 17,* 3–17.

Rotter, J. B. (1966). Generalized expectancies for internal versus external control of reinforcement. *Psychological Monographs, 80*(1, Whole No. 609).

Rubin, Z. (1970). Measurement of romantic love. *Journal of Personality and Social Psychology, 16,* 265–273.

Sampson, E. E. (1975). On justice as equality. *Journal of Social Issues, 31*(3), 45–64.

———. (1977). Psychology and the American ideal. *Journal of Personality and Social Psychology, 35,* 767–782.

———. (1978). Scientific paradigms and social values: Wanted—a scientific revolution. *Journal of Personality and Social Psychology, 36,* 1332–1343.

———. (1985). The decentralization of identity: Toward a revised concept of personal and social order. *American Psychologist, 40,* 1203–1211.

Schon, D. A. (1963). *Displacement of concepts.* London, England: Tavistock.

Seligman, C., Fazio, R. H., & Zanna, M. P. (1980). Effects of salience of extrinsic rewards on liking and loving. *Journal of Personality and Social Psychology, 38,* 453–460.

Smith, M. B. (1978). Perspectives on selfhood. *American Psychologist, 33,* 1053–1063.

Steck, L., Levitan, D., McLane, D., & Kelley, H. H. (1982). Care, need, and conceptions of love. *Journal of Personality and Social Psychology, 43,* 481–491.

Triandis, H. C. (in press). Collectivism vs. individualism: A reconceptualization of a basic concept in cross-cultural social psychology. In C. Bagley & G. K. Verma (Eds.), *Personality, cognition and values: Cross-cultural perspectives of childhood and adolescence.* London, England: Macmillan.

Walster (now Hatfield), E. (1965). The effect of self-esteem on romantic liking. *Journal of Experimental Social Psychology, 1,* 184–197.

Waterman, A. S. (1981). Individualism and interdependence. *American Psychologist, 36,* 762–773.

———. (1984). *The psychology of individualism.* New York: Praeger.

Wessman, A. E., & Ricks, D. F. (1966). *Mood and personality.* New York: Holt.

Ziller, R. C. (1973). *The social self.* New York: Pergamon.

PART IV

Theories of Love and Relationship Maintenance

CHAPTER THIRTEEN

Maintaining Loving Relationships

BY DONN BYRNE AND SARAH K. MURNEN

In the chronology of a relationship, three general time periods may be identified as initiation, maintenance, and—all too often—dissolution (Duck, 1985; Hatfield & Walster, 1985). Existing scientific data on these three periods are uneven. We know a great deal about how relationships are initiated (for example, Berscheid, 1985; Byrne, 1971; Duck & Gilmour, 1981a; Newcomb, 1961), and we have in recent years learned more and more about some of the antecedents and consequences of failed relationships (Baxter, 1984; Duck & Gilmour, 1981b, 1982; Rusbult, 1980, 1983; Rusbult & Zembrodt, 1983; Rusbult, Zembrodt, & Gunn, 1982). In the United States, a great many marriages now end in divorce, and one response has been an avalanche of trade books purporting to help women avoid that calamity by selecting the right mate in the first place (Kapp, 1986). It is possible that an improved selection process would solve the problem, but we suspect there is more to it than that.

The most glaring gap in our knowledge lies not in mate selection but in relationship maintenance. A close relationship can satisfy multiple needs—for affiliation, for friendship, and for love (Eidelson, 1980; Hatfield, 1983; McAdams & Losoff, 1984)—and the importance of such relationships in our lives should never be underestimated.

There seems to be an implicit assumption that we can understand how relationships are maintained if we simply extrapolate from the initiation and dissolution periods. It does not require extensive thought to recognize the weakness of that assumption. For example, we have abundant evidence that physical attractiveness plays a major role in determining attraction (Hatfield & Sprecher, 1986), but is it likely that two individuals in a well-established relationship spend significant amounts of time gazing at one another year after year, experiencing acute pleasure based on a partner's comeliness? We also know that deteriorating relationships are characterized by quarrels and bitter words; is the simple absence of such negative interactions a probable source of happiness and a sufficient condition to maintain love? We do not have a definitive answer to either question, but there is good reason to suspect that "no" is more probably accurate than "yes."

Our basic hypothesis is that relationship maintenance involves something beyond the mere repetition of those variables that initiated attraction in the first place and something besides the mere absence of the variables that are associated with relationship failure. At the same time, we propose that the *constructs* identified as crucial to attraction are also crucial to maintaining or failing to maintain a relationship. We will first describe a general conceptual framework and then apply it to three proposed classes of variables involved in maintenance.

THE AFFECTIVE MODEL OF ATTRACTION

A successful, satisfying, ongoing relationship can be defined as one involving lasting attraction between two partners. Simply stated, if two people continue to like each other, the relationship should endure. If that statement is accurate, we need to identify what determines their liking each other.

One approach to attraction research has been within the context of a formulation that stresses the importance of the association between one person and the emotional responses of another (Byrne, 1971; Byrne & Clore, 1970; Byrne, Clore, & Smeaton, 1986; Dixit, 1985). Another person is liked to the extent that he or she either evokes positive feelings or is simply associated with such feelings. In other words, the model says that if you feel good in the presence of a given individual, you will like that person (Clore & Byrne, 1974). Dislike is the result of the negative feelings evoked by or simply associated with another person. Bad feelings in the presence of another results in not liking that person. Because interactions almost always are characterized by a mixture of positive and negative emotions, we must take into account the number and relative strengths of positive and negative emotional responses associated with each person we know. Attraction toward someone at a given point in time is found to be determined by the proportion of positive feelings in the total array of positive and negative feelings aroused by that individual (Byrne, 1971).

The accuracy and usefulness of this formulation has been demonstrated in a wide variety of investigations in which positive or negative emotions were manipulated and attraction was found to vary as predicted. Support is also provided by investigations in which variables that determine attraction are shown to arouse emotional responses. To summarize, conditions that evoke positive feelings—good news, music one enjoys, amusing movies, extra credit for an assignment—lead to greater attraction for others in that same situation, whereas conditions that evoke negative feelings—hot and humid atmosphere, bad news, unpleasant music, sad movies—lead to decreased attraction or even dislike (Gouaux, 1971; Griffitt, 1968, 1970; May & Hamilton, 1980; Veitch & Griffitt, 1976. These factors also work in the reverse direction. That is, those variables that cause us to like another person—similar attitudes, physical attractiveness, positive evaluations—are also found to evoke positive feelings; those that cause us to dislike others—dissimilar attitudes, unattractiveness, negative evaluations—evoke negative feelings (Byrne & Clore, 1967; Clore & Gormly, 1974; Meadow, 1971; Singh, 1973).

Much of the research of the type just outlined has been conducted in experimental settings using college undergraduates as subjects. Such research can be characterized as dealing with the first impressions one has of a stranger after a brief exposure to the person. Although one might reasonably have doubts about how relevant this research is to real-life long-term relationships, it must be pointed out that the same factors found to operate in the laboratory are also found to operate in determining real-life friendship, love, courtship, and marriage (for example, Byrne, Ervin, & Lamberth, 1970; Griffitt & Veitch, 1974; Hunt, 1935; Kirkpatrick & Stone, 1935; Morgan & Remmers, 1935; Newcomb & Svehla, 1937; Pearson & Lee, 1903; Richardson, 1939; Schiller, 1932; Schuster & Elderton, 1906; Winslow, 1937). There is thus a convincing body of results indicating a parallel between what is found in the laboratory and what is found in actual relationships.

It is fair to say, then, that we now understand a great deal about the determinants of attraction. There is another point to consider, however—one that was suggested at the beginning of this chapter. Undoubtedly many *specific* variables at work in the initial stages of a relationship such as a romance become less important over time in a relationship such as marriage. For example, in the beginning stages of the "selection process" physical attractiveness is not the only crucial matter; an individual's decisions about another person are also influenced by the other person's acceptability to friends, what skills the person possesses such as dancing, and the leisure-time pursuits the two have in common. After several years of marriage, however, it is possible that none of these factors continues to play a role. At a higher level of abstraction, nevertheless, the importance of the *general* concept of emotional responses should remain constant. That is, we would hypothesize that the ratio of positive and negative feelings in a relationship determine how viable it is. The fact that different factors operate in the first year than in the seventh year is not at all inconsistent with the theory.

Given these considerations, what aspects of a relationship are likely to enhance feelings of love rather than interfere with them? We define romantic love as a strong emotional attachment between two adults that includes liking, feelings of tenderness and concern for one another's welfare, sexual desire, and—most often—a belief in sexual exclusivity (Berscheid & Walster, 1969; Goode, 1959; Rubin, 1974; Steck, Levitan, McLane, & Kelley, 1982). Although the following discussion is not meant to be all-inclusive, we will suggest three major realms of interpersonal interactions that are vital to maintaining or failing to maintain a loving relationship: similarity, habituation, and evaluation.

SIMILARITY: ATTITUDES, VALUES, BELIEFS, INTERESTS, AND PERSONALITY DISPOSITIONS

Our folklore tells us both that opposites attract and that birds of a feather flock together, but only the second adage is consistently supported by empirical data. Beginning with Galton's (1870) study of English marriages and continuing through current studies of couples in love, it is clear that the usual pattern is for an individual to select a mate who is similar in education, socioeconomic status, race, religion, degree of religiousness, desired family size, attitude toward sex roles, cultural background, general attitudes, physique, and physical attractiveness (Antill, 1983; Berscheid, 1985; Burchinal, 1964; Hill, Rubin, & Peplau, 1976; Kerckhoff, 1974; Price & Vandenberg, 1979). Those who marry have a greater than chance similarity in personality characteristics as diverse as authoritarianism (Byrne, Cherry, Lamberth, & Mitchell, 1973), erotophobia (Byrne, Becker, & Przybyla, 1986), Type A coronary-prone behavior (Becker, 1984), and needs (Meyer & Pepper, 1977). One investigation even reported significant husband-wife correlations in how well they can read an eye chart (Schooley, 1936).

If various types of similarity are characteristic of romantic partners, is dissimilarity a source of dissatisfaction? The answer would appear to be yes. In an early investigation of these issues, Terman and Buttenwieser

(1935) found greater similarity among happily married couples than among those who were unhappy or who had divorced. When couples are unequally matched on various dimensions, relationships can break down because of the negative emotional effects of dissimilarity per se or because of perceived inequity in the relationship (Utne, Hatfield, Traupmann, & Greenberger, 1984). In the Hill et al. (1976) study of college dating couples, those who broke up within a two-year period were less similar with respect to age, education, and attractiveness than those whose relationships endured for the same period. In a similar vein, happily married couples have been found to be more similar than unhappy couples on various personality scales (Cattell & Nesselroade, 1967; Dymond, 1954).

Given the apparent importance of similarity in determining initial attraction and in maintaining a positive relationship, how is it that relatively dissimilar pairs of individuals end up in a close relationship only to regret it? There appear to be two common causes of mismatches.

Getting to Know You, but Not Well Enough

It would seem that if the potential partners in a relationship knew one another sufficiently well in the first place, they would discover the degree to which they were similar or dissimilar and act accordingly. Unfortunately, we do not always behave in a rational, logical fashion in finding out all we need to know about prospective mates. There are, in effect, many paths from casual dating to marriage, and mate selection involves much more than simply seeking someone most like ourselves (Bolton, 1961; Cate, Huston, & Nesselroade, 1986; Levinger, Senn, & Jorgensen, 1970).

One major obstacle to learning about someone in a rational manner is the phenomenon of passionate love. According to a theory first advanced by Elaine Hatfield (Walster, 1971), passionate love is a powerful attraction response to another person that is based on culturally determined beliefs and the mislabeling of arousal cues. The all-consuming nature of the resulting emotional state is well documented (for example, Milardo, Johnson, & Huston, 1983; Murstein, 1980). Both laboratory and field studies have provided evidence that, in our culture, exposure to an opposite sex stranger under conditions of high arousal (fear, anxiety, stage fright, sexual excitement, and so on) results in sexually oriented attraction that is not based on any knowledge about the other individual's attitudes, values, beliefs, interests, or personality dispositions (Dutton & Aron, 1974; Istvan, Griffitt, & Weidner, 1983; Przybyla, Murnen, & Byrne, 1986). Presumably, these brief interactions observed in experiments constitute the prototype of "love at first sight" that occurs with surprising frequency in everyday life (Averill & Boothroyd, 1977). These sudden, emotionally determined experiences are characterized by such expressions as "falling head over heels in love" and "love is blind." It seems reasonable to hypothesize that any relationship that short-circuits the friendship process on the basis of someone's appearance, beliefs about love, and mislabeled emotions is not likely to involve the exchange of the necessary information that would reveal basic similarities and dissimilarities.

Consistent with this proposal about insufficient information is the finding that marital happiness is positively associated with the length of the courtship period (Grover, Russell, Schumm, & Paff-Bergen, 1985). Wives whose marriage was based on less than five months of dating were least happy, and those who had dated more than two years were happiest. The longer two individuals spend in building a relationship, the more likely their marriage will be a success, in part because time is required for two people to know one another well.

Similar Today, Dissimilar Tomorrow

The second problem with the role of similarity in maintaining a relationship is that people change over time (Levinger, 1980). Longitudinal studies of dispositional variables, for example, indicate that change is more common than stability (Kelly, 1955; Mischel, 1968, 1969; Worchel & Byrne, 1964). It has been commonly found that the younger an individual is, the more likely he or she is to alter beliefs, values, or whatever in subsequent years. In addition, young individuals are more likely than older ones to undergo change (and often differential change for the participants in a relationship) as a result of educational and vocational experiences. This tendency may well contribute to the finding that marriages among very young couples are least likely to succeed.

In addition to dispositional changes, individuals are beset by changing circumstances, and couples may find themselves responding quite differently to new experiences and issues. In this instance, knowledge of past behavior may be of little help in predicting how you or your partner will react. In the traditional, Norman Rockwell past, marriage often meant such new experiences as establishing patterns of sexual activity as well as the myriad details of daily life including eating, sleeping, housecleaning, budgeting, shopping, and all the rest. Couples who knew one another only as loving fiancés could well find themselves at odds over dozens of matters that arise each day when two people live together.

As the incidence of premarital intercourse and cohabitation rose stead-ily over the past few decades, many of these surprises were presumably eliminated—incompatibilities could be discovered prior to marriage. Nev-ertheless, a variety of new situations remain as potential sources of unpre-dictable dissimilarity. Few of us can know beforehand how we or the one we love will respond to parenthood, economic stress, in-laws, serious illness, spending increased amounts of discretionary income, moving, aging, or any of the other ever-changing events that are part of life. As the result of such situational changes and the new and unknown responses of each partner, extremely similar and compatible pairs can find themselves at odds about matters neither had even considered previously. Some of these changes are described in terms of the difficulties that individuals face in coping with role expectations (Burr, 1973; Rollins & Cannon, 1974). In part because of shifting role demands, the middle, child-rearing years of a marriage tend to be the most stressful and the least satisfying for a great many spouses (Hendrick & Hendrick, 1983).

Thus, similarity is of central importance in maintaining a loving rela-tionship, and every effort should be made to learn as much as possible about a potential mate. Nevertheless, such knowledge can never be com-plete, and changes in dispositions and/or in situational influences can bring about unexpected negative emotional responses based on dissimilarity.

HABITUATION: FAMILIARITY CAN BREED BOTH CONTEMPT AND BOREDOM

The tendency of a stimulus to change in its emotion-evoking properties over time is a well-known phenomenon. Repeated exposure to a neutral stim-ulus tends to evoke increasingly positive affective and evaluative responses to that stimulus (Moreland & Zajonc, 1979; Zajonc, 1968). Repeated exposure to a very positive stimulus leads to an increasingly negative emotional response to it. Endless repetitions of the same meal, the same television program, or the same song, for example, can result in an aversive response to something that one once enjoyed. It has been proposed that complex organisms have a need for variety or novelty; a change of stimulus conditions can thus be reinforcing (Berlyne, 1966; Denny, 1957; Kre-chevsky, 1937; Moon & Lodahl, 1956).

A considerable amount of research in the sexual realm indicates that repeated exposure to an erotic stimulus results in diminished sexual arousal and negative feelings—only the introduction of new stimuli can reinstate excitement and a pleasurable response (Kelley & Musialowski, 1986;

Mann, Berkowitz, Sidman, Starr, & West, 1974; Reifler, Howard, Lipton, Liptzin, & Widmann, 1971). A great many experiments indicate that the sexual response to a familiar partner is less intense than to a novel partner. When male animals are clearly satiated sexually and uninterested in further interaction with a mate, they nevertheless become rejuvenated and sexually responsive when a new partner is introduced (Clemens, 1967; Krames, Costanzo, & Carr, 1967; Michael & Zumpe, 1978; Symonds, 1979). The extension of these findings to human behavior has primarily been in the form of studies of declining interest in one's sexual partner in long-lasting marriages (Griffitt, 1981), observations of sexual performance among those engaged in mate swapping (O'Neill & O'Neill, 1970), and in jokes like the following: "A recovered heart patient asks his physician if it would be safe to resume having sexual relations. The doctor replies, 'There's no problem if you don't become too excited.' 'That's all right, doctor, I'll just have relations with my wife.'"

In the Hill et al. (1976) study of couples who broke up, the most frequently stated cause of the failed relationship was "boredom" for both males and females. Although this aspect of relationships has been largely ignored in research, there is considerable anecdotal evidence in advice columns and in novels and short stories that a major problem in long-term relationships is the extent to which people know one another "too well" because all novelty and surprise is gone. People find themselves in ruts, and life becomes routine; one obvious solution is to seek a new partner—not just for sexual novelty but for something different overall.

Solutions for the habituation effect have primarily been offered in popular how-to books dealing with ways to restimulate interest in the dining room and in the bedroom. The helpfulness of these advice books has not been established. What is badly needed is research that identifies why some couples succumb to boredom while others find ways to overcome it. At a commonsense level, it seems reasonable to suggest that spouses would benefit from being forewarned of this common problem and encouraged to develop ways to avoid it. For example, one couple might find it stimulating to seek new educational opportunities together, embark on a new shared hobby, or become involved in unfamiliar sports or games. Another couple may discover that planning, engaging in, and subsequently recalling the highlights of an annual family vacation provide new topics for conversation. Many other possibilities suggest themselves—from embarking on new household projects to joining a gourmet dining club to engaging in mate swapping. Ogden and Bradburn (1968) found that the number of shared pleasurable activities was a significant predictor of marital success. It is interesting to note that unsatisfied spouses report that their children are the greatest or only source of marital satisfaction; satisfied couples report many sources of satisfaction (Luckey & Bain, 1970). When their children grow up and leave home, it seems very likely that the unsatisfied pairs would find little reason to remain together.

Whatever the best solutions for a given couple, the alternative of monotonously doing precisely the same things in the same way over the years can easily lead to unhappiness and other negative emotions that are antithetical to a loving relationship.

EVALUATIONS: POSITIVE WORDS AND DEEDS VERSUS NEGATIVE WORDS AND DEEDS

The final, and probably most important, element in maintaining a loving relationship is the presence of positive evaluations and the absence of negative ones. Although people do not appear able to perceive how well they are liked by a partner on the basis of one date (Walster, Aronson, Abrahams, & Rottmann, 1966), when a relationship progresses further it is because mutual liking is communicated. The importance of interpersonal skills centered on communicating positive feelings and communicating negative ones nondestructively has been emphasized by many investigators (Bockus, 1975; D'Augelli, Deys, Guerney, Hershenberg, & Sborofsky, 1974; Sherwood & Scherer, 1975).

In both verbal and nonverbal behavior, couples in a newly developed loving relationship tend to indicate their positive response to one another through initiating physical closeness, making eye contact, expressing sexual interest, uttering kind words, holding hands, giving presents, and generally demonstrating their liking and love (Allgeier & Byrne, 1973; Byrne, Ervin, & Lamberth, 1970; Gold, Ryckman, & Mosley, 1984; Hays, 1984; Rubin, 1974). Very often, a given act—a thoughtful phone call informing a partner you will be late, a sexual interaction, or a birthday gift—is more important for the message of love it sends than for its intrinsic value.

As two people settle into the seeming security of a continuing relationship, these niceties tend to occur less frequently, and indications of negative evaluations gradually replace the positive expressions (Luckey, 1966). It has been found that unhappy couples differ from happy ones in many nonverbal behaviors such as amount of eye contact and touching (Beier & Sternberg, 1977; Vincent, Friedman, Nugent, & Messerly, 1979). We also seem to feel free in a close, loving relationship to criticize, nag, and complain. The song lyrics could be expanded to say "You not only don't bring me flowers anymore, you also made a fool of yourself at the party last Saturday." Compounding the problem is the fact that negative words and deeds from someone we like is unexpected and more upsetting than such responses from someone we dislike (Riordan, Quigley-Fernandez, & Tedeschi, 1982). Mutual understanding is made difficult by common attribution tendencies. Individuals tend to believe their own negative behaviors are the result of external, situational causes while their partner's negative behaviors are assumed to reflect internal factors such as personality and attitudes (Orvis, Kelley, & Butler, 1976).

The hypothesis that the ratio of positive to negative interactions is a key factor in maintaining a happy, loving relationship is supported by various types of data. For example, the more frequently a couple has sexual intercourse and the less frequently they argue, the more satisfied they are with their marriage (Howard & Dawes, 1976; Thornton, 1977). The relationship that was first established in laboratory experiments involving attraction has been found to be equally accurate as a description of marital satisfaction when one examines the ratio of positive to negative events in the interactions of spouses.

One very informative study of the role of evaluative interactions was conducted by Birchler, Weiss, and Vincent (1975) who compared distressed and nondistressed married couples. They hypothesized that distressed couples develop coercive patterns of interacting in which partners use negative social reinforcers and punishment as techniques for influencing one another's behavior. When these unpleasant techniques are used by one person, the partner tends to respond in a similar fashion, leading to an escalation of reciprocal aversiveness.

In their investigation, Birchler et al. (1975) observed couples interacting with one another; they also observed each member of the pair interacting with a stranger. Married couples generally used more negative and less positive social reinforcements toward spouses than toward strangers. With strangers, there was a tendency to agree and express approval; with the spouse there were many more complaints and criticisms. Moreover, these differences were more pronounced among the distressed than among the nondistressed couples. Self-reports about daily interactions involving such things as negative evaluations of the partner's appearance or behavior were most common among the distressed couples. These findings are consistent with those of other investigations of positive versus negative interactions between spouses (Billings, 1979; Koren, Carlton, & Shaw, 1980).

It is not immediately obvious whether these negative interactions are a cause or an effect of diminished love within a relationship. To the extent that such behavior plays a causative role, it might be possible to teach individuals to interact in nondestructive ways. In many interchanges, negative feelings are expressed more often than positive ones (Shimanoff, 1985). As one might guess, marital satisfaction is associated with the expression of positive rather than negative information (Levinger & Senn, 1967). Perhaps we need to be exposed to more role models like the Huxtables on the "Bill Cosby Show" and to fewer like the Bunkers on "All in the Family." At the simplest level, we should be able to learn to treat loved ones with as much politeness and kindness as we do strangers.

CONCLUSION

Because of the paucity of research directly focused on maintaining loving relationships, much of the foregoing discussion was based on extrapolations from what we know and on the identification of areas of potentially fruitful research.

The role of similarity seems to be well established, but we need to learn more about the kind of filtering process that occurs during relationship formation with respect to various types of similarity (Murstein, 1980). For example, what types of similarity-dissimilarity are crucial early in a relationship, and what types become more important over time? We need to know more about the internal and external changes that are likely to occur in a continuing relationship, and we need to seek ways to predict their impact on the individuals involved.

Knowledge about how to overcome the effects of routinized boredom is badly needed. Interestingly enough, we know more about the problems of monotony in the workplace and about techniques to relieve boredom there (Aldag & Brief, 1979; Gyllenhammar, 1977) than about the same problems in our relationships.

We have emphasized the proposition that reciprocal positive evaluative behavior plays a crucial role in maintaining a satisfying and loving relationship. If couples can reinforce one another, interact gently, and behave in ways that please each partner, their relationship should obviously benefit.

It is essential that we know as much about the mechanisms underlying successful relationships as we know about first impressions and reactions to relationship failure. It is our hope that this discussion will help provide an impetus to an increased amount of research on this central aspect of our lives.

REFERENCES

Aldag, R. J., & Brief, A. P. (1979). *Task design and employee motivation*. Glenview, IL: Scott, Foresman.

Allgeier, A. R., & Byrne, D. (1973). Attraction toward the opposite sex as a determinant of physical proximity. *Journal of Social Psychology, 90,* 213–219.

Antill, J. K. (1983). Sex role complementarity versus similarity in married couples. *Journal of Personality and Social Psychology, 45,* 145–155.

Averill, J. R., & Boothroyd, P. (1977). On falling in love in conformance with the romantic ideal. *Motivation and Emotion, 1,* 235–247.

Baxter, L. A. (1984). Trajectories of relationship disengagement. *Journal of Social and Personal Relationships, 1,* 29–48.

Becker, M. A. (1984). *Type A coronary-prone behavior and sexual interactions of 56 married couples*. Unpublished doctoral dissertation, State University of New York at Albany.

Beier, E. G., & Sternberg, D. P. (1977). Marital communication. *Journal of Communication, 27*(3), 92–97.

Berlyne, D. E. (1966). Curiosity and exploration. *Science, 153,* 25–33.

Berscheid, E. (1985). Interpersonal attraction. In G. Lindzey & E. Aronson (Eds.), *Handbook of social psychology* (Vol. 2). New York: Random House.

Berscheid, E., Dion, K., Walster, E., & Walster, G. W. (1971). Physical attractiveness and dating choice: A test of the matching hypothesis. *Journal of Experimental Social Psychology, 7,* 173–189.

Berscheid, E., & Walster, E. (1969). *Interpersonal attraction*. Reading, MA: Addison-Wesley.

Billings, A. (1979). Conflict resolution in distressed and nondistressed married couples. *Journal of Consulting and Clinical Psychology, 47,* 368–376.

Birchler, G. R., Weiss, R. L., & Vincent, J. P. (1975). Multimethod analysis of social reinforcement exchange between maritally distressed and nondistressed spouse and stranger dyads. *Journal of Personality and Social Psychology, 31,* 349–360.

Bockus, F. (1975). A systems approach to marital process. *Journal of Marriage and Family Counseling, 1,* 251–258.

Bolton, C. D. (1961). Mate selection as the development of a relationship. *Marriage and Family Living, 23,* 234–240.

Burchinal, L. G. (1964). The premarital dyad and love involvement. In H. T. Christensen (Ed.), *Handbook of marriage and the family* (pp. 623–674). Chicago: Rand McNally.

Burr, W. R. (1973). *Theory construction and the sociology of the family*. New York: Wiley.

Byrne, D. (1971). *The attraction paradigm*. New York: Academic Press.

Byrne, D., Becker, M. A., & Przybyla, D. P. J. (1986). *Similarity of sexual attitudes as a determinant of attraction, marital compatibility, and sexual dysfunction*. Unpublished manuscript, State University of New York at Albany.

Byrne, D., Cherry, F., Lamberth, J., & Mitchell, H. E. (1973). Husband-wife similarity in response to erotic stimuli. *Journal of Personality, 41,* 385–394.

Byrne, D., & Clore, G. L. (1967). Effectance arousal and attraction. *Journal of Personality and Social Psychology, 6*(4, Whole No. 638).

———. (1970). A reinforcement model of evaluative responses. *Personality: An International Journal, 1,* 103–128.

Byrne, D., Clore, G. L., & Smeaton, G. (1986). The attraction hypothesis: Do similar attitudes affect anything? *Journal of Personality and Social Psychology, 51,* 1167–1170.

Byrne, D., Ervin, C. R., & Lamberth, J. (1970). Continuity between the experimental study of attraction and "real life" computer dating. *Journal of Personality and Social Psychology, 16,* 157–165.

Cate, R. M., Huston, T. L., & Nesselroade, J. R. (1986). Premarital relationships: Toward the identification of alternative pathways to marriage. *Journal of Social and Clinical Psychology, 4,* 3–22.

Cattell, R. B., & Nesselroade, J. R. (1967). Likeness and completeness theories examined by Sixteen Personality Factor measures on stably and unstably married couples. *Journal of Personality and Social Psychology, 7,* 351–361.

Clemens, L. G. (1967). Effect of stimulus female variation on sexual performance of the male deermouse, Peromyscus Maniculatus. *Proceedings, 75th Annual Convention of the APA,* 119–120.

Clore, G. L., & Byrne, D. (1974). A reinforcement-affect model of attraction. In T. L. Huston (Ed.), *Foundations of interpersonal attraction* (pp. 143–170). New York: Academic Press.

Clore, G. L., & Gormly, J. B. (1974). Knowing, feeling, and liking: A psychophysiological study of attraction. *Journal of Research in Personality, 8,* 218–230.

D'Augelli, A., Deys, D., Guerney, B., Hershenberg, B., & Sborofsky, S. (1974). Interpersonal skill training for dating couples. *Journal of Counseling Psychology, 21,* 385–389.

Denny, M. R., Jr. (1957). Learning through stimulus satiation. *Journal of Experimental Psychology, 54,* 62–64.

Dixit, N. (1985). *The effect of verbal contact and spatial positioning on job satisfaction, job performance, and interpersonal attraction: An experimental investigation.* Unpublished doctoral dissertation, State University of New York at Albany.

Duck, S. (1985). Social and personal relationships. In S. R. Miller & M. L. Knapp (Eds.), *The handbook of interpersonal communication.* Beverly Hills, CA: Sage.

Duck, S., & Gilmour, R. (Eds.). (1981a). *Developing personal relationships.* London: Academic Press.

———. (1981b). *Personal relationships in disorder.* London: Academic Press.

———. (1982). *Dissolving personal relationships.* London: Academic Press.

Dutton, D. G., & Aron, A. P. (1974). Some evidence for heightened sexual attraction under conditions of high anxiety. *Journal of Personality and Social Psychology, 30,* 510–517.

Dymond, R. (1954). Interpersonal perception and marital happiness. *Canadian Journal of Psychology, 8,* 164–171.

Eidelson, R. J. (1980). Interpersonal satisfaction and level of involvement: A curvilinear relationship. *Journal of Personality and Social Psychology*, 39, 460–470.

Galton, F. (1870). *Hereditary genius: An inquiry into its laws and consequences.* (Republished, New York: Horizon, 1952.)

Gold, J. A., Ryckman, R. M., & Mosley, N. R. (1984). Romantic mood induction and attraction to a dissimilar other: Is love blind? *Personality and Social Psychology Bulletin*, 10, 358–368.

Goode, W. J. (1959). The theoretical importance of love. *American Sociological Review*, 24, 38–47.

Gouaux, C. (1971). Induced affective states and interpersonal attraction. *Journal of Personality and Social Psychology*, 20, 37–43.

Griffitt, W. (1968). Attraction toward a stranger as a function of direct and associated reinforcement. *Psychonomic Science*, 11, 147–148.

———. (1970). Environmental effects on interpersonal affective behavior: Ambient effective temperature and attraction. *Journal of Personality and Social Psychology*, 15, 240–244.

———. (1981). Sexual intimacy in aging marital partners. In J. Marsh & S. Kiesler (Eds.), *Aging: Stability and change in the family* (pp. 301–315). New York: Academic Press.

Griffitt, W., & Veitch, R. (1974). Preacquaintance attitude similarity and attraction revisited: Ten days in a fall-out shelter. *Sociometry*, 37, 163–173.

Grover, J. G., Russell, C. S., Schumm, W. R., & Paff-Bergen, L. A. (1985). Mate selection processes and marital satisfaction. *Family Relations*, 34, 383–386.

Gyllenhammar, P. G. (1977, July-August). How Volvo adapts work to people. *Harvard Business Review*, 102–113.

Hatfield, E. (1983). What do women and men want from love and sex? In E. R. Allgeier & N. B. McCormick (Eds.), *Changing boundaries: Gender roles and sexual behavior* (pp. 106–134). Palo Alto, CA: Mayfield.

Hatfield, E., & Sprecher, S. (1986). *Mirror, mirror . . . The importance of looks in everyday life.* Albany: State University of New York Press.

Hatfield, E., & Walster, G. W. (1985). *A new look at love.* Lanham, MD: University Press of America.

Hays, R. B. (1984). The development and maintenance of friendship. *Journal of Social and Personal Relationships*, 1, 75–98.

Hendrick, C., & Hendrick, S. (1983). *Liking, loving and relating.* Monterey, CA: Brooks/Cole.

Hill, C. T., Rubin, Z., & Peplau, L. A. (1976). Breakups before marriage: The end of 103 affairs. *Journal of Social Issues*, 32, 147–168.

Howard, J. W., & Dawes, R. M. (1976). Linear prediction of marital happiness. *Personality and Social Psychology Bulletin*, 2, 478–480.

Hunt, A. McC. (1935). A study of the relative value of certain ideals. *Journal of Abnormal and Social Psychology*, 30, 222–228.

Istvan, J., Griffitt, W., & Weidner, G. (1983). Sexual arousal and the polarization of perceived sexual attractiveness. *Basic and Applied Social Psychology*, 4, 307–318.

Kapp, I. (1986). Where the boys are. *New Republic*, 194(14), 38–41.

Kelley, K., & Musialowski, D. (1986). Repeated exposure to sexually explicit stimuli: Novelty, sex, and sexual attitudes. *Archives of Sexual Behavior, 15,* 487–498.

Kelly, E. L. (1955). Consistency of the adult personality. *American Psychologist, 10,* 659–681.

Kerckhoff, A. C. (1974). The social context of interpersonal attraction. In T. L. Huston (Ed.), *Foundations of interpersonal attraction* (pp. 61–78). New York: Academic Press.

Kirkpatrick, C., & Stone, S. (1935). Attitude measurement and the comparison of generations. *Journal of Applied Psychology, 19,* 564–582.

Koren, P., Carlton, K., & Shaw, D. (1980). Marital conflict: Relations among behaviors, outcomes, and distress. *Journal of Consulting and Clinical Psychology, 48,* 460–468.

Krames, L., Costanzo, D. J., & Carr, W. J. (1967). Responses of rats to odors from novel versus original sex partners. *Proceedings, 75th Annual Convention of the APA,* 117–118.

Krechevsky, I. (1937). Brain mechanisms and variability: II. Variability when no learning is involved. *Journal of Comparative Psychology, 23,* 139–163.

Levinger, G. (1980). Toward the analysis of close relationships. *Journal of Experimental Social Psychology, 16,* 510–544.

Levinger, G., & Senn, D. J. (1967). Disclosure of feelings in marriage. *Merrill-Palmer Quarterly, 13,* 237–249.

Levinger, G., Senn, D. J., & Jorgensen, B. W. (1970). Progress toward permanence in courtship: A test of the Kerckhoff-Davis hypothesis. *Sociometry, 33,* 427–443.

Luckey, E. B. (1966). Number of years married as related to personality perception and marital satisfaction. *Journal of Marriage and the Family, 28,* 44–48.

Luckey, E. B., & Bain, J. K. (1970). Children: A factor in marital satisfaction. *Journal of Marriage and the Family, 32,* 43–44.

Mann, J., Berkowitz, L., Sidman, J., Starr, S., & West, S. (1974). Satiation of the transient stimulating effect of erotic films. *Journal of Personality and Social Psychology, 30,* 729–735.

May, J. L., & Hamilton, P. A. (1980). Effects of musically evoked affect on women's interpersonal attraction and perceptual judgments of physical attractiveness of men. *Motivation and Emotion, 4,* 217–228.

McAdams, D. P., & Losoff, M. (1984). Friendship motivation in fourth and sixth graders: A thematic analysis. *Journal of Social and Personal Relationships, 1,* 11–27.

Meadow, B. L. (1971). *The effects of attitude similarity-dissimilarity and enjoyment on the perception of time.* Unpublished master's thesis, Purdue University, West Lafayette, IN.

Meyer, J. P., & Pepper, S. (1977). Need compatibility and marital adjustment in young married couples. *Journal of Personality and Social Psychology, 35,* 331–342.

Michael, R. P., & Zumpe, D. (1978). Potency in male rhesus monkeys: Effects of continuously receptive females. *Science, 200,* 451–453.

Milardo, R. M., Johnson, M. P., & Huston, T. L. (1983). Developing close relationships: Changing patterns of interaction between pair members and social networks. *Journal of Personality and Social Psychology, 44,* 964–976.

Mischel, W. (1968). *Personality and assessment.* New York: Wiley.

———. (1969). Continuity and change in personality. *American Psychologist, 24,* 1012–1018.

Moon, L. E., & Lodahl, T. M. (1956). The reinforcing effects of changes in illumination on lever-pressing in the monkey. *American Journal of Psychology, 69,* 288–290.

Moreland, R. L., & Zajonc, R. B. (1982). Exposure effects in person perception: Familiarity, similarity, and attraction. *Journal of Experimental Social Psychology, 18,* 395–415.

Morgan, C. L., & Remmers, H. H. (1935). Liberalism and conservatism of college students as affected by the depression. *School and Society, 41,* 780–784.

Murstein, B. I. (1980). Love at first sight: A myth. *Medical Aspects of Human Sexuality, 14*(9), 34, 39–41.

———. (1980). Mate selection in the 1970s. *Journal of Marriage and the Family, 42,* 777–792.

Newcomb, T. M. (1961). *The acquaintance process.* New York: Holt, Rinehart & Winston.

Newcomb, T. M., & Svehla, G. (1937). Intra-family relationships in attitudes. *Sociometry, 1,* 180–205.

O'Neill, G. C., & O'Neill, N. (1970). Patterns in group sexual activity. *Journal of Sex Research, 6,* 101–112.

Ogden, S. R., & Bradburn, N. M. (1968). Dimensions of marriage happiness. *American Journal of Sociology, 73,* 715–731.

Orvis, B. R., Kelley, H. H., & Butler, D. (1976). Attributional conflict in young couples. In J. H. Harvey, W. J. Ickes, & R. F. Kidd (Eds.), *New directions in attribution research* (Vol. 1). Hillsdale, NJ: Erlbaum.

Pearson, K., & Lee, A. (1903). On the laws of inheritance in man. I. Inheritance of physical characters. *Biometrika, 2,* 357–462.

Price, R. A., & Vandenberg, S. G. (1979). Matching for physical attractiveness in married couples. *Personality and Social Psychology Bulletin, 5,* 398–400.

Przybyla, D. P. J., Murnen, S., & Byrne, D. (1985). *Arousal and attraction: Anxiety reduction, misattribution, or response strength?* Unpublished manuscript, State University of New York at Albany.

Reifler, C. B., Howard, J., Lipton, M. A., Liptzin, M. B., & Widmann, D. E. (1971). Pornography: An experimental study of effects. *American Journal of Psychiatry, 128,* 575–582.

Richardson, H. M. (1939). Studies of mental resemblance between husbands and wives and between friends. *Psychological Bulletin, 36,* 104–120.

Riordan, C. A., Quigley-Fernandez, B., & Tedeschi, J. T. (1982). Some variables affecting changes in interpersonal attraction. *Journal of Experimental Social Psychology, 18,* 358–374.

Rollins, B., & Cannon, K. (1974). Marital satisfaction over the family life cycle: A reevaluation. *Journal of Marriage and the Family, 36,* 271–282.

Rubin, Z. (1974). From liking to loving: Patterns of attraction in dating relationships. In T. L. Huston (Ed.), *Foundations of interpersonal attraction* (pp. 383–402). New York: Academic Press.

Rusbult, C. E. (1980). Commitment and satisfaction in romantic associations. A test of the investment model. *Journal of Experimental Social Psychology, 16,* 172–186.

———. (1983). A longitudinal test of the investment model: The development (and deterioration) of satisfaction and commitment in heterosexual involvements. *Journal of Personality and Social Psychology, 45,* 101–117.

Rusbult, C. E., & Zembrodt, I. M. (1983). Responses to dissatisfaction in romantic involvements: A multidimensional scaling analysis. *Journal of Experimental Social Psychology, 19,* 274–293.

Rusbult, C. E., Zembrodt, I. M., & Gunn, L. K. (1982). Exit, voice, loyalty, and neglect: Responses to dissatisfaction in romantic involvements. *Journal of Personality and Social Psychology, 43,* 1230–1242.

Schiller, B. (1932). A quantitative analysis of marriage selection in a small group. *Journal of Social Psychology, 3,* 297–319.

Schooley, M. (1936). Personality resemblances among married couples. *Journal of Abnormal and Social Psychology, 31,* 340–347.

Schuster, E., & Elderton, E. M. (1906). The inheritance of psychical characters. *Biometrika, 5,* 460–469.

Sherwood, J., & Scherer, J. J. (1975). A model for couples: How two can grow together. *Small Group Behavior, 6,* 11–18.

Shimanoff, S. B. (1985). Expressing emotions in words: Verbal patterns of interaction. *Journal of Communication, 35,* 16–31.

Singh, R. (1973). *Affective implications of the weighting coefficient in attraction research.* Unpublished doctoral dissertation, Purdue University, West Lafayette, IN.

Steck, L., Levitan, D., McLane, D., & Kelley, H. H. (1982). Care, need, and conceptions of love. *Journal of Personality and Social Psychology, 43,* 481–491.

Symonds, D. (1979). *The evolution of human sexuality.* Oxford: Oxford University Press.

Terman, L. M., & Buttenwieser, P. (1935). Personality factors in marital compatibility: II. *Journal of Social Psychology, 6,* 267–289.

Thornton, B. (1977). Toward a linear prediction model of marital happiness. *Personality and Social Psychology Bulletin, 3,* 674–676.

Utne, M. K., Hatfield, E., Traupmann, J., & Greenberger, D. (1984). Equity, marital satisfaction, and stability. *Journal of Social and Personal Relationships, 1,* 323–332.

Veitch, R., & Griffitt, W. (1976). Good news, bad news: Affective and interpersonal effects. *Journal of Applied Social Psychology, 6,* 69–75.

Vincent, J. P., Friedman, L. C., Nugent, J., & Messerly, L. (1979). Demand characteristics in observation of marital interaction. *Journal of Consulting and Clinical Psychology, 47,* 557–566.

Walster, E. (1971). Passionate love. In B. I. Murstein (Ed.), *Theories of attraction and love* (pp. 85–99). New York: Springer.

Walster, E., Aronson, V., Abrahams, D., & Rottmann, L. (1966). Importance of physical attractiveness in dating behavior. *Journal of Personality and Social Psychology, 4*, 508–516.

Winslow, C. N. (1937). A study of the extent of agreement between friends' opinions and their ability to estimate the opinions of each other. *Journal of Social Psychology, 8*, 433–442.

Worchel, P., & Byrne, D. (Eds.). (1964). *Personality change*. New York: Wiley.

Zajonc, R. B. (1968). Attitudinal effects of mere exposure. *Journal of Personality and Social Psychology Monographs Supplement, 9*, 1–27.

CHAPTER FOURTEEN

Love within Life

BY WENDY M. WILLIAMS AND MICHAEL L. BARNES

DAUGHTER: "I'm just not satisfied with my life or my relationship—they don't seem to fit. My relationship isn't what it should be; it doesn't seem to be what's best for me. What a mess."

MOTHER: "Well, what kind of relationship is best for you? What kind of relationship would fit in with your life and make you happy?"

DAUGHTER: "I don't know!"

MOTHER: "Then who should I ask?"

What do you want out of your relationship? What type of relationship would best fit in with your life and make you most happy? Someone we know answered: "I want a meaningful, committed relationship with a partner perfectly suited to my needs. I want a high level of involvement with my family, and I expect my partner to share my feelings about family life. I also want an exciting, prestigious career in which I earn a lot of money and make a contribution to the world, and I expect a partner who has achieved the same. Still, I want a partner who shares hobbies and other interests of mine, and participates in them together with me and our family. I want each of us to have our own set of friends, but still to spend lots of time just being together, maintaining our closeness and our relationship."

Does this person sound familiar? Is he or she reading this chapter? We believe that many of us share the desires expressed above. We seem to want everything out of our lives and our relationships. But, for most of us, achieving all these goals is impossible. A consequence of functioning as a mature adult is making choices; everyone knows that this is so, but when it comes to our expectations about relationships, we often act as though very few choices should be necessary. When forced to make and accept choices, we feel cheated or slighted by fate. Most of us have finally reconciled the fact that we are not perfect—but what about our mate? He or she has a tremendous number of expectations to live up to—more than most mortals can accomplish (Hatfield, chap. 9, this book; Sternberg & Barnes, 1985). Maybe this is why so many people keep trying with yet another person— because human hope never dies. Many secretly believe that the elusive perfect mate is hiding out there somewhere; it's simply a matter of trial and error (Berscheid & Walster, 1978).

Because these perfect mates always seem to elude us, we must decide what is most important, and build a relationship with someone offering the highest probability of making us (and him- or herself) happy. The first step is accepting that we can't have everything; the next is knowing what is most important to us. People have very different sets of needs; hence, different people will be happy in widely disparate types of relationships (Lee, chap. 3, this book). For example, the sexes seem to differ, in certain areas, concerning what each desires in a good relationship (Barnes & Buss, 1985; Buss & Barnes, 1986; Peplau, 1983). This chapter concerns your thinking about and deciding what your needs are in order to learn what real-world relationship will make you happiest.

Researchers studying love have differing perspectives on what constitutes the central issue. Some work has centered on defining and understanding the phenomenon of love in a theoretical context (Brehm, Byrne, Dion & Dion, Hatfield, Huston, Levinger, Rubin, Sternberg, Tennov, and so on). This is a sort of "stimulus" approach to the study of love: learn what underlies the phenomenon to learn how it operates. Other researchers concentrate more on an "individual differences" approach; they study the diverse conceptions of love, the styles of loving that characterize human love relationships, and the consequences of love (Branden, Lee, Williams & Barnes, and so on).

Both these approaches are valid ways to enhance our understanding of what love is and how it operates and affects our behavior. However, after reading about love's theoretical constructs, principal modes of affect, evolutionary and biological bases, manifestations across culture and throughout time, literary and philosophical representation, individual perceptual significance, and so on—that is, after deepening our knowledge and understanding of love substantially—we are left to ponder its role in our own lives. Now we understand the phenomenon and its diversity; but what about our relationship?

In this chapter we present a conceptualization of a love relationship we have developed to illustrate the nature of differing types of love relationships. We discuss the nature of the general types of choices one must make to delineate one's own definition of a good love relationship, and we review some of the consequences that may result from these choices. In addition, we touch upon the role our model can play in understanding and improving relationships that are already in existence, and in understanding what happens as relationships evolve over time. Thus, our chapter is largely about getting to know yourself—what it takes to achieve happiness in the context of a real-world love relationship—because, as our opening quote states, who else but yourself can know?

A MODEL OF A LOVE RELATIONSHIP

We have conceptualized a way to represent love relationships that, we believe, helps clarify major areas of potential satisfaction or dissatisfaction within a relationship. Our model consists of a square representing the sum of the entire lives of the two members of a relationship (see figure 14.1). Each half of the square represents one member's life. Within this square is centered another, smaller square, representing the internal world of the relationship. This world consists of all the thoughts, feelings, and activities shared or participated in jointly by both partners. Again, half the internal world is theoretically contributed by each member, although in reality this distinction may be blurred. The size of the internal world of the relationship relative to the sum total of the two partners' lives is the first potential dimension of variability in our model—the inner or relationship square may be larger or smaller.

Three types of boundaries are defined by our model: the boundary between the partners within the internal world of the relationship, the boundary between the two partner's external lives, and the boundary separating each person's own external world from his or her part of the internal world of the relationship. The nature of these three types of boundaries can vary across relationships; boundaries may be fuzzy, permitting interchange, or well-defined, prohibiting interchange. The nature of these boundaries represents the second potential dimension of variability in our model. The third such dimension concerns the degree of symmetry displayed by the two members of a relationship within the context of our model. High symmetry implies that each person's half of the relationship diagram is essentially a mirror image of the partner's half.

Because a love relationship contains two people, our model displays a

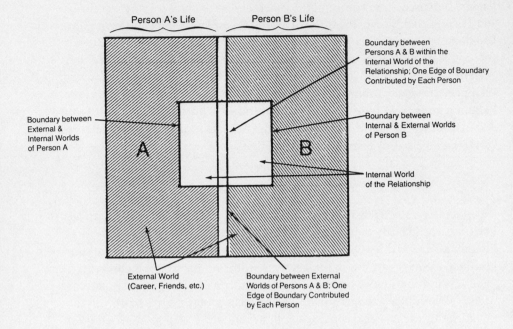

Fig. 14.1.   A Model of a Love Relationship

double boundary for each of the two types of boundaries that exist between the two. These boundaries are the boundary between the two partner's external worlds, and the boundary between the two partners within the internal world of the relationship. Consequently, the boundary that divides the internal world is double-edged, since each member of the relationship is characterized by his or her own type of boundary. For example, a woman might be more communicative and sharing than her partner; her boundary would be fuzzy, and his, well-defined. Similarly, the boundary dividing the two partners' external worlds is double-edged; a man might want his career and his wife's career to be intertwined, while his wife might want to keep her professional life completely separated from that of her husband. For these reasons, it is important to display pairs of boundaries wherever two people's lives may potentially interact. This allows us to represent relationships in which one person desires more interchange than the other in a given domain. In this sense, our model encompasses the variability in the symmetry of boundaries from one relationship to another.

Thus, our model allows for at least three potential types of variability within and across relationships (see figure 14.2). First, we shall consider the size of the inner or relationship square relative to the sum total of the two partners' lives. How much of the total lives of the partners is constituted by the internal world of the relationship? For some people, a relationship plays a much larger role in life than it does for other people.

The second area of potential variability in our model concerns the nature of the boundaries, both between and within the overall-life square and the relationship square. As discussed earlier, our model delineates three types of boundaries: the boundary between the partners within the internal world of the relationship, the boundary between the two partners' external worlds, and the boundary between each person's external world and the internal world of the relationship. The boundary between the two partners within the context of the internal world of the relationship may be more or less well-defined, with a fuzzier boundary signifying more communication and sharing between the partners. Some people share everything they think and feel with their partner; others are far more private.

The boundary between the partners' external worlds may also be fuzzy in some relationships, allowing for considerable flow or interchange between the partners. This might occur, for instance, between a husband and wife who run a joint family business, or a couple who works in the same company doing similar jobs. Conversely, if the two partners have vastly dissimilar external worlds—radically different types of career or other involvements—the boundary between their two external worlds may be well defined, with little interchange.

The final boundary exists within a person, rather than between persons, as is the case with the other two boundaries. This boundary separates the internal world of the relationship from the external world within an individual. In other words, it divides the person's relationship-oriented activities, thoughts, and feelings from his or her career, family, and other external interests, thoughts, and activities. Here again the boundary may be either fuzzy or more well defined. For some people, professional and personal life are very closely intertwined. For others, job and home life are distinct worlds with little overlap.

The third major area of potential variability in our model concerns the degree of symmetry within a relationship. Symmetry may involve all the

Fig. 14.2. Types of Variability in Love Relationships, Represented within the Context of Our Model

Nature of Difference	Diagram		Significance
Size of inner square	Big		Ratio of relationship-oriented to non-relationship-oriented activities and energy
	Small		(For example, casual lovers compared to deeply involved relationship.)
Types of Boundaries			
Between-person— internal	Dashed		Degree of communication and flow or amount of sharing between two areas of model.
	Solid	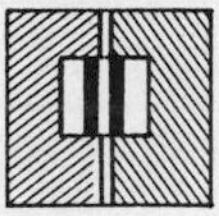	(For example, two people who share all their thoughts and feelings relevant to the relationship, compared with two private, withdrawn people.)
Between-person— external	Dashed	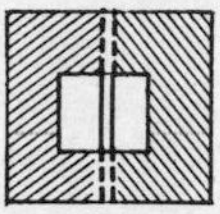	People whose external lives are highly interrelated versus people whose lives outside the relationship are separate.
	Solid		(For example, husband-and-wife psychologist team versus traditional American nuclear family.)
Within-person	Dashed	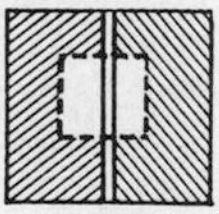	Degree of overlap between external and internal worlds of individual.
	Solid		(For example, people who mesh work and personal lives versus people who separate work and personal lives.)
Degree of Symmetry	High	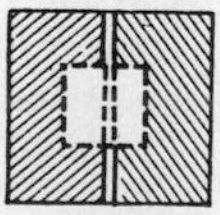	Good match between life-styles, love-styles, and conceptions of good relationship versus poor match.
	Low		(For example, two sharing partners with similar goals and life structures, versus bored housewife with workaholic, non-family-oriented husband.)

characteristics discussed above—size of internal world of relationship versus external world, nature of boundaries, and so on. Symmetry implies that the members of a relationship are similar with regard to their conception of a successful working relationship. Thus, in our model, their relationship would appear to be symmetrical, with one person's half of the diagram matching the other person's half very closely. We believe that, in general, symmetry is a positive thing for the success of a relationship. This premise has been borne out by research demonstrating both positive assortment in mating (Buss, 1984; Buss & Barnes, 1986; Plomin, DeFries, & Roberts, 1977; Price & Vandenberg, 1980; Vandenberg, 1972), and the role of similarity versus complementarity in relationship satisfaction (Buss & Barnes, 1986). Symmetry in our model implies shared beliefs and conceptualizations of how one should live, and of what constitutes a productive and successful relationship.

In response to those who would argue that too much similarity breeds contempt, however, we note the richness and diversity of each half of a successful love relationship. Similarity in feelings about life and the workings of a relationship in general hardly means that two people are identical in every respect. There is plenty of spice and novelty still present in a relationship well matched in terms of major values and general expectations. A bit of spice is nice; too much can cause an ulcer. Finding out that your partner loves NBA basketball and learning to share his or her zeal for a sky-hook is one thing; learning that your partner never wants to raise children when you are envisioning a modern-day equivalent of "The Waltons" in your future is an entirely different matter. Some things are much harder to compromise about and to learn to love and respect than are others.

Figure 14.3 depicts four relationships, two successful and two unsuccessful. Here we demonstrate how the many areas of potential variability interact within our model when the model is used to describe actual relationships. As this figure shows, good relationships come in many forms, as do bad ones. What we would like to stress is the match, the symmetry, of shared values and beliefs about life and love. Thus, we return to our original question—what kind of relationship do you want? What relationship will make you happiest within your life? In other words, what does your ideal relationship look like in the sense of our model? In the next section, we review the types of decisions that must be made to construct and understand the model of one's own maximally happy and productive relationship.

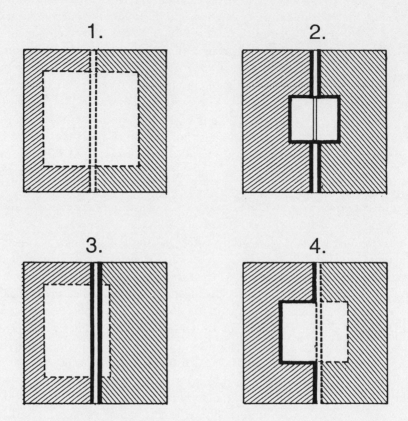

Fig. 14.3. A representation of four real-world relationships, two good and two bad. Relationships 1 and 2 are both successful. They are marked by symmetry in essential areas, although the relationships are different from one another. Relationships 3 and 4 are unsuccessful. They are marked by asymmetry in essential features. The asymmetrical aspect of relationship 3 concerns the proportion of life constituted by the relationship, whereas the asymmetry in relationship 4 involves conceptions of the degree of interchange desirable between various life domains. Relationship 1 might consist of a husband-and-wife psychologist team, working in the same department, for whom the relationship is the center of life. There is considerable interchange across all boundaries. Relationship 2 might represent a sailor and his wife. This sailor goes off to sea for months at a time, while his wife manages the household and is active in the community. Hence, the relationship forms less of life as a whole for this couple, their external worlds are radically different, and there is little interchange between either one's external world and the internal world of the relationship. The relationship works because both have similar expectations of it. Relationship 3 might be a bored housewife with a workaholic husband. She has little to do in her external life and wishes the

CHOICES AND CONSEQUENCES

We begin this discussion of the choices to be made, and some of the consequences of these decisions, with a cautionary note. Even though we phrase potential choices as polar in nature, in reality few things are this simple. We intend for the reader to envision choices as part of a continuum: "To what extent do I want this versus that?" rather than "Do I want this or that?" Whereas it may be difficult to wholly embrace an extreme opinion, it is likely that a more comfortable spot may be located along a continuum.

To avoid another potential misinterpretation of our discussion of choices and consequences, we note here that it is our intention that readers evaluate their desires within the context of a realistically attainable ideal relationship and that they should concentrate upon their general dispositional tendencies. Of course, everyone can visualize a partner for whom they can work up very little enthusiasm as easily as one for whom their motivation to form a successful relationship would be high. Underlying such situationally determined variability, however, are certain dispositional leanings (Costa & McCrae, 1980). To those who find themselves answering our questions with exclamations such as "But it depends on who my partner is!" we respond, "That may be true to *some* extent, but you yourself should try to uncover your personal desires, preferences, and feelings within the context of a realistically attainable ideal relationship."

Although it is possible that sometimes one may truly be "fifty-fifty" in one's degree of preference for a specific characteristic (for example, dominance versus submissiveness or extroversion versus introversion), usually most of us are closer to "eighty-twenty." We believe that most people *do* have definite preferences regarding the characteristics of a potential partner—for example, it is unlikely that a person would be equally happy with a dominant partner and a submissive partner, or with an outgoing extrovert and a quiet introvert. People who think they are "fifty-fifty" on many of the issues we raise are likely to be chronically dissatisfied with their interpersonal relationships because they themselves do not know what they want.

---

relationship were more fulfilling. He has a busy career that occupies most of his life, and he often brings work home. Communication is poor in this couple; similarly, because their external worlds are so different, there is no interchange between the two external worlds. Relationship 4 represents a couple with different beliefs about the interrelationship of work and personal life. Even though the relationship fills the same portion of each of their lives, one partner believes in melding his or her work and personal life. This difference of perspective results in extremely disparate conceptions of how time should be spent when the couple is together.

In addition, we caution our readers against stereotyping themselves too readily and absolutely. Ideas and people change. What worked at one point in a person's life may need to be reformulated ten years later (Byrne & Murnen, chap. 13, this book; Levinger, 1983). This longitudinal aspect of relationships is discussed in a later section of this chapter. For now, we begin with the premise that understanding what one wants today is necessary before one can predict what one will want tomorrow.

A final cautionary note concerns the order in which we discuss the choices below. Although we have attempted to present things logically, we make no judgment about the relative importance of these choices in a given relationship. Certain aspects of relationships may concern some people more than others; hence, some decisions will necessarily be more important than others within the context of their lives. Each person must decide the order in which to choose.

Our relationship model forms the basis of the points to follow. We will draw upon the model to illustrate our discussion of choices and some of their consequences in love relationships. The reader should recall that the type of boundary for one area of interaction in a relationship may differ from the type of boundary for another area in the same relationship. This is true even within an area for specific issues; for example, one partner might believe that his or her favorite sport has a much more defensible place in the relationship than his or her mother-in-law. In this case, this partner's boundary between the external world and the internal world of the relationship would be fuzzier for shared activities, such as participation in sports, than for best-done-alone activities, such as visiting parents. In this preliminary presentation of our model, we refer in general terms to the boundaries, communicating their characteristics in an average sense. We realize that the boundaries are more complex than this, but still, people do tend to exhibit trends in behavior, and it is trends that we are considering here, not specifics.

The first, and for many the biggest, issue concerns how much of one's life should be constituted by a relationship. What portion of life do you want your relationship to occupy? Do you want your relationship to be almost everything, or do you feel it has a clearly delineated place and nothing more? This question determines the size of the inner square in our model. Some people believe that all of life is incidental to their relationship—nothing else matters nearly as much. Related to this choice is the career versus relationship trade-off. Is it important to you to have an impressive career with a lot of prestige, in which you earn a high salary and work long hours? Or is your relationship clearly more important than your career? Which do you sacrifice for the other? Everyone experiences variability in time allocation from one day to the next, but when push comes to shove, do you prefer 80 percent career and 20 percent relationship, or the other way around? Someone whose career occupies most of his or her world will undoubtedly experience problems with a partner who wants low career involvement and high relationship involvement.

Other things that occupy a person's world external to the inner relationship are family members, children, hobbies, and other interests. These factors can all increase the amount of external involvements a person has, although if a person maintains fuzzily defined boundaries between his or her external world and the internal world of the relationship, these factors may enhance and occupy the internal world as well. We will discuss the nature of boundaries below. But aside from the extent to which these factors are incorporated into the internal world of the relationship, they remain as things that may reduce the size of the inner relationship square. Thus, decisions about the level of involvement one desires in these areas are relevant to our discussion at this point.

Questions that spring to mind include: How much time do you spend with your family and friends? Would you want your relationship to allow you plenty of involvement with other people? Or would you prefer to do most things alone with your partner? Here, as well as elsewhere in our model, fits the topic of children. Do you want to raise a family? Or do you believe children would take too much time away from your career or your mate? Some people cannot imagine *not* having children, whereas others cannot imagine making all the necessary sacrifices.

And what about hobbies, sports, social activities, and other outside interests? How much time do you want to devote to these things? If you want to participate with your partner, these activities will become part of an enlarged internal world of the relationship. But some people prefer to do these things alone or with others instead of with their partner. Do you enjoy a night out with your personal circle of friends, or would it be difficult for you to imagine having fun after work without your mate? Given one's answers to these types of questions and any others relevant to one's personal experiences, one should be able to decide on approximately the size of square that represents one's ideal relationship.

The next major area of decision making concerns the boundary between the two partners within the internal world of the relationship. How fuzzy or well defined do you want this boundary to be? How much communication is best for your relationship? Some would answer, "There is never enough communication"; others would argue that privacy and never hurting your partner's feelings are most important. This continuum is marked by complete honesty at one end and tactful sensitivity at the other. Do you want a partner who always tells you everything he or she is feeling, or is a more reserved partner your choice? Do you want to take the time to listen to someone else's thoughts and feelings, or does this idea turn you off?

Another example of the types of choices one encounters within this area relates to a partner's physical attributes and personality characteristics. Is it important for you to have an extremely good-looking partner? Are certain physical attributes necessary for you to feel attracted to someone? Is anyone who lacks these qualities going to make you more likely to withdraw? Would a fantastic-looking partner with a lot of money and influence make you more willing to be open and communicative within the internal world of the relationship? These are highly personal decisions that can make a substantial difference in the emotional realm of what constitutes an attractive partner.

The next series of decisions involves the degree of interrelatedness of the external worlds of the two individuals in a relationship. Here we are focusing upon the boundary between one's own and one's partner's external world. How much involvement do you want in your partner's life, outside of the context of the traditional internal world of the relationship? Perhaps you might enjoy working alongside your mate day in and day out. Or perhaps you feel it important to maintain your own individual identity in your work, keeping your work completely separate from your partner's work. Maybe you believe you will become competitive in a relationship with someone who does work similar to yours. Conversely, you may feel too distant from a partner unless you really know and understand what he or she does all day. Or perhaps you are more moderate and prefer to work in the same company but at a different job, for example. This would result in some meshing of your external world with that of your partner, but not in complete overlap.

Another option here is that of a traditional relationship with almost no overlap between the external worlds of the participants. Some women (or men) may choose to stay at home, raise the family, and do the housework, while their spouse goes off to work each day. For others, this idea is not an option—their self-esteem would suffer without more perceived equality, or perhaps they want to share in their partner's work life.

The next major area concerns the association between the two partners' external worlds and the internal world of the relationship. Here we are examining the boundary between the inner and outer square. How much separation do you believe there ought to be here? Do you bring your work-related problems home, or do you leave them at the office? How much do you want to involve your partner and relationship with your career, other family members, and hobbies? Do you prefer a well-defined relationship with its own sphere, or a relationship that essentially encompasses as much of your life as it can?

Also, how much do you want to be involved in your partner's career, outside family activities, sports, hobbies, and the like? Are you willing to give and take in these matters? Do you believe your relatives should be included in many of your activities with your partner? Or should the relationship be kept separate from these external involvements? Here again fits the topic of raising children—do you want children—who fall just outside the internal relationship in some families—to be highly integrated into the internal relationship in yours? Do you want to vacation with the kids along? Or do you want your children to go to boarding school, to make time for you to be alone with your spouse? Do you expect your spouse to spend a considerable amount of time with the children? Do you want someone for whom the boundary between the external and internal worlds of the relationship is fuzzy, allowing child and work involvement to overlap, or do you prefer a well-defined schedule for raising a family by more traditional guidelines, with less flow between the internal and external worlds within each partner?

Perhaps, also, you might desire a partner with a well-defined boundary between external and internal spheres—you may want him or her to make a lot of money, but not to discuss with you how it is done. Some people are too busy with their own external world to want a partner who expects them to be involved in his or her less clearly delineated external world.

Finally, we will touch upon the topic of symmetry. How much symmetry does one *require*, and how much asymmetry will one tolerate? It is hard to find a perfect match in the real world; and for some of us, in certain areas a bit of asymmetry may be desirable. (For example, if one has a tendency to withdraw too much in relationships, one might choose a partner who displays better communication skills so that one may improve one's own behavior in this area. This choice assumes that one wishes one were different and wants to change.) We note here, however, that we are not referring to symmetry in every characteristic of two people as being desirable! We are not referring to individual personality characteristics such as dominance and extraversion. We are most concerned with symmetry in major values and beliefs that guide us through life. Generally, we believe more of this kind of symmetry is better than less.

But perhaps some believe there is evidence for successful complementarity in their history. If this is true in your experience, can you describe where and how much complementarity existed or exists? We must all accept that some compromise is necessary in the real-world mate-selection process (Berscheid & Walster, 1978). But it is possible that one may wish to seek someone who differs from one in terms of how important that person believes a relationship is within the context of life, and how much involvement is desirable between each of the two partner's worlds. This sounds a bit risky to us; maybe some know it works for them. It seems to us that such a situation can be successful only when people want to change certain aspects of themselves—thus they choose a partner who exhibits the attributes they wish to acquire (Buss, 1984; Buss & Barnes, 1986). Otherwise, asymmetry will exist in a climate in which neither partner is willing to change. Consequently, we believe that asymmetry is a tricky thing to seek unless one is fully willing to change. For instance, to seek a partner who believes that a successful relationship means doing everything for his or her partner when one has no intention of reciprocating does not sound to us like a foundation for a mature love relationship (Branden, chap. 10, this book).

LONGITUDINAL APPLICATIONS OF OUR RELATIONSHIP MODEL

In presenting our relationship model, we have begun by considering relationships at a given moment in time. We have looked at the types of choices one must make to construct a model of a realistic ideal relationship today. By focusing on the present, we have not intended to imply that people's goals in relationships and conceptions of love are static. Rather, successful relationships may undergo evolution of their relationship model; these changes may be helpful positive aspects of a good mutual relationship. For example, a woman at age twenty might not desire a family as much as she will at age thirty. Do these types of attitude shifts render our model useless in application to real relationships?

Not at all. For a relationship to succeed over time, each member must change in ways acceptable and, it is hoped, desirable to the other member (Levinger, 1983). We view such successful development as a type of parallel evolution within a relationship. What makes this more likely to occur? We believe at least part of the answer is: a good match to start out with. Thus, maximization of symmetry and success in a relationship in the present is more likely to result in mutual growth of the relationship in the future. It is unlikely that most people will change radically in their fundamental beliefs and values about life and love, particularly if they are adults at the onset of the relationship. For these reasons, the best match one can find today will probably result in the best shot one can ever have at ensuring a happy and long-lasting relationship.

APPLICATIONS TO CURRENT RELATIONSHIPS

What about all the people who chose a partner (perhaps misguidedly) long before reading this chapter? What about all the relationships everywhere that are already in existence? In fact, it was through many hours of contemplation of this question that we developed our relationship model. Our thinking about current relationships led us to conceptualize the characteristics of our relationship model—because in so many relationships there are problems that we hope our model may help delineate and even diagnose.

Often, couples are aware that problems exist within their relationship, but have little idea of what is causing them, what their consequences are, and most important, how to begin to tackle them at their source. Our model may be useful in determining what is amiss; using it, couples may be able to locate a problem's position in the relationship and expose the nature of the imbalance between the two of them with regard to their conceptualization of the model of a good relationship.

For example, a young wife may want to incorporate her mother into her marriage by frequently consulting her for advice, inviting her over regularly, and so on. The husband, however, may not think *his* mother should play such a large role in his marriage. Thus, he may resent his wife's active inclusion of *her* mother in the relationship; this situation may lead to tension and multiple sources of conflict in the household. Our model depicts this imbalance as a more well-defined boundary between the external and internal worlds of the relationship for the husband, and a fuzzier boundary for the wife. For this couple to understand precisely what is at issue is a big improvement over general tension and dissatisfaction. Once the problem is defined and recognized by the couple to consist of a difference in the perception of a good relationship, positive movement toward reconciliation can be initiated. The solution may entail a change on the husband's part, the wife's part, or both. Or, of course, neither may change; the relationship is then likely to fail (Beach & Tesser, chap. 15, Branden, chap. 10, and Hatfield, chap. 9, this book); the key to success is knowing what the issues are.

So many people state that they experience a general sensation of discontentment within their relationship, without knowing the real bases of the bad feelings. Perhaps more tolerance may result from recognizing that a lack of symmetry in certain values or beliefs is a natural consequence of living in our society, in which people of diverse cultures meet and form relationships. When people grew up in a small area and married their childhood friend from down the block, most of the dimensions of our model were automatically held constant—the couple's values and beliefs about life and love were much the same, since they shared a common culture and common experiences. Today we face a far less dependable mate choice process, with many potential pitfalls (Lee, chap. 3, this book). As a consequence of this, there are a tremendous number of books, lectures, films, articles, and therapy groups devoted to remedying the problems of diversity and complexity inherent in forming and maintaining relationships in our society (Murstein, chap. 2, this book).

WHAT DOES OUR MODEL TELL US ABOUT LOVE?

Despite our basically individual differences–oriented approach to understanding love and relationships, we are in a position to make certain statements about what our model tells us about love. Theoretically, our model delineates certain specific aspects of any relationship: the role of the relationship in the individual partner's lives, the role of the partner's external lives in the internal world of the relationship, and the interrelationship of the two external lives brought together by the relationship. These aspects vary a great deal from one relationship to another. They also vary within a person over time, as a person develops and changes throughout life. Changing ideas about relationships are a consequence of development in life in general.

Our model views love within the context of life. Our focus is upon the interaction of love and life in general—our conception of the role love should play in life, and vice versa, given one's wants and needs. Much research on love and, indeed, much of this book focuses upon what is represented in our model by the inner square or internal world of the relationship. Here, researchers examine specific mechanisms underlying attraction, and the components of the love construct itself (for example, Sternberg, 1986). We have looked at the animal in its natural habitat—at love within life. Our model concerns *relationships*, not *love*, because it is the relationship that is the tangible, definable, measurable manifestation of love, which itself remains elusive, undefinable, and highly personal.

Thus, our chapter asks such questions as how much of one's life does one want one's relationship to be, and how does one want love to fit into the bigger picture? We have taken the position that too much concentration upon the stimulus approach to studying love removes research on love from reality. Love in daily life is not usually conceptualized and experienced by human beings as a construct with a given form. Rather, the experience most of us have is one of multiple opportunities that present us with the need to choose. Here it is essential to know what we want, and this has been the topic of most of our chapter. We hope to relate our theoretically based model to people's experience of love within life to better enable people to elucidate and elect what is ultimately best for them.

Upon reading some of the research centered on the love construct, one quickly realizes that the researcher's personal views and feeling are influencing his or her position (Branden, chap. 10, this book; Bakan, 1967). This is a natural consequence of human beings conducting research on such a personal issue. The problem that arises, however, is that many readers may be left wondering where their love life fits in. Which author thinks the way I do? Which sees love as I see it? Whose theory should I apply in my own life? All research has something to offer; but in this field, at least, readers may feel as though they have missed the love boat.

For example, in his chapter on romantic love in this volume, Nathaniel Branden (chap. 10) notes that in the past some have questioned whether his view of romantic love as an attainable life-long ideal is possible for them. Perhaps, for some readers, Branden's love reality is not a realistic possibility—perhaps they fail to share his goals. For some readers, romantic love may not even be what they are shooting for (Lee, chap. 3, this book).

For this reason, we have tried to help people delineate what they do want. (Then, they can even choose their favorite love researcher who sees things just as they do, and subscribe to whatever love philosophy they see fit.) Here we are in agreement with Lee, who discusses the multiplicity of love-styles characterizing human relationships. In an attempt to describe a method people can use to decide where they stand, we have presented a diagnostic aid for the home love doctor.

DIRECTIONS FOR FUTURE RESEARCH

Each of the three potential areas of variability in our model presents questions and opportunities for future research. Similarly, our model as a whole warrants research to investigate its applied value for people's romantic relationships within the context of their own lives.

The first area of variability—the size of the relationship square relative to both partners' lives—poses a general question concerning the value of our model. Are people more or less satisfied with relationships that form the focus of both partners' lives? Is more always better, or is there an ideal balance between external and internal involvements?

The second dimension of variability, the boundaries that exist in the relationship, raises the issue of the ideal amount of interchange across each of the three boundaries. Is overlap of the two partners' external worlds advantageous, and if so, to what extent? Is there an ideal amount of communication between the two members of a relationship? Within an individual, is greater satisfaction correlated with more or less incorporation of the external world into the internal world of the relationship? Are some things more satisfactorily included, and if so, for whom?

The final dimension of variability—symmetry—suggests the need to examine the role and value of symmetry in relationship satisfaction. Is symmetry very important in some areas, and less important in others? Do people tend to agree on the need for symmetry in certain areas, or do they tend to differ?

Finally, our model as a whole may be evaluated for its applied utility. Would teaching people to understand our model and the questions it raises enhance their likelihood of establishing and maintaining productive, happy relationships? This, for us, is the only true test of the value of our model. Because it was inspired by the lives of the people around us, we believe its worth should be measured in this arena.

In sum, we believe that there are as many ways of maintaining a successful, productive relationship as there are types of people. So often we look into other people's lives, finding it inconceivable that they are in a happy relationship with that person or under those terms. Or we see someone we know we could be happy with, but they're wasting themselves with so-and-so. Wouldn't it be simpler if they could all see it our way? Fortunately, we don't run others' lives—only our own. Certainly, our own relationship is a worthwhile place to start.

We have said very little in this chapter that hasn't been said before, in fact, a very long time ago. Socrates put it most simply: "Know thyself." If you don't know what you want out of your life and your relationship, who are you going to ask? Some might say, "Your model takes all the fun out of life and love. Unpredictability is exciting. We never can really know, so why bother trying? It's depressing to choose—I want it all." To this we respond, "Not choosing is choosing." We believe it is best to know what one wants and needs out of the major areas of life, and let the spice come from the less important areas. Making choices is part of mature adulthood. Few, if any, of us can ever really have it all, and the ones who do undoubtedly gave up on this chapter long ago.

REFERENCES

Bakan, D. (1967). *Toward a reconstruction of psychological investigation.* Baltimore: Jossey-Bass.

Barnes, M. L., & Buss, D. M. (1985). Sex differences in the interpersonal behavior of married couples. *Journal of Personality and Social Psychology, 48,* 654–661.

Berscheid, E., & Walster, E. H. (1978). *Interpersonal attraction.* Reading, MA: Addison-Wesley.

Buss, D. M. (1984). Toward a psychology of person-environment (PE) correlation: The role of spouse selection. *Journal of Personality and Social Psychology, 47,* 361–377.

Buss, D. M., & Barnes, M. L. (1986). Preference in human mate selection. *Journal of Personality and Social Psychology, 50,* 445–460.

Costa, P. T., & McCrae, R. R. (1980). Still stable after all these years: Personality as a key to some issues in aging. In P. B. Baltes & O. G. Brim (Eds.), *Life span development and behavior* (Vol. 3). New York: Academic Press.

Levinger, G. (1983). Development and change. In H. H. Kelley, E. Berscheid, A. Christensen, J. H. Harvey, T. L. Huston, G. Levinger, E. McClintock, L. A. Peplau, & D. R. Peterson (Eds.), *Close relationships.* San Francisco: Freeman.

Peplau, L. A. (1983). Roles and gender. In H. H. Kelley, E. Berscheid, A. Christensen, J. H. Harvey, T. L. Huston, G. Levinger, E. McClintock, L. A. Peplau, & D. R. Peterson (Eds.), *Close relationships.* San Francisco: Freeman.

Plomin, R., DeFries, J. C., & Roberts, M. K. (1977). Assortative mating by unwed biological parents of adopted children. *Science, 196,* 449–450.

Price, R. A., & Vandenberg, S. G. (1980). Spouse similarity in American and Swedish couples. *Behavior Genetics, 10,* 59–71.

Sternberg, R. J., (1986). A triangular theory of love. *Psychological Review, 93,* 119–135.

Sternberg, R. J., & Barnes, M. L. (1985). Real and ideal others in romantic relationships: Is four a crowd? *Journal of Personality and Social Psychology, 49,* 1586–1608.

Vandenberg, S. G., (1972). Assortative mating, or who marries whom? *Behavior Genetics, 2,* 127–157.

CHAPTER FIFTEEN

Love in Marriage

A Cognitive Account

BY STEVEN R. H. BEACH AND ABRAHAM TESSER

Stories of love and passion have been the mainstay of art and literature for many years. Love has been credited with producing sublime ecstasy as well as profound despair. Yet, it would be a mistake to assume that the frequency of themes of romantic love has been invariant in art and literature over time (cf. Swindler, 1980). Over the last two hundred years or so there appears to have been a shift in Western culture in the nature of marital relationships (cf. Scanzoni, 1979, 1983), with marriage becoming more egalitarian and more focused on mutual satisfaction. Over a similar period, there has been an increasing Western cultural preoccupation with the concept of romantic love (Branden, 1980). It is this gradual shift in values that has elevated love to the centerpiece of marriage. Although this shift in values clearly has its positive side, it has also undoubtedly contributed to the currently increasing national divorce rate (cf. Scanzoni, 1979; Slater, 1968). Perhaps increased divorce rates must be expected as couples find that it is harder to "stay in love" than it is to maintain a purely functional marriage. As love continues to claim a prominent place in peoples' conception of what a marriage should be and to play an important role in marital stability, love is appropriately and increasingly a focus of study for social scientists.

A formidable obstacle to the study of love by social scientists is the lack of a shared definition of love. As the preceding discussion implies, the popular definition has shifted over time and differs across cultures (Branden, 1980; Coppinger & Rosenblatt, 1968). In his history of the world, Durant (1954) describes love and its manifestations as differing markedly from culture to culture. He suggests that in ancient India romantic love was known, but that it was largely confined to symbolic religious literature and had little to do with marriage. In China, as in ancient Greece, love as a tender attachment appears to have been largely associated with relationships between men rather than between the sexes, and again it had little to do with marriage. In other, more primitive cultures, it is difficult to find evidence of romantic love as a distinct emotion. This led Durant to conjecture that love, at least romantic love, is a product of developed civilizations only (1954, p. 43).

Even within modern American culture, there appear to be pronounced individual differences in peoples' conceptions and experiences of love (Shaver & Hazan, 1985; Dion & Dion, 1985). Indeed, few terms have the variety of meanings or the idiosyncratic usage of the term *love*. Lee (1977), for example, has proposed a typology of love that defines six ways in which the term has been used. His proposed usages range from love that is largely physical (eros) to love that is largely spiritual (agape), from love that is primarily playful (ludus) to love that is primarily practical (pragma), and from love that is based on friendship (storge) to love that is based on obsession (mania). Certainly these definitions capture many facets of popular usage. They simultaneously, however, point out a difficulty in any discussion of love. If one is not careful, one could be talking about love in a way that is quite different from the reader's interpretation.

RECENT ATTEMPTS TO DEFINE LOVE

Fortunately, there do appear to be some elements of love that remain constant across the various discussions. Sternberg (1986) has recently done an admirable job of attempting to define love in terms of these common elements. In his definition, love is composed of three basic components: commitment, intimacy, and passion. Data from Maxwell tend to confirm that this description is consistent with modern usage of the term *love*. Maxwell (1985) found that people are more likely to use the word *love* to describe a relationship (1) if it is committed, (2) if closeness (intimacy) is involved, or (3) if there is a sexual component (or family tie). If we ignore the complicating presence of family tie in the factors that determine people's usage of the term *love*, then it can be seen that Sternberg comes very close to capturing the popular usage.

Nevertheless, it appears to us that the extent of the variation in popular usage of the term *love* over time and across individuals bodes ill for any attempt to force the term into static categories. It seems inevitable that a concept as important in people's lives as love will continue to evolve and change over time. Perhaps we would do best to acknowledge the provisional and culture-bound nature of any definition of love that is offered. Then we can focus our efforts on understanding the component parts that appear across a variety of discussions and that appear most relevant to a discussion of love in the context of our time and culture. If these components can be well defined from some theoretical vantage point, so much the better. Perhaps the interrelationships described from this more static and neutral vantage point will be stable over time and across individuals even if usage of the term *love* varies. Of course, it is important to discuss each of the components in the context of the others so that *love* does not get lost in the discussion of its parts. Accordingly, in this chapter we discuss the components of couples' relationships that most people currently associate with love. We will define and differentiate among these components using a cognitive theoretical perspective. We will also discuss the interaction of these components both within the individual and within the couple. It is hoped that the model developed will guide further efforts to understand love in the context of stable marital relationships.

COMPONENTS OF LOVE

We derive the components to be discussed from the work of Maxwell (1985), Sternberg (1986), and Spanier (1976). With Maxwell and Sternberg, we would include commitment as a discernible component of loving relationships. When we discuss commitment, it should be understood to comprise a constellation of cognitive, affective, and behavioral elements. A second discernible constellation of cognition, affect, and behavior derived from Sternberg's (1986) and Maxwell's (1985) analyses can best be labeled intimacy. Two other components that deserve mention may be derived from Spanier's (1976) factor analysis of the Dyadic Adjustment Scale. Spanier describes a component called cohesion, which assesses the amount of positive activities the couples share with each other. We suspect this influences judgments of closeness and so of love. Spanier also found that items having to do with sexual interaction clustered together as a discernible factor. Accordingly, we will discuss four components of marital relationships of relevance to understanding individual experiences of love: (1) commitment, (2) intimacy, (3) cohesion, and (4) sexual interaction.

First, we will consider each of the identified components of love individually from a cognitive perspective, and outline the interaction among cognitions, affects, and behaviors within each. Second, we will examine the systemic nature of the components that comprise love in marriage by examining the intra-individual links between the components. Finally, we will turn to an explication of the interpersonal links between the components of love experienced by one member of a couple and the components of love experienced by the spouse.

Commitment

Commitment is typically conceptualized as a set of cognitions, affects, and behaviors that comprise or serve as markers of an individual's disposition to continue a particular relationship (cf. Beach & Broderick, 1983; Johnson, 1982; Rosenblatt, 1977). From a cognitive perspective, one may view the decision to make a commitment to a relationship as the activation of a higher order schema—an implicit, naive theory of relationships in which the self and a particular other person are the principals. That is, becoming committed is the application of an existing cognitive structure, presumably learned in childhood and earlier relationship experiences, to this particular relationship with this particular person. This is not to say that new information cannot be incorporated into the schema as a result of subsequent relationship experiences. Indeed, becoming *more* committed to a relationship probably involves changes in the schema as well as its application to widening areas of one's life. As a relationship develops, one might expect that areas that had previously been seen as largely unrelated to the marriage, such as outside friendships and vocational choices, might increasingly be influenced by one's commitment to one's relationship. Thus, commitment to a relationship, from a cognitive perspective, should be a dynamic process over the life of a relationship rather than a static quantity.

In earlier work (for example, Tesser, 1978), we have used the term *cognitive schema* to refer to structures like "ideal lover." A cognitive schema, then, is a naive theory, and it functions much like a scientific theory. Scientific theories tell the scientist what he should attend to and what he should ignore regarding some subject. Similarly, a particular cognitive schema will make only selected aspects of a situation salient. In this way, schemas influence information search and retrieval processes (Snyder & Uranowitz, 1978; Snyder & Swann, 1978; Snyder, Tanke, & Berscheid, 1977). In the case of the commitment, one would expect to see a schema-driven bias toward searching for ways to increase personal satisfaction within the relationship rather than searching for options external to the relationship. One would expect the schema to lead an individual largely to ignore the range of options external to the relationship as being irrelevant (cf. Leik & Leik, 1977). Accordingly, one might expect the decision to commit oneself to a relationship to increase one's level of attention to one's spouse. A study by Berscheid, Graziano, Monson, and Dermer (1976) provides some support for this hypothesis. In this study, subjects agreed to date only the person assigned to them over a five-week period. It was found that subjects who believed they would be dating a partner exclusively for the five-week period attended to a taped presentation of the partner to a greater extent than persons who agreed to only one date. Thus, the greater the exclusivity of a relationship, the greater the attention given to the partner. At the level of the marital relationship, a similar effect might be expected. One would also expect increased attention to lead to polarization or more extreme affect in the committed individual (Tesser, 1978). Thus, the committed person should tend to feel more positively about his or her spouse. This process is discussed further below.

Scientific theories provide inference rules: if a scientist observes some value on dimension X, he can infer a particular value on dimension Y. Similarly, a cognitive schema provides an inference structure: if an individual observes some aspect of a stimulus to the extent that other aspects are unknown (or ambiguous), he will infer those aspects in a way that is consistent with the schema (Minsky, 1975; Fiske & Taylor, 1984). Likewise, when we are guided by a particular schema we will seek information in a way that maximizes the likelihood that the schema is confirmed (Rothbart, Evans, & Fulero, 1979; Snyder, 1981). Even more strikingly, we will influence others to behave in a way that confirms our schema. Thus, when a particular schema is guiding one's thoughts about one's spouse, one is likely to act in a way that forces the spouse to take on a congruent role. For example, if I act as if my spouse is committed to me, then all other things being equal, *she* will act as if she is committed to me. An interesting demonstration of this phenomenon comes from an ingenious study by Snyder et al. (1977). In this study, male subjects were randomly paired with a female subject and were instructed to get to know her via a ten-minute telephone conversation. All males were given photographs. One-half the males were presented with an attractive picture, whereas the other half were presented with an unattractive picture prior to their conversation. Later, judges who had neither seen the female subjects nor been shown the female's pictures and who only listened to the girl's track of the tape rated the girl more beautiful if her partner had been led to believe that she was more beautiful. It appears, then, that by believing the girl was beautiful, the males forced their partner to behave as though she were beautiful. Thus, in some cases, schemas can shape interpersonal reality. We will further develop the interpersonal impact of commitment in a later section.

No doubt, the exact contents of the cognitive schema activated by commitment varies from individual to individual. However, one would expect each schema to contain some specific information (for example, "Marriage is forever") as well as more general information in the form of rules (for example, "Things work out best if you focus on the relationship you have rather than pursuing a relationship you don't have"), or in the form of prototypic information (like "All divorces are painful, expensive, and time consuming"). Accordingly, the result of having become committed to a relationship and so having activated the commitment schema is that one should be able to "go beyond the information given" in the relationship (Tesser, 1978; Fiske & Taylor, 1984). Rather than responding only to the cues and contingencies provided by one's spouse, the person with a commitment to a relationship should also respond to the cues and contingencies suggested by the schema. Thus, committed individuals should be biased positively in their perceptions of their relationships. The commitment schema should allow relatively incomplete sets of information (for example, "I have been focusing on my marriage") to yield strong conclusions (for example, "Things are going to work out for the best in my relationship"). A corresponding positive bias might be anticipated in inferences regarding the spouse and the spouse's motivation for acting as part of a couple (cf. Fincham, Beach, & Nelson, 1987; Fincham & Beach, 1985).

The positive bias in information search, inference processes, and shaping of interpersonal reality would lead one to expect high levels of commitment to be associated with positive and stable feelings about one's life and one's relationship (cf. Kobasa, 1985). One might hypothesize on the basis of cognitive consistency theory (Festinger, 1957) as well that a certain optimism and buoyancy should derive from the positive expectations generated by a high level of commitment. Thus, on the average, commitment to a relationship should lead one to feel more satisfied with that relationship and should lead one to a variety of situations that confirm one's sense that one is basically satisfied and happy with one's relationship. Confirmation of this link, albeit indirect, comes from Spanier's (1976) factor analysis of the Dyadic Adjustment Scale. In this factor analysis, items related to commitment were related to the same factor as items related to general marital satisfaction.

Although the emphasis in our analysis has clearly been on the role of the cognitive subsystem in influencing behavior and affect, it should be noted that the behavior and affective subsystems may also influence each other as well as the cognitive subsystem. For example, it has been demonstrated that affect may help recruit and organize retrieval processes (Bower, 1981; Clark & Isen, 1982; Teasdale & Fogerty, 1979). The reciprocal relationship between affect, cognition, and behavior is discussed further below. The point we wish to emphasize here is that we view the commitment component of love as an interactive set of cognitive, behavioral, and affective processes. We suggest, however, that cognitive processes loom large in understanding the operation of this component.

Intimacy

Intimacy refers to a relationship state in which inner or innermost feelings, thoughts, and dispositions can be revealed or explored. Hatfield (1984) has provided a useful definition of intimacy as a process leading to closeness that involves the exploration of similarities and differences between two persons. Accordingly, confidences and self-disclosures would be among the behavioral markers of an intimate relationship. Self-disclosure implies a cognitive component of trust or willingness to take a risk with the other person (cf. Larzelere & Huston, 1980). At an emotional level, intimacy is typically thought to be related to particularly intense or "hot" emotions. Deep caring and passion, but also intense anger or depression, are accordingly potential emotional sequelae of intimacy.

From a cognitive perspective, the link between engaging in intimate disclosure and the production of passionate feelings is twofold. On the one hand, a confidence shared with a partner must involve uncertainty. That is, different possible outcomes of the disclosure can be imagined (cf. Abelson, 1983). Even where considerable trust exists, questions must nonetheless arise: How will my partner react? Will my disclosure be accepted? Laboratory investigations of uncertainty using considerably less meaningful consequences than potential censure from one's spouse have found increased arousal to be a function of subjective uncertainty (Deane, 1969; Elliot, 1966; Epstein & Roupenian, 1970). Likewise, it is to be expected that uncertainty in meaningful, real-life situations should be associated with strong arousal, and so, strong affect (Tomkins, 1962).

A second way in which intimate scripts should be linked to strong affect derives from Mandler's script-disruption hypothesis (Mandler, 1975, 1980; a "script" refers to an expected sequence of actions and interactions). According to this hypothesis, physiological arousal and so "hot" affect result from script disruption. Positive affect will result if the interruption is seen as benign or controllable, or if it results in the person completing his or her goal earlier than expected. Negative affect will occur if the interruption is not seen as benign, or is uncontrollable, or results in delay of goal completion. The scripts involved in intimate exchanges are by their very nature not well rehearsed. That is, if they were engaged in frequently with many other people, they would cease to be "intimate." Thus, a particular deep self-disclosure or other intimate behavior being poorly rehearsed should generate many opportunities for script disruption to occur. This in turn should set the stage for passion, deep emotion, anger, or despair.

One can imagine a scene in which a spouse is disclosing a personal concern long held secret from the world. He is prompted to do this self-disclosure because in his previous experience, his partner has been accepting and supportive. Nevertheless, as he begins his self-disclosure his words falter; he is not sure exactly what to say. Perhaps his partner gently prompts him to continue, bringing on a warm flush of positive emotion. Continuing, he finishes his self-disclosure and finds his spouse completely accepting. Uncertainty is now greatly reduced. A potentially problematic area is no longer threatening. A script has been successfully completed. A surge of strong emotion rushes over him, and he thinks to himself how deeply in love he really is.

Intimacy, then, is inherently tied to strong emotions because of the uncertainty and potential for script disruption that intimate behavior occasions. This perspective has some positive as well as some disturbing correlates. As partners engage in more and more intimate behavior, one would expect them to grow closer (cf. Hatfield, 1984), but also to develop relatively routine and predictable scripts involving those behaviors that are most often used (Schank & Abelson, 1977). Thus, as the marital relationship "improves" by becoming closer, it is likely to become more difficult to achieve the intensity of positive affect achieved earlier in the relationship (cf. Rook, 1985). Thus, over the course of the relationship, it may require greater ingenuity and a willingness to continue to explore new territory if the intense positive affect of earlier points in the relationship is to be maintained.

We have hypothesized that behaviors that are "intimate" at one point in a relationship may cease to be "intimate" as they are scripted into well-organized familiar sequences. What then becomes of these behaviors? Consider the example of a greeting kiss. Early in the relationship, the kiss can bring on a thumping heart and sweating palms, and the person may feel a sense of hesitancy about approaching the partner. When the kiss is returned, a surge of strong positive emotion may sweep over the one initiating the kiss. Clearly, at this stage in the relationship, the kiss is an intimate behavior and produces the appropriate emotions. Needless to say, few couples who have been married for very many years would describe the greeting kiss they give their spouse in terms of thumping hearts and sweating palms. The kiss may well remain a pleasant experience and one they would not give up, but it is no longer functioning as an intimate behavior. Rather, it has become part of a predictable script with little potential for script disruption. A greeting kiss has become part of the couple's ongoing pattern of cohesion. It is to this aspect of love that we now turn.

Cohesion

Dyadic cohesion refers to the degree of sharing and closeness in a relationship. As such, it should be the product of intimacy at earlier points in the relationship (cf. Hatfield, 1984), similar interests between the spouses, or other sources of mutual interaction. The items from the Dyadic Adjustment Scale that form the Dyadic Cohesion Subscale assess the behaviors of engaging in outside interests together, exchanging ideas, laughing together, discussing things calmly, and working on a project together. It can be seen that these are activities that are less likely to generate the hot emotions of intimate behavior. Cohesive behaviors might be expected to generate substantial positive affect, but without high levels of physical arousal.

From a cognitive perspective, the activities falling in the realm of cohesion are those that follow a well-elaborated script involving the spouse. There may be surprises on occasion, but they are likely to be minor and quickly resolved. As the number of activities in this realm grows, whether through repeated intimate interactions or discovery of new common ground, the couple becomes more cohesive. Cohesion might be expected to exert a strong influence on the individual's beliefs about the spouse and, more important, should influence which beliefs are most salient at any given time. That is, as the number of positive joint activities with the spouse increases, the number of thoughts about the spouse prompted by those interactions should also increase. Accordingly, the subset of beliefs about the spouse that is most salient, and that should play the largest role in determining an individual's moment-to-moment feelings about his spouse (cf. Salancik, 1974), are likely to be determined in large measure by the degree of cohesion that exists in the relationship. In addition, one might anticipate that the growth of familarity engendered by strong cohesion in a relationship should also lead to more positive feelings about the spouse (cf. Zajonc, 1968).

In a more speculative vein, one might expect the growth of cohesion in the relationship to be coincident with the growth of the stress-reducing capacity of the relationship. That is, since high-cohesion couples have an extensive repertoire of well-rehearsed scripts, they should have a variety of options for producing a calming effect when faced by stressors external to the relationship. Indeed, high cohesion might even help couples respond less negatively to stress produced by their own arguments and disagreements. A stressor that begins to raise uncertainty and so physiological arousal can be countered in high-cohesion couples by engaging in some well-elaborated script with the spouse. This might involve talking about the problem that has arisen, or distracting one's thoughts from the problem by engaging in some other relationship script. Thus, cohesion should play an important role in the individual functioning of the spouse as well as in their functioning as a couple.

Sexual Interaction

Sexual interaction refers to a variety of activities ranging from hand-holding and hugging to sexual intercourse. However, different types of sexual behavior may function differently for different couples. For some couples, particularly those in the early stages of their relationship, sexual interaction might be expected to function as other intimate behavior functions. That is, over and above the stimulus properties of the sexual interaction, one might expect to find strong affect which is generated by the fact that the scripts governing the interaction are not yet well developed and so hold considerable uncertainty and opportunity for either disruption or facilitation. Conversely, later in the relationship, this additional affective component may be attenuated. At this point, a well-elaborated script for sexual interaction may have developed, and sexual interaction may come to function more like other cohesive behaviors. (Indeed, for some couples entering therapy, sexual interaction has become so routine, it has lost all affective potential.) At this later point in the relationship, sexual interaction may be a shared positive activity that generates positive affect, but not necessarily the intense passion of the earlier relationship.

On this view, one would need to examine a particular couple's view of sexual interaction before knowing whether to categorize it as primarily intimacy-based or primarily cohesion-based. In factor analyses of large numbers of heterogenous couples, one would accordingly expect sexual interaction to emerge as a factor distinct from either intimacy or cohesion, but at a conceptual level and on a couple-by-couple basis, sexual behaviors should function either as the behaviors composing the intimacy component of the relationship or as the behaviors composing its cohesion component. Thus, from the cognitive perspective taken here, there are really *only three distinct components* of loving relationships that can be delineated and that follow different courses over the course of the marriage. First, there is commitment, which is hypothesized typically to be stable over long periods of the relationship and to exert strong pressure for consistent behavior and affect. Second, there is intimacy, the strength of which is largely determined by trust, or the willingness to take chances on unscripted and poorly scripted interactions with the spouse. This component might be expected to start off strong for most couples and then wax and wane over the course of the relationship (cf. Shaver & Hazan, 1985). And, third, there is cohesiveness, which is largely determined by the amount of available, well-scripted behavior patterns that involve the spouse. For nondysfunctional couples, this component might be expected to grow continuously over the course of the relationship. This leads us to the question of how these components may interact with each other.

INTRA-INDIVIDUAL LINKS IN THE PROPOSED RELATIONSHIP MODEL

The model that emerges from the preceding discussion is shown in figure 15.1. The figure shows the reciprocal relationships hypothesized to exist between the cognitive, affective, and behavioral elements within each component of the model. That is, despite our emphasis on the role of cognitive processes in defining and differentiating among the three relationship components discussed, we recognize the possibility for strong affect to lead to congruent memories and thoughts (Clark & Isen, 1982; Teasdale & Fogerty, 1979) and behavior (Isen & Levin, 1972), as well as behavior to elicit congruent affect and cognition (Bem, 1972; Freedman & Fraser, 1968; Hastorf & Cantril, 1954; Laird, 1974; Schacter, 1964). Thus, within each component, all arrows are bidirectional (cf. Isen, Shalker, Clark, & Karp, 1978). This suggests that although there may be some response system differences, there should also be considerable pressure for conformity across the response systems within each component of the model.

It can also be seen in figure 15.1 that each component of the system is expected to exert some influence on every other component. For example, a change in the commitment schema might have profound implications for

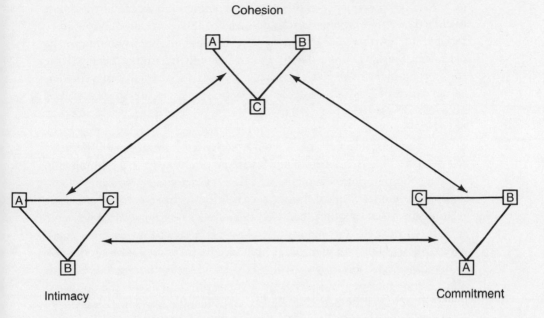

Fig. 15.1.

intimacy and cohesive behavior toward the partner. That is, if a spouse becomes less committed to the partner, then long-term potential payoffs vis-à-vis the partner are likely to assume a less salient position, whereas short-term payoffs may take on more salience. Thus, decisions to perform intimate behaviors and cohesive behaviors are likely to become more exchange-oriented and less communal in nature (Mills & Clark, 1982). This would be expected to produce less satisfying exchanges and fewer interactions overall. Thus, one would expect a decrease in commitment to push the couple toward the exchange pattern characteristic of unsatisfying relationships (cf. Holmes, 1981; Kiddler, Fagan, & Cohn, 1981). Accordingly, a change that originated in the commitment component could work its way through the entire system, eventually influencing intimacy and cohesion as well.

Consider an individual who, after some years of marriage, comes seriously to consider the possibility of divorce or separation from his spouse. Presumably, this could occur as the result of outside attractions and opportunities or because of decreased satisfactions (intimacy and cohesion) within the relationship (Levinger, 1976). The proposed model would suggest that one consequence of this lessened commitment would be to change the likelihood that intimate disclosures and cohesive interactions would be thought of. Further, even if they were thought of, they would not be considered valuable. Thus, overall rates of self-initiated interaction with the spouse should decrease if commitment decreases. Simultaneously, the perceived costs of possible negative outcomes vis-à-vis the spouse should decrease. Thus, risks may be taken that would never have been taken before, allowing for the possibility of intense affect. However, other more ordinary relationship behaviors would be expected to produce little positive arousal. That is, after someone loses his commitment to a relationship, normal cohesive relationship behavior that was previously meaningful and had an emotional impact should seem dull and lifeless. Only breaking relationship rules or other behavior perceived as extremely risky should suffice to produce strong emotion. As fewer cohesive behaviors are experienced as rewarding and so fewer are engaged in, there should be a reduction in thinking of the spouse positively. This should lead to even less positive affect about the spouse. Indeed, time spent thinking about the spouse is likely to focus on the negative affect that is being engendered, leading to further polarization of affect (Tesser, 1978). Increasing amounts of time may be spent thinking of other possible relationships, further decreasing commitment. Thus, changes in the intimacy and cohesion components would be hypothesized to feed back to influence further the commitment schema in a negative direction. Accordingly, one might expect a continuing erosion in all three components of the system until some new steady state is achieved or the relationship is dissolved.

Consider the situation of our hypothetical uncommitted spouse as the relationship approaches the point of dissolution. He begins to do fewer things with his spouse. Even those things he does try doing seem pointless and uninvolving. Eventually, he concludes that there is no real emotional potential left in the relationship. But when the relationship actually begins to dissolve, a variety of intense emotions return. An emotional roller coaster is launched. Perhaps all this emotion comes as a complete surprise to the spouse involved. Yet it is a straightforward prediction of the model presented here (see Berscheid, 1982, for a more complete discussion). As the scripts binding the couple together are dissolved, they should produce a great deal of disruption, arousal, and affect. Further, this effect should occur even though the relationship may have appeared relatively empty prior to the disruption. Indeed, the intensity of the reaction to the dissolution may convince the marital partners that they cared more for each other than they realized. Thus, the process of marital dissolution may in some cases provide the material needed by the couple to reestablish intimacy and commitment.

An example in which deterioration in the relationship does not result from a challenge to the commitment component can also be imagined. One can imagine a relationship that is high on intimacy and cohesion, but is faced with extremely attractive alternatives to the relationship. Although one's commitment might initially waver, the high level of positive thoughts of one's spouse and the perceived payoffs of the intimacy with the spouse would be inconsistent with a decrease in commitment to the relationship. The pull for consistency between the components of the system would be expected to shore up one's wavering commitment. This should lead one to not consider the alternatives any further. One might distract oneself by engaging in cohesive behaviors or seek the highly charged reinforcement of intimacy, but in either case, one's relationship might be expected to emerge stronger and more resistant to future temptations as a result of the experience (Bem, 1972).

It can be seen in the examples above that each component is expected to exert an influence on the other components, and this influence is bidirectional in each case. Although other examples are possible, it is interesting to note that the primary links between components of the system consistently lie at the cognitive level in the examples considered. Indeed, we would hypothesize that it is largely via the cognitive elements that the pull for consistency in the intra-individual system arises (cf. Festinger, 1957). However, another possible source of consistency might include affective states recruiting mood-congruent cognitions or behavior across components or affective states recruiting other similarly valenced affects across components (cf. Zillman, 1978). These various possibilities should be examined further empirically.

ANOTHER COGNITIVE CONSIDERATION: ATTENTION

Cognitive considerations have been discussed as they appeared relevant to each component and the interaction of the components within the system. However, each of the components of the system described above has implications for attentional processes. We hypothesize that commitment to one's spouse should increase the time allocated to thinking about and interacting with the spouse, that the intense affective discharge associated with intimate behavior should increase the salience of one's spouse in awareness, and that high levels of cohesive behavior should provide increased numbers of opportunities for positive thoughts about the spouse.

What should we expect to happen, then, when an individual begins to think more about the spouse? Will feelings change?

There are experimental and correlational data that are consistent with the expectation that simply thinking about someone can polarize feelings about that individual (Ickes, Wickland, & Ferris, 1973; Sadler & Tesser, 1973; Tesser, 1976; Tesser & Conlee, 1973; Tesser & Leone, 1977). In the context of dating, Tesser and Paulhus (1976) found that the more an individual thought about the person she or he had dated, the greater the love that was indicated on the Rubin love scale (Rubin, 1970). In the context of marriage, we would expect a similar polarization to occur. If a particular set of negative thoughts about the spouse is salient, the more time one spends thinking about one's spouse, the more negative one's feelings should become. Conversely, if a set of positive thoughts about the spouse is most salient, the more time one spends thinking about one's spouse, the more positive one's feelings should become.

One way in which polarization should occur is to add consistent positive beliefs about one's spouse as a function of thinking about him or her. It seems likely, however, that this type of process would be easier when little information about another person is available than when much information is available. Indeed, a study by Tesser and Cowan (1975) found that thought produced greater polarization when little information was available. These data suggest that this form of polarization is not likely to figure prominently in established long-term relationships. A second way in which polarization could occur is to change or reinterpret known facts about one's spouse (Tesser & Cowan, 1975). For example, a spouse's unavailability for recreational activities could be interpreted as either a reflection of his or her hard-working disposition or as a deliberate rejection. Clearly, any fact can be attributed to very different characteristics. This type of interpretive process could quickly change many "positive facts" to "negative facts" or vice versa. Given the inherent uncertainty in attributions for behavior (cf. Brickman, Ryan, & Wortman, 1975), one might expect considerable change in this domain as a function of prolonged thought about the partner (for a more extended discussion of the effect of thought in romantic relationships, see Tesser & Reardon, 1983). Indeed, attributional differences have been found between satisfied and unsatisfied couples (Fincham & Beach, 1985; Fincham, Beach, & Nelson, 1987). Thus, one might hypothesize that as one pays more attention to one's spouse's behavior, one's attributions for that behavior become increasingly polarized with subsequent effects on affect and behavior.

INTERINDIVIDUAL RELATIONSHIPS

Thus far, in our explication of love, we have focused on the individual. Love, of course, occurs in the context of the couple. Thus, it is important to consider the ramifications of different aspects of the components of loving relationships on a potential partner. The various components of love are expected to have different degrees of relevance in terms of impact on the spouse. From a cognitive perspective, it is assumed that rather than the actual level of the various components, it is their levels as perceived by the spouse that are most important in determining the impact on the spouse. Thus, each component is expected to have greater relevance as its level of observability increases. The components of love may be rank-ordered in terms of their accessibility to an outside observer. The most observable of the three components is cohesion.

Cohesion in the Couple

Cohesion is assumed to index the extent to which well-elaborated scripts are available for a variety of situations involving the spouse. Accordingly, the level of cohesion might be expected to be relatively symmetrical between the spouses. That is, to the extent that one is engaging in a variety of pleasant activities with one's spouse, the spouse should also be engaging in a variety of pleasant relationship activities. This should be relatively observable to the spouse and produce similar affect in the spouse as in one's self (cf. Hoffman, 1978, 1983, 1984). A possible mismatch could occur if the activities that are enjoyable to one spouse are boring to the other (that is, an overly elaborated script) or are unpleasant (that is, involve blocking or delay of desired outcomes for the other spouse). For example, one can imagine a couple who spend a good deal of time together doing only what the husband enjoys, say, going to hockey games. In this case, the husband might report a high level of cohesion while the wife would report a lower level. Nevertheless, we would hypothesize that, in general, cohesion involves shared and observable activities that are mutually gratifying. Accordingly, it should be the component of love that is most likely to be equally strong or equally weak for the two spouses. In addition, it should be the component of love that impacts most directly on the corresponding component of the spousal system. Thus, in figure 15.2, the heaviest line connecting the spousal systems is drawn between the cohesion components.

One might also hypothesize that a high level of cohesion would influ-

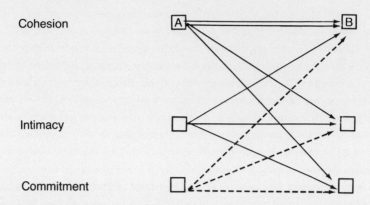

Cohesion

Intimacy

Commitment

Fig. 15.2.

ence the partner's levels of commitment and intimacy. It has been argued above that cohesive behaviors should provide cues for thinking about one's spouse positively. More specifically, if one sees one's spouse involved in a variety of cohesive behaviors, one should be more likely to attribute one's spouse's behavior to positive traits. This should make one more optimistic about the future course of one's relationship. Accordingly, one is likely to believe that the relationship has a more durable future and that one's spouse is unlikely to be rejecting if one were to reveal negative information about oneself. The first train of thought would be expected to lead to elevated levels of commitment, while the second train of thought would be expected to lead to elevated levels of trust and therefore intimate behavior. Thus, it can be argued that cohesion should have an impact on all three components of the spousal system. In addition to its direct effect on increasing the spouse's cohesive behavior, it is also expected to have a less direct effect on the spouse's cognitions regarding commitment and intimacy. Since these relationships are hypothesized to be less direct and somewhat weaker, they are indicated by somewhat lighter lines in figure 15.2.

Intimacy in the Couple

The component of intimacy is hypothesized to be somewhat less observable to the spouse than is cohesion. Nevertheless, there are likely to be behavioral and affective cues that are observable to the spouse. A particularly deep self-revelation, if it is recognized as such by the spouse, may elicit a variety of thoughts. Likewise, a surge of positive affect by one's spouse is likely to elicit a corresponding surge of affect in oneself (cf.

Hoffman, 1978). Similarly, behavior such as self-disclosure may prompt reciprocal self-disclosure or other positive behavior on the part of the spouse (Derlega, Wilson, & Chaikin, 1976). Thus, one would expect a fairly high level of reciprocated affect in intimate exchanges and reciprocated intimate behavior on the part of the spouse. Accordingly, a relatively strong link is hypothesized to connect the intimacy components of the spouses. However, because there is more room for ambiguity and misinterpretation, this link is indicated to be less strong than that connecting the cohesion components of the spouses.

Intimate behavior, when recognized, might also be hypothesized to influence the spouse's thoughts concerning commitment and thoughts about engaging in cohesive behavior. For example, the occurrence of intimate behavior may lead to thoughts about the partner as approachable and attractive. This would be anticipated to influence the decision to engage in increased levels of cohesive behavior. Seeing one's spouse as highly emotionally involved in the relationship might also be expected to influence thoughts about the likely maintenance of the relationship over the long run. That is, if one sees one's spouse as highly affectively involved in the relationship, one might expect greater investment and effort on one's spouse's part to make the relationship last. Accordingly, one's own expectation that the relationship can work over the long run should be increased. Thus, in addition to the direct effect of intimacy on reciprocated intimacy, we would hypothesize a link between intimacy and both commitment and cohesion. As can be seen in figure 15.2, however, owing to the decreased observability of intimacy, these direct effects are represented as being of the same magnitude as the indirect effects of cohesion.

Commitment in the Couple

Commitment is perhaps the least observable of the three components of love discussed in this chapter. Indeed, its primary defining characteristic is a nonevent—not getting out of the relationship. Given the well-known difficulty of assimilating information conveyed via nonevents, one would expect spouses to have difficulty (1) perceiving commitment accurately and (2) responding to its indicators (Nisbett & Ross, 1980). Of course, verbal expression of one's level of commitment or behaviors indicating the pursuit of alternative relationships may be observable under some circumstances. When behavioral indicators of commitment are called for and are not forthcoming, or are generated spontaneously even though not called for, we expect that they would have an impact on the spouse. It is hypothesized, however, that commitment is typically not overtly expressed and so is more often inferred by the spouse from intimacy and cohesion rather than from overt markers of commitment. Accordingly, although we see commitment playing a critical role in the intra-individual system, it should play a less important role overall in the relationship.

However, as can be seen in figure 15.2, the links between commitment and the components of the partners' experience of love are hypothesized to be relatively weak compared to the effects of cohesion and intimacy on the partner. If the expressions of commitment are noticed and are appraised by the spouse as being reliable, this should have a positive impact on trust. One should be more inclined to trust a highly committed partner than an uncommitted partner. Accordingly, one should expect commitment that is noticed to increase the likelihood of future intimate behavior. Also, indications of commitment would be expected to influence the overall attractiveness of the spouse and so increase rates of cohesive behaviors. Finally, the belief that one's spouse is committed may be important in maintaining one's own commitment in the face of marital difficulties. Thus, when commitment is perceived, it would be expected to have an impact on the partner's commitment, intimacy, and cohesion.

Overall, it can be seen that cohesion on the part of spouse A is hypothesized to be a powerful determinant of cohesion and to have a strong impact on intimacy and commitment in the spouse. Owing to its lesser observability, intimacy is seen as influencing intimacy, cohesion, and commitment, but less powerfully overall than the impact exerted by cohesion. Finally, as commitment typically is the least observable of the components of love, it is hypothesized to be weakly related to all three components on the part of the spouse. Thus, it can be seen that cohesion would be expected to play an extremely important role in maintaining equal levels of love over the family life cycle. It is not that love would necessarily disappear without high levels of cohesion, but rather that discrepancies in the partners' experienced level of love should more easily arise when levels of cohesion are not high.

LOVE VERSUS MARITAL ADJUSTMENT

Perhaps the most widely researched topic in the marital area is marital adjustment. Accordingly, it behooves us to distinguish love as it is presented here from the construct of marital adjustment as it has been typically investigated. Traditional measures of marital adjustment such as the Locke-Wallace Marital Adjustment Test (Locke & Wallace, 1959) or the Dyadic

Adjustment Scale (Spanier, 1976) include items that would be expected to tap some aspects of the construct of love as it has been portrayed in this chapter and by theorists in the area. Indeed, two of the components discussed were derived from Spanier's (1976) factor analysis of his widely used marital adjustment measure. Items are often included in measures of marital adjustment that assess commitment and cohesion in the relationship, and level of sexual and affectionate behavior. However, these scales also typically assess a number of problem areas, conflict-resolution methods, and overall level of upset with the relationship. These types of items would seem to fall somewhat outside the realm of love and more squarely in the domain of marital skills or marital role functioning. One way of differentiating love from marital adjustment, then, is that love is a more specific construct than is marital adjustment. Marital adjustment may be considered a broad construct including components of marital role functioning, skills relevant to marriage such as problem-solving ability and conflict resolution, and overall marital happiness/unhappiness, and some components of love in the marriage as well.

There are strong theoretical reasons to anticipate that the components of love should be empirically related to other components of marital adjustment. Certainly, conflicts and the inability to resolve them would be expected to impair cohesion. In a similar vein, global satisfaction has been hypothesized to be a strong determinant of commitment (Rusbult, 1983). Nevertheless, we would hypothesize that it is possible for the components of love to be strong even in a dysfunctional relationship. That is, one may love his or her spouse even though the relationship is currently frustrating and problems have been difficult to resolve. Thus, we view an increased focus on the component of love in marital relationships as a move toward increased specificity in the study of marital relationships and thus as a positive development in the marital area. It is hoped that, by focusing on more specific categories in describing the marital relationship and moving away from a single global description, we will be better able to investigate the intricate dynamics of marriage (cf. Fincham & Bradbury, 1985).

LOVE VERSUS ATTACHMENT

Another widely researched construct is that of attachment. Although attachment has historically been studied in the context of infant care–giver relationships (Ainsworth, Blehar, Waters, & Wall, 1978), it is certainly appropriate to investigate attachment between adults (cf. Shaver & Hazan, 1985). Attachment may be considered to include any of the emotional processes that bind two people together. In this sense, love is one of several forces contributing to attachment. Other forces that may contribute to attachment could include fear of the unknown, need for affection or self-enhancement, a desire to dominate, sexual attraction, or inertia. Although these other emotional forces may result in some form of attachment, it is not always clear that this attachment should be labeled as love.

Recently, Shaver and Hazan (1985) have presented a conceptualization of love as an attachment process. This perspective has led them to categorize lovers into secure versus anxious/ambivalent versus avoidant lovers, paralleling the three types of attachment documented in early childhood (Ainsworth et al., 1978). They found that the experience of love appeared different for members of each category. The secure lovers experienced love as waxing and waning over the course of the relationship but at times reaching the intensity experienced at the start of the relationship. The avoidant lovers appeared not to experience the same depth of feeling in love relationships as either the secure or the anxious/ambivalent lovers. The distinguishing feature of the anxious/ambivalent lovers was that they frequently fell in love (or began to), but found it hard to stay in love. In terms of the model we have presented, it appears that Shaver and Hazan's (1985) typology captures individual differences in the intimacy component of love. The secure lovers are able to trust their partner and so increase the intimacy of their relationships over time. Accordingly, they find that the level of intense affect in their relationships decreases at times, but they are also able to recapture it by moving to a deeper level of intimacy. The avoidant lovers, on the other hand, are not able to trust their partners sufficiently to engage in deeply intimate behaviors. Accordingly, they are confined to less intense affect in their relationships. Conversely, the anxious/ambivalent lovers, who expect rejection, are nonetheless motivated initially to engage in some intimacy. One might hypothesize that their expectation of rejection leads to uncertainty even in low levels of intimacy. Thus, they may experience high levels of intense affect early in relationships. Over time, however, their fear of rejection should lead them to stop deepening the level of intimacy in their relationships. Thus, in the long run, the intense affective experience of love should fade for the anxious/ambivalent lovers, and not be recaptured. If Shaver and Hazan (1985) are correct that these adult styles reflect learning that occurred in early childhood, then perhaps the thing that is learned is basic trust. This would indeed be expected to affect all subsequent interpersonal relationships to some degree. It would also be expected to have particularly profound implications for close relationships.

The empirical work by Shaver and Hazan (1985) highlights the fruitfulness of thinking of adult relationships in terms of attachment. It should be noted, however, that love as it has been presented in this chapter, while being more specific in some respects than "attachment," is also more than an attachment process. Love as we view it is an integrated set of processes that serve to bind individuals together in sharing, caring, committed relationships. As such, love in marriage is a dynamic growth process with implications for the individuals involved that go beyond their level of attachment to each other.

This chapter should be seen not primarily as an attempt to present an all-inclusive model of love but rather as an attempt to present a cognitive perspective on some relationship processes that appear to be relevant to love. Love is a construct with meanings that vary with the individual, and it seems unlikely that any model will adequately capture the full range of popular usage. It is important, however, that the processes responsible for love's growth, decay, and maintenance be better understood. For better or for worse, love is a highly valued aspect of marital relationships. For most couples, love is the reason to marry and its disappearance is the reason to divorce. Accordingly, we offer the cognitive perspective developed in this chapter as a heuristic for future investigation.

REFERENCES

Abelson, R. P. (1983). Whatever became of cognitive consistency theory? *Personality and Social Psychology Bulletin, 9,* 37–54.

Ainsworth, M. D. S., Blehar, M. C., Waters, E., & Wall, S. (1978). *Patterns of attachment: A psychological study of the strange situation.* Hillsdale, NJ: Erlbaum.

Beach, S. R. H., & Broderick, J. E. (1983). Commitment: A variable in women's responses to marital therapy. *American Journal of Family Therapy, 11,* 16–24.

Bem, D. J. (1972). Self-perception theory. In L. Berkowitz (Ed.), *Advances in experimental social psychology* (Vol. 6, pp. 1–62). New York: Academic Press.

Berscheid, E. (1982). Attraction and emotion in interpersonal relationships. In M. S. Clark & S. T. Fiske (Eds.), *Affect and cognition: The 17th annual Carnegie symposium on cognition.* Hillsdale, NJ: Erlbaum.

Berscheid, E., Graziano, W., Monson, T., & Dermer, M. (1976). Outcome dependency: Attention, attribution, and attraction. *Journal of Personality and Social Psychology, 34,* 978–989.

Bower, G. H. (1981). Emotional mood and memory. *American Psychologist, 36,* 129–148.

Branden, N. (1980). *The psychology of romantic love.* New York: Bantam.

Brickman, P., Ryan, K., & Wortman, C. B. (1975). Causal chains: Attribution of responsibility as a function of immediate and prior causes. *Journal of Personality and Social Psychology*, 32, 1060–1067.

Clark, M. S., & Isen, A. M. (1982). Toward understanding the relationship between feeling states and social behavior. In A. Hastorf & A. Isen (Eds.), *Cognitive social psychology*. New York: Elsevier North Holland.

Coppinger, R. M., & Rosenblatt, P. C. (1968). Romantic love and subsistency dependence of spouses. *Southwestern Journal of Anthropology*, 24, 310–319.

Deane, G. E. (1969). Cardiac activity during experimentally induced anxiety. *Psychophysiology*, 6, 17–30.

Derlega, V. J., Wilson, M., & Chaikin, A. L. (1976). Friendship and disclosure reciprocity. *Journal of Personality and Social Psychology*, 34, 578–587.

Dion, K. K., & Dion, K. L. (1985). Personality, gender, and the phenomenology of romantic love. In P. R. Shaver (Ed.), *Self situations and behavior: Review of personality and social psychology* (Vol. 6, pp. 209–239). Beverly Hills, CA: Sage.

Durant, W. (1954). *Our Oriental heritage*. New York: Simon & Schuster.

Elliot, R. (1966). Effects of uncertainty about the nature and advent of a noxious stimulus (shock) upon heart rate. *Journal of Personality and Social Psychology*, 3, 353–356.

Epstein, S., & Roupenian, A. (1970). Heart rate and skin conductance during experimentally induced anxiety: The effect of uncertainty about receiving a noxious stimulus. *Journal of Personality and Social Psychology*, 16, 20–28.

Festinger, L. (1957). *A theory of cognitive dissonance*. Stanford, CA: Stanford University Press.

Fincham, F., & Beach, S. R. H. (1985). *Attributions to the self and partner in distressed and nondistressed relationships*. Paper presented at the symposium, Cognition and Marital Therapy: Current Research, at the 19th Annual Convention of the Association for the Advancement of Behavior Therapy, Houston, TX.

Fincham, F., Beach, S. R. H., & Nelson, G. (1987). Attribution process in distressed and nondistressed couples: 3. Causal and responsibility attributions for spouse behavior. *Cognitive Therapy and Research*.

Fincham, F. D., & Bradbury, T. N. (1985). *The assessment of marital quality: Implications for research on marriage*. Unpublished manuscript, University of Illinois, Champaign, IL.

Fiske, S. T., & Taylor, S. E. (1984). *Social cognition*. Reading, MA: Addison-Wesley.

Freedman, J., & Fraser, S. (1966). Compliance without pressure: The foot in the door technique. *Journal of Personality and Social Psychology*, 4, 195–202.

Hastorf, A., & Cantril, H. (1954). They saw a game: A case study. *Journal of Abnormal and Social Psychology*, 49, 129–134.

Hatfield, D. (1984). The dangers of intimacy. In V. Derlega (Ed.), *Communication, intimacy, and close relationships* (pp. 207–220). New York: Academic Press.

Hoffman, M. L. (1978). Empathy, its development and prosocial implications. In C. B. Keasey (Ed.), *Nebraska symposium on motivation* (Vol. 25, pp. 169–217). Lincoln: University of Nebraska Press.

———. (1983). Affective and cognitive processes in moral internalization. In E. T.

Higgins, D. N. Ruble, & W. W. Hartup (Eds.), *Social cognition and social development: A sociocultural perspective* (pp. 236–274). Cambridge: Cambridge University Press.

———. (1984). Empathy, its limitations, and its role in a comprehensive moral theory. In W. M. Kurtines & J. J. Gewirtz (Eds.), *Morality, moral behavior, and moral development* (pp. 283–302). New York: Wiley-Interscience.

Holmes, J. G. (1981). The exchange process in close relationships: Microbehavior and micromotives. In M. J. Lerner & S. C. Lerner (Eds.), *The justice motive in social behavior.* New York: Plenum.

Ickes, W. J., Wickland, R. A., & Ferris, L. B. (1973). Objective self-awareness and self-esteem. *Journal of Experimental Social Psychology, 9,* 202–219.

Isen, A. M., & Levin, P. F. (1972). The effect of feeling good on helping: Cookies and kindness. *Journal of Personality and Social Psychology, 21,* 284–388.

Isen, A. M., Shalker, T. E., Clark, M. S., & Karp, L. (1978). Affect, accessibility of material in memory, and behavior: A cognitive loop? *Journal of Personality and Social Psychology, 36,* 1–12.

Johnson, M. P. (1982). Social and cognitive features of the dissolution of commitment to relationships. In S. Buck (Ed.). *Personal relationships* (Vol. 4). London: Academic Press.

Kiddler, L. H., Fagan, M. A., & Cohn, E. S. (1981). Giving and receiving: Social justice in close relationships. In M. J. Lerner & S. C. Lerner (Eds.), *The justice motive in social behavior.* New York: Plenum.

Kobasa, S. C. O. (1985). Personality and health: Specifying and strengthening the conceptual links. In P. Shaver (Ed.), *Self, situations, and social behavior: Review of personality and social psychology* (Vol. 6). Beverly Hills, CA: Sage.

Laird, J. D. (1974). Self attribution of emotion: The effects of expressive behavior on the quality of emotional experience. *Journal of Personality and Social Psychology, 29,* 475–486.

Larzelere, R. E., & Huston, T. L. (1980). The dyadiac trust scale: Toward understanding interpersonal trust in close relationships. *Journal of Marriage and the Family, 42,* 575–604.

Lee, J. A. (1977). A typology of styles of loving. *Personality and Social Psychology Bulletin, 3,* 173–182.

Leik, R., & Leik, S. A. (1977). Transition to interpersonal commitment. In R. L. Hamblin & J. H. Kunkel (Eds.), *Behavioral theory in sociology.* New Brunswick, NJ: Transaction Books.

Levinger, G. (1976). A social psychological perspective on marital dissolution. *Journal of Social Issues, 32,* 21–47.

Locke, H., & Wallace, U. (1959). Short marital adjustment and prediction tests: Their reliability and validity. *Marriage and Family Living, 21,* 251–255.

Mandler, G. (1975). *Mind and emotion.* New York: Wiley.

———. (1980). The generation of emotion: A psychological theory. In R. Plutchik & H. Kellerman (Eds.), *Emotion: Theory, research and experience: Vol. 1. Theories of emotion.* New York: Academic Press.

Maxwell, G. M. (1985). Behavior of lovers: Measuring closeness of relationships. *Journal of Social and Personal Relationships, 2,* 215–238.

Mills, J., & Clark, M. S. (1982). Exchange and communal relationships. In L.

Wheeler (Ed.), *Review of personality and social psychology* (Vol. 3). Beverly Hills, CA: Sage.

Minsky, M. (1975). A framework for representing knowledge. In P. H. Winston (Ed.), *The psychology of computer vision*. New York: McGraw-Hill.

Nisbett, R., & Ross, L. (1980). Human inference: Strategies and shortcomings of social judgment. Englewood Cliffs, NJ: Prentice-Hall.

Rook, K. S. (1985, August). *Nonsupportive aspects of social relationships*. Paper presented to the Annual Meeting of the American Psychological Association, Los Angeles.

Rosenblatt, P. C. (1977). Needed research on commitment in marriage. In G. Levinger & H. L. Raush (Eds.), *Close relationships: Perspectives on the meaning of intimacy*. Amherst: University of Massachusetts Press.

Rothbart, M., Evans, M., & Fulero, S. (1979). Recall for confirming events: Memory processes and the maintenance of social stereotypes. *Journal of Experimental Social Psychology, 15*, 343–355.

Rubin, Z. (1970). Measurement of romantic love. *Journal of Personality and Social Psychology, 16*, 265–273.

Rusbult, C. E. (1983). A longitudinal test of the investment model: The development (and deterioration) of satisfaction and commitment in heterosexual involvements. *Journal of Personality and Social Psychology, 45*, 101–117.

Sadler, O., & Tesser, A. (1973). Some effects of salience and time upon interpersonal hostility and attraction during social isolation. *Sociometry, 36*, 99–112.

Salancik, J. R. (1974). Inference of one's attitude from behavior recalled under linguistically manipulated cognitive sets. *Journal of Experimental Social Psychology, 10*, 415–427.

Scanzoni, J. (1979). A historical perspective on husband-wife bargaining power and marital dissolution. In G. Levinger & O. C. Moles (Eds.), *Divorce and separation*. New York: Basic Books.

———. (1983). *Shaping tomorrow's family: Theory and policy for the 21st century*. Beverly Hills, CA: Sage.

Schacter, S. (1964). The interaction of cognitive and psychological determinants of emotional states. In L. Berkowitz (Ed.), *Advances in experimental social psychology*. New York: Academic Press.

Schank, R., & Abelson, R. (1977). *Scripts, plans, goals, and understanding*. Hillsdale, NJ: Erlbaum.

Shaver, P., & Hazan, C. (1985, August 25). *Romantic love conceptualized as an attachment process*. Paper presented at the 93rd Annual Convention of the American Psychological Association, Los Angeles.

Slater, P. E. (1968). Some social consequences of temporary systems. In W. G. Bennes & P. E. Slater (Eds.), *The temporary society*. New York: Harper & Row.

Snyder, M. (1981). Seek, and ye shall find: Testing hypotheses about other people. In E. T. Higgins, C. P. Herman, & M. P. Zanna (Eds.), *Social cognition: The Ontario symposium*. Hillsdale, NJ: Erlbaum.

Snyder, M., & Swann, W. B. (1978). Hypothesis-testing processes in social interaction. *Journal of Personality and Social Psychology, 36*, 1202–1212.

Snyder, M., Tanke, E. D., & Berscheid, E. (1977). Social perception and interpersonal behavior: On the self-fulfilling nature of social stereotypes. *Journal of Personality and Social Psychology, 33,* 656–666.

Snyder, M., & Uranowitz, S. W. (1978). Reconstructing the past: Some cognitive consequences of person perceptions. *Journal of Personality and Social Psychology, 36,* 941–950.

Spanier, G. B. (1976). Measuring dyadic adjustment: New scales for assessing the quality of marriage and similar dyads. *Journal of Marriage and the Family, 38,* 15–28.

Sternberg, R. J. (1986). A triangular theory of love. *Psychological Review, 93,* 119–135.

Swindler, A. (1980). Love and adulthood in American culture. In J. Smelser & E. H. Erikson (Eds.), *Themes of work and love in adulthood.* Cambridge, MA: Harvard University Press.

Teasdale, J. D., & Fogerty, S. J. (1979). Differential effects of induced mood on retrieval of pleasant and unpleasant events from episodic memory. *Journal of Abnormal Psychology, 88,* 248–257.

Tesser, A. (1976). Thought and reality constraints as determinants of attitude polarization. *Journal of Research in Personality, 10,* 183–194.

––––––. (1978). Self-generated attitude change. In L. Berkowitz (Ed.), *Advances in experimental social psychology* (Vol. 11). New York: Academic Press.

Tesser, A., & Conlee, M. C. (1973). Some effects of time and thoughts on attitude polarization. *Journal of Personality and Social Psychology, 31,* 262–270.

Tesser, A., & Cowan, C. L. (1975). Some effects of thought and number of cognitions on attitude change. *Social Behaviors and Personality, 3,* 165–173.

Tesser, A., & Leone, C. (1977). Cognitive schemas and thought as determinants of attitude change. *Journal of Experimental Social Psychology, 13,* 340–356.

Tesser, A., & Paulhus, D. L. (1978). Toward a causal model of love. *Journal of Personality and Social Psychology, 34,* 1095–1105.

Tesser, A., & Reardon, R. (1981). Perceptual and cognitive mechanisms in human sexual attraction. In M. Cook (Ed.), *The bases of human sexual attraction.* London: Academic Press.

Tomkins, S. S. (1962). *Affect, imagery, and consciousness* (Vol. 1). New York: Springer.

Zajonc, R. B. (1968). The attitudinal effects of mere exposure. *Journal of Personality and Social Psychology Monograph Supplement, 9*(2, pt. 2).

Zillman, D. (1978). Attribution and misattribution of excitatory reactions. In J. H. Harvey, W. Ickes, & R. F. Kidd (Eds.), *New directions in attribution research* (Vol. 2). New York: Wiley.

PART V

Overview

CHAPTER SIXTEEN

Some Comments on Love's Anatomy

Or, Whatever Happened to Old-fashioned Lust?

BY ELLEN BERSCHEID

An invitation to write a few words on the subject of love for a collection of essays such as this is to be prized for the opportunity it presents to set down personal observations on the phenomenon and its study that are not afforded by the more usual scholarly contexts, those of developing a line of theoretical argument or of narrow reportage of empirical results, where one is required to suppress doubts and uncertainties, to clip off loose threads, to ignore dangling embarrassments, and, in general, to appear more confident than one feels. As this suggests, what follows are some comments on love that, although not entirely random in nature, for they stem from almost two decades of hard, if sporadic, labor on the rockpile of love, simply represent some current musings on the subject.

The first of these comments about the phenomenon of human love and its study is immediately prompted by the title of this chapter, which refers to the "anatomy" of love and which was prompted by the editors' early intention to use this phrase to label their entire collection of chapters. The word *anatomy* with reference to love is somewhat misleading, of course, in that it implies not only the existence of a corpus to be dissected, a body with some cohesiveness and integrity, but also that the phenomenon has been captured, subdued, and placed on a marble slab in the laboratory. No such progress has been made in the arena of love (and perhaps this is why the title of this volume was changed), but that substantial advances have been made in a very few years is undebatable. For example, the fact that the editors have been able to bring together such a distinguished array of knowledgeable contributors to a book on love to be published by one of the nation's most respected university presses is perhaps more remarkable than anything expressed within the pages of this volume—and undoubtedly more remarkable than the average layperson, or psychology graduate student for that matter, is likely to appreciate. What the fact of this book attests to is that the study of human love in all its forms has become an acceptable topic for systematic study by behavioral and social scientists.

It was not always so. It was not so even ten years ago. The relatively unsophisticated nature of much available theory and information on love, the anomalies, omissions, and contradictions, cannot be understood without also understanding that, first, until very recently the psychologist who studied love automatically stained his or her scientific mantle. The subject was considered to be a frivolous one (as contrasted, for example, to such respectable enterprises as outlining the intricacies of classical eyelid conditioning or descriptively detailing the mating habits of the stickleback fish), and it was thought not to be amenable to systematic observation, analysis, and understanding (poets and philosophers being regarded by most scientists and laypersons alike as the proper authorities on the subject). Not only did an interest in love bring disapproving stares from one's peers, but psychologists who with federal research grant funding looked up from the study of such mild and innocuous forms of attraction as "liking" to contemplate the strong form, "love," found themselves embroiled in seemingly endless congressional and media controversy and debate. As one of those publicly reproached for studying "romantic love," I can testify that the international firestorm of publicity and controversy extracted, at a minimum, two years from my personal and professional life. (This, however, was not without precedent; the drubbing that was earlier endured by the late, great Harry Harlow from congressional panels of inquiry and from the press when it was discovered that he was investigating the development of affectional systems in monkeys was far worse.)

I will not spend any of these few pages allotted me defending the worthiness of the enterprise of understanding love, taking it as a given that anyone with even half a human brain and two eyes to look about in the world of human affairs can readily appreciate the superordinate role it plays in each individual's life and in determining the welfare and survival of homo sapiens as a class (and trusting also that such a defense is offered elsewhere between these covers and, if not, referring doubting Thomases to other justificatory treatises on the subject—for example, Berscheid, 1984). Rather, I shall, as was originally suggested by the editors, pick up the scalpel and commence the vivisection. But, first, one has to find the body—or attempt to answer the first question the editors posed to their contributors, "What is love?"

THE SEARCH FOR THE BODY OF "LOVE"

Queen Victoria's venerable behavioral scientist, Sir Henry Finck, spoke to that question almost a century ago by announcing (after giving the matter a good deal of thought) that "love is such a tissue of paradoxes, and exists in such a variety of forms and shades, that you may say almost anything about it that you please, and it is likely to be correct" (Finck, 1891, p. 224). Finck's succinct, if pessimistic, answer to the problem of identifying love stands up even in the age of star wars.

The behavioral scientist can deal only with observable behavioral events (a person doing or saying something), and so, the first step in the analysis of love is a description of the events that fall within this behavioral domain. The problem is, as Sir Finck noted, that the word *love* in the English language refers to a vast territory of human behavioral events that have in common one person's thinking, feeling, or doing something positive toward another person—at least as perceived by the person doing the thinking, feeling, or acting, or by the recipient of the action, or by other people observing the event (all of whom, of course, may vary in their interpretations of how positive the event really is, of what the object of the action truly is, and so forth). Some, of course, would even quarrel with this sweeping characterization of the common denominator of these events. (For example, Oscar Wilde, who gloomily observed that "you always hurt the one you love," would object to the characterization of behavior associated with love as "positive.") However, few would deny that the central problem is that the number and diversity of behavioral events that someone, somewhere, has regarded as an instance of "love" are huge. And, yet, it is with such events that any analysis of love must begin.

To illustrate what needs to be the grist for an analysis of love, imagine that we had at our disposal a research assistant who was both omnipotent and omniscient (and, for the sake of exposition, named Mr. Feinmind), and that we asked Feinmind to go find us the body of love and bring it back to the lab so that we could dissect it. Feinmind, with his extraordinary powers, might, first, freeze the entire world of human social intercourse at this very moment and, second, from the billions of flash-frozen slides of human behavior that resulted, subsequently select out for us all those slides that reflected actions clearly directed toward another person (as opposed to other animals or inanimate objects) and that, also, had at least some positive quality to them (they reflected favorable thoughts about the other, facilitated the welfare of the other, promoted proximity to the other, and so on). If Feinmind then put all these frames of human behavior together in a sack (and only a very *large* sack could hold them all), dragged it back to the laboratory, and heaved it up onto the marble slab, we would have secured the "body" of love and our analysis could begin.

This collection of behavioral events, then, roughly constitutes the domain of interest to the social scientist seeking an understanding of love. Rummaging through Feinmind's sack, we would find all the eye-popping and bewildering paradoxes of which Finck spoke and with which all of us are familiar in our own lives—of people running away from those they desperately desire to be near (perhaps as a short-term stratagem to effect long-term closeness), of beating about the head and shoulders those they most care about (sometimes "for their own good"), and on and on. It is a fascinating bag of human behavior, and so it is no wonder that men and women have, for ages, poked through it, extracted one or more of the more remarkable oddities it contains, held that specimen up to the light and marveled—in prose, poetry, and analyses of love—often with the assumption that if the whole universe can be reflected in a single blade of grass plucked by Walt Whitman, then certainly the whole of the collection of events constituting love can be fathomed from minute scrutiny of a single, often unusual if not bizarre, item in it. This, of course, is the *anecdotal* route to an understanding of love, and well traveled though it still may be, it doesn't seem to go anywhere, the fruit of the exercise being primarily in the pleasures afforded by the journey itself. For no matter how scrupulous an analysis one does on single instances of love, there are a multitude of other items in the sack to be reckoned with and, inevitably, someone else will come along and thrust *his* hand into the sack, hold a different specimen up to inspection, and say reproachfully, "But, here, how do you account for *this*?"

The corpus problem, then, is that love is not a single distinct behavioral phenomenon with clearly recognizable outlines and boundaries. Rather, the genus love is a huge and motley collection of many different behavioral events whose only commonalities are that they take place in a relationship with another person (in that they are caused by and/or affect the behavior of another; see Kelley et al., 1983) and that they have some sort of positive quality to them. Thus, the first step in analysis is to reduce this impossibly huge array down to a more manageable size by some means, or to begin to sort the behavioral events in the love domain according to the properties they have in common and to deal with the resultant smaller piles of events. These smaller piles, each made up of events that seem more similar to each other than to events in a different pile, may be termed the "species" of love (or more frequently, the "varieties" of love). This sorting task, however, is much more difficult than it sounds because we have neither God nor Mr. Feinmind as a research assistant—someone who can present us with that critical representative sample of frozen slides of behavioral events in the love domain that we may then describe and classify.

DISSECTION INTO VARIETIES OF LOVE

Two general approaches to this difficulty have been devised, with one more systematic and seemingly more scientific than the other. The systematic approach is to gather together a sample of people and ask them to describe to us their thoughts, feelings, and actions toward others whom they ostensibly love. Thus, for example, husbands and wives may be asked to describe their behavior toward their spouses (the assumption often being that men and women love their spouses). Then, these statements (or this collection of slides of behavioral events associated with love) are subjected to an analysis of commonality of properties, often via factor analysis, which statistically boils down the collection of statements and indicates the dimensions that seem to underlie the whole (for a brief review of some of such studies, see Berscheid, 1984, and for one of the better examples, see Sternberg & Grajek, 1984). "Caring," for example, is a dimension that is found in some studies.

Such factor analytic studies are valuable, not least because they begin with actual descriptions of behavioral events (albeit by the person doing the acting and not by an external observer whose description of the behaviors of the loving person and their effect on the loved one may differ appreciably from the actor's). On the other hand, it is one of the more regrettable facts of a behavioral scientist's life that the magical qualities of factor analytic techniques are limited by the imagination and preconceptions of the investigator using them. If he or she, for example, happens to put only oranges and apples in the sack, then only an orange factor and an apple factor (and, sometimes, an "oraple" or an "appange" factor) can emerge. If the domain properly also includes lemons, but none was included in the sample, then no lemon dimension can appear. In other words, what appears in the sample is, naturally, heavily determined by the investigator's notion of what love is; if "caring" is part of that conception, for example, then one can be certain that respondents will be asked to tell whether they exhibit caring behaviors toward the loved one. There are other limitations, many of which are similar to those typical of conceptions of emotion that rely on self-report of behavior (see Berscheid, 1984).

The other approach to identifying the varieties of love is more common. The love theorist mulls over his or her own life experiences and personal observations of the experiences of others (these then constituting the sample of behavioral events to be classified), attends to their similarities and differences, and comes up with some sort of classification scheme that purports to distinguish among the varieties of love. An example, and there are many, is the scheme presented by C. S. Lewis in *The Four Loves* (1960), which suggests that, as his title implies, it is useful to think of at least four species of love.

Lewis's scheme shall be briefly outlined here not only because it once seemed particularly compelling to me but because his varieties bear good correspondence to many of the dimensions that emerge from factor analytic studies. They correspond, as well, to many of the distinctions people seem to make among different types of love in their daily lives (this latter being information not to be sniffed at, as the fruits of Heiderian analyses of commonsense psychology have demonstrated). Lewis's four species follow closely from the Greek distinctions of types of love and are as follows:

1. *Agape*: behavior directed toward another that has the intended effect of furthering the survival and welfare of the other and that is performed with no thought of receiving rewards from the other in return. This is what has been called altruistic or "Christian" love, what Maslow called "B-love" (or love for another's being as opposed to "D-love," or deficit love that stems from personal needs one believes the other can satisfy). It is the kind of love Erich Fromm discussed at length in his classic *The Art of Loving*, a book purchased by many undergraduate psychology students with the expectation of reading about something very different.

2. *Affection*: what may be also called *attachment* in that the behavioral events in this class primarily seem to be proximity-seeking or proximity-maintaining behaviors (presumably reflecting a desire to have the object of affection nearby and accessible for interaction even if it rarely occurs). Affection appears to require familiarity with the other.

3. *Philias*: friendship. Sometimes called pragmatic love, philias seems to be based on the expectation and/or receipt of concrete rewards from another in the course of interaction with them, with a quid pro quo giving of rewards in return; expressions of admiration, support, and the attribution of positive qualities to the other (intelligence, humor, and so on) seem to be behavioral events typical of this class of love.

4. *Eros*: romantic love. The definitive behavioral events in this class (although surprisingly overlooked in many contemporary analyses

of romantic love, a point to which we shall return) have to do with sexual desire; its other seemingly distinctive qualities—its short life, the ability of the loved other to dominate the person's fantasy, idealization of the loved other, desire for possession and exclusivity—have been outlined in perhaps a hundred discussions on romantic love (for example, see Berscheid & Walster, 1974; Walster & Walster, 1979).

One reason these four are attractive candidates for any treatise on the "anatomy" of love is that each class of behavioral events may occur in a relationship quite independently of the others. That is, as discussed elsewhere (Berscheid, 1984):

1. People not infrequently act to further the welfare of those they do not know and feel no affection toward, people they do not think highly of in terms of the other's personal qualities, people from whom they expect no reward in return for caring behavior, and, moreover, people they feel not the slightest sexual desire toward. That is, people not infrequently exhibit altruistic love toward another person while not exhibiting any of the behaviors in the other three classes of events. On the other hand, and as the aforementioned factor analytic studies reveal, caring behavior often occurs alongside the other types of loving behaviors—in friendships and in romantic affairs, for example—but it need not, which argues for its distinctiveness as a class of loving behavior.

2. People not infrequently act to maintain physical proximity to a person they have never lifted a finger to help (and never would), a person they do not feel possesses good qualities (and who may, in fact, be perceived to possess unfavorable attributes), a person who is not particularly rewarding to the individual and, of course, for whom they feel no sexual attraction and to whom they give no serious thought—as long as the other remains accessible. They simply don't feel good—or safe—if the other person isn't around. A child who wants her parents in the background as she goes about her business and a husband who treats his spouse like a household fixture (but is distressed if the fixture suddenly disappears) are examples. Again, the affection/attachment class of behaviors *may* occur independently of behaviors in the other three classes and may, as Bowlby (1973, for example) has suggested, represent the most basic affectional mechanism the human is born with. But again, too, these behaviors do often accompany the others.

3. People not infrequently feel they are "in love" with someone they know to be an unworthy scoundrel, a person who is not only not a friend but sometimes appears to be one's worst enemy, and they sometimes perpetrate extraordinarily destructive acts upon the "loved" one—never

mind fail to help them when help is needed. Romantic love may appear, in other words, devoid of the elements of agape, philias, or affection.

Or, in sum, the prototypical behavioral events of each of these four varieties of love *may* occur in a relationship with another in the absence of behavioral events that are representative of the other types of love. How frequently they do appear in isolation from one another is not known, since we do not have that representative sample of behavioral instances of love, but it is clear that they very frequently appear together, as lumping them all under the genus love would suggest they ought. Some theorists have speculated, however, that when eros appears in a relationship, probably the other three types of events—altruistic behaviors, attachment behaviors, friendship behaviors—usually appear also, but the reverse is not true. In other words, the other three types of behavior frequently appear together without eros, leading some to suggest that the most useful classification of love is only twofold: eros, or romantic love, and something often called companionate love, a stew of the remaining three types of behavioral events.

Of what use are such classification schemes? They obviously have enormous popular entertainment value, with many wishing for the experts to identify for them (perhaps through some sort of test) the variety of love characteristic of their relationship with another (or, perhaps more usually, the variety of love characteristic of the other's relationship with them). Apart from such parlor games, however, there is little or no value to anatomical exercises if they are not followed through in some way.

THE DYNAMICS OF LOVE

Classification schemes, then, should be a beginning, but too frequently they are the end. The object of the classification enterprise is to aid in the discovery and understanding of the dynamics of love, which importantly includes identification of the causal antecedents of the various types of love behaviors in a relationship, the conditions that inhibit or prevent their development, and the consequences of the presence or absence of these love behaviors in the relationship for a multitude of other events of significance to the partners or to those whose fate and fortunes depend on that relationship.

Some of the events of particular concern, and to which the type and extent of love in a relationship are believed to be intimately associated, are the likelihood of relationship initiation, relationship development toward closeness, relationship maintenance and stability, and the physical and mental health of the partners in the relationship, including the degree of emotional distress they experience upon its dissolution. To classify a relationship according to the type of love behaviors present (and the type absent)—to say, for example, this is primarily a friendship, with altruistic love, eros, and affection notably absent—is to say not much of anything of value or interest if one does not also know the causal conditions that produced this type of love relationship rather than another, the nature of the causal conditions whose appearance (or disappearance) will cause the relationship to change its character, as well as the consequences for the participants and for others of the relationship being of that particular character (such as philias).

One value of even rough diagrams of the anatomy of love, such as the fourfold scheme outlined here, is that they reveal that we know a great deal more about the dynamics of love than is commonly recognized. When all manner of loving behaviors remain jumbled together in that very large sack labeled love, Finck's observation that love is so full of paradoxes you can say almost anything you like about it and be correct is true. When these behavioral events are sorted into even preliminary smaller piles, however, many of the paradoxes disappear; you can no longer say what you like and be in accord with the evidence about the causes and consequences of that variety of love.

The causal antecedents of altruistic (or "prosocial") behavior, for example, have been investigated to a fare-thee-well. What is know about these sorts of behaviors currently fills books as well as at least one standard chapter in every introductory social psychology text. For another example, attachment, most extensively investigated in children, is now coming to be recognized as an adult phenomenon as well, just as Bowlby (1973) theorized, and the effects of growing familiarity with another, as well as the kinds of circumstances that lead to a heightened desire to be in close physical proximity to a familiar person (for example, stress), are now being explored.

Perhaps most of our current knowledge applies to the causal determinants of friendship, or of pragmatic love, and this knowledge also currently fills books as well as yet another standard chapter in introductory social psychology texts, a chapter often entitled "interpersonal attraction." Here, one most certainly cannot say anything you please and be correct. One can no longer say, for example, that "opposites attract." They don't; the evidence for homogamy—in background, interests, attitudes, and, indeed, almost any characteristic one can name—is overwhelming, with exceptions only proving the rule. For just one other example, one can no longer say that "absence makes the heart grow fonder," at least when one is speaking of friendships. It doesn't; physical distance, or any difficulty of accessibility to the partner, adds to the costs of maintaining a relationship, and in the end, the evidence dictates that one would be much safer betting on "out of sight, out of mind."

EROS

The litany of self-congratulation about how much we do know about love comes to an end, however, when we come to eros, or romantic love. Here, we haven't done so well, and, unfortunately, when most people express thirst for a knowledge of the dynamics of love, it's not altruism, attachment, or friendship they're talking about. Moreover, it is this sort of love that is closely associated with the prediction of other events of great consequence to the relationship partners and to others with whom they interact, primarily because of the close association of romantic love with marriage in our culture. The belief that romantic love is a precondition for the marital contract has been growing in recent years, not diminishing, mainly because of the dramatic increase in the numbers of women who maintain that they will not marry a man they are not "in love" with, even if he possesses all the other qualities they desire in a spouse. (Men for years have maintained that they would not marry unless they were in love with the woman; it is women who have changed over the past two decades and who are now also emphasizing the role of romantic love in marriage.) Thus, at least among college men and women, over 80 percent now say that they will not consider marrying a person they are not in love with, and over half consider falling out of love a good reason to dissolve the marriage (see Simpson, Campbell, & Berscheid, 1986). And, even apart from its consequences for marriage, romantic love appears to play an extremely important role in the lives of young adults. For example, when unmarried and unengaged college men and women were asked to identify their "closest" relationship with another human being, over 50 percent named a romantic partner—*not* a father, mother, brother, sister, friend, or coworker (Berscheid & Snyder, in preparation).

(It should be noted parenthetically here, in keeping with an insistence that it is important for students of love to keep the different varieties of love in mind and to resist jumbling them together under the one rubric "love," that many men and women make a serious distinction between the statements "I love you" and "I'm *in* love with you," the latter phrase usually signifying a state of romantic love. As discussed elsewhere [Berscheid, 1984], it is most probably a mistake for researchers not to attend carefully to this distinction in meaning when interpreting self-reports of experience or in phrasing questionnaires and interview questions about love. To illustrate, in a recent biography of Ingrid Bergman [Leamer, 1986], the author tells of a man who was besotted with Bergman. She cared deeply about him and enjoyed and valued his friendship, but she finally was forced to tell him that although she loved him very much, she simply was not in love with him—whereupon he committed suicide. This tale says much about the value of plain, unvarnished love—of agape, affection, and philias—to a person suffering from the "awesome, burning power" of romantic love; all three together often do not seem an adequate recompense for unrequited romantic love.)

Romantic love, as Walster and I (1974) argued early on, is a different animal from the other forms of love. Since this point, too, has been discussed elsewhere, only two elements of that argument shall be repeated here. First, it seems quite clear that more and more liking for another does not, in the end, lead to romantic love; more and more liking just leads to a lot of liking. Liking for another—whether affection or philias in form—and romantic love are not different points of quantitative intensity on the same dimension; the two are on different tracks altogether. This, of course, can be testified to by anyone who has earnestly desired to be in love with another, often because the other *is* so likable, or because they *do* have all those qualities one desires (or ought to desire) in a mate, or because it would please one's parents, friends, or the other person; one can like the other so hard one's nose bleeds, but that—still—does not, and seemingly cannot, cause the liking state to be transcended and romantic love to appear.

Second, the probability that romantic love is a different animal from the other varieties of love is argued for by the fact that some of the conditions that are conducive to the development of, say, philias are not conducive to the development of romantic love and may even be detrimental to it. Philias (as well as affection), for example, appears to grow, other things being equal, with increases in the familiarity of the other and with the predictability of his or her behavior; novelty and uncertainty, on the other hand, appear to be associated with romantic love.

Which brings us to the misleading nature of many schemes that classify love into its varieties. The four-faceted scheme discussed here is, regrettably, no exception. Each of the words representing the four types of love in this scheme refers to an *emotion*: agape, affection, philias, and eros. But the representative events in each class are not emotional events but, rather, behaviors that either intend or actually achieve some kind of effect (for example, helping another, staying in physical proximity to another, exchanging rewarding experiences with the other, promoting sexual mating with the other, and so forth). This is an important difference. The emotions (or emotional events) that accompany each behavioral event directed toward the other may be congruent with it, may be entirely absent, or may be incongruent with it. Consider agape, for example. Behavioral events falling in this category might include dropping a dime in the collection can on the counter to help someone, driving the elderly to church on Sunday, or cleaning up the vomit of a very sick person one is taking care of. How frequently are such behaviors accompanied by a *feeling* of agape, an emotion of brotherly love? Probably not very often; dropping a dime in the can is often a mindless behavior and the only emotion that accompanies driving the old folks to church every Sunday may be mild irritation and wonderment that one every got roped into the "Mobile Helpers Program." If one were to classify only those behavioral events that were also accompanied by the appropriate (or congruent) emotions as constituting loving behaviors in that class, one likely would have many empty classes of loving behavior even in the most loving of relationships.

The point here is simply that many typologies of love often confuse the so-called loving emotions with other types of behavioral events diagnostic of the varieties of love and that, more important, typologies of love alone do not take us very far toward understanding the emotions that are reputed to accompany (or, according to some, to constitute) the various types of love.

Which brings us back again to romantic love, for of all the types of love, it is most often regarded and spoken of as an emotion. But herein lies another confusion—a confusion between a short-term emotional experience and a general state of affairs that extends much longer in time. If romantic love is a strong emotion, then like any other intense emotion, it is precipitated by a particular concatenation of stimulus events; it is characterized by strong peripheral physiological arousal, by changes in facial and other musculature, by changes in focal attention and cognitive processing, and so forth, and these bodily and cognitive events run their course within a limited time (seconds, minutes, or hours as opposed to days, weeks, and months). However, and apart from the possibility that it is useful to think of an emotion of romantic love, the term *romantic love* most certainly should be regarded as a state or condition of the "in love" individual that usually extends for a much longer period of time (months or years) than does—or can—any single emotional experience. Or, in other words, intense emotions are bodily alarm or emergency reactions, and when the alarm rings too insistently for too long, the person dies; obviously, then, people do not experience an intense emotion of romantic love for very long.

Thus, when we speak of an individual being in love with another, we usually do not mean that the individual has experienced *an* emotion precipitated by the other, or even that the person has experienced that one emotion many times in association with the other. Rather, we mean that the individual has exhibited many behaviors, some of which are emotional and some of which are not, that have been precipitated by or directed toward another and that fall within the eros class of behavioral events. Moreover (although this is a point that needs systematic investigation), the kinds of emotions typical of the *state* of romantic love may be varied, ranging all over the emotional map in intensity, in positivity and negativity, and in quality. Thus, again, as we theorized early on (Berscheid & Walster, 1974), the state of romantic love is often characterized by a "hodgepodge of emotions"—fear, anger, sexual desire, and so on—and not all these emotions are positive. To give a well-worn example, we really weren't surprised to discover that the item "X has been the cause of my worst depressions" discriminates well between friends and romantic lovers, with lovers endorsing the statement and friends not (Berscheid & Fei, 1977). One of the emotions in that hodgepodge of emotions associated with romantic love, then, is most probably depression. What the other emotions are and how frequently they occur in the syndrome have not been investigated, to my knowledge.

Given this general state of our understanding of eros, I personally have arrived at three conclusions. First, if you want to understand the dynamics of romantic love, or that cluster of emotional experiences and other events people frequently call by that name, then it is necessary to understand the dynamics of human emotional experience in general, as well as how these translate into the context of a relationship with another. I have put my efforts where my conviction is and have presented elsewhere a theoretical model for the experience of emotions in close relationships (for example, Berscheid, 1983). Such an understanding of how emotional experiences of all kinds are generated in a relationship with another is especially vital, not just for understanding the *emotion* of romantic love (again, if there is a single emotion), but for understanding the causal antecedents of the *state* of romantic love, or the complex of emotions experienced over some extended period of time in association with another that together are called romantic love (and I have no doubt that there is such a syndrome, that it is identifiable, and that its determinants may be discovered).

Second, however, I conclude that with respect to understanding the dynamics of eros, an understanding of the emotions as they occur in a relationship with another (or fail to occur) is only a beginning. Essential also is knowledge of how the occurrence (or absence) of emotional experiences of various kinds and intensities are *interpreted* by the person doing the experiencing. Or, in other words, what emotions, of what intensities and hedonic sign, experienced in what sequences in association with another person lead the individual to characterize his or her state as one of being in romantic love? Does the experience of even intense negative emotions make that characterization more likely? What other nonemotional conditions need to be present for an individual to characterize his or her state as romantic love? The answer to that question depends, of course, on what the individual believes romantic love *is*, and Karen Dion and her associates (for example, Dion & Dion, 1973), as well as others, have explored popular beliefs about it. There clearly are individual differences in belief, and those who do not believe there is such a thing as romantic love are not likely to think they are in love no matter what their experiences in the relationship—for these people, the occurrence of such events is like a tree falling in the forest with no one to hear.

Of special interest, then, are the *consequences to the relationship* of one individual interpreting a course of events as signifying romantic love while another individual, experiencing exactly the same events in the same sequence, does not. It should make a difference to the future of the relationship. For example, if both partners believe that it is necessary to be in love with the other in order to contemplate marriage, then the partner who also has characterized his or her state as one of being in love has satisfied that prerequisite to marriage and the other has not. Or, in other words, the nature of the individual's characterization of his or her relationship with another has consequences *apart from* the occurrence of the events that gave rise to the characterization.

My third, and final, conclusion (to which I've already alluded) is that the role of sexual desire and experience has been neglected in contemporary discussions of romantic love. It is all very well to look down one's nose at Sigmund Freud's cursory analysis of romantic love as repressed, suppressed, or frustrated sexual desire, but, for me at least, Freud seems to have gotten much smarter as I've gotten older. And, surely, it is no accident that the wisest of the romantic love theorists, Theodore Reik, entitled his classic book *Of Love and Lust* (1941) (and not, by the way, "Of Love and Liking").

The student of romantic love who agrees that sex has been an unfortunate omission from recent discussions and who wishes to learn about sexual desire need not rush to one of the myriad human sexuality texts currently inflicted upon college undergraduates; there, he or she will find only endless diagrams of the plumbing involved in sexual intercourse and reproduction, lengthy discussions of diseases and perversions of every description, and endless statistics on the frequencies of this or that. There isn't much there about human sexual desire (although there is much discussion of the mechanisms of sexual arousal in rodents, chickens, and apes, since this seems to be the kind of information available—useful, it might be noted, only if the individual asking where sexual desire and romantic love have fled in his relationship happens to be a chimpanzee).

The emotion theorists haven't done much better with emotions of a sexual nature, with at least one confessing "You know, we haven't done a very good job with sex" (George Mandler, personal communication), the extent of the analysis largely being Mandler's musing in *Mind and Emotion* (1975) that sympathetic arousal, characteristic of most intense emotions, seems to be inhibitory of sexual arousal (that being—maybe—characterized by parasympathetic arousal, at least in the initial stages). Perhaps one of the most intelligent discussions of the subject is still Albert Ellis's *An American Sexual Tragedy* (1954), which at least pointed up the relationship between the physical attractiveness of the partner and sexual desire, although whether this is a learned cultural phenomenon or a genetically wired-in preference (given the association between outward symptoms of health and standards of physical attractiveness) is not clear.

I end this chapter by returning to the first question the editors asked their contributors to confront—"What is love?"—by confessing that, in the case of romantic love, I don't really know—but, if forced against a brick wall to face a firing squad who would shoot if not given the correct answer, I would whisper "It's about 90 percent sexual desire as yet not sated." And I would also hope that they did not realize this is, still, a very complex and inadequate answer. If asked for the evidence, unfortunately, one of my prize exhibits would still have to be an overlooked study conducted by Dermer and Pyszczynski (1978), which serves to demonstrate that in leading men (women weren't studied) to exhibit behaviors associated with romantic love, sexual arousal goes a very long way. At the least, I am certain that to continue to discuss romantic love without also prominently mentioning the role sexual arousal and desire plays in it is very much like our printing a recipe for tiger soup that leaves out the main ingredient.

REFERENCES

Berscheid, E. (1983). Emotion. In H. H. Kelley, E. Berscheid, A. Christensen, J. Harvey, T. L. Huston, G. Levinger, E. McClintock, A. Peplau, & D. R. Peterson, *Close relationships*. San Francisco: Freeman.

————. (1984). Interpersonal attraction. In G. Lindzey and E. Aronson (Eds.), *The handbook of social psychology* (3rd ed.). Hillsdale, NJ: Erlbaum.

Berscheid, E., and Fei, J. (1977). Sexual jealousy and romantic love. In G. Clinton & G. Smith (Eds.), *Sexual jealousy: An anthology of research and reflection* (pp. 101–109). Englewood Cliffs, NJ: Prentice-Hall.

Berscheid, E., & Snyder, M. (in preparation). *The measurement of relationship closeness.*

Berscheid, E., & Walster, E. (1974). A little bit about love. In T. L. Huston (Ed.), *Foundations of interpersonal attraction.* New York: Academic Press.

Bowlby, J. (1973). Affectional bonds: Their nature and origin. In R. S. Weiss (Ed.), *Loneliness: The experience of emotional and social isolation.* Cambridge, MA: MIT Press.

Dermer, M., & Pyszczynski, T. (1978). Effects of erotica upon men's loving and liking responses for women they love. *Journal of Personality and Social Psychology, 36,* 1302–1309.

Dion, K. L., & Dion, K. K. (1973). Correlates of romantic love. *Journal of Consulting Clinical Psychology, 41,* 51–56.

Ellis, A. (1954). *The American sexual tragedy.* New York: Twayne.

Finck, H. T. (1891). *Romantic love and personal beauty: Their development, causal relations, historic and national peculiarities.* London: Macmillan.

Fromm, E. (1956). *The art of loving.* New York: Harper & Row.

Kelley, H. H., Berscheid, E., Christensen, A., Harvey, J., Huston, T. L., Levinger, G., McClintock, E., Peplau, A., & Peterson, D. R. (1983). The analysis of close relationships. In H. H. Kelley, E. Berscheid, A. Christensen, J. Harvey, T. L. Huston, G. Levinger, E. McClintock, A. Peplau, and D. R. Peterson, *Close relationships.* San Francisco: Freeman.

Leamer, L. (1986). *As time goes by.* New York: Harper & Row.

Lewis, C. S. (1960). *The four loves.* New York: Harcourt, Brace & World.

Mandler, G. (1975). *Mind and emotion.* New York: Wiley.

Reik, T. (1941). *Of love and lust.* New York: Bantam Books.

Simpson, J. A., Campbell, B., & Berscheid, E. (1986). The association between romantic love and marriage: Kephart (1967) twice revisited. *Personality and Social Psychology Bulletin,* 363–372.

Sternberg, R. J., & Grajek, S. (1984). The nature of love. *Journal of Personality and Social Psychology: Interpersonal Processes, 47,* 312–329.

Walster, E. H., & Walster, W. (1979). *A new look at love.* Reading, MA: Addison-Wesley.

Contributors and Editors

MICHAEL BARNES is a graduate student in psychology at Yale University.

STEVEN BEACH is a postdoctoral fellow in psychology at the University of Georgia.

ELLEN BERSCHEID is a professor of psychology at the University of Minnesota.

DONNA BRADSHAW is a postdoctoral fellow in psychology at Harvard University.

NATHANIEL BRANDEN is a psychotherapist in California.

SHARON BREHM is a professor of psychology at the University of Kansas.

DAVID BUSS is a professor of psychology at the University of Michigan.

DONN BYRNE is a professor of psychology at the State University of New York.

KAREN DION is a professor of psychology at the University of Toronto.

KENNETH DION is a professor of psychology at the University of Toronto.

ELAINE HATFIELD is a professor of psychology at the University of Hawaii at Manoa.

CINDY HAZAN is a graduate student at the University of Denver.

JOHN ALAN LEE is a professor of sociology at the University of Toronto.

GEORGE LEVINGER is a professor of psychology at the University of Massachusetts.

SARAH MURNEN is a graduate student at the State University of New York.

BERNARD MURSTEIN is a professor of psychology at Connecticut College.

STANTON PEELE is a psychotherapist in New Jersey.

ZICK RUBIN is a professor of psychology at Brandeis University.

PHILLIP SHAVER is a professor of psychology at the University of Denver.

ROBERT STERNBERG is a professor of psychology at Yale University.

ABRAHAM TESSER is a professor of psychology at the University of Georgia.

WENDY WILLIAMS is a graduate student at Yale University.

Index